The Color Nature Library
DOGS

By
PEGGY WRATTEN

Designed by
DAVID GIBBON

Produced by
TED SMART

CRESCENT BOOKS

First published in Great Britain by Colour Library International Ltd.

Designed by David Gibbon. Produced by Ted Smart.

© Text: Peggy Wratten. © Illustrations: Colour Library International Ltd.

Colour separations by La Cromolito, Milan, Italy.

Display and Text filmsetting by Focus Photoset, London, England.

Printed and bound by L.E.G.O. Vicenza, Italy.

Published by Crescent Books, a division of Crown Publishers Inc.

Library of Congress Catalogue Card No. 77-17787

CRESCENT 1978

The dog was almost certainly the first animal to be fully domesticated. For many thousands of years it has given Man faithful friendship and co-operation. Wild dogs are social animals, living in packs or family groups, showing loyalty to a leader and conforming to the rules of the pack. Even domesticated dogs that have gone feral will readily form packs under a leader, so man found it relatively easy to train dogs to work for him and obey him. Consequently, the traditional role of the dog is a working one.

Over the years different breeds have been selectively developed to serve different purposes. The hound has been used for hunting from prehistoric times down to the present day. The sheepdog was bred especially to herd sheep under the direction of the shepherd. In polar regions, in spite of modern inventions, the husky dog is still used for pulling sledges and, for many years before the advent of the automobile, the dog was used in many countries for draught work. Special breeds with more than average intelligence and learning

left: Old English Sheepdog pup
right: Wire-haired Fox Terrier
below: Shetland Sheepdog and Old English Sheepdog

ability are today trained for police tracking work and crowd control. Guard dogs are valued for guarding large premises at night and even the domestic pet dog will usually alert the household to possible danger by barking. More recently certain breeds have been trained as guide dogs for blind people. No other animal species has rendered such a diversity of service.

It is only in relatively recent times that dogs have been kept solely as domestic pets. Today the dog is a familiar and much loved member of many households all over the world. Many different breeds and varieties have been produced to satisfy man's whims and fancies, as well as his needs, and some pedigree breeds bear little resemblance to their wild ancestors. The Dog Show is now a firmly based institution in many countries.

left: Dalmatian and Smooth-haired Dachshund
right: Welsh Corgi (Cardigan)
below: Welsh Corgi (Pembroke)

Origin and Domestication

The dog first appeared on earth some twenty million years ago and according to the findings of bones in prehistoric middens it probably first became domesticated, at least to some extent, about 10,000 years ago. Some authorities put the time at nearer 15,000 years. The dog was probably first domesticated in the warmer parts of Europe and southwest and southern Asia, judging from firmer evidence based on more complete skeletons dating from about 8000 B.C. This dog was almost certainly of a similar type to the modern pariahs and the Dingo. The latter was almost certainly taken to Australia from Polynesia about 3000 years ago by the ancestors of the present-day Aboriginals. Around this time, too, a second small breed of dog seems to have been bred in Europe. Probably dogs were first kept by man to provide him with food. Even today some primitive people eat dogs. Once man and dog became associated, however, the value of the animal as a hunter, as a guard or as a draught animal probably soon came to be recognized.

Added to the uncertainty as to the period when the dog first became of use to man, there has long been speculation about its origin. There are several theories: that its ancestor was the wolf; that the dog is derived from the wolf with some admixture of jackal; and that the dog came from a wild species distinct from both wolf and jackal, that has since become extinct. From the little real evidence we have, the first of these theories seems the most acceptable especially since the behaviour and characteristics of the wolf have been more extensively studied during recent years. However, it has to be admitted that much of the evidence is purely circumstantial and the correct answer will probably never now be established.

The problem has been made more difficult because no other domestic animal shows so much variation in colour, coat, size and behaviour as the dog. The smallest is the Chihuahua (pronounced chi-wa-wa), a breed developed from the Mexican hairless dog and only 6-9 in high and up to 6 lb weight (sometimes as little as 1½ lb!). The largest are the Mastiff, up to 30 in high and 165 lb weight and the St. Bernard up to 28 in high and 200 lb weight.

left above: Pyrenean Mountain Dog
left below: Pointer
right: St. Bernard

The Chief Senses

Smell is a dog's dominant sense, although the degree to which sight is used varies from breed to breed. In general, to a dog the world around presents a pattern of smells just as to us it presents a pattern of visual details. In the best tracker dogs the smelling membrane in the nose contains about 220 million receptor cells compared with only 5 million in the human nose, and each cell works more efficiently than ours.

Like most other mammals, a dog in the wild is a territorial animal and the boundaries of its territory are marked by its urine. The smell of the urine will tell other male dogs to keep away and inform a bitch of the presence of a possible mate. The messages it conveys are, however, much more numerous than this and usually more subtle. Even the domestic dog urinates repeatedly

left: Smooth-haired Dachshunds
right: Scottish Terriers
bottom: Pekingese pups

9

when taken for a walk to tell other dogs that it has passed that way. When two dogs meet they first sniff noses and then sniff each other's hindquarters for later recognition.

A dog's sense of taste, so closely allied to smell, is not particularly discerning. In fact it has fewer taste buds on the tongue than we have. A dog, like most carnivores, once it has sniffed its food to see that it is to its liking, will swallow it whole with little or no chewing.

Although a dog predominantly uses its sense of smell, its sight is reasonably good and, like cats, it has a faint colour vision. The eyes are positioned to look straight ahead and as would be expected, sight is sharpest in working dogs and sporting dogs. Gun dogs particularly, that point and retrieve game, are almost entirely dependent on vision, at least in the duties for which they are kept.

A dog's sense of hearing is very acute and, like the cat, its hearing extends beyond the range of the human ear into the higher frequencies. The 'silent' dog whistle, inaudible to our ears, is easily heard by canines. Usually dogs with pricked ears have better hearing than those with floppy ears. Hearing is particularly necessary to some working dogs in conjunction with their other senses. Sheepdogs, guard dogs and guide dogs especially need an acute sense of hearing to do their work efficiently.

left: Bearded Collie
bottom: Shetland Sheepdogs
right: Collie pups

Communication

The familiar bark of the domestic dog so expressive of many moods seems only to have developed during domestication because wild dogs do not bark. Small pet dogs seem to bark and yap a lot but the larger working dogs are quieter and bark only when necessary or when excited. The growl is a sign of aggression and the whine a sign of disquiet. Many dogs yawn at each other as wolves do before setting off to hunt.

Apart from vocal sounds, the dog has a whole range of gestures to convey different moods. It will prick its ears at sudden noises, wag its tail when pleased. The way the tail is held is also indicative of mood. It will raise its hackles, stiffen its body, bare its teeth and snarl when about to attack. It will roll over with legs in the air as a sign of submission.

left: Miniature Poodle
right: Standard Poodle
bottom: Toy Poodle pups

top, overleaf: Dobermann Pinscher and Yorkshire Terrier
bottom: Longcoat Chihuahua, Pekingese and St. Bernard
right: Cocker Spaniels

Courtship and Family Life

As a result of domestication the reproductive cycle of the dog has altered from that of its wild counterparts. Sexual maturity occurs earlier in domestic dogs, at one year instead of two. Bitches come into heat twice a year at any season and males are able to mate at any time.

If courtship and mating are allowed naturally, the dog is attracted by the smell of a bitch on heat. He will show increasing interest in her, inviting play by springing up and down on his forelegs in front of her, cocking his head on one side. The male will attempt to mount her but the bitch will not allow mating until she reaches full oestrus. Once receptive the bitch allows the dog to mount her and copulation is unusual in that the pair become locked together (knotted) for about 20 minutes, sometimes for as much as an hour. The gestation of the dog is about 63 days.

A litter may comprise anything up to a dozen or more puppies, the largest recorded being 22. After the birth of each puppy the mother will clean off the birth membranes, bite through the umbilical cord, lick the puppy clean and eat the placenta (afterbirth). The puppy's first reaction is to find a nipple and suck milk from its mother. The puppies are born more or less helpless, blind and deaf. At first the mother stays with them nearly all the time, keeping them warm, suckling and grooming them. When later she leaves them for short periods, they will huddle together for warmth.

The puppies' eyes open at 9 to 14 days and hearing begins at 10 to 12 days. After about three to four weeks the puppies show signs of independence and the mother begins to detach herself from the litter, although she will be quick to help any pup in difficulties. The puppies start trying to feed themselves, although they are not fully weaned until four to eight weeks old. To teach them self-sufficiency the mother cuffs them for any wrongdoing, she teaches them to keep the sleeping basket clean and joins in their play. Much as the puppies seem to enjoy their play, in the wild this would be a preparation for adult life and even in domestic dogs the play shows all the pattern of the dog's hunting behaviour.

After about eight weeks the puppies will be fully independent of their mother.

left: Bulldog
top right: Boston Terrier
middle right: Pug
bottom right: Bulldog

Hunting and Feeding

Although today the family dog is fed mainly from tins of prepared food and its meals are regular and sufficient, almost any dog, given the opportunity, will go out hunting into the fields and woods.

Being a carnivore, the dog gulps its food with little or no chewing, but it loves to gnaw a bone and will bury it in the garden for future enjoyment. A dog's teeth are characteristic of a carnivore: incisors for gripping small prey, dagger-like canines for making slashing cuts at large prey or enemies and cheekteeth which include the carnassials for slicing flesh or crunching bones.

It is said that half the small dogs at a vet's surgery today are there because of gum disease caused by too easy a diet. If dogs do not use their teeth properly to tear flesh and crack bones or hard biscuits, the teeth become encrusted with tartar. This inflames the gums and teeth may have to be extracted. However, dogs need never wear dentures, they can manage perfectly well without teeth!

left: King Charles Spaniels
bottom, left: Pomeranian
bottom, right: Cocker Spaniel
right: Cocker Spaniel

Intelligence

The dog has always been thought to be highly intelligent, at least by its owner, largely because it is usually trainable, obedient and able to learn simple tricks. This does not by any means prove that a dog is intelligent, however, and some scientists have even gone so far as to deny that any animal, other than a human, can show intelligence.

One of the many definitions of intelligence is that it is the ability to recognise a problem, formulate a solution and quickly act upon it. The working sheepdog seems to prove by its cleverness and initiative that it is indeed capable of this. There are many stories of a sheepdog being ordered to go out on a pitch-black night to round up a flock that had scattered widely. By daylight, unassisted, the sheepdog had rounded them all up. Anyone who has watched sheepdog trials can testify to the sheepdog's ability to use its initiative to solve a difficult problem of herding.

There are many other stories of other breeds of dog alerting their owners to danger of fire or disaster and helping humans selflessly without any regard for their own safety.

Four pictures of Alsatians

Types of breeds

The classification of breeds of dogs has always presented problems ever since different breeds were recognized. Today this classification varies in different countries. There are over a hundred distinct breeds now recognized, more if one includes varieties of breeds, and a convenient grouping, which does not of course satisfy everyone, is recognized by the American Kennel Club. It indicates broadly the uses to which the various dogs are put as follows:

1. Sporting breeds: includes Pointers, Retrievers, Setters and Spaniels.
2. Hound breeds: includes those hounds that use scent such as Bloodhound, Foxhound and Beagle, and those that use sight such as Greyhound, Afghan, Borzoi and Dachshund.
3. Working breeds: includes those used as sledge dogs, sheepdogs, guide dogs, St. Bernard and Boxer.

left: Irish or Red Setter
right: English Setters
bottom: Gordon Setter

4. Terrier breeds: familiar small dogs such as Fox Terrier and Scottish Terrier.
5. Toy Dogs: includes the Pekingese and Chihuahua.
6. Non-sporting Dogs: includes those difficult to classify elsewhere such as the Bulldog, Dalmation and Poodle.

left: Border Collie
below: Collies herding sheep
right: Rough Collie

Sporting Dogs

To assist him when out shooting game-birds, man has trained sporting dogs to find and flush the birds and, although they do not assist in the actual killing, they help to find dead or wounded game. In Britain they are known as Gundogs.

At the start of the shoot, the Pointer or Setter ranges widely to get an airborne scent of the bird long before it is alarmed enough to fly to safety. They then come to a complete stop and remain rigid, pointing in the direction of the game until the 'gun' comes up, when they either lead him nearer the game until the bird flies, or drop to the ground at the shot.

The Pointer is thought to have originally come from Spain and been evolved especially for work with game-birds, able to gallop fast and range widely over fields and moors and with excellent sight and smell. Well-built, with high head-carriage and a long, muscular neck, it is a big dog standing 24 to 27in. at the shoulder, with a short fine coat.

The English, Irish and Gordon Setters are similar in build to the Pointer but the head is longer and finer-skulled and the coat long. The Gordon Setter, bred for the Scottish moors is particularly strongly built with a heavy coat.

The Retriever walks at heel or sits by its master until the bird is shot when it is ordered to pick up the game, either dead or wounded, and bring it back. The Retrievers are all large, active dogs, with good heads and necks, strong bodies and muscular hindquarters. The muzzles are wide, suitable for carrying any size of bird. The Golden Retriever, so popular as a domestic pet, is also a good gundog with a soft mouth. The Labrador Retrievers either Black or Golden are both great gundogs with wonderful noses for finding game. They have a dense undercoat to keep them warm when swimming even in icy waters.

The Spaniel does not lead its handler to the game like the Pointer but hunts about close to the 'gun' until it has found and flushed a bird, then after the game is shot, retrieves it to hand. The Cocker Spaniel with a height of 15-16in., is a lively, active dog, very strong and muscular for its size. Originally bred in Britain for flushing woodcock, it is now bred mainly for show and as a companion.

left: Boxer pups
right, top: Bloodhounds
right, below: Boxer

27

Hounds

Probably man's first use of the dog, apart from using it as food, was for hunting. As the dog is by nature a hunter it would have required little training for this. It is thought that the first breed used was possibly of the greyhound type. Today, different varieties of hound are still used by man for the chase, although most of them will also settle down quite happily to a domestic life, if given plenty of exercise. There are two types of hound: those that hunt by scent and those that hunt by sight.

Most of the scent hounds are of ancient origin. The Basset Hound as long ago as the 16th century was used in France to hunt badgers, wolves and smaller animals. It is a handsome hound, with long droopy ears and a soulful expression. The long body, only 12-18in. at the shoulder, the short sturdy hindlegs and crooked forelegs make it seem slightly out of proportion. It is still used as a pack hound for hunting on foot but also makes a splendid family pet. The Beagle is another ancient

left: Golden Retriever
right: Deerhound
bottom: Great Dane

breed used today, particularly in Britain, for hunting on foot like the Basset Hound. Beagles are compactly built, active hounds with a wide domed head and long ears. They are particularly attractive as puppies. The Bloodhound is the oldest of the scent hounds. With a heavy build and large head it has folds of loose skin falling over the forehead and sides of the face. It has been used particularly for tracking down criminals.

Although viewed with disfavour by the conservationists, hunting the fox, deer and otter with the help of pack hounds still goes on in Britain and in other countries, although not so frequently as in former years. The modern Foxhound in England has the reputation of being the most efficient working animal used by man. The American Foxhound is similar but a heavier animal. All Foxhounds need good noses, good staying power and good voices to co-operate with the huntsmen. Although the Dachshund was first bred in Germany as a badger dog to go down holes it is today popular as a companion and show dog. It is characterised by its long body and very short legs and is familiarly called a 'sausage dog'.

All the sight hounds are bred for speed. One of the most popular today as a show dog and one of the most beautiful is the Afghan Hound. In its native Afghanistan it is used as a guard dog and for hunting deer and wolves. Shaped rather like a Greyhound it stands 24-29in. high and has a long, thick, silky coat. The Borzoi, or Russian Wolfhound, is perhaps the most elegant of all hounds and one of the swiftest. Originally kept in packs by the Russian nobles for hunting wolves, it is now a popular show dog in Britain and the United States. Similar in build but smaller the Saluki has also become popular in recent years. It is the modern coursing dog of the Arabs.

Of all the swift hounds perhaps the Greyhound has altered least over the years. It was once used for coursing the hare and, in Ancient Egypt, for running down the gazelle. Today it is popular as a racing animal on the Greyhound track in the United States and Britain, where Greyhound racing has become big business. Greyhounds are easily recognized by their long sharp muzzles, long bodies, arched loins, very long limbs and long thin tails.

left, top: Pointer
left, below: Smooth-haired Fox Terrier
right: Basset Hound

Working Dogs

The name for this group of dogs is not very satisfactfory as originally all breeds of dog worked for man. However, it is convenient to include in this group such working dogs as sheepdogs, guard dogs, draught dogs and guide dogs.

left: Beagle pups
bottom: Bearded Collie pups
right: English Cocker Spaniel

Sheepdogs and Herders

It must have been many thousands of years ago when man first trained dogs to herd and guard his flocks. This was a remarkable achievement, going against a dog's natural instincts, as cattle and sheep would have been its natural prey. Today there are sheepdogs or herding dogs all over the world and their ability and intelligence while at work are supreme among dogs. Any sheepdog trial will demonstrate this. The Collie breeds are universally known and although they make good family dogs and show dogs they are at their best as working sheepdogs. The Rough Collie is still used in Austrailia for controlling large flocks of sheep. In Britain most of

left: Dalmatian
right: English Springer Spaniel
bottom: Rough Collie, Great Dane, Border Terrier, Boston Terrier, Smooth-haired Fox Terrier, Borzoi, Alsatian.
overleaf top, left: Dalmatian pup
top, right: Jack Russell Terrier pups
right: Great Dane and pups
bottom: Golden Cocker Spaniel pups

the working sheepdogs are Welsh or Border Collies. Renowned for intelligence, stamina and speed, they excel at obedience trials. The Shetland Sheepdog or 'Sheltie' was originally used in the Shetland Isles for herding sheep but today, like the Old English Sheepdog it is more popular as a family pet dog. The beautiful Pyrenean Mountain Dog with thick long white coat and dense neck frill was used in the Middle Ages to protect flocks from bears and wolves, as a dog of war armed with a spiked collar, and for guard work. It still serves as a guide and pack dog today.

Some dogs were bred as cattle herders. Most famous, but rarely used for this purpose today, are the Welsh Cardigan and Pembroke Corgis. They were used in cattle droves from Wales to Smithfield Market in London and were known as heelers as they nipped the heels of stragglers. With bat ears, compact bodies and short coats, the Corgis stand only 12in. at the shoulder and make excellent house dogs for small homes. The only active cattle-herding breed in the world today is the Australian Cattle Dog. A large dog standing 18in. at the shoulder and weighing 40lb. this sturdy dog has been bred to cope with the strain and heat of cattle-driving.

left: English Setter
right: Black Labrador Retriever
bottom: Yellow Labrador Retriever

39

Guard Dogs, Police Dogs and Guide Dogs

When man first trained dogs to guard his home and property he did not find it a difficult task as a dog naturally has a well-developed sense of territory. In Ancient Egypt and Rome guard dogs were used extensively. They were large, powerful animals of the Mastiff type. Today, first among the guard dogs is the Alsatian or German Shepherd Dog. First used as a herd dog, the Alsatian is intelligent, reliable and strong. It is used by the Police and the Military and is also used as a guide dog for the blind. It is invaluable to the Police for tracking and crowd control. Although also popular as a family pet, many people distrust it, probably because of its wolf-like looks. Other German breeds seem to excel at guarding and Police work. The Dobermann Pinscher makes a splendid guard dog and is used in Police work in Europe and the United States. The Great

left: Borzoi
bottom right: Salukis
bottom left: Afghan Hound
right: Greyhound

Dane was once used for fighting and hunting and is still used sometimes today for guarding because of its formidable size, yet it is not in any way a ferocious animal and makes a good family dog if it has plenty of room for exercise. The Boxer, with its broad square head and muzzle, smooth short coat and well-muscled body has a reputation for affection and reliability and some have been trained as guide dogs for the blind.

In time of war dogs have been used for rescue work, particularly as a help to Red Cross workers, finding wounded and leading ambulance workers to them.

Another dog with a reputation as a guide dog is the St. Bernard. Although it was supposed to be sent out from the St. Bernard Monastery, in the Swiss Alps, to find lost travellers in the snow, this story is now discounted because the St. Bernard is of such a massive build that it would have quickly sunk in the snow and its thick coat would have become clogged. It was however, used to guide monks up and down the mountain passes.

left: Weimaraner
right: Pyrenean Mountain Dog
bottom: Dobermann Pinscher

Draught Dogs

The use of dogs for haulage seems to have been confined mainly to Europe and the polar regions. In Europe today the dog is still seen occasionally pulling milk-carts and bakers' vans but the practice is dying out. The Leonberger, rather like a large Golden Retriever, has been used for this work in parts of northern Europe and the Bernese Mountain Dog was a popular Swiss draught dog.

Today the only dogs still used extensively for pulling loads are the 'Huskies' of the Arctic and Antarctic regions. They are invaluable for pulling sleds and will work till they drop in fifty-below-zero temperatures. Although popularly all sled dogs are called 'Huskies' there are many distinct breeds in regular use as sled dogs. The best sled dogs are fairly short and sturdy with thick coats to keep out the cold. They must have powerful chest muscles for pulling and plenty of stamina to keep going for many miles on a very limited fish diet.

left: Shih Tzu pup
bottom: Yorkshire Terrier
right: Border Terrier

above: Chow
left: Boxer

above: Airedale Terrier
bottom: Bulldog, Rough Collie

Terriers

Terriers, generally, are among the hardiest of all dogs. They were originally bred for entering fox earths and badger setts and for the destruction of vermin. They are all fairly small dogs, sturdy and robust with a strong body and rather long head, some long-legged, some short-legged. Most varieties have short, rough coats. Above all they are active, enthusiastic dogs with an eagerness for work and a very friendly nature. Although most of them today, whether pedigree or merely 'mongrel', are household pets, they are at their best when working. Even the domesticated Terrier, on seeing a rat or mouse, will instinctively chase and kill it.

The Terrier was originally a British breed and at one time nearly every district in the country had its own individual variety. Today, many breeds are popular on the Continent, in the United States and other countries. There is only room here to describe a few.

Scotland is the home of many rough-haired, short-legged Terriers. Probably the original was the Cairn Terrier. It is a good sturdy game-working dog and

left: Rough Collie
bottom: Husky Dogs
right: Cairn Terrier and
West Highland White Terrier

excellent ratter. Its coat is harsh and thick with a dense undercoat. Although very popular as a pet it is at its best when working. The Scottish Terrier or 'Scottie' is one of the most popular Terriers. It is small with a very long head and short legs and a thick wiry coat, usually black. It is popular as a show dog or companion in Britain and the United States.

One of the longer-legged Terriers is the Airedale Terrier from Yorkshire. It is the largest of the British Terriers and was widely used as an army dog in World War I. The head is long with a long powerful muzzle. The coat is short and rough. The Airedale Terrier is not so popular as formerly as a family dog but is still used occasionally as a guard dog.

The Smooth-haired Fox Terrier is one of the best-known of all the Terriers and popular today in many countries. Although an excellent companion in a town house, it is a very capable ratter in the country. The head is flat and narrow with strong jaws and small ears that drop forwards. The very short smooth coat is white, marked with black or tan.

left: Pointer
right: Harlequin Great Dane
bottom: St. Bernard

Toy Dogs

The Toy Dogs today are bred solely as pets. They have no other purpose in life except to give pleasure, especially to ladies. Some breeds are so small as to seem almost grotesque.

Of all the Toy breeds one of the most popular and one of the smallest is the Yorkshire Terrier. Although originally used by Yorkshire mill workers for catching mice and rats in the woollen factories, today Yorkshire Terriers are kept solely as pets or show dogs. The coat is normally long, straight and glossy, a dark steel blue with tan on the chest. Some specimens are bred as small as 2-4lb.

The Pekingese, a firm favourite, and pampered pet of women in many countries is, in fact, one of the oldest breeds of small dog. It has a Chinese ancestry dating back to the 8th century. Small varieties were called 'Sleeve Pekes' and were carried in the wide sleeves of the Mandarins. It is a member of the Spaniel family and has a long straight coat with a profuse mane forming a frill round the neck. The head is wide with a short muzzle and large eyes.

left: Beagle
bottom: a gathering of Foxhounds
right: a working English Springer Spaniel

The origin of the Pug is rather obscure but it is said to have been brought from China by Dutch traders. It has an affectionate and gentle nature but is more popular on the Continent than in Britain or the United States. It has all the features of a miniature Mastiff with a round head, short muzzle and wrinkled face, short square body and strong legs.

The smallest dog in the world is the Chihuahua originating from Mexico and now very popular in the United States. One specimen has been recorded as weighing only 24 oz, an appalling example of the dictates of fashion. Most are, however, between 2 and 6 lb. There are two varieties: Long-coated and Short-coated. The head is round with large erect ears and prominent eyes. The coat is usually white with tan, blue or black markings. Although comfort-loving, male Chihuahuas may be aggressive and fight other males or females.

left: Long-haired Dachshund puppy
bottom: Poodle
right: Yellow Labrador Retrievers

Non-sporting Dogs

This group, sometimes called Utility Dogs, contains those breeds excluding the Toys, that are simply household pets and companions and are not used by man for sport or for herding or any other utilitarian purpose. They are no less popular or attractive.

Perhaps the best-known and most popular are the Poodles. They are very suitable for town houses and flats because of their small size and because they do not smell or moult, although they should have daily brushing to keep their coats in good condition. They are bred in Standard (large) and Miniature (medium) and there is also a very small one that is classified under Toy Dogs.

left: Irish or Red Setter
right: Smooth-haired Dachshund
       (black and tan)
bottom: Bloodhound

The Poodle was originally a Water Spaniel from Germany and clipped to facilitate swimming. If not clipped into too grotesque a fashion the Poodle is a very attractive dog.

A dog very popular in the United States is the Boston Terrier. It looks more like a Bulldog and was originally produced by crossing English and French Bulldogs and Old English Terriers. Also included in this group is the Bulldog, one of Britain's oldest breeds and accepted as the British 'National dog'.

left: West Highland White Terrier puppy
right: West Highland White Terrier
bottom: Cairn Terrier
overleaf:
top left: Shetland Sheepdog
top right: Airedale Terrier
bottom: Yellow Labrador Retriever
right: Shetland Sheepdogs

The Family Dog

Much has been said in this book about different breeds of dogs and especially those that man uses to work for him. Perhaps now we should end with a few words about the ordinary family dog, be it pedigree or just plain 'mongrel'. The relationship between man and his dog companion is unique. If given a good home, regular food and exercise and, especially, friendly treatment the dog will repay you with years of faithful service. It will sit with its head on your feet when you are relaxing in the evening by the fire or will run joyously before you when taken for a walk in the countryside. It may even catch the odd mouse or rat and bark to warn you of visitors or strangers to the house.

The dog, unlike the cat, however, is far happier if its owner trains it to be obedient and if done wisely and well the dog will not only love its master but will also respect him.

below: Clumber Spaniel pups
right: Bloodhound

INDEX

Photographs supplied by:
Colour Library International Ltd., 80-82 Coombe Road, New Malden, Surrey, England.
and
Bruce Coleman Ltd., 16a-17a Windsor Street, Uxbridge, Middlesex, England.

JE

AMERICA'S
TEST KITCHEN

also by the editors at america's test kitchen

The Complete Slow Cooker

The Complete Make-Ahead Cookbook

The Complete Mediterranean Cookbook

The Complete Vegetarian Cookbook

The Complete Cooking for Two Cookbook

Nutritious Delicious

Cooking at Home with Bridget and Julia

What Good Cooks Know

Cook's Science

The Science of Good Cooking

The Perfect Cookie

Bread Illustrated

Master of the Grill

Kitchen Smarts

Kitchen Hacks

100 Recipes: The Absolute Best Ways to Make the True Essentials

The New Family Cookbook

The America's Test Kitchen Cooking School Cookbook

The Cook's Illustrated Meat Book

The Cook's Illustrated Baking Book

The Cook's Illustrated Cookbook

The America's Test Kitchen Family Baking Book

The Best of America's Test Kitchen (2007–2018 Editions)

The Complete America's Test Kitchen TV Show Cookbook 2001–2018

Food Processor Perfection

Pressure Cooker Perfection

Vegan for Everybody

Naturally Sweet

Foolproof Preserving

Paleo Perfected

The How Can It Be Gluten-Free Cookbook: Volume 2

The How Can It Be Gluten-Free Cookbook

The Best Mexican Recipes

Slow Cooker Revolution Volume 2: The Easy-Prep Edition

Slow Cooker Revolution

The Six-Ingredient Solution

The America's Test Kitchen D.I.Y. Cookbook

THE COOK'S ILLUSTRATED ALL-TIME BEST SERIES

All-Time Best Sunday Suppers

All-Time Best Holiday Entertaining

All-Time Best Appetizers

All-Time Best Soups

COOK'S COUNTRY TITLES

One-Pan Wonders

Cook It in Cast Iron

Cook's Country Eats Local

The Complete Cook's Country TV Show Cookbook

FOR A FULL LISTING OF ALL OUR BOOKS

CooksIllustrated.com

AmericasTestKitchen.com

praise for other america's test kitchen titles

"A terrifically accessible and useful guide to grilling in all its forms that sets a new bar for its competitors on the bookshelf. . . . The book is packed with practical advice, simple tips, and approachable recipes."
PUBLISHERS WEEKLY (STARRED REVIEW) ON *MASTER OF THE GRILL*

"This encyclopedia of meat cookery would feel completely overwhelming if it weren't so meticulously organized and artfully designed. This is *Cook's Illustrated* at its finest."
THE KITCHN ON *THE COOK'S ILLUSTRATED MEAT BOOK*

Selected as the Cookbook Award Winner of 2017 in the Baking Category
INTERNATIONAL ASSOCIATION OF CULINARY PROFESSIONALS (IACP) ON *BREAD ILLUSTRATED*

"With 1,000 photos and the expertise of the America's Test Kitchen editors, this title might be the definitive book on bread baking."
PUBLISHERS WEEKLY ON *BREAD ILLUSTRATED*

"The editors at America's Test Kitchen pack decades of baking experience into this impressive volume of 250 recipes. . . . You'll find a wealth of keeper recipes within these pages."
LIBRARY JOURNAL (STARRED REVIEW) ON *THE PERFECT COOKIE*

Selected as one of Amazon's Best Books of 2015 in the Cookbooks and Food Writing Category
AMAZON ON *THE COMPLETE VEGETARIAN COOKBOOK*

"This book is a comprehensive, no-nonsense guide . . . a well-thought-out, clearly explained primer for every aspect of home baking."
THE WALL STREET JOURNAL ON *THE COOK'S ILLUSTRATED BAKING BOOK*

"Cooks with a powerful sweet tooth should scoop up this well-researched recipe book for healthier takes on classic sweet treats."
BOOKLIST ON *NATURALLY SWEET*

"The 21st-century *Fannie Farmer Cookbook* or *The Joy of Cooking*. If you had to have one cookbook and that's all you could have, this one would do it."
CBS SAN FRANCISCO ON *THE NEW FAMILY COOKBOOK*

"The go-to gift book for newlyweds, small families, or empty nesters."
ORLANDO SENTINEL ON *THE COMPLETE COOKING FOR TWO COOKBOOK*

"The sum total of exhaustive experimentation . . . anyone interested in gluten-free cookery simply shouldn't be without it."
NIGELLA LAWSON ON *THE HOW CAN IT BE GLUTEN-FREE COOKBOOK*

"A one-volume kitchen seminar, addressing in one smart chapter after another the sometimes surprising whys behind a cook's best practices. . . . You get the myth, the theory, the science, and the proof, all rigorously interrogated as only America's Test Kitchen can do."
NPR ON *THE SCIENCE OF GOOD COOKING*

"The perfect kitchen home companion. . . . The practical side of things is very much on display . . . cook-friendly and kitchen-oriented, illuminating the process of preparing food instead of mystifying it."
THE WALL STREET JOURNAL ON *THE COOK'S ILLUSTRATED COOKBOOK*

"Another winning cookbook from ATK. . . . The folks at America's Test Kitchen apply their rigorous experiments to determine the facts about these pans."
BOOKLIST ON *COOK IT IN CAST IRON*

"Some 2,500 photos walk readers through 600 painstakingly tested recipes, leaving little room for error."
ASSOCIATED PRESS ON *THE AMERICA'S TEST KITCHEN COOKING SCHOOL COOKBOOK*

"An exceptional resource for novice canners, though preserving veterans will find plenty here to love as well."
LIBRARY JOURNAL (STARRED REVIEW) ON *FOOLPROOF PRESERVING*

HOW TO
roast
everything

A Game-Changing Guide to Building Flavor in Meat, Vegetables, and More

the editors at
America's Test Kitchen

Library of Congress Cataloging-in-Publication Data

Names: America's Test Kitchen (Firm)
Title: How to roast everything : a game-changing guide
    to building flavor in meat, vegetables, and more /
    the editors at America's Test Kitchen.
Description: Boston, MA : America's Test Kitchen,
    [2018] | Includes index.
Identifiers: LCCN 2017039248 | ISBN 9781945256226
Subjects: LCSH: Roasting (Cooking) | LCGFT:
    Cookbooks.
Classification: LCC TX690 .H69 2018 | DDC 641.7/1--
    dc23
LC record available at https://lccn.loc.gov/2017039248

AMERICA'S
TEST KITCHEN ®

AMERICA'S TEST KITCHEN
21 Drydock Avenue, Boston, MA 02210
Manufactured in the United States of America

10 9 8 7 6 5 4 3 2 1

Distributed by Penguin Random House
Publisher Services
Tel: 800.733.3000

Pictured on front cover: Bacon-Wrapped Pork Loin
with Peach Sauce (page 166) and Roasted Sweet Potato
Wedges (page 363)
Pictured on back cover: Roasted Bone-In Chicken
Breasts (page 36), Roasted Salmon Fillets with
Tangerine and Ginger Relish (page 54), Roast Beef
Tenderloin with Mushroom and Caramelized Onion
Stuffing (page 134), and One-Pan Roast Pork Tenderloin
with Green Beans and Potatoes (page 156)

Chief Creative Officer JACK BISHOP

Editorial Director, Books ELIZABETH CARDUFF

Executive Editor JULIA COLLIN DAVISON

Executive Food Editor DAN ZUCCARELLO

Senior Managing Editor DEBRA HUDAK

Senior Editor SARA MAYER

Associate Editors RACHEL GREENHAUS AND RUSSELL SELANDER

Assistant Editor SAMANTHA RONAN

Editorial Assistant ALYSSA LANGER

Design Director, Books CAROLE GOODMAN

Deputy Art Director ALLISON BOALES

Graphic Designer KATIE BARRANGER

Production Designer REINALDO CRUZ

Photography Director JULIE BOZZO COTE

Photography Producer MARY BALL

Senior Staff Photographer DANIEL J. VAN ACKERE

Staff Photographer STEVE KLISE

Additional Photography KELLER + KELLER AND CARL TREMBLAY

Food Styling DANIEL CELLUCCI, CATRINE KELTY, KENDRA MCKNIGHT,
MARIE PIRAINO, ELLE SIMONE SCOTT, AND SALLY STAUB

Photoshoot Kitchen Team
    Manager TIMOTHY MCQUINN
    Associate Editor DANIEL CELLUCCI
    Assistant Test Cooks MADY NICHAS AND JESSICA RUDOLPH

Production Director GUY ROCHFORD

Senior Production Manager JESSICA LINDHEIMER QUIRK

Production Manager CHRISTINE SPANGER

Imaging Manager LAUREN ROBBINS

Production and Imaging Specialists HEATHER DUBE, DENNIS NOBLE,
AND JESSICA VOAS

Copy Editor CHERYL REDMOND

Proofreader ELIZABETH WRAY EMERY

Indexer ELIZABETH PARSON

CONTENTS

Welcome to America's Test Kitchen

This book has been tested, written, and edited by the folks at America's Test Kitchen. Located in Boston's Seaport District in the historic Innovation and Design Building, it features 15,000 square feet of kitchen space including multiple photography and video studios. It is the home of *Cook's Illustrated* magazine and *Cook's Country* magazine and is the workday destination for more than 60 test cooks, editors, and cookware specialists. Our mission is to test recipes over and over again until we understand how and why they work and until we arrive at the best version.

We start the process of testing a recipe with a complete lack of preconceptions, which means that we accept no claim, no technique, and no recipe at face value. We simply assemble as many variations as possible, test a half-dozen of the most promising, and taste the results blind. We then construct our own recipe and continue to test it, varying ingredients, techniques, and cooking times until we reach a consensus. As we like to say in the test kitchen, "We make the mistakes so you don't have to." The result, we hope, is the best version of a particular recipe, but we realize that only you can be the final judge of our success (or failure). We use the same rigorous approach when we test equipment and taste ingredients.

All of this would not be possible without a belief that good cooking, much like good music, is based on a foundation of objective technique. Some people like spicy foods and others don't, but there is a right way to sauté, there is a best way to cook a pot roast, and there are measurable scientific principles involved in producing perfectly beaten, stable egg whites. Our ultimate goal is to investigate the fundamental principles of cooking to give you the techniques, tools, and ingredients you need to become a better cook. It is as simple as that.

To see what goes on behind the scenes at America's Test Kitchen, check out our social media channels for kitchen snapshots, exclusive content, video tips, and much more. You can watch us work (in our actual test kitchen) by tuning in to *America's Test Kitchen* or *Cook's Country from America's Test Kitchen* on public television or on our websites. Listen in to test kitchen experts on public radio (SplendidTable.org) to hear insights that illuminate the truth about real home cooking. Want to hone your cooking skills or finally learn how to bake—with an America's Test Kitchen test cook? Enroll in one of our online cooking classes. However you choose to visit us, we welcome you into our kitchen, where you can stand by our side as we test our way to the best recipes in America.

facebook.com/AmericasTestKitchen

twitter.com/TestKitchen

youtube.com/AmericasTestKitchen

instagram.com/TestKitchen

pinterest.com/TestKitchen

google.com/+AmericasTestKitchen

AmericasTestKitchen.com
CooksIllustrated.com
CooksCountry.com
OnlineCookingSchool.com

ROASTING
BASICS

Introduction

Something magical happens when you roast a chicken, beef tenderloin, a pork shoulder—or fish, vegetables, or even fruit. The alchemy of heat, caramelization, fat, and flavorings is transformative, but only if you have the right techniques. The art of roasting is timeless, so we are not discovering it here in this book but rather drawing on years of test kitchen experience and inventive recipe development to provide the widest array of roasting recipes. And we take the guesswork and fear out of the process while we're at it. Because who hasn't overcooked an expensive cut of beef or turned out a wan-looking roast chicken? What's great about roasting is that there are so many methods for achieving stellar results; none of them are hard, but the steps are exacting. Take whole roast chicken: There is the classic version, which uses a roasting pan and a rack; the weeknight version that relies on a preheated skillet (and the oven turned off for the last 25 minutes); chicken and vegetable combos; glazed whole chicken (made on a vertical roaster); and butterflied lemon chicken roasted on the grill.

How to Roast Everything covers the entire roasting landscape, from classics like Boneless Rib Roast with Yorkshire Pudding and Jus (page 138) and Roasted Rack of Lamb (page 194) to new favorites like Chinese Barbecued Roast Pork Shoulder (page 181) and Bulgur-Stuffed Roasted Eggplant (page 340). Along the way, we supply the secrets to success, whether you want to make a foolproof Thanksgiving turkey, the best rolled and stuffed pork loin, succulent whole fish, perfectly roasted chicken parts, or garlicky roasted mussels. We show you how to both master the basics and take your roasting game to the next level by trying new recipes and techniques like salting and slow-roasting an inexpensive boneless eye round to tender perfection. There is nothing more satisfying than pulling a gorgeously burnished and garlic-infused leg of lamb out of the oven or a sheet pan full of browned and nutty roasted cauliflower, a simple side turned star of the meal.

While you can dive into the book at any point and choose the recipes that interest you, we've organized it with an informative guide to the basics of roasting in the pages that follow and a starter chapter called Ten Essential Roasts. Cook your way through this chapter and you will have completed a mini tutorial on technique and mastered simple, foolproof recipes like Easy Roast Turkey Breast (page 43) and Roasted Salmon Fillets with Tangerine and Ginger Relish (page 54) that you will make again and again.

All About Chicken and Game Birds

Roast chicken is high on just about everyone's list given its versatility. From the simplest weeknight whole roast chicken to perfectly bronzed chicken parts to grill-smoked bourbon chicken, you'll find dozens of recipes for succulent roasted chicken throughout the book.

BUYING CHICKEN

Chicken is relatively inexpensive and low in fat, and it's become America's favorite type of meat. There are an overwhelming number of chicken choices at the supermarket with confusing labels and a wide range in cost. Here's what you need to know when buying chicken.

buy organic

"USDA Organic" isn't all hype: The poultry must eat organic feed that doesn't contain animal byproducts, be raised without antibiotics, and have access to the outdoors. Similar sounding terms including "Raised without Antibiotics," "Natural/All-Natural," "Hormone-Free," and "Vegetarian Diet/-Fed" can be very misleading and are often unregulated or not strictly enforced.

buy air-chilled

How the chicken was processed makes a big difference in its flavor and texture once cooked. Avoid chickens that have been "water-chilled" (soaked in a water bath in which they absorb up to 14 percent of their weight in water) or "enhanced" (injected with broth and flavoring) because they will have a spongy texture; the water gain must be shown on the product label, so these should be easy to identify. Instead, look for chicken that has been "air-chilled." Without the excess water weight, we found these chickens to be less spongy (but still plenty juicy) and to taste more chicken-y.

OUR FAVORITE WHOLE CHICKEN

We did an extensive tasting of eight brands of whole chickens and can highly recommend these two brands.

The test kitchen's winning whole chicken is **Mary's Free Range Air-Chilled Chicken**, which is air-chilled and has a higher percentage of fat than most brands. Calling its flavor clean and its meat juicy and very chicken-y, our tasters dubbed this brand "really perfect." Our runner up is **Bell & Evans Air Chilled Premium Fresh Chicken**; it had the highest fat percentage of any bird in our lineup. Tasters found its white meat to be perfectly moist with concentrated chicken flavor and really fresh and clean-tasting.

CHICKEN FOR ROASTING

When it comes to buying chicken for roasting, you'll find many options at the supermarket, including whole chickens of various sizes, cut-up whole chickens, and a variety of chicken parts. The problem with buying prepackaged chicken parts is that you can't really tell what you are buying and often you'll wind up with parts of widely varying sizes, which makes it difficult to cook them through properly. If you have the time, consider buying a whole chicken and butchering it yourself. Here are the various cuts of chicken that we use in the roasting recipes in this book.

THIGH

Thighs have bones and skin and weigh between 5 and 7 ounces each. They consist of all dark meat and are rich with fat.

DRUMSTICK

Drumsticks have bones and skin and weigh between 5 and 6 ounces each. They are usually sold together in family-size packages. Look for full, round tipped drumsticks that are evenly covered with skin; a poorly butchered drumstick will have the top lopped off with the meat.

SPLIT BREAST

Split chicken breasts have bones and skin, and weigh between 10 and 12 ounces each. Be sure to buy breasts that are the same size so that they will cook at the same rate. To ensure evenly sized pieces, we prefer to buy a whole chicken breast (see below) and split it in half ourselves. See page 4 for how to do this.

WHOLE BREAST

These chicken pieces have both bones and skin, and usually weigh about 1½ pounds each. These can be cooked whole or split in half.

WHOLE CHICKEN

Whole chickens can range dramatically in size from 2½ to 7 pounds. Small, young birds that weigh between 2½ and 4 pounds are called broilers or fryers. Slightly older birds that weigh between 5 and 7 pounds are called roasters. A stewing chicken is an older laying hen and is best used for stews since the meat is tougher and more stringy.

GAME BIRDS FOR ROASTING

There are a few other birds you can roast besides chicken and turkey. Game birds—such as our Cumin-Coriander Roasted Cornish Hens (page 111) and Crisp Roast Duck with Port Wine Glaze (page 107)—are just as easy to prepare but look and feel special.

QUAIL

These tiny game birds weigh about 5 ounces each. They are often sold with the neck still attached; you can remove it with kitchen shears before roasting. One bird is the perfect size for an appetizer, but plan on serving two birds per person if serving for dinner. See page 109 for Roast Pomegranate-Glazed Quail.

CORNISH HENS

These hens weigh about 1½ pounds each, and one whole bird will serve one person for dinner. They feature small breasts and a high ratio of fatty skin to meat. See recipes for Cornish hens on pages 111–112 and 260.

DUCK

Ducks weigh about 4½ pounds on average and one duck will serve two to three people for dinner. They are almost always sold frozen, and need to be thawed before cooking. Ducks have a larger, heavier bone structure than chickens and contain a lot of fat. For our duck recipes, see pages 107 and 258.

DON'T RINSE POULTRY

Both the U.S. Department of Agriculture and the Food and Drug Administration advise against washing poultry. According to their research, while rinsing may remove some bacteria, the only way to ensure that all bacteria are killed is through proper cooking. Moreover, splashing bacteria around the sink can be dangerous, especially if water lands on food that is ready to be served. All the same, some people will argue that chicken should be rinsed for flavor—not safety—reasons. After sitting in its own blood and juices for days, they argue, chicken should be unwrapped and refreshed under running water. To find out if rinsing had any impact on flavor, we roasted four chickens—two rinsed, two unrinsed—and held a blind tasting. Tasters couldn't tell the difference.

KEY PREP TIPS

Here are some basic techniques that you need to know when preparing a whole chicken and chicken breasts for roasting. For how to carve a whole bird, see page 8.

---

trimming chicken

We trim excess fat and skin from chicken to prevent greasiness.

Using chef's knife or kitchen shears, trim excess fat and skin from chicken breasts or whole chicken prior to cooking.

---

splitting a chicken breast

You can buy a package of split chicken breasts, but sometimes it's hard to tell what you're getting. Buying one whole breast and splitting it yourself guarantees evenly sized pieces.

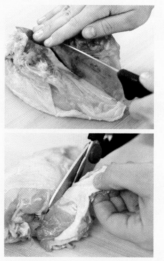

1 With chicken skin side down on cutting board, place knife on breastbone and press firmly to cut through breast plate.

2 Using kitchen shears, trim off rib section of each breast, following vertical line of fat from tapered end of breast up to socket where wing was attached.

butterflying a chicken

Butterflying a chicken (also known as "spatchcocking") means cutting out the backbone and pressing the bird flat. We've found the easiest way to do this is with a sturdy pair of kitchen shears.

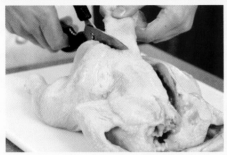

1 Cut through bones on either side of backbone and trim any excess fat and skin around neck.

2 Flip chicken over and use heel of your hand to flatten breastbone.

3 Cover chicken with plastic wrap and pound breast to be same thickness as legs and thighs.

cutting up a whole chicken

Cutting up a whole chicken is easy and guarantees evenly sized pieces. It's also very economical.

1 Using chef's knife, cut off legs, one at a time, by severing joint between leg and body.

2 Cut each leg into 2 pieces—drumstick and thigh—by slicing through joint that connects them (marked by thin white line of fat).

3 Flip chicken over and remove wings by slicing through each wing joint.

4 Turn chicken on its side and, using kitchen shears, remove back.

5 Flip breast skin side down and, using chef's knife, cut in half through breast plate (marked by thin white line of cartilage).

6 Flip each breast piece over and cut in half crosswise.

All About Turkey

The test kitchen knows how to talk turkey, whether you want a foolproof way to roast a turkey to feed a crowd (see page 102) or are looking to make a one-pan family meal like Spice-Rubbed Roast Turkey Breast with Green Beans (page 93).

BUYING TURKEY

Since most turkeys are bought for a special occasion, the stakes are a bit higher than for your average weeknight supper. Here's what you need to know when buying a turkey.

buy untreated

Avoid "pre-basted" turkey (injected with a solution) because it often tastes weak and washed out, mushy, and waterlogged. We found the flavor of kosher turkeys (which are covered in kosher salt and then rinsed multiple times during processing) to be mild and sometimes spongy. We prefer untreated turkeys because they have a clean flavor and are juicy without being mushy. Also, untreated turkeys are slightly higher in fat than the injected turkeys, which means more flavor.

buy vegetarian-fed

What the turkey was fed is another factor in how good it will taste. Giving turkeys a vegetarian diet (of primarily corn and soy) helps to ensure the birds have a clean flavor, but it is an expensive way to breed turkeys. Up to 70 percent of the cost of producing a turkey relates to feed, so many companies look for ways to cut corners. Many turkeys are fed commercial diets that may contain antibiotics, animal products, and byproducts that meet dietary requirements but affect their flavor.

OUR FAVORITE TURKEY

The holidays are no time to gamble, so we tasted 120 pounds of supermarket turkey to find the best-tasting bird. Avoid those listing anything other than "turkey" on the ingredient list. Our winner is from the same company that produces our winning chicken and heritage turkey. **Mary's Free-Range Non-GMO Verified Turkey** ($34.97 for a 13-pound turkey) has relatively high fat levels and is fed a vegetarian diet. As a result it has clean, robust turkey flavor and is very tender with a juicy texture. Our Best Buy, at half the price of our winner, is **Plainville Farms Young Turkey** ($15.47 for a 13-pound turkey). Tasters especially liked the texture and rich, meaty flavor of the dark meat, which had the highest fat level in our lineup. It was so good there was no need for gravy.

TURKEY FOR ROASTING

Most of us purchase a whole turkey or turkey breast just a few times a year so we want to get it right. Here's what you need to look for to shop wisely. For brining instructions, see page 22.

BONELESS TURKEY BREAST 	Boneless turkey breasts can range in size from 2 to 5 pounds. Often, two boneless breasts are packaged together in netting. The skin is usually left intact, but is often torn or ragged at the edges. For evenly sized breasts with skin that covers the meat, we like to buy a bone-in turkey breast (see below) and remove the bone ourselves; for how to do this, see page 253. A boneless turkey breast is a great choice for a family meal. It cooks more quickly than a whole turkey and is easy to stuff, roll, and roast, as in our recipe for Stuffed Roast Turkey Breast (page 95).
BONE-IN TURKEY BREAST 	Bone-in turkey breasts can range in size from 5 to 7 pounds and include both the skin and rib bones. They are usually sold fresh, not frozen, and come in two different styles: regular (aka true cut) and hotel (aka country-style). The hotel-cut breast comes with wings attached, as well as a bag containing the neck and giblets for making gravy; see page 7 for more information. We think this is a highly underutilized cut and perfected a fool-proof roasting method for Easy Roast Turkey Breast (page 43) that delivers flavorful moist white meat every time.
WHOLE TURKEY 	Whole turkeys range in size from 10 to 24 pounds and are sold fresh, frozen, and mail order. A bag containing the neck and giblets can usually be found in the body or neck cavity for making gravy; see page 7 for more information.
HERITAGE TURKEY 	Heritage turkeys are often only available via special-order or mail-order. They have long legs and wings, a more angular breast and high keel bone, almost bluish-purple dark meat (a sign of well-exercised birds), and traces of dark pin-feathers in the skin around the tail. They have an even ratio of white to dark meat and require special cooking instructions.

KEY PREP AND SERVING TIPS

Here are some key steps for preparing turkey, from defrosting a frozen turkey to attractively carving your perfectly cooked bird. Some steps appear in the recipe pages: For how to turn a bone-in breast into a boneless roast, see page 253. For how to remove the backbone from a turkey breast, see page 91. For how to butterfly a turkey, see page 105.

thawing a frozen bird

In the Refrigerator

The best way to defrost a frozen turkey is in the refrigerator. Plan on one day of defrosting for every 4 pounds of turkey; for example, a 12-pound turkey will take about three days. To prevent a mess, place the wrapped turkey in a large bin or rimmed baking sheet to catch the drips.

In Cold Water

If you don't have time to thaw the bird in the refrigerator, use a cold water bath. Fill a large bucket with cold water and place the wrapped bird in the water; change the water every hour to guard against bacteria growth. Plan on 30 minutes of defrosting for every pound of turkey; for example, a 12-pound turkey will take about 6 hours.

skip the truss

We found no benefit from trussing the turkey completely before roasting. Trussing holds the bird in a compact shape during cooking, which makes the bird cook unevenly. Rather, we found it best to simply tuck the wings out of the way and tie the drumsticks together to prevent them from splaying out.

tucking turkey wings and securing legs

Tucking the wings under the bird prevents them from burning and also makes the turkey look neater.

1 Using your hands, twist wing back behind bird—it should stay in place by itself.

2 Remove and discard any plastic trussing. Using kitchen twine, tie legs together at ankles.

WHAT'S IN THE GIBLET BAG?

When you buy a turkey, there is usually a small bag containing the neck and giblets, which are helpful for making gravy. See Giblet Pan Gravy for a Crowd (page 102).

Neck The neck is the large muscle with a bone through the center. It contains some very flavorful meat. Cut it into several pieces for easy browning and then simmer it in the broth. Discard after straining the broth.

Heart The heart is the small, dark-colored organ. Brown it along with the neck and gizzard and then simmer it in the broth. Reserve it after straining the broth and then dice it and return it to the gravy before serving.

Gizzard The gizzard is the grinding organ from the bird's digestive tract, recognizable by a butterfly-shaped strip of connective tissue. Cut the gizzard in half, brown it along with the heart and neck, and reserve it after straining the broth. Dice the gizzard and return it to the gravy along with the heart.

Liver The liver is the brownish, flat organ. We usually don't recommend using it to make gravy.

---

loosening poultry skin

Carefully separating the skin from the meat makes it easy to apply butter, a spice rub, or other seasonings directly to the flesh.

With Your Fingers

Insert your fingers between meat and skin, starting at bottom of breast. Gently loosen skin, being careful not to break it.

With a Spoon

Insert handle of spoon between meat and skin, starting at bottom of breast. Gently loosen skin, being careful not to break it.

carving a whole bird

Before you start, make sure that you've let the bird rest so the juices can redistribute. We've found that a chef's knife works better than a carving knife for this task. The same technique is used for carving a whole roast chicken.

1 Remove any kitchen twine. Start by slicing turkey through skin between leg and breast to expose hip joint.

2 Pull leg quarters away from carcass. Separate joint by gently pressing leg out to side and pushing up on joint. Carefully cut through joint.

3 Cut through joint that connects drumstick to thigh. Repeat on second side. Slice meat off drumsticks and thighs, leaving some skin attached to each slice.

4 Pull wings away from carcass and carefully cut through joint between wing and breast to remove wings. Cut wings in half for easier eating.

5 Cut down along 1 side following breastbone, pulling meat away from bone as you cut. Continue until breast has been removed.

6 Cut breast meat crosswise into slices for serving.

All About Beef

From a classic Sunday roast beef to company-worthy beef tenderloin, the options for roasting beef are endless. Careful shopping and the right techniques make the difference between a mediocre roast beef and a great one. Here is what you need to know.

PRIMAL CUTS

Before choosing a cut of beef for roasting, it helps to understand the anatomy of a cow. Eight different cuts of beef are sold at the wholesale level. From this first series of cuts, known in the trade as primal cuts, butchers make the retail cuts that you find at the market.

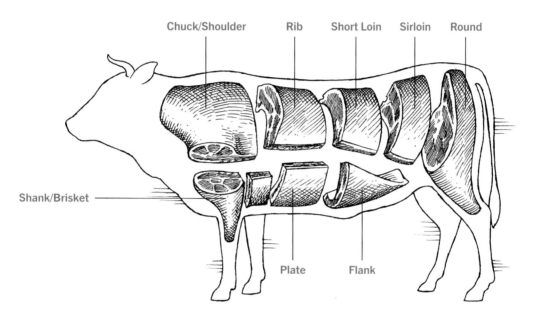

Chuck/Shoulder The chuck (also called the shoulder) runs from the neck down to the fifth rib. There are four major muscles in this region, and meat from the chuck tends to be flavorful and fairly fatty, which is why ground chuck makes the best hamburgers. Chuck also contains a fair amount of connective tissue, so when the meat is not ground it generally requires a long cooking time to become tender.

Rib The rib section extends along the back of the animal from the sixth to the 12th rib. The prime rib comes from this area, as do rib-eye steaks. Rib cuts have excellent beefy flavor and are quite tender, making them the ultimate cut for roasting.

Short Loin The short loin (also called the loin) extends from the last rib back through the midsection of the animal to the hip area. It contains two major muscles—the tenderloin and the shell. The tenderloin is extremely tender, has quite a mild flavor, and may be sold whole as a roast or sliced crosswise into steaks called filets mignons. The shell is a much larger muscle and has a more robust beef flavor as well as more fat.

Sirloin The sirloin contains relatively inexpensive cuts that are sold as both steaks and roasts. We found that sirloin cuts are fairly lean and tough although top sirloin makes a decent roast.

Round Roasts and steaks cut from the round are usually sold boneless. They are quite lean and can be tough, but with the test kitchen's innovative techniques they can be roasted with great success.

Shank/Brisket, Plate, and Flank Moderately thick boneless cuts are removed from the three primal cuts that run along the underside of the animal. The brisket (also called shank) is rather tough and contains a lot of connective tissue, which usually requires a long braise to become tender, but we get foolproof results via oven roasting. The plate is rarely sold at the retail level (it is used to make pastrami). The flank is a leaner cut that tastes great as a steak or in a braise.

COMMON BEEF ROASTS

There are many cuts of beef to pick from when choosing a roast, from the already-tender tenderloin to the leaner top sirloin and eye-round roasts. Here are the test kitchen's top picks for beef roasts. We've also listed the primal cut (see page 9) from which each roast is cut.

**CHUCK-EYE ROAST
(Chuck/Shoulder)**

This tender, juicy boneless roast is cut from the center of the first five ribs and it contains an abundant amount of fat. It is also called boneless chuck roll and boneless chuck fillet. We like the chuck-eye roast for its compact, uniform shape, deep flavor, and tenderness in slow-roasted applications. This roast should always be tied (see page 12 for tying instructions).

**RIB ROAST, FIRST
CUT (Rib)**

Butchers tend to cut a rib roast, which consists of ribs 6 through 12 if left whole, into two distinct cuts. The more desirable half contains the large, single rib-eye muscle and consists of ribs 10 through 12, sometimes called the loin end, the small end, or the first cut. Whatever it is called, it is preferable because it has more meat and less fat. The second cut consists of ribs 6 through 9 and is fattier and more irregularly shaped but still a great roast.

**BONE-IN RIB-EYE
STEAK (Rib)**

Rib-eye steaks are deeply marbled, tender, and beefy. The bone contributes flavor and protects against overcooking when roasted. The exterior band of fat and meat on a rib eye is called the deckle; connoisseurs say it is the most flavorful part of the cow.

**TENDERLOIN ROAST
(Short Loin)**

The tenderloin (also called the whole filet) is the most tender piece of beef you can buy and requires careful roasting to preserve its buttery texture. Its flavor is pleasantly mild, almost non-beefy. "Peeled" roasts have scattered patches of fat that need not be removed. "Unpeeled" tenderloins come with a thick layer of exterior fat still attached, which should be removed. For more information, see page 12.

**TOP SIRLOIN ROAST
(Sirloin)**

Other parts of the sirloin are lean and tough, but top sirloin roast is a great inexpensive roast. This cut from the hip area tastes incredibly meaty and has plenty of marbling, which makes for a succulent roast. Aside from an unpleasant vein of gristle that runs through it, this roast is tender and juicy with big, beefy flavor.

**SIRLOIN TRI-TIP
ROAST (Sirloin)**

Also known as a triangle roast, this boomerang-shaped roast is cut from the bottom sirloin and is popular in the American West. This mild-flavored roast is moist but can have a spongy texture. We like to roast tri-tip on the grill (see page 266).

**BOTTOM ROUND
RUMP ROAST
(Round)**

This inexpensive cut makes a juicy, relatively beefy roast. Because it is not particularly tender, this roast is best served in thin slices as recommended in Bottom Round Roast Beef with Zip-Style Sauce (page 126).

**EYE-ROUND ROAST
(Round)**

This boneless roast is quite inexpensive but not nearly as flavorful as the top cuts. However, it does have a nice shape that slices neatly, making it a better choice than other round or rump roasts. In order to make this lean cut as tender as possible, we roast it in a very low oven (see page 46) and slice it paper-thin for serving.

BRISKET

This large, rectangular cut is often divided into two subcuts, the flat cut and the point cut. We prefer the flat cut when roasting because it is leaner, thinner, and more widely available. Look for a flat-cut brisket with a decent fat cap on top.

**ENGLISH-STYLE
SHORT RIBS**

These meaty ribs can be cut from various locations on the cow, although they commonly come from the underside of the animal. In most markets, each rib bone has been separated and cut crosswise so that a large chunk of meat is attached to one side of the bone.

BUYING BEEF

There are not only a large number of beef roasts to choose from, but there are a variety of other factors (and price tags) to consider when picking one out at the butcher's counter. Here's what is helpful to know when buying beef.

buy choice or prime

The U.S. Department of Agriculture (USDA) assigns different quality grades to beef and beef that is graded should bear a USDA grade stamp, though it may not be visible to the consumer. Most meat available to consumers is confined to the top three grades: prime, choice, and select. Prime is the highest grade and the meat is heavily marbled with intramuscular fat, which makes for a tender, flavorful steak. Choice is the second highest grade and it is generally moderately marbled with intramuscular fat; the majority of graded beef is choice. Select is the third highest grade and it has little marbling. In a blind tasting of all three grades (using rib steaks), we found that prime ranked first for its tender, buttery texture and rich beefy flavor, followed by choice with good meaty flavor and a little more chew. The select steak was ranked last, with a tough stringy texture and barely acceptable flavor. If you can find and afford prime quality beef, go for it, but choice quality is a fine option.

buy organic

The government regulates the use of the term "organic" on beef labels, but producers set their own guidelines when it comes to the term "natural." If you want to ensure that you're buying meat raised without antibiotics or hormones and fed an organic diet (and no mammalian or aviary products), then look for the USDA's organic seal.

grain-fed versus grass-fed beef

Most U.S. beef is raised on grain but grass-fed beef is becoming an increasingly popular option. Grain-fed beef is generally considered to be richer and fattier, while grass-fed beef is leaner, chewier, and more gamy—or at least that's the conventional wisdom. In our taste tests, we pitted grain-fed and grass-fed rib-eye steaks and strip steaks against each other. We found differences among the various strip steaks to be quite small. The grain-fed rib eyes had a milder flavor compared with the nutty, complex flavor of the grass-fed beef, but our tasters' preferences were evenly split. The texture of all samples was similar, but we did find that the grass-fed beef cooked slightly faster than grain-fed beef, so be sure to check the meat for doneness at the beginning of a recommended time range.

THE ROLE OF BONES

While some recipes require careful deboning, a great many roast recipes keep the bones intact, and for good reason. Because bone is very porous and thus a relatively poor conductor of heat, the meat located next to the bone doesn't cook as quickly as the rest of the meat—a phenomenon that helps to prevent overcooking and moisture loss and contributes to a noticeably juicier end product. Bones are also lined with fat, and as the fat melts during the roasting process, it bastes the meat, increasing the perceived juiciness. And it doesn't end there. Bones actually add flavor directly to the meat. Here, the credit goes to the marrow, where blood cells are made, which is rich in fat and other flavorful substances. While bone-in cuts cook, the marrow's flavor compounds slowly migrate through the porous bone into the surrounding meat.

KEY PREP AND SERVING TIPS

Here are some of the fundamental techniques you need to employ to prepare and serve different kinds of beef roasts.

two ways to tie a roast

Most roasts are unevenly shaped, which leads to uneven cooking. For long, cylindrical cuts, such as beef or pork tenderloin, we even out thickness with a series of ties down the length. You can also fold the thin end under the roast and tie it in place. For squat roasts such as the eye round, wrap longer pieces of kitchen twine around the perimeter to cinch in the sides and give the roast a neater shape.

For Long Roasts

Fold thin end, if needed, under roast. Wrap piece of kitchen twine around roast and fasten with double knot, repeating along length of roast, spacing ties about 1½ inches apart.

For Squat Roasts

Wrap piece of kitchen twine around roast about 1 inch from bottom and tie with double knot. Repeat with second piece of twine, wrapping it about 1 inch from top.

cutting a crosshatch into a beef or pork roast

To help the meat absorb a salt rub and help the fat render during cooking, we score a crosshatch pattern into the fat cap of the roast.

Using sharp knife, cut evenly spaced slits in crosshatch pattern in fat cap, being careful not to cut into meat.

slicing thinly

Carving a boneless roast, such as a top sirloin or eye round, into wafer-thin slices across the grain helps the beef to taste more tender.

After removing roast from oven and letting it rest, slice meat crosswise as thin as possible.

trimming a whole tenderloin

Buying a beef tenderloin that is already trimmed is both convenient and saves you prep time, but a trimmed tenderloin is expensive—roughly $25 per pound. An untrimmed tenderloin costs about $14 per pound (and can sell for as little as $9 per pound at warehouse clubs); given the huge savings in cost, we prefer to do the work ourselves.

1 Pull away outer layer of fat to expose fatty chain of meat.

2 Pull chain of fat away from roast, cut it off, and discard chain.

3 Scrape silverskin at creases in thick end to expose lobes, then trim by slicing under it and cutting upward. Remove remaining silverskin in creases and fat from underside.

All About Pork

We love pork in all of its incarnations, from large shoulder roasts to weeknight-friendly pork tenderloin. Roasting today's lean cuts of pork can be a challenge but our kitchen-tested methods, such as brining and salting, eliminate any issues.

PRIMAL CUTS

Four different cuts of pork are sold at the wholesale level. From this first series of cuts, known in the trade as primal cuts, a butcher (usually at a meatpacking plant in the Midwest but sometimes on-site at your market) will make the retail cuts that you bring home.

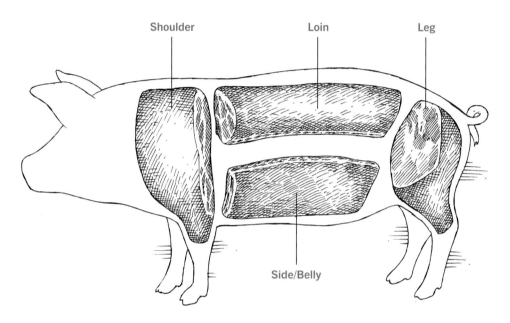

Shoulder   Cuts from the upper portion of the shoulder (called the blade shoulder) are well marbled with fat and contain a lot of connective tissue, making them ideal candidates for slow-cooking methods like braising, stewing, or barbecuing. Cuts from the arm, or picnic shoulder, are a bit more economical than those from the blade area but are otherwise quite similar.

Loin   The area between the shoulder and back legs is the leanest, most tender part of the animal. Rib and loin chops are cut from this area, as are pork loin roasts and tenderloin roasts. These cuts will be dry if overcooked.

Leg   The rear legs are often referred to as "ham." This primal cut is sold as large roasts and is available fresh or cured.

Side/Belly   The underside is the fattiest part of the animal and is the source of bacon and spareribs.

COMMON PORK ROASTS

Not all pork roasts are alike. This chart helps you understand their differences so you can shop with confidence. These are the cuts of pork we roast most often in the test kitchen.

**PORK BUTT
(Blade Shoulder)**

This large, flavorful cut (often labeled Boston butt or pork shoulder) can weigh as much as 8 pounds when sold with the bone in. Many markets take out the bone and sell this cut in smaller chunks. This cut is ideal for slow-roasted shredded pork dishes.

**SHOULDER
ARM PICNIC
(Arm Shoulder)**

This affordable cut (often labeled "picnic roast" at markets) can be sold bone-in or boneless. It is rich in fat and connective tissue. Like pork butt, it's best roasted low and slow.

RIB CHOP (Loin)

Cut from the rib section of the loin, these chops have a relatively high fat content, rendering them flavorful and unlikely to dry out during roasting. These chops are easily identified by the bone that runs along one side and the one large eye of loin muscle.

**TENDERLOIN
ROAST (Loin)**

This lean, delicate, boneless roast cooks very quickly because it's so small, usually weighing just about 1 pound. Since there is very little marbling, overcooking this roast destroys its texture. Tenderloins are often sold two to a package. Many tenderloins sold in the supermarket are enhanced (see page 15); look for one that has no ingredients other than pork on the label.

**BONELESS
BLADE-END
ROAST (Loin)**

This boneless roast is cut from the shoulder end of the loin and has plenty of fat and flavor. Unfortunately this cut can be hard to find, but the more readily available boneless center-cut loin roast serves as a strong stand-in.

**BONELESS
CENTER-CUT LOIN
ROAST (Loin)**

This boneless roast is widely available and a good choice for roasting. We prefer the more flavorful boneless blade-end roast, but the two cuts can be used interchangeably. Make sure to buy a center-cut roast with a decent fat cap on top.

RIB ROAST (Loin)

Often referred to as the pork equivalent of prime rib or rack of lamb, this mild, fairly lean roast consists of a single muscle with a protective fat cap. It is available as a center-cut roast with anywhere from five to eight ribs or as a bone-in blade-end roast.

**CROWN ROAST
(Loin)**

Butchers tie two bone-in center-cut rib or center-cut loin roasts together to create this impressive-looking roast. We find that a crown roast with 16 to 20 ribs is the best choice, as smaller and larger roasts are harder to cook evenly.

**FRESH HAM,
SHANK END (Leg)**

The leg is divided into two cuts—the tapered shank end and the more rounded sirloin end. The sirloin end has a lot of bones that make carving tricky. We prefer the shank end. This cut is usually covered in a thick layer of fat and skin, which should be scored before roasting. Despite the visible fat, this cut benefits from brining.

COUNTRY HAM (Leg)

Country hams are porky and robust because they are dry-cured—salted, spiced, smoked, and aged for anywhere from three months to years. We prefer purchasing uncooked whole hams, but cooked and sliced varieties are available. Hams aged from three to six months are the most widely sold. Our favorite: Harper's Grand Champion Whole Country Ham.

**SPIRAL-SLICED
BONE-IN HAM (Leg)**

This is our favorite wet-cured ham because the meat is not pumped up with water (the label should read "ham with natural juices") and because it is so easy to carve. Bone-in hams taste best, and although packages are not labeled as such, look for a ham from the shank rather than from the sirloin end. You can pick out the shank ham by its tapered, more pointed end opposite the flat cut side of the ham. The sirloin ham has more rounded or blunt ends. Our favorite: Johnston County Spiral-Sliced Smoked Ham.

**PORK BELLY
(Side/Belly)**

This unctuous, ultraflavorful cut with its alternating layers of meat and fat is nothing more than unsliced, uncured bacon. Low roasting turns the meat and fat tender and sumptuous and the skin supremely crisp.

BUYING PORK

The majority of pork sold in today's supermarkets bears little resemblance to the pork our grandparents consumed. New breeding techniques and feeding systems have slimmed down the modern pig, which contains a third less fat than it did 30 years ago. As you might imagine, leaner pork is not as flavorful and is prone to drying out as it cooks. Here's what you need to know when buying pork.

buy pink pork

Raw pork can range in color from a pasty white to a deep pink, and color is an indication of quality. The color of pork reflects the meat's pH, and even small differences in pH can have a significant impact on flavor and texture. In fact, a high pH can be even more important than fat in determining flavor. Compared to rosy-pink high-pH pork, pork with low pH is paler, softer, and relatively bland. So don't be fooled into thinking that pork is "the other white meat," but rather pick out the pinkest pork you can find at the market.

buy unenhanced or natural pork

Because modern supermarket pork is so lean and prone to dryness, many producers now inject their fresh pork products with a sodium solution. So-called enhanced pork is now the only option at many supermarkets, especially for lean cuts like the tenderloin. To be sure, read the label; if the pork has been enhanced it will have an ingredient list.

berkshire pork

Chefs and consumers pay top dollar for specialty, heritage pork breeds, such as Berkshire (known as Kurobuta in Japan) and Duroc. They are touted as being fattier, juicier, and much more flavorful. Putting this claim to the test, we tasted both Berkshire and Duroc pork in a side by side test against regular supermarket pork. The Berkshire pork consistently came out on top for being the juiciest and most intensely flavored. Some stores carry Berkshire pork and you can order it online, but it does costs much more than supermarket pork.

KEY PREP TIPS

Here are a few essential steps that help to prepare various cuts of pork for roasting. For instructions on cutting a crosshatch pattern into the fat cap of a pork loin or ham, see page 12.

preventing curled pork chops

Pork chops come covered in a thin layer of fat and connective tissue (or silverskin). This layer contracts faster than the rest of the meat, causing buckling and leading to unevenly cooked chops. Cutting slits in this layer solves the problem.

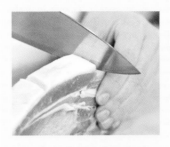
For each chop, cut 2 slits about 2 inches apart through fat and connective tissue.

trimming silverskin from pork tenderloin

Silverskin, the translucent connective tissue running along the tenderloin, is chewy and unpalatable and should be removed.

To remove it, slip knife under silverskin, angle it slightly upward, and use gentle back-and-forth motion to remove it; discard skin.

tying a pork loin

Tying a pork loin helps maintain its shape during cooking so that it cooks evenly.

Use double knots to secure pieces of kitchen twine at 1½-inch intervals (about 3 fingers' width apart).

All About Lamb

Lamb is undergoing a renaissance of late and is no longer relegated to the Easter table. And for good reason. It takes particularly well to roasting, both in the oven and on the grill, and its rich flavor can't be beat.

PRIMAL CUTS
Lamb is initially divided into five primal (or major) cuts.

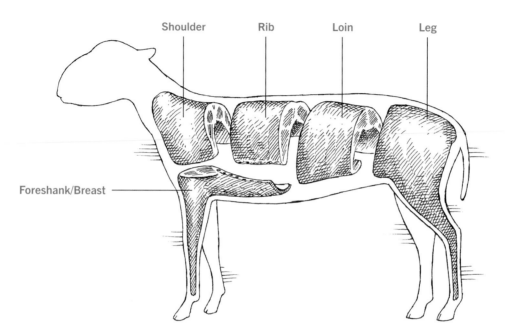

Shoulder This area extends from the neck through the fourth rib. Meat from this area is flavorful, although it contains a fair amount of connective tissue and can be tough. Chops, roasts, and boneless stew meat all come from the shoulder.

Rib The rib area is directly behind the shoulder and extends from the fourth to the 12th rib. The rack (all eight ribs from this section) is cut from the rib. When cut into individual chops, the meat is called rib chops. Meat from this area has a fine, tender grain and a mild flavor.

Loin The loin extends from the last rib down to the hip area. The loin chop is the most familiar cut from this part of the lamb. Like the rib chop, it is tender and has a mild, sweet flavor.

Leg The leg area runs from the hip down to the hoof. It may be sold whole or broken into smaller roasts and shanks (one comes from each hind leg). These roasts may be sold with the bones in, or they may be butterflied and sold boneless.

Foreshank/Breast The foreshank and breast is cut from the underside of the animal. This area includes the two front legs (each yields a shank) as well as the breast, which is rarely sold in supermarkets.

BUYING LAMB

Lamb is becoming more popular. It can be relatively inexpensive and is easy to turn into something special with the right recipes. Note that most markets contain just a few of our favorite cuts, so you may need to special-order lamb.

buy young lamb

Most lamb sold in the supermarket has been slaughtered when 6 to 12 months old. When the animal is slaughtered past the first year, the meat must be labeled mutton. Generally, younger lamb has a milder flavor that most people prefer. The only indication of slaughter age at the supermarket is size. A whole leg of lamb weighing 9 pounds is likely to have come from an older animal than a whole leg weighing just 6 pounds.

domestic versus imported lamb

While almost all the beef and pork sold in American markets is raised domestically, you can purchase imported as well as domestic lamb. Domestic lamb is distinguished by its larger size and milder flavor, while lamb imported from Australia or New Zealand has a stronger, gamier taste. The reason for this difference in taste boils down to diet and the chemistry of lamb fat. Imported lamb is pasture-fed on mixed grasses, while lamb raised in the United States begins on a diet of grass but finishes with grain.

COMMON LAMB ROASTS

These are the test kitchen's favorite lamb cuts for roasting.

BONELESS LEG OF LAMB

A boneless leg is a whole lamb leg that has been completely deboned, and it usually weighs between 6 and 8 pounds. You can also purchase a boneless half leg of lamb, which is simply this roast cut in half. There is usually a thin layer of fat covering the meat on the outside. Often, the interior of the meat (where the bone was located) requires some serious trimming before cooking.

BONE-IN LEG OF LAMB

The whole leg generally weighs 6 to 10 pounds and includes both the wider sirloin end and the narrower shank end. Often the hip bone and aitch bone will be removed for easier carving; this is sometimes referred to as a "semiboneless" leg of lamb. Also, the sirloin and shank ends can be sold separately.

RACK OF LAMB

The equivalent to prime rib from a cow, this cut is extremely flavorful and tender. It's also very expensive. This roast contains either eight or nine rib bones, depending on how the meat has been butchered.

KEY PREP TIPS

Here are some important steps you need to know to prepare a rack or leg of lamb for roasting.

trimming a boneless leg of lamb

Trimming the lamb of excess fat and silverskin will give it a cleaner flavor and the meat will be less chewy.

Place lamb on cutting board with fat cap facing down. Using sharp knife, trim any pockets of fat and connective tissue from underside of lamb.

pounding a boneless leg of lamb

Pounding the lamb will even out the thickness of the meat so that it roasts more evenly or is easier to roll into a tidy roast.

Place rough side of meat (side that was closest to bone) facing up on counter or cutting board. Pound meat to desired thickness to ensure even cooking.

preparing a rack of lamb

1 Using boning knife, scrape ribs clean of any scraps of meat or fat (this is known as frenching). Trim off outer layer of fat, then trim flap of meat underneath it and fat underneath that flap.

2 Remove silverskin by sliding boning knife between silverskin and flesh.

All About Fish and Shellfish

Roasting is a popular way to prepare salmon fillets, but there's a whole ocean out there. We also like to roast white fish fillets, whole fish, and shellfish, from a big batch of mussels in the oven to oysters on the grill.

BUYING SEAFOOD

Buying top-quality fish is just as important as utilizing the proper cooking technique. Here's what to look for from either a fishmonger or in the supermarket.

buy fresh fish

Buying fresh fish is key for good flavor and texture. Try to always buy fish from a trusted source, preferably one with high volume to help ensure freshness. Both the store, and the fish in it, should smell like the sea (not fishy or sour), and all the fish should be on ice or properly refrigerated. Fillets and steaks should look bright, shiny, and firm, not dull or mushy. Whole fish should have moist, taut skin, clear eyes, and bright red gills. It is always better to have your fishmonger slice steaks and fillets to order rather than buying precut pieces that may have been sitting around.

keep it cold

It is important to keep your fish very cold. If you have a long ride home, ask for a plastic bag of ice that you can put under the fish. Because fish is so perishable, it's best to buy it the day it will be cooked. If that's not possible, unwrap the fish, pat it dry, put it in a zipper-lock bag, press out the air, and seal the bag. Set the fish on a bed of ice in a bowl or container (to hold the water once the ice melts), and place it in the back of the fridge, where it is coldest. If the ice melts before you use the fish, replenish it. The fish should keep for one day.

understand your choice of salmon: farmed versus wild

Salmon is perhaps the most popular fish as it is easily accessible around the country. Roasting it is easy and there are many ways to dress up simple roasted salmon fillets or a side of salmon. There is a lot of debate about farmed versus wild salmon and which you should buy. So what's the difference between wild and farmed salmon? Plenty, and each variety has its virtues. Wild salmon hails from the Pacific and has a deep pink hue due to its crustacean-based diet. The texture is firm and meaty and it's only available from late spring to early fall. Farmed salmon is raised primarily in Norway, Scotland, Chile, and Canada and is available year-round. It is naturally gray but pigments added to its feed turn it pink. The texture is soft and buttery. We roast farmed salmon more often than we do wild; farmed salmon becomes firm yet silky when cooked to 125 degrees, while wild varieties taste dry at this temperature and are best cooked to just 120 degrees.

buy mussels and oysters with closed shells

The key to buying bivalves is freshness. They should smell clean and the shells should look moist. Look for tightly closed shells and avoid any that are broken or sitting in a puddle of water. Some clam and mussel shells may gape slightly, but they should close when they are tapped. Discard any that won't close; they may be dead and should not be eaten. Every bag of mussels, oysters, and clams that is harvested commercially must be tagged by the grower. And the retailer is required to keep the tag attached to the original container until that container is empty. Any legitimate seller will show you the tag upon request and, if the date is within a couple of days of your purchase, you know you have a fresh product. See page 21 for information on storing bivalves properly.

buy frozen shrimp

Virtually all shrimp sold in supermarkets today were frozen at some point. Because it's hard to know how long "fresh" (defrosted) shrimp have been sitting at the fish counter, we recommend buying bags of still-frozen shrimp and defrosting them at home. Shell-on shrimp tend to be sweeter, and make sure your shrimp are preservative-free (shrimp should be the only thing on the ingredient list). Shrimp are sorted and sold by size; see below for more information.

SORTING OUT SHRIMP SIZES

Shrimp are sold both by size (small, medium, etc.) and by the number needed to make 1 pound, usually given in a range. Choosing shrimp by the numerical rating is more accurate, because the size labels vary from store to store. Here's how the two sizing systems generally compare:

Small	51 to 60 per pound
Medium	41 to 50 per pound
Medium-Large	31 to 40 per pound
Large	26 to 30 per pound
Extra-Large	21 to 25 per pound
Jumbo	16 to 20 per pound

FISH AND SHELLFISH FOR ROASTING

This chart lists all of the fish that we think are best suited for roasting and that have recipes in the book. It explains what they are and shows what you can expect to see at the supermarket.

HALIBUT

Sold as whole steaks, belly steaks, and fillets, this firm, lean white fish is mild but rich, ideal for robust flavor pairings. Steaks are your best bet for roasting.

COD

Cod is a white fish with a medium-firm, meaty texture and a clean, mild flavor. We like roasting skinless cod fillets.

HADDOCK

Usually sold as skin-on fillets, haddock is a very mild white fish with a medium-firm texture. It is a good substitute for cod or halibut.

RED SNAPPER

Perfect for roasting whole, snapper is a flaky but firm white fish with a mild to moderate flavor that can hold its own against bold flavors.

SEA BASS

Sea bass is a sweet, mild white fish with a medium-firm texture. We like roasting sea bass whole as well as in fillets.

FLOUNDER

Flounder's delicate, flaky texture and sweet, mild flavor make it a great candidate for stuffing before roasting.

SOLE

Sole is interchangeable with flounder.

SALMON

We roast salmon both as a whole side and as fillets. We use mild-flavored, silky-textured, marbled farm-raised salmon more often than leaner wild salmon, but both have a firm enough texture for a variety of roasting recipes. Like most filleted fish, salmon is sold deboned, but it's prudent to check for pinbones (see page 20).

TROUT

Due to its delicate, flaky texture, this is another fish best roasted whole. Trout is rich and flavorful and is particularly tasty when stuffed.

MACKEREL

While most people are familiar with the pungency of smoked mackerel, this moist, firm yet flaky fish is rich in flavor when roasted fresh. We roast mackerel whole.

SHRIMP

Shrimp are sold by size as well as by the number needed to make 1 pound, usually given in a range. Choosing shrimp by the numerical rating is more accurate, because the size label can vary from store to store. See the size chart for shrimp on page 18.

LOBSTER TAILS

Unlike fresh whole lobsters, lobster tails are widely available year-round, which is why we developed a recipe for roasted stuffed lobster tails (page 228). We found that frozen tails weighing between 5 and 6 ounces had just the right amount of meat without being too pricey. Frozen tails from the Northeast (rather than the Caribbean) tend to be sweeter and more tender.

MUSSELS

We discovered that the most foolproof method for cooking mussels is roasting them (page 232). Roasting concentrates their earthy flavor and ensures that a big batch cooks evenly, which is not the case with steaming. The two main varieties you will see at the store are the Atlantic blue mussel and the Pacific green-lipped (also called New Zealand) mussel. These mussels are interchangeable when it comes to cooking, although some think the green-lipped mussels are slightly chewier. Most mussels sold today are farmed or rope-cultured, which is good because they are less gritty. Make sure that shells are tightly closed and avoid any that are open or gaping; they may be dying or dead. Be sure to remove the beard before cooking (see page 20).

OYSTERS

There are many varieties of oysters available throughout the United States. Contrary to old fish lore, there is no true "oyster season" thanks to modern cultivation methods and the fact that various types spawn at different times. We prefer oysters from cold northern waters because they tend to be briny with a flavor that's more crisp than oysters from warmer southern waters. Make sure that shells are tightly closed and avoid any that are open or gaping; they may be dying or dead.

CLAMS

There are many varieties of clams available throughout the United States, but they generally fall into two categories: hard-shelled and soft-shelled. Hard-shell clams have thick, hard shells; the two most common varieties are littleneck clams and cherrystone clams. Soft-shell clams have thin, brittle shells and common varieties include steamers and razor clams. Make sure that shells are tightly closed and avoid any that are open or gaping; they may be dying or dead. Clams must be scrubbed to remove sand and grit before cooking (see page 20).

KEY PREP AND SERVING TIPS

Here's what you should do when getting ready to roast fish and shellfish.

removing skin from a fish fillet

Some recipes recommend removing the skin from the fish before cooking.

Using tip of boning knife or sharp chef's knife, cut skin away from fish at corner of fillet. When sufficient skin is exposed, grasp skin firmly with paper towel, hold it taut, and slice remaining skin off flesh.

removing pinbones from salmon

Pinbones can sometimes be hidden inside a piece of salmon. Always check the salmon for these bones before cooking.

1 Drape fillet over inverted bowl to help any pinbones protrude. Then, working from head end to tail end, locate pinbones by running your fingers along length of fillet (they will feel like tiny bumps).

2 Use needle-nose pliers or tweezers to grasp tip of bone. To avoid tearing flesh, pull slowly but firmly at slight angle in direction bone is naturally pointing rather than straight up. Repeat until all pinbones are removed.

cutting salmon into fillets

Buying a large piece of salmon and cutting it into fillets at home ensures that the pieces are the same thickness and will cook at the same rate.

Buy one 1½-pound skinless salmon fillet. Using sharp chef's knife, cut it into 4 evenly sized portions.

scrubbing mussels, oysters, and clams

Bivalves often have fine bits of sand and grit stuck within the crags of their shells, and need to be scrubbed before cooking.

Place mussels, oysters, or clams in colander and scrub briefly with vegetable brush under cold running water. Discard any that are cracked or open.

debearding mussels

There can be a small, weedy beard protruding from the side of the mussel that needs to be removed before cooking.

Holding mussel in your hand, pull beard firmly out of shell, using your thumb and side of paring knife to grip it firmly.

peeling and deveining shrimp

It's better to buy shrimp with their peels intact and then peel and devein them yourself because the shrimp will have better flavor.

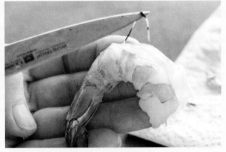

1 Break shell on underside, under swimming legs. Leave tail end intact if desired, or tug tail end to remove shell.

2 Use paring knife to make shallow cut along back of shrimp to expose vein.

3 Using tip of knife, lift vein out. Discard vein by wiping knife blade against paper towel.

serving a whole roasted fish

If properly roasted, a whole fish should need just a few strategic cuts in order to easily remove the meat from the bones in a single piece.

1 Using sharp knife, make vertical cut just behind head from top of fish to belly.

2 Make another cut along top of fish from head to tail.

3 Use large, flat spatula to lift meat from bones, starting at head and lifting out fillet. Repeat on other side of fish. Discard head and skeleton.

STORING FISH PROPERLY

Because fish is so perishable, it's best to buy it the day it will be cooked. If that's not possible, it's important to store it properly. Properly stored fish should keep for one day.

Unwrap the fish, pat it dry, put it in a zipper-lock bag, press out the air, and seal the bag. Set the fish on a bed of ice in a bowl and place it in the back of the fridge.

Storing Bivalves

Storing mussels, oysters, and clams properly will ensure they stay fresh before serving. They need to be kept moist and cold and have access to oxygen. Do not place them inside a sealed plastic bag or submerge them in water or they will die.

Store mussels, oysters, and clams in a colander of ice set over a bowl with a damp towel draped over the top. Stored properly they should keep for up to three days.

Brining and Salting

BRINING POULTRY AND PORK

Brining means soaking meat in a solution of water and salt (and sometimes sugar) before cooking. The meat absorbs the brine as it soaks and then retains it during cooking, which improves both its flavor and tenderness. On a molecular level, the salt water fills up gaps in the protein structure and stays there during cooking. We have found that brining inhibits browning, and it requires fitting a brining container in the fridge. It works especially well with lean cuts of meat, like chicken, turkey, and pork; do not brine kosher birds or enhanced pork. We prefer to use table salt for brining because it dissolves quickly and has a standard crystal size that measures uniformly from brand to brand.

brining directions

Dissolve the salt in the water in a container or bowl large enough to hold the brine and meat, following the amounts in the chart. Submerge the meat completely in the brine. Cover and refrigerate, following the times in the chart (do not brine for longer or the meat will become overly salty). Remove the meat from the brine and pat dry with paper towels.

CUTS	COLD WATER	TABLE SALT	TIME
Chicken			
1 (3- to 8-pound) whole chicken	2 quarts	½ cup	1 hour
2 (3- to 8-pound) whole chickens	3 quarts	¾ cup	1 hour
4 pounds bone-in chicken pieces (whole breasts, split breasts, whole legs, thighs, and/or drumsticks)	2 quarts	½ cup	½ to 1 hour
Boneless, skinless chicken breasts (up to 6 breasts)	1½ quarts	3 tablespoons	½ to 1 hour
Turkey			
1 (12- to 17-pound) whole turkey	2 gallons	1 cup	6 to 12 hours
1 (18- to 24-pound) whole turkey	3 gallons	1½ cups	6 to 12 hours
Bone-in turkey breast	1 gallon	½ cup	3 to 6 hours
Pork			
Bone-in pork chops (up to 6)	1½ quarts	3 tablespoons	½ to 1 hour
Boneless pork chops (up to 6)	1½ quarts	3 tablespoons	½ to 1 hour
1 (2½- to 6-pound) pork roast	2 quarts	¼ cup	1½ to 2 hours

SALTING MEAT AND POULTRY

Sprinkling meat with salt and letting it sit for a while before cooking is similar to brining. As the meat sits, the salt is absorbed by the meat which both seasons it and helps alter the protein structure. Compared to brining, salting is the best choice for meats that are already relatively juicy and/or well marbled. We prefer to use kosher salt for salting because it's easier to distribute the salt evenly. We use Diamond Crystal Kosher Salt; if using Morton Kosher Salt, reduce the amounts listed by 33 percent (e.g., use ⅔ teaspoon Morton Kosher Salt or 1 teaspoon Diamond Crystal).

not all kosher salt is the same

Unlike table salt, kosher salt is fairly easy to spread and won't clump. But the two leading brands of kosher salt are not the same. Because of its more open crystal structure, a teaspoon of Diamond Crystal acutally contains less salt than a teaspoon of Morton kosher salt.

CUTS	TIME	KOSHER SALT	METHOD
Meat			
Steaks, Lamb Chops, Pork Chops	1 hour	¾ teaspoon per 8-ounce chop or steak	Apply salt evenly over surface and let rest at room temperature, uncovered, on wire rack set in rimmed baking sheet.
Beef, Lamb, and Pork Roasts	At least 6 hours and up to 24 hours	1 teaspoon per pound	Apply salt evenly over surface, wrap tightly with plastic wrap, and let rest in refrigerator.
Poultry			
Whole Chicken	At least 6 hours and up to 24 hours	1 teaspoon per pound	Apply salt evenly inside cavity and under skin of breast and legs and let rest in refrigerator on wire rack set in rimmed baking sheet. (Wrap with plastic wrap if salting for longer than 12 hours.)
Bone-In Chicken Pieces, Boneless or Bone-In Turkey Breast	At least 6 hours and up to 24 hours	¾ teaspoon per pound	If poultry is skin-on, apply salt evenly between skin and meat, leaving skin attached, and let rest in the refrigerator on wire rack set in rimmed baking sheet. (Wrap with plastic wrap if salting for longer than 12 hours.)
Whole Turkey	At least 24 hours and up to 2 days	1 teaspoon per pound	Apply salt evenly inside cavity and under skin of breast and legs, wrap tightly with plastic wrap, and let rest in refrigerator.

Doneness Temperatures for Meat, Poultry, and Fish

Do not guess at doneness: Use a thermometer (for tips, see page 25). We list below the final cooking temperatures of meat, poultry, and fish. Note that the temperature of beef and pork (but not poultry or fish) will continue to rise after cooking (this is known as carryover cooking). For this reason, we list both the cooking and serving temperatures.

FOR THIS INGREDIENT...	COOK TO THIS TEMPERATURE
Beef and Lamb	
Chops, Steaks, and Roasts	
Rare	115 to 120 degrees (120 to 125 degrees after resting)
Medium-Rare	120 to 125 degrees (125 to 130 degrees after resting)
Medium	130 to 135 degrees (135 to 140 degrees after resting)
Medium-Well	140 to 145 degrees (145 to 150 degrees after resting)
Well-Done	150 to 155 degrees (155 to 160 degrees after resting)
Pork	
Chops and Tenderloin	
Medium-Well	145 degrees (150 degrees after resting)
Well-Done	160 degrees
Loin Roasts	
Medium-Well	140 degrees (145 degrees after resting)
Well-Done	160 degrees
Poultry	
Breasts	160 degrees
Thighs and drumsticks	175 degrees
Fish	
Rare	110 degrees (for tuna only)
Medium-Rare	125 degrees (for tuna or salmon)
Medium	135 to 140 degrees (for white-fleshed fish)

USING A THERMOMETER

A thermometer is the best tool for determining if your food is cooked properly—as long as you use it correctly. Here are some tips.

how to temp a whole bird

Because breast meat cooks faster than thigh meat, you should take the temperature of both when cooking poultry.

For breast meat

Insert thermometer from neck end, holding thermometer parallel to bird. It should register 160 degrees.

For thigh meat

Insert thermometer at an angle into area between drumstick and breast, taking care not to hit bone. It should register 175 degrees.

how to temp a steak, chop, or small roast

When taking the temperature of thin steaks or pork chops, it can be hard to get the tip of the thermometer into the very center unless you pick the meat up with tongs. You can also use this technique for pork tenderloin or rack of lamb; just lift the meat with a pair of tongs and insert the thermometer into the end, parallel to the meat.

Using tongs to hold meat away from cooking area, insert thermometer through side of meat, into center where temperature will be lowest.

look for the lowest temperature

It is key to always look for the lowest temperature when determining the doneness of meat. For large roasts, we recommend taking the temperature in a few places to find the lowest temperature because there often are hotter and cooler spots. The lowest temperature should be your guide.

Sink probe far into meat and let it adjust for a minute, then very slowly pull it out again, taking note of lowest temperature you find. (Do this in two different locations to help ensure that you've nailed the doneness perfectly.)

RESTING

Resting meat and poultry (and fish, depending on the recipe) is crucial. It allows the meat to relax and reabsorb its juices, so there's less juice on the cutting board and more inside the meat itself. Small steaks, chops, and cutlets need only 5 to 10 minutes of resting time, while larger roasts require 15 to 20 minutes. An entire turkey, on the other hand, should rest for 30 minutes before being carved. To keep meat warm while it rests, tent it loosely with aluminum foil, unless it has a crisp coating or skin that you don't want to turn soggy. To protect the bottom crust of grilled meat from turning soggy, set the meat on a wire rack as it rests.

CALIBRATE YOUR THERMOMETER

You should check that your thermometer takes accurate readings when you first buy it and then again periodically over time.

Put a mixture of ice and cold tap water in a glass and let it sit for several minutes to allow the temperature to stabilize. Put the probe in the slush, being careful not to touch the sides or bottom of the glass or bowl. On a digital thermometer, press the "calibrate" button to 32 degrees; on a dial-face thermometer, turn the dial to 32 degrees (the method differs from model to model; you may need pliers to turn a small knob on the back).

Finishing Touches: Sauces and More

A perfectly roasted piece of meat or fish is delicious on its own but add a simple sauce, a chutney, or a compound butter and suddenly you've elevated your meal from good to great. Here are some of the test kitchen's favorite basic yet versatile sauces and what to pair with them.

HORSERADISH SAUCE

makes about 1 cup

Buy refrigerated prepared horseradish, not the shelf-stable kind.
Great with: beef, lamb, and salmon

½ cup sour cream
½ cup prepared horseradish
1½ teaspoons kosher salt
⅛ teaspoon pepper

Combine all ingredients in bowl. Refrigerate for at least 30 minutes.

SALSA VERDE

makes about 1½ cups

This sauce is best served immediately after it is made, but can be refrigerated for up to 2 days. If refrigerated, bring the sauce to room temperature and stir to recombine before serving.
Great with: chicken, turkey, beef, pork, lamb, white fish, and salmon

2 slices hearty white sandwich bread
1 cup extra-virgin olive oil
¼ cup lemon juice (2 lemons)
4 cups fresh parsley leaves
¼ cup capers, rinsed
4 anchovy fillets
2 small garlic cloves, minced
¼ teaspoon salt

1 Toast bread in toaster on lowest setting until surface is dry but not browned, about 15 seconds. Remove crust and cut bread into rough ½-inch pieces (you should have about 1½ cups).

2 Process bread, oil, and lemon juice in food processor until smooth, about 10 seconds. Add parsley, capers, anchovies, garlic, and salt. Pulse until mixture is finely chopped (mixture should not be smooth), about 5 pulses, scraping down sides of bowl with rubber spatula after 3 pulses. Transfer mixture to bowl.

CHERMOULA SAUCE

makes about 1 cup

To keep the sauce from becoming bitter, whisk in the olive oil by hand. The sauce can be refrigerated for up to 2 days. If refrigerated, bring the sauce to room temperature and rewhisk before serving.
Great with: beef (especially grilled), lamb, white fish, and cauliflower

¾ cup fresh cilantro leaves
4 garlic cloves, minced
1 teaspoon ground cumin
1 teaspoon paprika
¼ teaspoon cayenne pepper
¼ teaspoon salt
3 tablespoons lemon juice
½ cup extra-virgin olive oil

Pulse cilantro, garlic, cumin, paprika, cayenne, and salt in food processor until coarsely chopped, about 10 pulses. Add lemon juice and pulse briefly to combine. Transfer mixture to medium bowl and slowly whisk in oil until incorporated and mixture is emulsified. Cover with plastic wrap and let stand at room temperature for at least 1 hour.

FENNEL-APPLE CHUTNEY
makes about 2 cups
Great with: white fish and pork

1 tablespoon extra-virgin olive oil
1 large fennel bulb, stalks discarded, bulb halved, cored, and cut into ¼-inch pieces
1 onion, chopped fine
2 Granny Smith apples, peeled, cored, and cut in ½-inch pieces
1 cup rice vinegar
¾ cup sugar
2 teaspoons grated lemon zest
1 teaspoon salt
½ teaspoon red pepper flakes

Heat oil in medium saucepan over medium heat until shimmering. Add fennel and onion and cook until softened and lightly browned, about 10 minutes. Add apples, vinegar, sugar, lemon zest, salt, and pepper flakes. Bring to simmer and cook until thickened, about 20 minutes. Cool to room temperature, about 2 hours, or refrigerate overnight.

RED WINE–ORANGE SAUCE
makes about 1½ cups
Medium-bodied red wines are best for this sauce.
Great with: turkey, beef, and lamb

6 tablespoons unsalted butter, cut into 6 pieces and chilled
3 shallots, minced
1½ tablespoons tomato paste
1 tablespoon sugar
4 garlic cloves, minced
1 tablespoon all-purpose flour
3 cups beef broth
1½ cups red wine
⅓ cup orange juice
1½ tablespoons Worcestershire sauce
1 sprig fresh thyme
Salt and pepper

1 Melt 2 tablespoons butter in medium saucepan over medium-high heat. Add shallots, tomato paste, and sugar and cook, stirring frequently, until deep brown, 4 to 5 minutes. Stir in garlic and flour and cook until garlic is fragrant and vegetables are well coated with flour, about 30 seconds.

2 Stir in broth, wine, orange juice, Worcestershire, and thyme sprigs, scraping up any browned bits. Bring to boil, reduce heat to medium, and cook at low boil until reduced to 2 cups, about 40 minutes.

3 Strain sauce through fine-mesh strainer set over bowl; discard solids. Return sauce to pot and place over low heat. Whisk in remaining 4 tablespoons butter, 1 piece at a time. Season with salt and pepper to taste.

MUSTARD-CREAM SAUCE
makes about 1 cup
Great with: chicken, beef, and pork

½ cup sour cream
½ cup heavy cream
2 large egg yolks
5 teaspoons Dijon mustard
1 tablespoon white wine vinegar
Salt and pepper
⅛ teaspoon sugar
1 tablespoon minced fresh chives

Whisk sour cream, heavy cream, egg yolks, mustard, vinegar, ¼ teaspoon salt, and sugar together in small saucepan. Cook over medium heat, whisking constantly, until sauce thickens and coats back of spoon, 4 to 5 minutes. Transfer to serving bowl, stir in chives, and season with salt and pepper to taste. Serve warm or at room temperature.

GARLIC-HERB COMPOUND BUTTER
makes about 1 cup
A compound butter—butter mixed with fresh herbs and other potent ingredients like garlic—is an easy way to add savory flavor to plain roasted foods. Compound butter can be refrigerated for up to 4 days or frozen, wrapped tightly in plastic, for up to 2 months.
Great with: beef, pork, lamb, white fish, broccoli, carrots, and potatoes

8 tablespoons unsalted butter, softened
2 tablespoons minced fresh sage or 1½ teaspoons dried
1 tablespoon minced fresh parsley
1 tablespoon minced fresh thyme or ¾ teaspoon dried
2 garlic cloves, minced
¼ teaspoon salt
¼ teaspoon pepper

Combine all ingredients in bowl. Wrap in plastic wrap and let rest to blend flavors, about 10 minutes, or roll into log and refrigerate.

CUCUMBER-YOGURT SAUCE
makes about ¾ cup

A spoon makes easy work of removing the cucumber seeds. Using Greek yogurt here is key; don't substitute regular plain yogurt, or the sauce will be very watery.

Great with: lamb and salmon

½ cucumber, peeled, halved lengthwise, and seeded
½ cup plain whole Greek yogurt
1 tablespoon extra-virgin olive oil
1 tablespoon chopped fresh mint
1 tablespoon chopped fresh dill
1 small garlic clove, minced
¼ teaspoon pepper
⅛ teaspoon salt

Shred cucumber on large holes of box grater. Combine yogurt, oil, mint, dill, garlic, pepper, salt, and shredded cucumber in bowl. Cover and refrigerate until chilled, about 20 minutes.

SWEET AND SOUR CHILI SAUCE
makes about 1 cup

Great with: pork and whole fish

¾ cup sugar
⅓ cup water
¼ cup distilled white vinegar
5 Thai chiles, sliced thin
4 garlic cloves, minced
½ teaspoon salt

Bring all ingredients to boil in small saucepan over medium-high heat. Cook, stirring occasionally, until mixture thickens to thin syrup, 4 to 6 minutes. Let cool completely before serving.

ALL-PURPOSE GRAVY
makes 2 cups

If you would like to double the recipe, use a Dutch oven to give the vegetables ample space for browning and increase the cooking times by roughly 50 percent. Finished gravy can be frozen for up to 1 month. To thaw either single or double recipe, place gravy and 1 tablespoon water in saucepan over low heat and bring slowly to simmer. Gravy may appear broken or curdled as it thaws, but vigorous whisking will recombine it.

Great with: chicken, turkey, beef, pork, and potatoes

1 small carrot, peeled and chopped
1 small celery rib, chopped
1 small onion, chopped
3 tablespoons unsalted butter
¼ cup all-purpose flour
2 cups chicken broth
2 cups beef broth
1 bay leaf
¼ teaspoon dried thyme
5 whole black peppercorns
Salt and pepper

1 Pulse carrot in food processor until broken into rough ¼-inch pieces, about 5 pulses. Add celery and onion; pulse until all vegetables are broken into ⅛-inch pieces, about 5 pulses.

2 Melt butter in large saucepan over medium-high heat. Add vegetables and cook, stirring often, until softened and well browned, about 7 minutes. Reduce heat to medium; add flour and cook, stirring constantly, until thoroughly browned and fragrant, about 5 minutes. Slowly whisk in chicken broth and beef broth; bring to boil, skimming off any foam that forms on surface. Add bay leaf, thyme, and peppercorns, reduce to simmer, and cook, stirring occasionally, until thickened and measures 3 cups, 20 to 25 minutes.

3 Strain gravy into clean saucepan or bowl, pressing on solids to extract as much liquid as possible; discard solids. Season with salt and pepper to taste.

CLASSIC CRANBERRY SAUCE
makes 2¼ cups

If you are using frozen cranberries, do not defrost them before use; just pick through them and add about 2 minutes to the simmering time. Cranberry sauce can be covered and refrigerated for up to 7 days; let stand at room temperature for 30 minutes before serving.

Great with: chicken, turkey, duck, and pork

1 cup sugar
¾ cup water
¼ teaspoon salt
1 (12-ounce) bag cranberries, picked through

Bring sugar, water, and salt to boil in medium saucepan over high heat, stirring occasionally to dissolve sugar. Stir in cranberries; return to boil. Reduce heat to medium; simmer until saucy and slightly thickened and about two-thirds of berries have popped open, about 5 minutes. Transfer to bowl and let cool to room temperature.

Recommended Roasting Equipment

There are some key pieces of equipment that will help you be more successful when roasting. From a quality roasting pan, a heavy baking sheet, and a sturdy skillet to a reliable thermometer and other tools, the right equipment just makes the job easier.

ROASTING PANS, SKILLETS, AND MORE

Roasting Pan

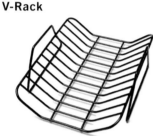

It goes without saying that if you are going to roast a variety of large cuts of meat—never mind your Thanksgiving turkey—you need to invest in a good, heavy roasting pan. Our winning roasting pan is sold with a U-shaped rack.

OUR FAVORITE Calphalon Contemporary Stainless Roasting Pan with Rack ($99.99)

V-Rack

These racks are meant for heavy loads, so go for the biggest and sturdiest rack available. U- and V-shaped racks are best for cradling a roast, and a good set of handles makes safe work of lifting the food out of the pan for carving.

OUR FAVORITE All-Clad Nonstick Large Rack ($24.95)

Traditional Skillet

We are big fans of pan roasting, where we sear meat or fish in a skillet and then transfer it to a hot oven to finish cooking. We also like to build a pan sauce in the skillet while the meat rests. Buy a good traditional skillet and you will have it for a lifetime of cooking. Look for an ovensafe model with balanced weight, sturdy construction, and flared sides for good evaporation. It's also good to have a tight-fitting lid.

OUR FAVORITE All-Clad 12-Inch Stainless Steel Fry Pan with Lid ($96.85)

Nonstick Skillet

Look for an ovensafe model with a broad cooking area, a dark finish, and a grippy, stay-cool handle. It's also good to have a tight-fitting lid.

OUR FAVORITE OXO Good Grips Non-Stick 12-Inch Open Fry Pan ($39.99)

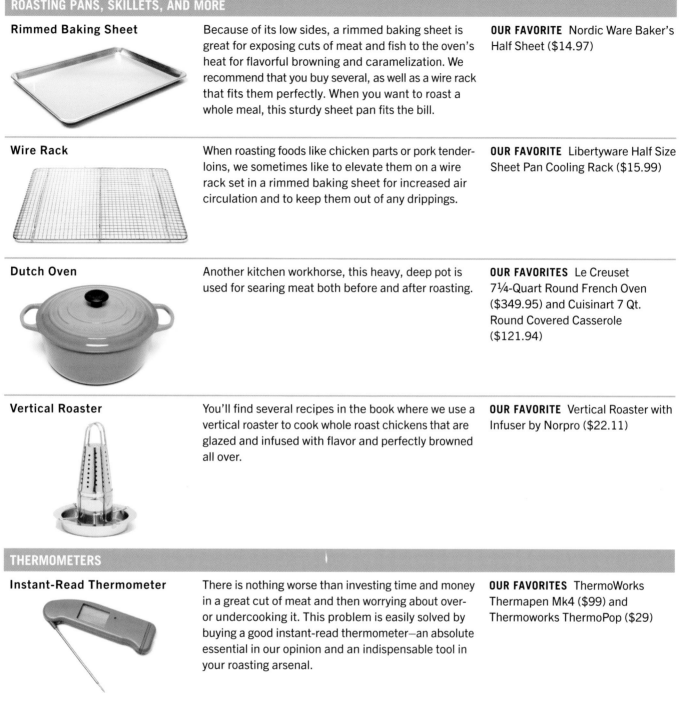

Rimmed Baking Sheet

Because of its low sides, a rimmed baking sheet is great for exposing cuts of meat and fish to the oven's heat for flavorful browning and caramelization. We recommend that you buy several, as well as a wire rack that fits them perfectly. When you want to roast a whole meal, this sturdy sheet pan fits the bill.

OUR FAVORITE Nordic Ware Baker's Half Sheet ($14.97)

Wire Rack

When roasting foods like chicken parts or pork tenderloins, we sometimes like to elevate them on a wire rack set in a rimmed baking sheet for increased air circulation and to keep them out of any drippings.

OUR FAVORITE Libertyware Half Size Sheet Pan Cooling Rack ($15.99)

Dutch Oven

Another kitchen workhorse, this heavy, deep pot is used for searing meat both before and after roasting.

OUR FAVORITES Le Creuset 7¼-Quart Round French Oven ($349.95) and Cuisinart 7 Qt. Round Covered Casserole ($121.94)

Vertical Roaster

You'll find several recipes in the book where we use a vertical roaster to cook whole roast chickens that are glazed and infused with flavor and perfectly browned all over.

OUR FAVORITE Vertical Roaster with Infuser by Norpro ($22.11)

Instant-Read Thermometer

There is nothing worse than investing time and money in a great cut of meat and then worrying about over- or undercooking it. This problem is easily solved by buying a good instant-read thermometer—an absolute essential in our opinion and an indispensable tool in your roasting arsenal.

OUR FAVORITES ThermoWorks Thermapen Mk4 ($99) and Thermoworks ThermoPop ($29)

Oven Thermometer

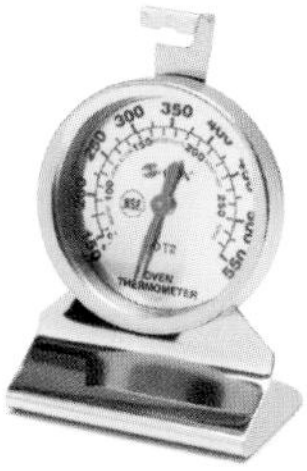

For reliable, consistent results when roasting, an accurate oven thermometer is critical to ensure your oven is calibrated perfectly.

OUR FAVORITE CDN Pro Accurate Oven Thermometer ($8.70)

KNIVES AND OTHER TOOLS

Tongs

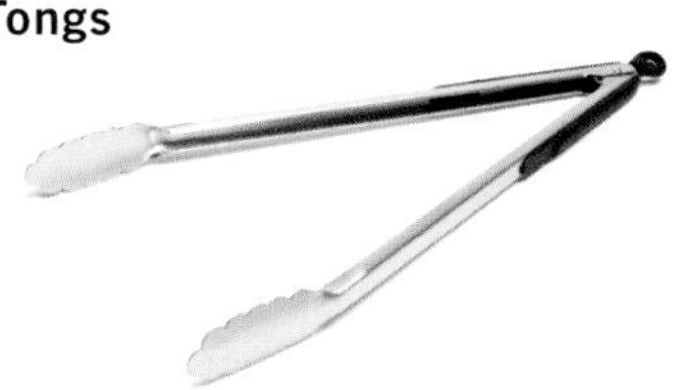

A good pair of tongs is essential for grabbing and turning all kinds of food on the stovetop, in the oven, and on the grill.

OUR FAVORITE OXO Good Grips 12-Inch Locking Tongs ($12.09)

Meat Pounder

This sturdy tool makes it easy to flatten butterflied meat to even thickness with control and steady force.

OUR FAVORITE Norpro GRIP-EZ Meat Pounder ($17.50)

Cutting Board

The right durable cutting board ensures safe slicing and dicing.

OUR FAVORITES Proteak Edge Grain Teak Cutting Board ($84.99) and OXO Good Grips Carving & Cutting Board ($21.99)

Carving Board

Designed with trenches to contain escaping drippings and a well to hold a roast in place, this board is essential for slicing a wide variety of meats.

OUR FAVORITE J.K. Adams Maple Reversible Carving Board ($69.95)

Kitchen Twine

Essential for tying roasts into shape and birds' legs together, this strong, no-fray cotton twine stays in place without singeing or splitting during roasting.

OUR FAVORITE Librett Cotton Butcher's Twine ($8.29)

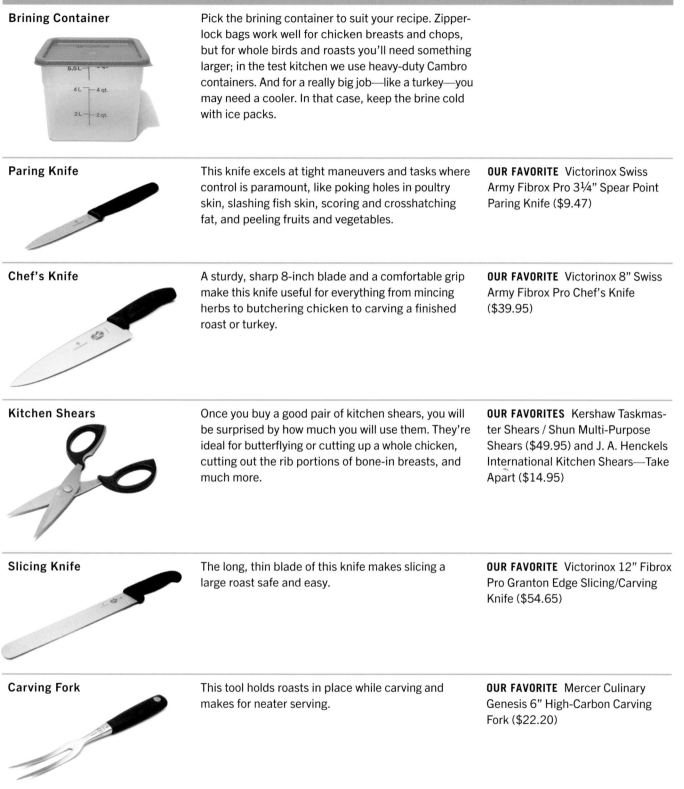

Brining Container

Pick the brining container to suit your recipe. Zipper-lock bags work well for chicken breasts and chops, but for whole birds and roasts you'll need something larger; in the test kitchen we use heavy-duty Cambro containers. And for a really big job—like a turkey—you may need a cooler. In that case, keep the brine cold with ice packs.

Paring Knife

This knife excels at tight maneuvers and tasks where control is paramount, like poking holes in poultry skin, slashing fish skin, scoring and crosshatching fat, and peeling fruits and vegetables.

OUR FAVORITE Victorinox Swiss Army Fibrox Pro 3¼" Spear Point Paring Knife ($9.47)

Chef's Knife

A sturdy, sharp 8-inch blade and a comfortable grip make this knife useful for everything from mincing herbs to butchering chicken to carving a finished roast or turkey.

OUR FAVORITE Victorinox 8" Swiss Army Fibrox Pro Chef's Knife ($39.95)

Kitchen Shears

Once you buy a good pair of kitchen shears, you will be surprised by how much you will use them. They're ideal for butterflying or cutting up a whole chicken, cutting out the rib portions of bone-in breasts, and much more.

OUR FAVORITES Kershaw Taskmaster Shears / Shun Multi-Purpose Shears ($49.95) and J. A. Henckels International Kitchen Shears—Take Apart ($14.95)

Slicing Knife

The long, thin blade of this knife makes slicing a large roast safe and easy.

OUR FAVORITE Victorinox 12" Fibrox Pro Granton Edge Slicing/Carving Knife ($54.65)

Carving Fork

This tool holds roasts in place while carving and makes for neater serving.

OUR FAVORITE Mercer Culinary Genesis 6" High-Carbon Carving Fork ($22.20)

TEN ESSENTIAL ROASTS

ROASTED BONE-IN CHICKEN BREASTS

serves 4

4 (12-ounce) bone-in split chicken breasts, trimmed

¾ teaspoon salt

1 tablespoon vegetable oil

Why This Recipe Works Roasted bone-in chicken breasts are everyone's choice for an easy route to dinner. And if you want crisp skin and tender meat, this method really delivers. For reliably moist meat and crisp skin, we employed a reverse-searing method, using the oven first and finishing on the stovetop. After carefully peeling back the skin and salting the meat to season it and help it retain moisture, we pricked the skin to allow the fat to render and slid the breasts into the oven to roast gently. Once the surrounding heat cooked the meat through, we pulled out a skillet to sear the breasts. This direct heat imparted a burnished finish to the skin and gave the chicken a serious flavor boost. These chicken breasts taste great on their own, but you can also prepare a quick sauce (recipes follow) while they roast.

1 Adjust oven rack to lower-middle position and heat oven to 325 degrees. Line rimmed baking sheet with aluminum foil. Working with 1 breast at a time, use your fingers or handle of spoon to carefully separate chicken skin from meat. Peel skin back, leaving it attached at top and bottom of breast and at ribs. Sprinkle salt evenly over all chicken, then lay skin back in place. Using metal skewer or tip of paring knife, poke 6 to 8 holes in fat deposits in skin. Arrange breasts, skin side up, on prepared sheet. Roast until chicken registers 160 degrees, 35 to 45 minutes.

2 Heat 12-inch skillet over low heat for 5 minutes. Add oil and swirl to coat surface. Add chicken, skin side down, and increase heat to medium-high. Cook chicken, without moving it, until skin is well browned and crispy, 3 to 5 minutes. Using tongs, flip chicken and prop against side of skillet so thick side of breast is facing down; continue to cook until browned, 1 to 2 minutes longer. Transfer to serving dish and let rest 10 minutes before serving.

JALAPEÑO AND CILANTRO SAUCE

makes 1 cup

For a spicier sauce, reserve and add some of the chile seeds to the blender.

1 cup fresh cilantro leaves and stems, trimmed and chopped coarse

3 jalapeño chiles, stemmed, seeded, and minced

½ cup mayonnaise

1 tablespoon lime juice

2 garlic cloves, minced

½ teaspoon kosher salt

2 tablespoons extra-virgin olive oil

Process cilantro, jalapeños, mayonnaise, lime juice, garlic, and salt in blender for 1 minute. Scrape down sides of blender jar and continue to process until smooth, about 1 minute. With blender running, slowly add oil until incorporated. Transfer to bowl.

TAHINI AND HONEY SAUCE

makes ½ cup

A rasp-style grater makes quick work of turning the garlic into a paste.

¼ cup tahini

2 tablespoons lemon juice

2 tablespoons extra-virgin olive oil

1 tablespoon water

2 teaspoons honey

1 garlic clove, minced to paste

¾ teaspoon kosher salt

⅛ teaspoon ground cumin

Pinch cayenne pepper

2 tablespoons chopped fresh cilantro

Whisk tahini, lemon juice, oil, water, honey, garlic, salt, cumin, and cayenne in bowl until smooth. Stir in cilantro.

SKILLET-ROASTED BUTTERFLIED CHICKEN

serves 4

1 (3½- to 4-pound) whole chicken, giblets discarded, brined if desired

Salt and pepper

2 tablespoons extra-virgin olive oil

Why This Recipe Works It takes just a few minutes (and a good pair of kitchen shears) to butterfly a chicken, allowing it to be easily browned in a skillet before roasting. Adding a weighted Dutch oven kept the whole chicken flat in the skillet so the skin picked up deep browning on the stovetop. With the skin well on its way to burnished perfection, we removed the weight, flipped the chicken skin side up, and transferred it to a hot oven where the meat cooked through quickly, preserving its crisp exterior. A brush of olive oil (or one of our bold flavor variations) allowed the skin to pick up even more color and flavor in the oven's dry heat. You will need a 12-inch ovensafe skillet and a Dutch oven for this recipe. The chicken may slightly overhang the skillet at first, but once browned it will shrink to fit. For butterflying instructions, see page 5. If using kosher chicken, do not brine. If brining the chicken, do not season with salt in step 1. For brining instructions, see page 22. Serve with lemon wedges.

1 Adjust oven rack to lowest position and heat oven to 450 degrees. With chicken breast side down, use kitchen shears to cut through bones on either side of backbone; discard backbone. Flip chicken over and press on breastbone to flatten. Tuck wingtips behind back. Pat chicken dry with paper towels and season with salt and pepper.

2 Heat 1 tablespoon oil in 12-inch ovensafe skillet over medium-high heat until just smoking. Add chicken, skin side down, and reduce heat to medium. Place Dutch oven loaded with 2 bricks or heavy cans on top of chicken and cook until evenly browned, about 8 minutes. After 5 minutes, chicken should be golden brown; if it is not, increase heat to medium-high and continue to cook until well browned.

3 Remove skillet from heat and remove Dutch oven and weights. Gently flip chicken skin side up. If more than 3 tablespoons fat have collected in skillet, remove chicken from skillet temporarily and drain excess fat from skillet. Brush chicken with remaining 1 tablespoon oil. Transfer skillet to oven and roast chicken until breast registers 160 degrees and thighs register 175 degrees, about 15 minutes. Transfer chicken to carving board and let rest for 20 minutes. Carve chicken and serve.

Skillet-Roasted Butterflied Chicken with Garlic and Rosemary

Combine 2 tablespoons extra-virgin olive oil, 1 minced garlic clove, ½ teaspoon minced fresh rosemary, pinch red pepper flakes, ⅛ teaspoon salt, and ⅛ teaspoon pepper in bowl; substitute for oil in step 3.

Skillet-Roasted Butterflied Chicken with Sesame and Ginger

Combine 1 tablespoon toasted sesame oil, 1 tablespoon extra-virgin olive oil, 1 teaspoon grated fresh ginger, ½ teaspoon five-spice powder, ⅛ teaspoon salt, and pinch red pepper flakes in bowl; substitute for oil in step 3.

WEEKNIGHT ROAST CHICKEN

serves 4

1 (3½- to 4-pound) whole chicken, giblets discarded, brined if desired

1 tablespoon vegetable oil

Salt and pepper

Why This Recipe Works When you want a hands-off, absolutely foolproof way to roast a chicken, this is the recipe to use. In fact, we think everyone should memorize it—it's that good. Rather than fussing with a V-rack or flipping the chicken, we simply preheated a skillet in the oven. Direct contact with the superhot pan jump-started the thighs' cooking. Roasting the chicken in a 450-degree oven and then turning the oven off allowed the more delicate white meat to remain moist and tender as the bird finished cooking in the oven's residual heat. We prefer to use a 3½- to 4-pound chicken for this recipe. If using kosher chicken, do not brine. If brining the chicken, do not season with salt in step 1. For brining instructions, see page 22. If roasting a larger bird, increase the time when the oven is on in step 2 to 35 to 40 minutes. You will need a 12-inch ovensafe skillet for this recipe. Serve with a pan sauce (recipes follow), if desired. If making a sauce, be sure to save 1 tablespoon of the pan drippings.

1 Adjust oven rack to middle position, place 12-inch ovensafe skillet on rack, and heat oven to 450 degrees. Pat chicken dry with paper towels. Rub entire surface with oil and season with salt and pepper. Tie legs together with kitchen twine and tuck wingtips behind back.

2 Transfer chicken, breast side up, to hot skillet in oven. Roast chicken until breast registers 120 degrees and thighs register 135 degrees, 25 to 35 minutes. Turn oven off and leave chicken in oven until breast registers 160 degrees and thighs register 175 degrees, 25 to 35 minutes. Transfer chicken to carving board and let rest for 20 minutes. Carve chicken and serve.

TARRAGON-LEMON PAN SAUCE

While chicken rests, remove all but 1 tablespoon fat from now-empty skillet (handle will be very hot) using large spoon, leaving any fond and jus in skillet. Place skillet over medium-high heat, add 1 minced shallot, and cook until softened, about 2 minutes. Stir in 1 cup chicken broth and 2 teaspoons Dijon mustard, scraping up any browned bits. Simmer until reduced to ¾ cup, about 3 minutes. Off heat, whisk in 2 tablespoons unsalted butter, 2 teaspoons minced fresh tarragon, and 2 teaspoons lemon juice. Season with pepper to taste; cover and keep warm. Serve with chicken.

THYME–SHERRY VINEGAR PAN SAUCE

While chicken rests, remove all but 1 tablespoon fat from now-empty skillet (handle will be very hot) using large spoon, leaving any fond and jus in skillet. Place skillet over medium-high heat, add 1 minced shallot, 2 minced garlic cloves, and 2 teaspoons minced fresh thyme; cook until softened, about 2 minutes. Stir in 1 cup chicken broth and 2 teaspoons Dijon mustard, scraping up any browned bits. Simmer until reduced to ¾ cup, about 3 minutes. Off heat, whisk in 2 tablespoons unsalted butter and 2 teaspoons sherry vinegar. Season with pepper to taste; cover and keep warm. Serve with chicken.

EASY ROAST TURKEY BREAST

serves 6 to 8

4 tablespoons unsalted butter, softened

3 garlic cloves, minced

Salt and pepper

1 (5- to 7-pound) bone-in turkey breast, brined if desired

Why This Recipe Works We think bone-in turkey breasts are an underutilized cut. Cooked right, they are flavorful and deliver lots of moist, tender meat. The trick, we found, was to use two different oven temperatures. Rather than trying to sear the cumbersome breast on the stovetop, we elevated it in a V-rack and started it out in a blazing hot oven to kick-start the browning process. Dropping the temperature to 325 degrees allowed the meat to gently finish cooking so it stayed moist and tender. Loosening the skin and applying some flavored butter to the meat before roasting gave it an extra dose of richness and moisture. If using a self-basting turkey (such as a frozen Butterball) or a kosher turkey, do not brine. If brining the turkey, do not season the butter with salt in step 1, and do not season the turkey with salt in step 3. For brining instructions, see page 22.

1 Adjust oven rack to middle position and heat oven to 425 degrees. Set V-rack inside roasting pan and spray with vegetable oil spray. Combine butter, garlic, 1 teaspoon salt, and ¼ teaspoon pepper in bowl.

2 Using kitchen shears, cut through ribs following vertical line of fat where breast meets back, from tapered end of breast to wing joint. Using your hands, bend back away from breast to pop shoulder joint out of socket. With paring knife, cut through joint between bones to separate back from breast; discard backbone. Trim excess fat from breast.

3 Place turkey, breast side up, on counter. Using your fingers or handle of spoon, gently loosen skin covering each side of breast. Pat turkey dry with paper towels and season with salt and pepper. Using spoon, place butter mixture under skin, directly on meat in center of each side of breast. Gently press on skin to distribute butter mixture over meat.

4 Place turkey, skin side up, on prepared V-rack and add 1 cup water to pan. Roast turkey for 30 minutes.

5 Reduce oven temperature to 325 degrees and continue to roast until turkey registers 160 degrees, about 1 hour. Transfer turkey to carving board and let rest for 20 minutes. Carve turkey and serve.

Easy Roast Turkey Breast with Lemon and Thyme

Add 2 tablespoons minced fresh thyme and 1 teaspoon grated lemon zest to butter mixture in step 1.

Easy Roast Turkey Breast with Orange and Rosemary

Add 1 tablespoon minced fresh rosemary, 1 teaspoon grated orange zest, and ¼ teaspoon red pepper flakes to butter mixture in step 1.

CLASSIC ROAST BEEF WITH GRAVY

serves 6 to 8

1 (4-pound) center-cut boneless top sirloin roast, fat trimmed to ¼ inch and tied at 1½-inch intervals

Kosher salt and pepper

1 tablespoon vegetable oil

8 ounces white mushrooms, trimmed and chopped

2 onions, chopped fine

1 carrot, peeled and chopped

1 celery rib, chopped

¼ cup all-purpose flour

4 garlic cloves, minced

1 tablespoon tomato paste

4 cups beef broth

1 cup dry red wine

1 teaspoon Worcestershire sauce

Why This Recipe Works For a classic Sunday roast beef with gravy, we turned to top sirloin roast for its beefy flavor, tender texture, and reasonable price. Selecting a roast with a fat cap meant the fat would render in the oven, basting the meat and keeping it moist. Allowing the salted beef to rest for at least an hour ensured thoroughly seasoned meat and improved its already rich flavor. Before sliding the roast into the oven, we gave it a good sear in a Dutch oven to build up a flavorful crust. Using a V-rack meant the oven's dry heat would further brown the entire exterior. Roasting the beef low and slow allowed it to cook through gently and retain its juices. Even without drippings, we were able to build a rich gravy from the flavorful browned bits left in the pot from the beef's stovetop sear. We added layers of savory, complex flavor with mushrooms, umami-boosting tomato paste, beef broth, and red wine. We strained out the solids and stirred in Worcestershire sauce for a smooth texture and truly meaty taste. For the best flavor and texture, refrigerate the roast overnight after salting. If you don't have a V-rack, cook the roast on a wire rack set in a rimmed baking sheet. We prefer this roast cooked to medium-rare, but if you prefer it more or less done, see our guidelines on page 24.

1 Pat roast dry with paper towels and rub evenly with 4 teaspoons salt. Refrigerate, uncovered, for at least 1 hour or up to 24 hours.

2 Adjust oven rack to lower-middle position and heat oven to 275 degrees. Set V-rack inside roasting pan and spray with vegetable oil spray. Pat roast dry with paper towels and season with 1 teaspoon pepper. Heat oil in Dutch oven over medium-high heat until just smoking. Brown roast well on all sides, 8 to 12 minutes; reduce heat if pan begins to scorch. Transfer roast to prepared V-rack (do not wipe out pot). Roast until beef registers 120 to 125 degrees (for medium-rare), 1½ to 2 hours.

3 Meanwhile, add mushrooms to fat left in pot and cook over medium-high heat until golden, about 5 minutes. Add onions, carrot, and celery and cook until softened and lightly browned, 6 to 8 minutes. Add flour, garlic, and tomato paste and cook, stirring constantly, until fragrant, about 2 minutes. Stir in broth and wine, scraping up any browned bits and smoothing out any lumps. Bring to boil, then reduce heat to medium and simmer until thickened, about 10 minutes. Strain gravy through fine-mesh strainer set over bowl, then stir in Worcestershire and season with salt and pepper to taste. Transfer gravy back to pot; cover and keep warm.

4 Transfer roast to carving board and let rest for 20 minutes. Remove twine and slice into ¼-inch-thick slices. Serve with gravy.

SLOW-ROASTED BEEF

serves 6 to 8

1 (3½- to 4½-pound) boneless
eye-round roast, trimmed

4 teaspoons kosher salt

5 teaspoons vegetable oil

2 teaspoons pepper

Why This Recipe Works It's good to have a recipe for roasting an inexpensive beef roast like boneless eye-round in your repertoire. You will be surprised (and delighted) at how the test kitchen's low and slow method delivers remarkably succulent meat from a cut that starts out relatively tough. The method is similar to that of our classic roast beef but with a few twists. By roasting the meat elevated on a wire rack at a very low 225 degrees and turning off the oven toward the end of cooking, we ensured that the beef's tough connective tissue would gradually break down, rewarding us with notably tender meat. If the roast has not reached the desired temperature in the time specified in step 4, reheat the oven to 225 degrees for 5 minutes, then shut it off and continue to cook the roast to the desired temperature. We don't recommend cooking this roast past medium. For a smaller (2½- to 3½-pound) roast, reduce the amount of kosher salt to 1 tablespoon and pepper to 1½ teaspoons. For a larger (4½- to 6-pound) roast, cut the meat in half crosswise before cooking to create two smaller roasts. Note that this recipe requires refrigerating the salted meat for at least 18 hours or up to 24 hours before cooking (a longer salting time is preferable). Serve with Horseradish Sauce (page 27), if desired.

1 Pat roast dry with paper towels and rub salt evenly over roast. Refrigerate, uncovered, for at least 18 hours or up to 24 hours.

2 Adjust oven rack to middle position and heat oven to 225 degrees. Pat roast dry with paper towels, rub with 2 teaspoons oil, and season with pepper.

3 Heat remaining 1 tablespoon oil in 12-inch skillet over medium-high heat until just smoking. Brown roast well on all sides, 12 to 16 minutes; reduce heat if pan begins to scorch. Transfer roast to wire rack set in rimmed baking sheet and roast until meat registers 115 degrees (for medium-rare), 1¼ to 1¾ hours, or 125 degrees (for medium), 1¾ to 2¼ hours.

4 Turn off oven and leave roast in oven, without opening door, until meat registers 120 to 125 degrees (for medium-rare), 30 to 50 minutes.

5 Transfer roast to carving board and let rest for 20 minutes. Slice meat as thin as possible. Serve.

PAN-SEARED OVEN-ROASTED PORK TENDERLOIN

serves 4

2 (12- to 16-ounce) pork tenderloins, trimmed

Salt and pepper

1 tablespoon vegetable oil

1 recipe pan sauce (optional)

Why This Recipe Works Pork tenderloin has a lot going for it—it's supremely tender, cooks quickly, and has a nice mild flavor. For an easy preparation that would up the flavor of this speedy roast while also producing juicy meat, we seasoned it with salt and pepper to lay the groundwork for a flavorful crust. After thoroughly browning the pork in a skillet, we transferred the tenderloins to a baking sheet and into the oven to finish cooking. Following 10 minutes of oven roasting and a 10-minute rest, we had perfectly cooked pork. A pan sauce made with the fond left in the skillet provided a flavorful finish. To ensure that the tenderloins don't curl during cooking, remove the silverskin from the meat (see page 15). We strongly prefer natural pork in this recipe. If the pork is enhanced (injected with a salt solution), do not salt in step 1. Because two are cooked at once, tenderloins larger than 1 pound apiece will not fit comfortably in a 12-inch skillet. For best results, season the tenderloins up to 30 minutes before cooking. A pan sauce (recipes follow) can be made while the tenderloins are in the oven; if you intend to make a sauce, ready the sauce ingredients before cooking the pork.

1 Adjust oven rack to middle position and heat oven to 400 degrees. Pat tenderloins dry with paper towels and season with salt and pepper. Heat oil in 12-inch skillet over medium-high heat until just smoking. Brown tenderloins well on all sides, about 5 minutes. Transfer tenderloins to rimmed baking sheet (reserve skillet if making pan sauce) and roast until pork registers 145 degrees, 10 to 16 minutes. (Begin pan sauce, if making, while pork roasts.)

2 Transfer tenderloins to carving board (continue with pan sauce, if making); let rest for 10 minutes. Slice tenderloins into ½-inch-thick slices, transfer to serving dish, and spoon sauce (if using) over. Serve.

SHALLOT-BALSAMIC SAUCE WITH ROSEMARY AND MUSTARD

makes ½ cup

4 tablespoons unsalted butter, cut into 4 pieces
2 shallots, sliced thin
2 tablespoons water
1 teaspoon packed light brown sugar

¾ cup balsamic vinegar
2 teaspoons minced fresh rosemary
1 tablespoon Dijon mustard
Salt and pepper

1 Immediately after placing pork in oven, add 1 tablespoon butter to still-hot skillet. When melted, stir in shallots, water, and sugar. Cook over medium-low heat, stirring frequently, until shallots are browned and caramelized, 7 to 10 minutes. (If pan is browning too quickly, add 2 tablespoons water and scrape up any browned bits with wooden spoon.) Set skillet aside off heat.

2 While pork is resting, set skillet over medium-low heat and add vinegar; simmer, scraping up any browned bits, until mixture is slightly thickened, 5 to 7 minutes. Add rosemary and any accumulated pork juices; continue to simmer until syrupy and reduced to about ⅓ cup, about 2 minutes longer. Off heat, whisk in mustard and remaining 3 tablespoons butter, 1 piece at a time. Season with salt and pepper to taste.

GARLICKY LIME SAUCE WITH CILANTRO
makes ½ cup

A rasp-style grater makes quick work of turning the garlic into a paste. Remove green sprouts or shoot from garlic before grating.

10 garlic cloves, grated to fine paste (2 tablespoons)
2 tablespoons water
1 tablespoon vegetable oil
2 teaspoons packed light brown sugar
¼ teaspoon red pepper flakes
¼ cup chopped fresh cilantro
3 tablespoons lime juice (2 limes)
1 tablespoon chopped fresh chives
4 tablespoons unsalted butter, cut into 4 pieces
Salt and pepper

1 Immediately after placing pork in oven, mix garlic paste with water in small bowl. Add oil to still-hot skillet and swirl to coat; add garlic paste mixture and cook with skillet's residual heat, scraping up any browned bits, until sizzling subsides, about 2 minutes. Set skillet over low heat and continue cooking, stirring frequently, until garlic is sticky, 8 to 10 minutes; set skillet aside off heat.

2 While pork is resting, set skillet over medium heat; add sugar and pepper flakes to skillet and cook until sticky and sugar is dissolved, about 1 minute. Add cilantro, lime juice, and chives; simmer to blend flavors, 1 to 2 minutes. Add any accumulated pork juices and simmer 1 minute longer. Off heat, whisk in butter, 1 piece at a time. Season with salt and pepper to taste.

MAPLE-GLAZED PORK ROAST

serves 4 to 6

½ cup maple syrup

⅛ teaspoon ground cinnamon

Pinch ground cloves

Pinch cayenne pepper

1 (2½-pound) boneless blade-end pork loin roast, brined if desired, tied at even intervals along length with 5 pieces kitchen twine

1½ teaspoons kosher salt

½ teaspoon pepper

2 teaspoons vegetable oil

Why This Recipe Works An unexpected (and easy) technique yields tender, juicy pork with a rich, clingy glaze that packs pure maple flavor—all in one pan. We used a boneless blade-end loin roast here because it has the most fat and a lot of flavor. Tied into an even bundle, the roast fit into a skillet for a quick sear on the stovetop to build flavor. A maple glaze kept the exterior of the roast from becoming tough and dry. Reducing the glaze in the skillet after the roast was browned ensured that the fond left in the pan contributed meaty flavor. Roasting and turning the pork in the glaze made covering the whole roast easy and kept the pork plenty moist. The blade-end roast is our first choice; however, a center-cut roast will also work in this recipe. In either case, look for a roast with a thin fat cap (about ¼ inch thick) and don't trim this thin layer of fat. We prefer the stronger, richer flavor of grade A maple syrup labeled as "dark, robust" but lighter-colored syrup will work, too. You will need a 10-inch ovensafe skillet for this recipe.

1 Adjust oven rack to middle position and heat oven to 325 degrees. Stir maple syrup, cinnamon, cloves, and cayenne together in measuring cup or bowl; set aside. Pat roast dry with paper towels, then season with salt and pepper.

2 Heat oil in 10-inch ovensafe skillet over medium-high heat until just smoking. Place roast fat side down in skillet and cook until well browned, about 3 minutes. Using tongs, rotate roast one-quarter turn and cook until well browned, about 2½ minutes; repeat until roast is well browned on all sides. Transfer roast to large plate. Reduce heat to medium and pour off fat from skillet; add maple syrup mixture and cook until fragrant, about 30 seconds (syrup will bubble immediately). Off heat, return roast to skillet; using tongs, roll to coat roast with glaze on all sides.

3 Place skillet in oven and roast until pork registers 140 degrees, 35 to 45 minutes, using tongs to roll and spin roast to coat with glaze twice during roasting time (skillet handle will be hot). Transfer roast to carving board; set skillet aside to cool slightly and thicken glaze, about 5 minutes. Pour glaze over roast and let rest 15 minutes longer. Remove twine, cut roast into ¼-inch-thick slices, and serve.

Maple-Glazed Pork Roast with Orange Essence

Add 1 tablespoon grated orange zest to maple syrup along with spices.

Maple-Glazed Pork Roast with Rosemary

Substitute 2 teaspoons minced fresh rosemary for cinnamon, cloves, and cayenne.

Maple-Glazed Pork Roast with Smoked Paprika

Add 2 teaspoons smoked hot paprika to maple syrup along with spices.

Maple-Glazed Pork Roast with Star Anise

Add 4 star anise pods to maple syrup along with spices.

SLOW-ROASTED BONE-IN PORK RIB ROAST

1 (4- to 5-pound) center-cut bone-in pork rib roast, chine bone removed

2 tablespoons packed dark brown sugar

1 tablespoon kosher salt

1½ teaspoons pepper

1 recipe Port Wine–Cherry Sauce (recipe follows)

Why This Recipe Works The pork equivalent of prime rib, a center-cut pork rib roast is sure to impress but requires some prep work, some tricks, and some time to get it right. To guarantee a juicy, flavorful, and beautifully browned roast (without searing), we applied a brown sugar and salt rub and let it rest overnight. Removing the bones allowed the rub to penetrate the meat, and tying them back in place before roasting safeguarded the pork's juices. Roasting low and slow prevented over-cooking and allowed the crosshatched fat cap to melt and baste the pork. A final blast under the broiler crisped and caramelized the brown sugar for a perfect mahogany crust, and a rich accompanying sauce made for a perfect finish. This recipe requires refrigerating the salted meat for at least 6 hours and up to 24 hours before cooking (a longer salting time is preferable). For easier carving, ask the butcher to remove the chine bone. We strongly prefer natural pork in this recipe. If the pork is enhanced (injected with a salt solution), do not salt in step 1.

1 Using sharp knife, remove roast from bones, running knife down length of bones and following contours as closely as possible. Reserve bones. Combine sugar and salt in small bowl. Pat roast dry with paper towels. If necessary, trim thick spots of surface fat layer to about ¼-inch thickness. Using sharp knife, cut slits, spaced 1 inch apart and in crosshatch pattern, in surface fat layer, being careful not to cut into meat. Rub roast evenly with sugar mixture. Refrigerate, uncovered, for at least 6 hours or up to 24 hours.

2 Adjust oven rack to lower-middle position and heat oven to 250 degrees. Pat roast dry with paper towels and season with pepper. Place roast back on ribs so bones fit where they were cut; tie roast to bones with lengths of kitchen twine between ribs. Transfer roast, fat side up, to wire rack set in rimmed baking sheet. Roast until pork registers 140 to 145 degrees, 3 to 4 hours.

3 Remove roast from oven (leave roast on sheet) and let rest for 30 minutes.

4 Adjust oven rack 8 inches from broiler element and heat broiler. Return roast to oven and broil until top of roast is well browned and crispy, 2 to 6 minutes.

5 Transfer roast to carving board; remove twine and remove meat from ribs. Slice pork into ¾-inch-thick slices. Serve, passing sauce separately.

PORT WINE–CHERRY SAUCE
makes about 1¾ cups

2 cups tawny port

1 cup dried cherries

½ cup balsamic vinegar

4 sprigs fresh thyme, plus 2 teaspoons minced

2 shallots, minced

¼ cup heavy cream

16 tablespoons unsalted butter, cut into ½-inch pieces and chilled

1 teaspoon salt

½ teaspoon pepper

1 Combine port and cherries in bowl and microwave until steaming, 1 to 2 minutes. Cover and let stand until plump, about 10 minutes. Strain port through fine-mesh strainer into medium saucepan, reserving cherries.

2 Add vinegar, thyme sprigs, and shallots to port and bring to boil over high heat. Reduce heat to medium-high and reduce mixture until it measures ¾ cup, 14 to 16 minutes. Add cream and reduce again to ¾ cup, about 5 minutes. Discard thyme sprigs. Off heat, whisk in butter, few pieces at a time, until fully incorporated. Stir in cherries, minced thyme, salt, and pepper. Cover pan and hold, off heat, until serving. (Sauce can be refrigerated for up to 2 days. To serve, heat in small sauce-pan over medium-low heat, stirring frequently, until warm.)

butchering a pork rib roast

1 Using sharp knife, remove roast from bones, running knife down length of bones and closely following contours.

2 Trim surface fat to ¼ inch and score with crosshatch slits; rub roast with sugar mixture and refrigerate for at least 6 hours.

3 Pat roast dry, sprinkle with pepper, then place roast back on ribs. Using kitchen twine, tie roast to bones between ribs.

ROASTED SALMON FILLETS WITH TANGERINE AND GINGER RELISH

serves 4

Tangerine and Ginger Relish

4 tangerines

1 scallion, sliced thin

1½ teaspoons grated fresh ginger

2 teaspoons lemon juice

2 teaspoons extra-virgin olive oil

Salt and pepper

Salmon Fillets

1 (1¾- to 2-pound) center-cut skin-on salmon fillet, 1½ inches thick

2 teaspoons vegetable oil

Salt and pepper

Why This Recipe Works Ever popular and easy to dress up, roasted salmon fillets are a weeknight workhorse, but they also make great company fare. That's why we created this hybrid roasting technique, which offers a hands-off way to serve up silky fish with a nicely browned exterior. Rather than sear the fillets on the stovetop, we preheated a baking sheet in a 500-degree oven. While the pan heated up, we readied the fillets for roasting, slashing the skin so the fat would render in the oven. We dropped the temperature to 275 degrees just before placing the fillets on the pan, skin side down for a layer of insulation. The initial contact with the hot pan helped crisp the skin, and the heat of the gradually cooling oven cooked the fillets gently. To ensure uniform pieces of fish, buy a whole center-cut fillet and cut it into four pieces. If your knife is not sharp enough to cut through the skin easily, try a serrated knife. It is important to keep the skin on during cooking; remove it afterward if desired. Oranges can be substituted for the tangerines in the Tangerine and Ginger Relish. You can serve the salmon with Cucumber-Yogurt Sauce (page 29), Fennel-Apple Chutney (page 28), or lemon wedges instead of the relish if desired.

1 For the tangerine and ginger relish Cut away peel and pith from tangerines. Quarter tangerines, then slice crosswise into ½-inch-thick pieces. Place pieces in fine-mesh strainer set over bowl and drain for 15 minutes.

2 Pour off all but 1 tablespoon tangerine juice from bowl; whisk in scallion, ginger, lemon juice, and oil. Stir in tangerine pieces and season with salt and pepper to taste.

3 For the salmon fillets Adjust oven rack to lowest position, place rimmed baking sheet on rack, and heat oven to 500 degrees. Cut salmon crosswise into 4 fillets. Make 4 or 5 shallow slashes diagonally, about 1 inch apart, on skin side of each fillet, being careful not to cut into flesh. Pat salmon dry with paper towels, rub with oil, and season with salt and pepper.

4 Reduce oven temperature to 275 degrees and remove sheet. Carefully place salmon, skin side down, on sheet. Roast until center is still translucent when checked with tip of paring knife and registers 125 degrees (for medium-rare), 9 to 13 minutes. Transfer salmon to plates and serve with relish.

slashing salmon skin

Using sharp or serrated knife, cut 4 or 5 shallow slashes diagonally, about 1 inch apart, through skin of each piece of salmon, being careful not to cut into flesh.

POULTRY

PAN-ROASTED CHICKEN BREASTS WITH SHALLOT-THYME SAUCE

serves 4

Chicken

4 (12-ounce) bone-in split chicken breasts, trimmed, brined if desired

Salt and pepper

1 tablespoon vegetable oil

Sauce

1 large shallot, minced

¾ cup chicken broth

½ cup dry vermouth or white wine

2 sprigs fresh thyme

3 tablespoons unsalted butter, cut into 3 pieces and chilled

Salt and pepper

Why This Recipe Works To develop a bone-in chicken breast recipe that produced moist meat, crisp skin, and a quick pan sauce, we turned to pan roasting, where the chicken is browned in a skillet on the stovetop and then slid, skillet and all, into a very hot oven to finish cooking. This method helped to protect the delicate white meat, which doesn't have a lot of fat, from drying out. The chicken was added skin side down in a smoking hot skillet, where it formed a gorgeous brown crust and produced plenty of fond. After lightly browning the second side of the chicken, we moved the skillet to a 450-degree oven where the chicken roasted for just 15 minutes. While the chicken rested, we used the browned bits left in the pan to make a flavorful pan sauce. You will need a 12-inch ovensafe skillet for this recipe. If using kosher chicken, do not brine. If brining the chicken, do not season with salt in step 1. For brining instructions, see page 22.

1 For the chicken Adjust oven rack to middle position and heat oven to 450 degrees. Pat chicken dry with paper towels and season with salt and pepper.

2 Heat oil in 12-inch ovensafe skillet over medium-high heat until just smoking. Cook breasts, skin side down, until well browned, 6 to 8 minutes. Flip breasts and brown lightly on second side, about 3 minutes. Flip breasts skin side down, transfer skillet to oven, and roast until chicken registers 160 degrees, 15 to 18 minutes.

3 Remove skillet from oven (skillet handle will be hot). Transfer chicken to serving dish and let rest while making sauce.

4 For the sauce Being careful of hot skillet handle, pour off all but 1 teaspoon fat left in skillet. Add shallot and cook over medium heat until softened, about 2 minutes. Stir in broth, vermouth, and thyme sprigs, scraping up any browned bits, and simmer until thickened and measures ⅔ cup, about 6 minutes.

5 Discard thyme sprigs and stir in any accumulated chicken juices. Reduce heat to low and whisk in butter, 1 piece at a time. Off heat, season with salt and pepper to taste. Spoon sauce over chicken and serve.

Pan-Roasted Chicken Breasts with Garlic-Sherry Sauce

Substitute 7 sliced garlic cloves for shallot and cook, stirring often, until garlic turns golden but not brown, about 1½ minutes. Substitute dry sherry for dry vermouth. Stir ½ teaspoon lemon juice into sauce before seasoning with salt and pepper.

Pan-Roasted Chicken Breasts with Sage-Vermouth Sauce

Use dry vermouth, not white wine, and substitute 4 fresh sage leaves, torn in half, for thyme sprigs.

Pan-Roasted Chicken Breasts with Onion-Ale Sauce

Substitute ½ onion, sliced thin, for shallot; ½ cup brown ale for dry vermouth; and bay leaf for 1 sprig of thyme. Add 1 tablespoon brown sugar to skillet along with broth, ale, thyme sprig, and bay leaf. After adding chicken juices, return to simmer and cook for 30 seconds. Off heat, discard thyme sprig and bay leaf and whisk in butter, 1 piece at a time. Stir in ½ teaspoon cider vinegar and season with salt and pepper to taste.

ROASTED CHICKEN BREASTS WITH ORANGE-HONEY GLAZE

serves 4

1½ cups plus 2 tablespoons orange juice (4 oranges)

⅓ cup light corn syrup

3 tablespoons honey

1 tablespoon Dijon mustard

1 tablespoon distilled white vinegar

⅛ teaspoon red pepper flakes

Salt and pepper

½ cup all-purpose flour

4 (12-ounce) bone-in split chicken breasts, trimmed, brined if desired

2 tablespoons vegetable oil

1 shallot, minced

Why This Recipe Works Glazed chicken breasts are a family favorite, and our method delivers perfect flavor and texture without overcomplicating (or oversweetening) them. Using bone-in split breasts meant glaze-grabbing skin and a built-in layer of insulation to prevent overcooked white meat; dredging the chicken in flour before searing created a more substantial crust for the glaze to cling to. After searing the breasts, we used the rendered fat to build the glaze, whisking together and reducing a sweet but balanced mixture of orange juice, corn syrup, honey, Dijon mustard, vinegar, and red pepper flakes. We coated the breasts in the citrusy glaze, arranged them skin side down in the skillet, and moved them to the oven to roast, flipping them halfway through to crisp the skin and caramelize the glaze. While the chicken rested, we reduced the glaze further, adding an additional hit of orange juice before spooning it over the waiting chicken. If the glaze looks dry during baking, add up to 2 tablespoons more orange juice to the pan. You will need a 12-inch ovensafe skillet for this recipe. If using kosher chicken, do not brine. If brining the chicken, do not season with salt in step 2. For brining instructions, see page 22.

1 Adjust oven rack to middle position and heat oven to 375 degrees. Whisk 1½ cups orange juice, corn syrup, honey, mustard, vinegar, pepper flakes, ⅛ teaspoon salt, and ⅛ teaspoon pepper together in bowl.

2 Spread flour in shallow dish. Pat chicken dry with paper towels and season with salt and pepper. Working with 1 breast at a time, dredge breasts in flour, shaking off excess, and transfer to large plate.

3 Heat oil in 12-inch ovensafe skillet over medium heat until shimmering. Add breasts, skin side down, and cook until well browned, 6 to 8 minutes. Flip breasts and lightly brown second side, about 3 minutes; transfer to second large plate.

4 Pour off all but 1 teaspoon fat left in skillet. Add shallot and cook over medium heat until softened, about 2 minutes. Add orange juice mixture, scraping up any browned bits, bring to simmer, and cook, stirring occasionally, until mixture is syrupy and measures 1 cup, 6 to 10 minutes. Off heat, tilt skillet to 1 side so glaze pools in corner of pan. Using tongs, roll each breast in pooled glaze to coat evenly, then place skin side down in skillet.

5 Transfer skillet to oven and roast until chicken registers 160 degrees, 25 to 30 minutes, flipping chicken skin side up halfway through roasting.

6 Remove skillet from oven (skillet handle will be hot). Transfer chicken to serving dish and let rest while finishing glaze.

7 Being careful of hot skillet handle, place skillet over high heat and cook glaze, stirring constantly, until thick and syrupy, about 1 minute. Off heat, whisk in remaining 2 tablespoons orange juice. Spoon 1 teaspoon glaze over each breast and serve, passing remaining glaze separately.

Roasted Chicken Breasts with Apple-Maple Glaze

Substitute apple cider for orange juice and 2 tablespoons maple syrup for honey.

Roasted Chicken Breasts with Pineapple–Brown Sugar Glaze

Substitute pineapple juice for orange juice and 2 tablespoons packed brown sugar for honey.

ROASTED STUFFED CHICKEN BREASTS

serves 4

4 (12-ounce) bone-in split chicken breasts, trimmed, brined if desired

Salt and pepper

¼ cup vegetable oil

½ cup finely chopped onion

2 teaspoons grated lemon zest plus 1 tablespoon juice

2 garlic cloves, minced

2 teaspoons minced fresh thyme

2 teaspoons Dijon mustard

1 teaspoon minced fresh rosemary

2 ounces sliced Genoa salami, chopped fine

2 ounces Parmesan cheese, grated (1 cup)

2 tablespoons capers, chopped

½ cup chicken broth

Why This Recipe Works Stuffed chicken breasts are impressive—if the chicken is moist and the filling is worthy and stays where it's supposed to. We created a savory stuffing and found a way to make it stay put: First we sliced a pocket into each chicken breast, which we filled with a briny, nutty combination of Parmesan, salami, and capers along with an intense mixture of lemon zest, herbs, and Dijon. Then we tied the breasts closed with kitchen twine to securely seal in the filling. We browned the stuffed breasts in a skillet on the stovetop before flipping them skin side up, pouring in chicken broth, and transferring the skillet to the oven. The broth kept the meat juicy as it roasted, and once the chicken and stuffing were fully cooked, the reduced broth served as a rich pan sauce that needed only a splash of lemon juice and more of the mustard-herb blend for a vibrant finish. High-quality Parmesan makes a difference here. You will need a 12-inch ovensafe nonstick skillet for this recipe. If using kosher chicken, do not brine. If brining the chicken, do not season with salt in step 1. For brining instructions, see page 22.

1 Adjust oven rack to middle position and heat oven to 400 degrees. Working with 1 breast at a time, place skin side down on counter with breastbone side facing your knife hand. Press on breast with your opposite hand to flatten slightly and, using sharp paring knife, cut 3-inch-long horizontal pocket in breastbone side of breast, stopping ½ inch from rib side so halves remain attached. Using your fingers and tip of knife, make interior of pocket wider without increasing 3-inch opening. Season breasts inside and out with salt and pepper; set aside.

2 Heat 1 tablespoon oil in 12-inch ovensafe nonstick skillet over medium heat until shimmering. Add onion and ⅛ teaspoon salt and cook until softened and lightly browned, 4 to 6 minutes. Set aside to cool slightly, about 5 minutes.

3 Combine lemon zest, garlic, thyme, mustard, rosemary, and 2 tablespoons oil in bowl; set aside 2 teaspoons oil mixture for sauce. Stir onion, salami, Parmesan, capers, 1 teaspoon pepper, and ¼ teaspoon salt into remaining oil mixture, mashing against side of bowl with back of spoon until stuffing mixture clumps together.

4 Place about 3 tablespoons stuffing mixture into pocket of each breast, pressing into ends of pockets with your fingers to fill completely and evenly. Fold breast over to enclose. Tie each breast with 3 evenly spaced pieces of kitchen twine. Wipe skillet clean with paper towels.

5 Heat remaining 1 tablespoon oil in now-empty skillet over medium-high heat until just smoking. Cook breasts skin side down until well browned, 6 to 8 minutes, reducing heat if pan begins to scorch.

6 Flip breasts, add broth to skillet, and transfer to oven. Roast until thickest part of stuffing registers 160 degrees, 30 to 37 minutes. Remove skillet from oven (skillet handle will be hot). Transfer breasts to carving board and let rest for 10 minutes.

7 Meanwhile, being careful of hot skillet handle, pour pan juices into liquid measuring cup. Let liquid settle for 5 minutes. Using spoon, skim off fat. Stir in lemon juice and reserved oil mixture; season with salt and pepper to taste. Remove twine, then carve breasts from bones. Slice ½ inch thick, transfer to serving dish, and drizzle with sauce. Serve.

stuffing chicken breasts

1 Place breast skin side down on cutting board with breastbone side facing your knife hand. Press breast with opposite hand to flatten, and use paring knife to cut 3-inch-long horizontal pocket in breastbone side of breast, stopping ½ inch from rib side.

2 Use your fingers and tip of knife to make pocket wider without increasing 3-inch opening.

3 Fill pockets with about 3 tablespoons stuffing, fold breast over to enclose, and tie breast with 3 evenly spaced pieces of kitchen twine to seal.

ROASTED SPICE-RUBBED CHICKEN

serves 6 to 8

3 tablespoons packed brown sugar

2 tablespoons chili powder

2 tablespoons paprika

1 tablespoon salt

2 teaspoons pepper

¼–½ teaspoon cayenne pepper

5 pounds bone-in chicken pieces (split breasts cut in half, drumsticks, and/or thighs), trimmed

Why This Recipe Works Cold barbecued chicken is a classic. The secret to our ultimate picnic-ready chicken is to coat bone-in parts with a robust salty spice rub overnight. This method seasons the chicken throughout and keeps it moist, even during high-heat roasting. A little extra prep work helped with the flavor, texture, and appearance of the parts. Scoring the skin (but not the meat) provided outlets for the melting fat, yielding more fully rendered, paper-thin skin. Applying the spice rub on and beneath the skin ensured flavor inside and out; air-drying the rubbed parts on a rack in the refrigerator for at least 6 hours gave the flavors time to penetrate while also drying out the skin. We started the chicken in a 425-degree oven and finished it with a final blast of higher heat to nicely crisp the skin. Thanks to the salty rub and two-temperature roasting, our chicken was bursting with barbecue flavor after it cooled and had delicate, not flabby, skin. If using large chicken breasts (about 1 pound each), cut each breast into three pieces. We use toothpicks to secure the skin on the breast pieces; otherwise it will shrink considerably in the oven, leaving the meat exposed and prone to drying out. This recipe requires refrigerating the rubbed chicken for at least 6 hours or up to 24 hours before cooking (a longer time is preferable). If you plan to serve the chicken later on the same day that you cook it, refrigerate it after it has cooled and let it come back to room temperature before serving. For spicier chicken, use the greater amount of cayenne.

1 Set wire rack in rimmed baking sheet. Combine sugar, chili powder, paprika, salt, pepper, and cayenne in bowl.

2 Using sharp knife, make 2 or 3 short slashes into skin of each piece of chicken, taking care not to cut into meat. Coat chicken with spice mixture, gently lifting skin to distribute spice mixture underneath but leaving it attached to chicken. Transfer chicken, skin side up, to prepared rack (if desired, secure skin of each breast piece with 2 or 3 toothpicks placed near edges of skin). Tent chicken with aluminum foil and refrigerate for at least 6 hours or up to 24 hours.

3 Adjust oven rack to middle position and heat oven to 425 degrees. Remove foil and roast chicken until smallest piece registers 140 degrees, 15 to 20 minutes. Increase oven temperature to 500 degrees and continue roasting until chicken is browned and crisp and breast pieces register 160 degrees, 5 to 8 minutes. (Smaller pieces may cook faster than larger pieces. Remove pieces from oven as they reach correct temperature.) Continue to roast thighs and/or drumsticks until they register 175 degrees, about 5 minutes. Transfer chicken to wire rack and let cool completely before refrigerating or serving.

TANDOORI CHICKEN WITH RAITA

serves 4

Raita

1 cup plain whole-milk yogurt

2 tablespoons minced fresh cilantro

1 garlic clove, minced

Salt

Cayenne pepper

Chicken

2 tablespoons vegetable oil

6 garlic cloves, minced

2 tablespoons grated fresh ginger

1 tablespoon garam masala

2 teaspoons ground cumin

2 teaspoons chili powder

1 cup plain whole-milk yogurt

¼ cup lime juice (2 limes), plus lime wedges for serving

2 teaspoons salt

3 pounds bone-in chicken pieces (split breasts cut in half, drumsticks, and/or thighs), skin removed, trimmed, brined if desired

Why This Recipe Works Traditional tandoori chicken is marinated in yogurt and spices and roasted in a superhot tandoor oven to produce tender meat beneath beautifully charred skin. To make an authentic-tasting version at home, we started by peeling the skin off of bone-in chicken parts and slashing the surface of the meat so the flavors could penetrate deeply. We built a fragrant paste, blooming ginger and garlic in oil before adding garam masala, cumin, and chili powder and binding everything together with lime juice. We used this paste twice over, applying some directly to the exposed meat and stirring the rest into whole-milk yogurt. The spices imparted plenty of flavor and the yogurt marinade gave our chicken tang. Arranged on a wire rack placed in a rimmed baking sheet, our chicken roasted gently and evenly in a moderate oven, and a final few minutes under the broiler delivered the charred finish we wanted. A cool, creamy raita sauce offered the perfect complement to our flavorful tandoori-style chicken. If using large chicken breasts (about 1 pound each), cut each breast into three pieces. If using kosher chicken, do not brine. If brining the chicken, omit salt from garlic–lime juice mixture in step 2. For brining instructions, see page 22. To serve eight, double all the ingredients, adjust the oven racks to the upper-middle and lower-middle positions, arrange the chicken on two baking sheets in step 4, and broil each sheet of chicken individually in step 5. We prefer whole-milk yogurt for this recipe.

1 **For the raita** Combine yogurt, cilantro, and garlic in bowl and season with salt and cayenne to taste. Refrigerate until ready to serve. (Raita can be refrigerated for up to 24 hours.)

2 **For the chicken** Heat oil in 10-inch skillet over medium heat until shimmering. Add garlic and ginger and cook until fragrant, about 30 seconds. Stir in garam masala, cumin, and chili powder and continue to cook until fragrant, about 30 seconds. Transfer half of garlic mixture to medium bowl, stir in yogurt and 2 tablespoons lime juice, and set aside. In large bowl, combine remaining garlic mixture, remaining 2 tablespoons lime juice, and salt.

3 Using sharp knife, make 2 or 3 short slashes into each piece of chicken. Transfer chicken to bowl with garlic–lime juice mixture and rub until all pieces are evenly coated. Let sit at room temperature for 30 minutes.

4 Adjust oven rack to upper-middle position and heat oven to 325 degrees. Set wire rack in aluminum foil–lined rimmed baking sheet. Pour yogurt mixture over chicken and toss until chicken is evenly coated with thick layer. Arrange chicken pieces, scored side down, on prepared rack. Discard excess yogurt mixture. Roast chicken until breast pieces register 125 degrees and thighs and/or drumsticks register 130 degrees, 15 to 25 minutes. (Smaller pieces may cook faster than larger pieces. Remove pieces from oven as they reach correct temperature.)

5 Adjust oven rack 6 inches from broiler element and heat broiler. Return chicken to wire rack, scored side up, and broil until chicken is lightly charred in spots and breast pieces register 160 degrees and thighs and/or drumsticks register 175 degrees, 8 to 15 minutes. Transfer chicken to serving dish and let rest for 10 minutes. Serve with raita and lime wedges.

ONE-PAN ROASTED CHICKEN WITH ROOT VEGETABLES

serves 4

12 ounces Brussels sprouts, trimmed and halved

12 ounces red potatoes, unpeeled, cut into 1-inch pieces

8 ounces shallots, peeled and halved

4 carrots, peeled and cut into 2-inch pieces, thick ends halved lengthwise

6 garlic cloves, peeled

4 teaspoons minced fresh thyme

1 tablespoon vegetable oil

2 teaspoons minced fresh rosemary

1 teaspoon sugar

Salt and pepper

2 tablespoons unsalted butter, melted

3½ pounds bone-in chicken pieces (2 split breasts cut in half, 2 drumsticks, and 2 thighs), trimmed, brined if desired

Why This Recipe Works It's easy to understand the appeal of preparing chicken parts and root vegetables together on one sheet pan, but without the right technique, you are apt to wind up with unevenly cooked meat and greasy, soggy vegetables. For a pan packed with well-browned, herb-flecked chicken and vegetables that roasted at the same rate, we arranged our ingredients on a sheet pan with their cooking times in mind. After tossing the root vegetables with fresh thyme and rosemary, we arranged halved Brussels sprouts in the center of the pan and the denser items—chunky pieces of red potatoes and carrots and halved shallots—around the edges. Likewise, to ensure that the chicken breasts stayed moist while the meatier thighs and drumsticks cooked through, we placed the breasts in the center of the pan atop the sprouts and the thighs and drumsticks around the perimeter where they would take on (and benefit from) more direct contact with the oven's intense heat. Brushing the parts with herb butter promised added richness and browning. Roasted together in a hot oven, the chicken parts and vegetables emerged browned and perfectly cooked in about 35 minutes. Use Brussels sprouts no bigger than golf balls, as larger ones are often tough and woody. If using kosher chicken, do not brine. If brining the chicken, do not season with salt in step 2. For brining instructions, see page 22.

1 Adjust oven rack to upper-middle position and heat oven to 475 degrees. Toss Brussels sprouts, potatoes, shallots, carrots, garlic, 2 teaspoons thyme, oil, 1 teaspoon rosemary, sugar, ¾ teaspoon salt, and ¼ teaspoon pepper together in bowl. Combine butter, remaining 2 teaspoons thyme, remaining 1 teaspoon rosemary, ¼ teaspoon salt, and ⅛ teaspoon pepper in second bowl; set aside.

2 Pat chicken dry with paper towels and season with salt and pepper. Place vegetables in single layer on rimmed baking sheet, arranging Brussels sprouts in center. Place chicken, skin side up, on top of vegetables, arranging breast pieces in center and leg and thigh pieces around perimeter of sheet.

3 Brush chicken with herb butter and roast until breasts register 160 degrees and thighs/drumsticks register 175 degrees, 35 to 40 minutes, rotating sheet halfway through roasting. Transfer chicken to serving platter and let rest for 10 minutes. Toss vegetables in pan juices and transfer to platter with chicken. Serve.

One-Pan Roasted Chicken with Fennel and Parsnips

Replace Brussels sprouts and carrots with 1 fennel bulb, stalks discarded, bulb halved, cored, and sliced into ½-inch wedges, and 8 ounces (4 medium) parsnips, peeled and cut into 2-inch pieces.

ROASTED HONEY MUSTARD–GLAZED CHICKEN DRUMSTICKS WITH SWEET POTATO COINS

serves 4

2 pounds sweet potatoes, peeled, trimmed, and sliced into ¾-inch-thick rounds

2 tablespoons vegetable oil

¼ teaspoon cayenne pepper

Salt and pepper

½ cup honey

¼ cup soy sauce

¼ cup yellow mustard

2 teaspoons cornstarch

8 (6-ounce) chicken drumsticks, skin removed, brined if desired

Why This Recipe Works Inexpensive but meaty chicken drumsticks taste great when glazed and roasted. Here, we set out to roast drumsticks in a sweet yet sophisticated honey-mustard glaze alongside plenty of spiced sweet potatoes. To achieve our goal, we removed the drumsticks' skin (which tended to turn flabby beneath a thick glaze), seasoned the meat, and tossed the drumsticks in a thick mixture of honey, soy sauce, mustard, and cornstarch. To get the chicken and sweet potatoes to roast at the same rate, we sliced the potatoes into thick rounds, tossed them with cayenne for a touch of heat, and microwaved them just long enough to soften their dense texture. The potatoes picked up flavorful browning just as the chicken's coating began to caramelize. Applying more glaze partway through roasting gave the drumsticks an attractive sheen, and flipping the potatoes ensured even browning. Our two elements finished roasting right on cue, making for a fuss-free dinner from a single pan. Chicken drumsticks come in various sizes; if your chicken drumsticks are smaller than 6 ounces each, you may need to adjust the baking time. If you opt not to peel the sweet potatoes, be sure to scrub them well before slicing. If using kosher chicken, do not brine. If brining the chicken, do not season with salt in step 4. For brining instructions, see page 22.

1 Adjust oven rack to middle position and heat oven to 450 degrees. Line rimmed baking sheet with aluminum foil and spray with vegetable oil spray.

2 Toss sweet potatoes with oil and cayenne, season with salt and pepper, and arrange in single layer on large plate. Microwave potatoes until they begin to soften but still hold their shape, 6 to 8 minutes, flipping them halfway through microwaving.

3 Whisk honey, soy sauce, mustard, and cornstarch together in large bowl. Microwave glaze, whisking occasionally, until slightly thickened, 3 to 5 minutes. Let glaze cool slightly.

4 Pat chicken dry with paper towels, season with salt and pepper, and toss with half of glaze. Arrange chicken on one side of prepared sheet. Spread sweet potatoes in single layer on other side of prepared sheet. Roast chicken and sweet potatoes for 20 minutes.

5 Brush chicken with remaining glaze and carefully flip sweet potatoes over with spatula. Continue to roast chicken and potatoes until glaze is well browned, chicken registers 175 degrees, and sweet potatoes are lightly browned, 15 to 20 minutes. Let chicken and sweet potatoes rest on sheet for 10 minutes before serving.

CLASSIC ROAST CHICKEN

serves 4

1 (3½- to 4-pound) whole chicken, giblets discarded, brined if desired

2 tablespoons unsalted butter, softened

1 tablespoon vegetable oil

Salt and pepper

Why This Recipe Works There are many ways to roast a whole chicken, but the challenges are always the same: getting the white and dark meat to each roast to perfection while also developing a crisp, golden skin. Although you'll find our Weeknight Roast Chicken in Chapter 1 (page 41), this recipe takes a more classic approach, using a roasting pan and rack instead of a skillet. To guarantee great color and crisp skin, we preheated the oven with the roasting pan on the oven rack and rubbed the chicken's skin with oil. Lifting the skin broke up the fat deposits that inhibit crisping and applying butter directly to the breast provided some extra moisture to the lean white meat. Leaving the chicken untrussed allowed the dark meat to cook more quickly. We placed the chicken in a V-rack for even air circulation, arranging it wing side up (then flipping it to the other side) so the breast had a chance to cook through without too much close exposure to the hot pan. A final flip, placing the chicken breast side up, allowed the dark meat to finish cooking. We recommend using a V-rack to roast the chicken. If you don't have a V-rack, set the bird on a regular roasting rack and use balls of aluminum foil to keep the chicken propped up on its side. If using kosher chicken, do not brine. If brining the chicken, do not season with salt in step 2. For brining instructions, see page 22.

1 Adjust oven rack to lower-middle position, place roasting pan on rack, and heat oven to 400 degrees. Spray V-rack with vegetable oil spray.

2 Using your fingers or handle of spoon, gently loosen center portion of skin covering each side of breast. Using spoon, place 1 tablespoon butter underneath skin over center of each side of breast. Gently press on skin to distribute butter over meat. Tuck wingtips behind back. Rub skin with oil and season with salt and pepper. Place chicken, wing side up, on prepared V-rack. Place V-rack in preheated roasting pan and roast for 15 minutes.

3 Remove roasting pan from oven. Using 2 large wads of paper towels, rotate chicken so that opposite wing side is facing up. Return roasting pan to oven and roast for another 15 minutes.

4 Using 2 large wads of paper towels, rotate chicken again so that breast side is facing up, and continue to roast until breast registers 160 degrees and thighs register 175 degrees, 20 to 25 minutes. Transfer chicken to carving board and let rest for 20 minutes. Carve and serve.

GLAZED ROAST CHICKEN

Chicken

1 (6- to 7-pound) whole chicken, giblets discarded

2½ teaspoons salt

1 teaspoon baking powder

1 teaspoon pepper

2 cups beer

Glaze

1 teaspoon cornstarch

½ cup maple syrup

½ cup orange marmalade

¼ cup cider vinegar

2 tablespoons unsalted butter

2 tablespoons Dijon mustard

1 teaspoon pepper

Why This Recipe Works To serve up a whole roast chicken in a mahogany-colored glaze, we focused on getting (and keeping) the skin really crisp, cooking the meat evenly, and making the glazing as simple as possible. Using a vertical roaster to elevate and hold the chicken upright as it roasted guaranteed even heat circulation in the oven; plus, it allowed us access to every nook and cranny when applying the glaze. For a crisp exterior that stood up to a syrupy coating, we separated the skin from the meat and pricked holes in it so the fat could render easily. A salt-and-baking-powder rub and 30 minutes, uncovered, in the refrigerator dehydrated the skin for better crisping. Roasting the chicken at two temperatures was key: Starting out in a moderate oven gently cooked the meat and a 500-degree blast provided a burnished finish. Removing the chicken while the oven heated to its final temperature prevented overcooking. Reducing a marmalade-based glaze on the stovetop and brushing it on toward the end of roasting gave the glaze just enough time to caramelize without harming the skin, and another coating while the chicken rested gave the bird a luminous sheen. As a bonus, we had glaze left over to use in a serving sauce. This recipe calls for a vertical poultry roaster; our favorite is the Vertical Roaster with Infuser by Norpro. If you don't have one, you can substitute a 16-ounce can of beer. Open the beer and pour out about half of the liquid. Spray the can lightly with vegetable oil spray and proceed with the recipe. Taste your marmalade before using it; if it is overly sweet, reduce the amount of maple syrup in the glaze by 2 tablespoons.

1 For the chicken Place chicken breast side down on cutting board. Using tip of sharp knife, make four 1-inch incisions along back of chicken. Using your fingers or handle of spoon, gently loosen skin covering breast and thighs. Using metal skewer, poke 15 to 20 holes in fat deposits on top of breast and thighs. Tuck wingtips behind back.

2 Combine salt, baking powder, and pepper in bowl. Pat chicken dry with paper towels. Sprinkle salt mixture evenly all over chicken. Rub mixture in with your hands, coating entire surface evenly. Transfer chicken, breast side up, to wire rack set in rimmed baking sheet and refrigerate, uncovered, for at least 30 minutes or up to 1 hour.

3 Adjust oven rack to lowest position and heat oven to 325 degrees. Place vertical roaster on rimmed baking sheet. Slide chicken onto vertical roaster so drumsticks reach down to bottom of roaster, chicken stands upright, and breast is perpendicular to bottom of pan. Roast chicken until skin just begins to turn golden and breast registers 140 degrees, 1¼ to 1½ hours. Carefully remove chicken with sheet from oven and increase oven temperature to 500 degrees.

4 For the glaze While chicken roasts, stir cornstarch and 1 tablespoon water together in bowl until no lumps remain. Bring maple syrup, marmalade, vinegar, butter, mustard, and pepper to simmer in medium saucepan over medium-low

heat and cook, stirring occasionally, until reduced to ¾ cup, 6 to 8 minutes. Slowly whisk in cornstarch mixture; return to simmer and cook for 1 minute. Remove saucepan from heat.

5 When oven temperature reaches 500 degrees, pour 1½ cups water in bottom of sheet and return to oven. Roast until chicken skin is evenly browned and crisp, breast registers 160 degrees, and thighs register 175 degrees, 24 to 30 minutes. (Check chicken halfway through roasting; if top is becoming too dark, place 7-inch square piece of aluminum foil over neck and wingtips of chicken and continue to roast. If pan begins to smoke and sizzle, add additional ½ cup water to sheet.)

6 Brush chicken with ¼ cup glaze and continue to roast until browned and sticky, about 5 minutes. (If glaze starts to stiffen, return to low heat to soften.) Carefully remove sheet from oven; with chicken still on vertical roaster brush on ¼ cup glaze. Let chicken rest for 20 minutes.

7 While chicken rests, strain juices from pan through fine-mesh strainer into fat separator; let liquid settle for 5 minutes. Whisk ½ cup juices into remaining ¼ cup glaze in saucepan and set over low heat. Using 2 large wads of paper towels, carefully lift chicken off vertical roaster and onto carving board. Carve chicken, adding any accumulated juices to sauce. Serve with sauce.

PERUVIAN ROAST CHICKEN WITH GARLIC AND LIME

¼ cup fresh mint leaves

3 tablespoons vegetable oil

6 garlic cloves, chopped coarse

1 tablespoon salt

1 tablespoon pepper

1 tablespoon ground cumin

1 tablespoon sugar

2 teaspoons smoked paprika

2 teaspoons dried oregano

2 teaspoons grated lime zest plus ¼ cup juice (2 limes)

1 teaspoon minced habanero chile

1 (3½- to 4-pound) whole chicken, giblets discarded

Why This Recipe Works When you want to roast a chicken but you're looking to infuse it with bold exotic flavors, this Peruvian chicken fits the bill. Treating the meat and skin with a paste of salt, garlic, fresh mint, oregano, paprika, and habanero chile delivered this dish's signature spicy, smoky flavor, and refrigerating the rubbed bird for at least 6 hours deeply seasoned the meat. We placed the chicken on a vertical roaster for allover browning (much like you'd get from a rotisserie) and employed two different oven temperatures to get the crisp skin and perfectly cooked meat we were after. Starting out in a 325-degree oven produced tender, juicy meat, but before the chicken was fully cooked, we pulled it from the oven, upped the heat to 500 degrees, and gave the chicken a final 20 minutes to brown its skin. A homemade spicy mayo made for an authentic finish. If habanero chiles are unavailable, 1 tablespoon of minced serrano chile can be substituted. Wear gloves when working with hot chiles. Note that this recipe requires refrigerating the rubbed chicken for at least 6 hours or up to 24 hours before cooking (a longer time is preferable). If using kosher chicken, omit salt in step 1. This recipe calls for a vertical poultry roaster; our favorite is the Vertical Roaster with Infuser by Norpro. If you don't have one, you can substitute a 16-ounce can of beer. Open the can and pour out about half of the liquid. Spray the can lightly with vegetable oil spray and proceed with the recipe. Serve with Spicy Mayonnaise (recipe follows) and lime wedges.

1 Process mint, oil, garlic, salt, pepper, cumin, sugar, paprika, oregano, lime zest and juice, and habanero in blender until smooth paste forms, 10 to 20 seconds. Pat chicken dry with paper towels. Using your fingers or handle of spoon gently loosen skin covering breast and thighs; place half of paste under skin, directly on meat of breast and thighs. Gently press on skin to distribute paste over meat. Spread entire exterior surface of chicken with remaining paste. Tuck wingtips behind back. Place chicken in 1-gallon zipper-lock bag and refrigerate for at least 6 hours or up to 24 hours.

2 Adjust oven rack to lowest position and heat oven to 325 degrees. Place vertical roaster on rimmed baking sheet. Slide chicken onto vertical roaster so drumsticks reach down to bottom of roaster, chicken stands upright, and breast is perpendicular to bottom of pan. Roast chicken until skin just begins to turn golden and breast registers 140 degrees, 45 to 55 minutes. Carefully remove chicken with sheet from oven and increase oven temperature to 500 degrees.

3 When oven temperature reaches 500 degrees, pour 1 cup water in bottom of sheet and return to oven. Roast until chicken skin is evenly browned and crisp, breast registers 160 degrees, and thighs register 175 degrees, about 20 minutes, rotating baking sheet halfway through roasting. (Check chicken halfway through roasting; if top is becoming too dark, place 7-inch square piece of aluminum foil over neck and wingtips of chicken and continue to roast. If sheet begins to smoke and sizzle, add additional water to sheet.)

4 Carefully remove sheet from oven and let chicken rest, still on vertical roaster, for 20 minutes. Using 2 large wads of paper towels, carefully lift chicken off vertical roaster and onto carving board. Carve chicken and serve.

SPICY MAYONNAISE
makes about 1 cup

If you have concerns about consuming raw eggs, ¼ cup of an egg substitute can be used in place of the egg.

1 large egg
2 tablespoons water
1 tablespoon finely chopped onion
1 tablespoon lime juice
1 tablespoon minced fresh cilantro
1 tablespoon minced jarred jalapeños
1 garlic clove, minced
1 teaspoon yellow mustard
¼ teaspoon salt
1 cup vegetable oil

Process egg, water, onion, lime juice, cilantro, jalapeños, garlic, mustard, and salt in food processor until combined, about 5 seconds. With processor running, slowly drizzle in oil in steady stream until mixture reaches mayonnaise-like consistency, scraping down sides of bowl as needed.

THAI ROAST CHICKEN WITH CHILE DIPPING SAUCE

serves 4

Chicken

1 cup fresh cilantro leaves and stems, trimmed and chopped coarse

6 garlic cloves, peeled and smashed

¼ cup packed light brown sugar

2 teaspoons ground white pepper

2 teaspoons ground coriander

2 teaspoons salt

¼ cup fish sauce

1 (3½- to 4-pound) whole chicken, giblets discarded

Dipping Sauce

½ cup distilled white vinegar

½ cup granulated sugar

1 tablespoon minced Thai chiles

3 garlic cloves, minced

¼ teaspoon salt

Why This Recipe Works This full-flavored chicken takes its inspiration from *gai yang*, a Thai street food, and features a pungent marinade and a spicy, sweet, and sour dipping sauce. To build authentic flavor, we made a thick marinade from a pantry-friendly mixture of spices, cilantro leaves and stems, brown sugar, and fish sauce that offered the same intensity imparted by traditional (but hard-to-find) Thai ingredients. We rubbed the marinade both on and under the skin and let the flavors penetrate for at least 6 hours in the refrigerator. To ensure the chicken had crisp skin and perfectly cooked meat, we roasted it on a vertical roaster, starting it out in a gentle 325-degree oven before ramping up the heat to 500 degrees. To finish, we paired our roast chicken with a simple but potent sauce of vinegar, sugar, garlic, and Thai chiles. Note that this recipe requires refrigerating the marinated chicken for at least 6 hours or up to 24 hours before cooking (a longer time is preferable). To make the sauce less spicy, remove the ribs and seeds from the chiles before mincing. This recipe calls for a vertical poultry roaster; our favorite is the Vertical Roaster with Infuser by Norpro. If you don't have one, you can substitute a 16-ounce can of beer. Open the can and pour out about half of the liquid. Spray the can lightly with vegetable oil spray and proceed with the recipe.

1 For the chicken Pulse cilantro, garlic, sugar, pepper, coriander, and salt in food processor until finely chopped, 10 to 15 pulses, scraping down sides of bowl as needed; transfer to small bowl. Stir in fish sauce until combined. Pat chicken try with paper towels. Using your fingers or handle of spoon, gently loosen skin covering breast and thighs. Place half of paste under skin, directly on meat in center of each side of breast and on thighs. Gently press on skin to distribute paste over meat. Spread entire exterior surface of chicken with remaining paste. Tuck wingtips behind back. Place chicken in 1-gallon zipper-lock bag and refrigerate for at least 6 hours or up to 24 hours.

2 Adjust oven rack to lowest position and heat oven to 325 degrees. Place vertical roaster on rimmed baking sheet. Slide chicken onto vertical roaster so drumsticks reach down to bottom of roaster, chicken stands upright, and breast is perpendicular to bottom of pan. Roast chicken until skin just begins to turn golden and breast registers 140 degrees, 45 to 55 minutes. Carefully remove chicken with sheet from oven and increase oven temperature to 500 degrees.

3 For the dipping sauce While chicken cooks, bring vinegar and sugar to boil in small saucepan. Reduce heat to medium-low and simmer, stirring occasionally, until vinegar mixture is slightly thickened, about 5 minutes. Off heat, let vinegar mixture cool completely. Stir in chiles, garlic, and salt; set aside until ready to serve. (Sauce can be refrigerated for up to 2 weeks. Bring to room temperature before serving.)

4 When oven temperature reaches 500 degrees, pour 1 cup water in bottom of sheet and return to oven. Roast until chicken skin is evenly browned and crisp, breast registers 160 degrees, and thighs register 175 degrees, about 20 minutes, rotating sheet halfway through roasting. (Check chicken halfway through roasting; if top is becoming too dark, place 7-inch square piece of aluminum foil over neck and wingtips of chicken and continue to roast. If sheet begins to smoke and sizzle, add additional water to sheet.)

5 Carefully remove sheet from oven and let chicken rest, still on vertical roaster, for 20 minutes. Using 2 large wads of paper towels, carefully lift chicken off vertical roaster and onto carving board. Carve chicken and serve with sauce.

LEMON ROAST CHICKEN

serves 4

1 (3½- to 4-pound) whole chicken, giblets discarded, brined if desired

3 tablespoons grated lemon zest plus ⅓ cup juice (3 lemons)

1 teaspoon sugar

Salt and pepper

2 cups chicken broth

1 cup plus 1 tablespoon water

1 teaspoon cornstarch

3 tablespoons unsalted butter, cut into 3 pieces

1 tablespoon minced fresh parsley

Why This Recipe Works Infusing a chicken with great lemon flavor takes more than stuffing it with lemon wedges. For a bird bursting with clear citrus flavor, we butterflied a whole chicken so it would lay flat. We grated some lemon zest and combined it with salt and sugar to create a rub; the sugar tempered the lemon's acidity. After loosening the skin, we applied some of the rub directly to the meat. Next, we made a lemony braising liquid by adding the remaining rub and fresh lemon juice to chicken broth. We poured the citrus-boosted broth into a roasting pan and laid the butterflied bird in it, breast side up, to begin roasting with the skin safely above the surface of the liquid. With the broth protecting the bird from drying out, we were able to roast it at a hot 475 degrees. Our chicken emerged with lemony, juicy meat beneath a supremely crisp skin, and while it rested we reduced and thickened the liquid into a rich sauce. Avoid using nonstick or aluminum roasting pans in this recipe. The former can cause the chicken to brown too quickly, while the latter may react with the lemon juice, producing off-flavors. For butterflying instructions, see page 5. If using kosher chicken, do not brine. If brining the chicken, do not season with salt in step 1. For brining instructions, see page 22.

1 Adjust oven rack to middle position and heat oven to 475 degrees. With chicken breast side down, use kitchen shears to cut through bones on either side of backbone; discard backbone. Flip chicken over and press on breastbone to flatten. Tuck wingtips behind back.

2 Combine lemon zest, sugar, and 1 teaspoon salt in small bowl. Pat chicken dry with paper towels. Using your fingers or handle of spoon, gently loosen skin covering breast and thighs. Rub 2 tablespoons zest mixture under skin of chicken, directly onto meat. Season chicken with salt and pepper and transfer skin side up to roasting pan. (Seasoned chicken can be refrigerated for up to 2 hours.)

3 Whisk together broth, 1 cup water, lemon juice, and remaining zest mixture, then pour into roasting pan. (Liquid should just reach skin of thighs. If it does not, add enough water to reach skin of thighs.) Roast until skin is golden brown and thighs register 175 degrees, 40 to 45 minutes. Transfer to carving board and let rest for 20 minutes.

4 Stir cornstarch and remaining 1 tablespoon water together in bowl until no lumps remain. Pour liquid from pan, along with any accumulated chicken juices, into saucepan (you should have about 1½ cups). Using spoon, skim fat. Bring to simmer over medium-high heat and cook until reduced to 1 cup, about 5 minutes. Slowly whisk in cornstarch mixture; return to simmer and cook until slightly thickened, about 2 minutes. Off heat, whisk in butter, 1 piece at a time, and parsley and season with salt and pepper to taste. Carve chicken and serve, passing sauce separately.

ZA'ATAR-RUBBED ROAST CHICKEN WITH MINT VINAIGRETTE

serves 4

5 tablespoons plus 1 teaspoon extra-virgin olive oil

2 tablespoons za'atar

1 (3½- to 4-pound) whole chicken, giblets discarded, brined if desired

Salt and pepper

1 tablespoon minced fresh mint

¼ preserved lemon, pulp and white pith removed, rind rinsed and minced (1 tablespoon)

2 teaspoons white wine vinegar

½ teaspoon Dijon mustard

Why This Recipe Works This lively pan-roasted butterflied chicken gets its impactful flavor from a thick za'atar paste. *Za'atar* is the Arabic name for wild thyme but the word now commonly denotes a blend of thyme, sumac, and sesame. To keep those bold flavors intact, we began roasting the bird before introducing the za'atar. Starting on the stovetop, we kept the chicken flat and flush against a hot skillet with the help of a Dutch oven weighted down with bricks to render the fat quickly and crisp the skin. After the chicken picked up plenty of color and flavor, we removed the pot, flipped the chicken breast side up, and brushed it with a thick paste of za'atar and extra-virgin olive oil before transferring it to a hot oven. As the chicken roasted, the paste turned into a distinct, aromatic crust. To brighten up the finished dish, we prepared a zesty mint vinaigrette. You can find za'atar in the international aisle of the supermarket. If you can't find preserved lemons, you can substitute 1 tablespoon lemon zest. You will need a 12-inch ovensafe skillet and a Dutch oven for this recipe. For butterflying instructions, see page 5. If using kosher chicken, do not brine. If brining the chicken, do not season with salt in step 1. For brining instructions, see page 22.

1 Adjust oven rack to lowest position and heat oven to 450 degrees. Combine 2 tablespoons oil and za'atar in small bowl. With chicken breast side down, use kitchen shears to cut through bones on either side of backbone; discard backbone. Flip chicken over and press on breastbone to flatten. Tuck wingtips behind back. Pat chicken dry with paper towels and season with salt and pepper.

2 Heat 1 teaspoon oil in 12-inch ovensafe skillet over medium-high heat until just smoking. Add chicken skin side down and reduce heat to medium. Place Dutch oven loaded with 2 bricks or heavy cans on top of chicken and cook until evenly browned, about 25 minutes. After 20 minutes, chicken should be golden brown; if it is not, increase heat to medium-high and continue to cook until well browned.

3 Off heat, remove pot and carefully flip chicken. Brush skin with za'atar mixture, transfer skillet to oven, and roast until breast registers 160 degrees and thighs register 175 degrees, 10 to 20 minutes.

4 Transfer chicken to carving board and let rest for 20 minutes. Meanwhile, whisk mint, preserved lemon, vinegar, mustard, ⅛ teaspoon salt, and ⅛ teaspoon pepper in bowl until combined. Whisking constantly, slowly drizzle in remaining 3 tablespoons oil until emulsified. Carve chicken and serve with vinaigrette.

SKILLET ROAST CHICKEN AND POTATOES

serves 4

3 tablespoons vegetable oil

2 teaspoons minced fresh thyme

1½ teaspoons smoked paprika

1½ teaspoons grated lemon zest, plus lemon wedges for serving

Salt and pepper

1 (3½- to 4-pound) whole chicken, giblets discarded, brined if desired

2 pounds Yukon Gold potatoes, peeled, ends squared off, and sliced into 1-inch-thick rounds

Why This Recipe Works There is almost nothing more delicious than a whole chicken, roasted to perfection, atop a bed of perfectly browned potatoes. To achieve this ideal, we started by choosing a skillet instead of a roasting pan. To fit a full 2 pounds of potatoes into a 12-inch skillet we cut them into thick rounds and gave them a jump-start on the stovetop to get a crust started. For a full-flavored bird, we carefully separated the skin from the breast and thighs and applied a fragrant blend of fresh thyme, smoked paprika, and lemon zest. Keeping the potatoes in the skillet and roasting the chicken on top of them not only elevated the bird for greater exposure to the oven's heat, but also allowed the potatoes to soak up the chicken's tasty drippings. Once the chicken was fully cooked, we let it rest while we covered the potatoes and returned them to the oven. By the time the chicken was ready to be served, the potatoes were perfectly tender. Use uniform, medium potatoes. You will need a 12-inch ovensafe nonstick skillet with a tight-fitting lid for this recipe. If using kosher chicken, do not brine. If brining the chicken, do not season with salt in step 1. For brining instructions, see page 22.

1 Adjust oven rack to lower-middle position and heat oven to 400 degrees. Combine 2 tablespoons oil, thyme, paprika, lemon zest, 1 teaspoon salt, and ½ teaspoon pepper in bowl. Pat chicken dry with paper towels. Using your fingers or handle of spoon, gently loosen skin from breast and thighs. Rub oil mixture all over chicken and underneath skin of breast, directly onto meat. Tie legs together with kitchen twine and tuck wingtips behind back.

2 Toss potatoes with 1½ teaspoons salt, ½ teaspoon pepper, and remaining 1 tablespoon oil. Arrange potatoes, flat sides down, in single layer in 12-inch ovensafe nonstick skillet. Place skillet over medium heat and cook potatoes, without moving them, until brown on bottom, 7 to 9 minutes (do not flip).

3 Place chicken, breast side up, on top of potatoes and transfer skillet to oven. Roast until breast registers 160 degrees and thighs register 175 degrees, 1 to 1¼ hours. Remove skillet from oven (skillet handle will be hot). Transfer chicken to carving board and let rest while finishing potatoes.

4 Meanwhile, being careful of hot skillet handle, cover skillet, return potatoes to oven, and roast until tender, about 20 minutes. Carve chicken and serve with potatoes and lemon wedges.

TWIN ROAST CHICKENS WITH ROOT VEGETABLES AND TARRAGON VINAIGRETTE

serves 8

1½ pounds red potatoes, unpeeled, cut into 1-inch pieces

1 pound carrots, peeled and cut into 1-inch pieces

1 pound parsnips, peeled and cut into 1-inch pieces

6 shallots, peeled and halved

5 tablespoons extra-virgin olive oil

Salt and pepper

2 (3½- to 4-pound) whole chickens, giblets discarded, brined if desired

6 tablespoons minced fresh tarragon

⅓ cup minced fresh parsley

2 tablespoons sherry vinegar

1 teaspoon Dijon mustard

Why This Recipe Works Roasting two whole chickens together is as simple as cooking one, provided you employ the right method (and the right vessel). To ensure that our two birds roasted evenly, we placed them side by side on a V-rack with breasts facing down to jump-start browning while allowing maximum air circulation for even cooking. We then flipped them to finish cooking, giving the birds an allover golden hue. To turn our chickens into dinner, we spread fresh tarragon beneath the skin and scattered a mix of root vegetables (carrots, parsnips, shallots, and potatoes) into the bottom of the pan, where they readily soaked up the chicken juices as they, too, roasted and turned brown. The vegetables were not quite tender when the chickens were done, so while the birds rested we shifted the roasting pan to the stovetop, straddled it over two burners, and continued cooking the vegetables, stirring them with the pan drippings. For a fresh finish, we whisked together a quick tarragon vinaigrette that echoed the chickens' herbal flavor. If using kosher chickens, do not brine. If brining the chickens, do not season with salt in step 3. For brining instructions, see page 22.

1 Adjust oven rack to middle position and heat oven to 475 degrees. Toss potatoes, carrots, parsnips, shallots, 1 tablespoon oil, ½ teaspoon salt, and ½ teaspoon pepper together in bowl. Spread vegetables evenly into roasting pan. Spray V-rack with vegetable oil spray and nestle into pan with vegetables.

2 Pat chickens dry with paper towels. Using your fingers or handle of spoon, gently loosen skin covering breasts and thighs. Spread 3 tablespoons tarragon under skin of chickens, directly onto meat. Tie legs together with kitchen twine and tuck wingtips behind back.

3 Season exterior of chickens with salt and pepper. Place chickens, breast side down, in prepared V-rack. Roast for 20 minutes.

4 Using 2 large wads of paper towels, flip chickens breast side up and continue to roast until breasts register 160 degrees and thighs register 175 degrees, 50 minutes to 1 hour.

5 Remove pan from oven. Transfer chicken to carving board and let rest for 20 minutes. Being careful of hot pan handles, place pan over medium-high heat on stovetop (over 2 burners, if possible) and cook vegetables, stirring gently, until lightly browned and glistening, 8 to 10 minutes.

6 Whisk remaining ¼ cup oil, remaining 3 tablespoons tarragon, parsley, vinegar, and mustard together in small bowl. Carve chickens and serve with vegetables and vinaigrette.

ROAST CHICKEN AND STUFFING

serves 4

1 (3½- to 4-pound) whole chicken, giblets discarded, brined if desired

6 tablespoons unsalted butter

2 tablespoons minced fresh sage

2 tablespoons minced fresh thyme

Salt and pepper

2 onions, chopped fine

2 celery ribs, minced

7 ounces Italian bread, cut into ½-inch cubes (6 cups)

⅓ cup chicken broth

Why This Recipe Works To enjoy a roast chicken and stuffing without employing a pile of pots and pans, we roasted the bird on top of the savory stuffing. Not only did this method streamline the process, but it also allowed the chicken juices to flavor the stuffing—a bonus you don't get when cooking the two components separately. A brush of herb butter guaranteed flavorful, well-seasoned skin, and sautéing chopped onions and minced celery established an aromatic base for the stuffing. We placed the chicken on top of the vegetables, scattered bread cubes all around the bird, and roasted everything in the oven. As the chicken browned and gently cooked through, the bread cubes turned toasty even as they soaked up the rich rendered fat. When the chicken was fully cooked, we let it rest and finished the stuffing, first letting it sit to continue soaking up the surrounding flavors and then adding a splash of broth to tie it all together. You can find Italian bread in the bakery section of your grocery store. You will need a 12-inch ovensafe skillet with a tight-fitting lid for this recipe. If using kosher chicken, do not brine. If brining the chicken, omit the salt in step 1. For brining instructions, see page 22.

1 Adjust oven rack to lower-middle position and heat oven to 375 degrees. Pat chicken dry with paper towels. Melt 4 tablespoons butter in small bowl in microwave, about 45 seconds. Stir in 1 tablespoon sage, 1 tablespoon thyme, 1 teaspoon salt, and ½ teaspoon pepper. Brush chicken with herb butter. Tie legs together with kitchen twine and tuck wingtips behind back.

2 Melt remaining 2 tablespoons butter in 12-inch ovensafe skillet over medium heat. Add onions, celery, ½ teaspoon salt, and ½ teaspoon pepper and cook until vegetables are softened, about 5 minutes. Add remaining 1 tablespoon sage and remaining 1 tablespoon thyme and cook until fragrant, about 1 minute. Off heat, place chicken, breast side up, on top of vegetables. Arrange bread cubes around chicken in bottom of skillet.

3 Transfer skillet to oven and roast until breast registers 160 degrees and thighs register 175 degrees, about 1 hour, rotating skillet halfway through roasting.

4 Remove skillet from oven (skillet handle will be hot). Carefully transfer chicken to carving board and let rest while finishing stuffing. Being careful of hot skillet handle, stir bread and vegetables in skillet to combine; cover and let stand for 10 minutes.

5 Stir broth and any accumulated chicken juices into stuffing to combine. Warm stuffing, uncovered, over low heat until heated through, about 3 minutes. Remove from heat, cover, and let sit while carving chicken. Carve chicken and serve with stuffing.

ROAST TURKEY BREAST WITH GRAVY

serves 6 to 8

1 (5- to 7-pound) bone-in turkey breast

Kosher salt and pepper

2 tablespoons unsalted butter, melted

2 teaspoons extra-virgin olive oil, plus extra as needed

1 small onion, chopped into ¼-inch pieces

1 small carrot, chopped into ¼-inch pieces

1 small celery rib, chopped into ¼-inch pieces

2 sprigs fresh thyme

1 bay leaf

5 cups water

¼ cup all-purpose flour

¼ cup dry white wine

Why This Recipe Works A perfectly roasted whole turkey breast, complete with gravy, can be just the ticket for smaller holiday gatherings. We started by removing the backbone so the breast sat flat in the oven for even browning and to make carving easier. Salting the turkey both seasoned it and helped it to retain more of its juices as it cooked. Brushing the skin with melted butter promoted deep browning and contributed rich flavor. We roasted the breast in a skillet, instead of a roasting pan, to contain the drippings so they didn't scorch. Starting the breast at 325 degrees gently cooked the white meat, while finishing it at 500 degrees deeply bronzed the skin. While the bird cooked, we used the backbone to make a simple stock for our gravy, which we built in the skillet with the drippings. You will need a 12-inch ovensafe skillet for this recipe. Note that this recipe requires refrigerating the salted breast for 24 hours. If using a self-basting turkey (such as a frozen Butterball) or a kosher turkey, do not salt the breast in step 2. If your turkey breast comes without a back, substitute 1 pound of chicken wings. Serve with Classic Cranberry Sauce (page 29), if desired.

1 Using kitchen shears, cut through ribs following vertical line of fat where breast meets back, from tapered end of breast to wing joint. Using your hands, bend back away from breast to pop shoulder joint out of socket. With paring knife, cut through joint between bones to separate back from breast. Reserve back for gravy. Trim excess fat from breast.

2 Place turkey, breast side up, on counter. Using your fingers or handle of spoon, gently loosen and separate skin from each side of breast. Peel skin back, leaving it attached at top and center of breast. Rub 1 teaspoon salt onto each side of breast, then lay skin back in place. Rub 1 teaspoon salt into underside of bird's cavity. Refrigerate turkey, uncovered, for 24 hours.

3 Adjust oven rack to middle position and heat oven to 325 degrees. Pat turkey dry with paper towels. Arrange turkey breast, skin side up, in 12-inch ovensafe skillet, tucking ribs under breast and arranging so narrow end of breast is not touching skillet. Brush melted butter evenly over turkey and sprinkle with 1 teaspoon salt. Roast until thickest part of breast registers 130 degrees, 1 to 1¼ hours.

4 While turkey is roasting, heat oil in large saucepan over medium-high heat. Add reserved back, skin side down, and cook until well browned, 6 to 8 minutes. Add onion, carrot, and celery and cook, stirring occasionally, until vegetables

are softened and lightly browned, about 5 minutes. Add thyme sprigs, bay leaf, and water and bring to boil. Reduce heat to medium-low and simmer for 1 hour. Strain broth through fine-mesh strainer into container. Discard solids and set broth aside (you should have about 4 cups of broth). (Broth can be refrigerated for up to 24 hours.)

5 Remove turkey from oven (skillet handle will be hot) and increase temperature to 500 degrees. When oven reaches 500 degrees, return turkey to oven and roast until skin is deeply browned and thickest part of breast registers 160 degrees, 15 to 30 minutes. Transfer to carving board and let rest for 30 minutes.

6 Being careful of hot skillet handle, pour off fat in skillet. You should have about ¼ cup; add oil as needed to equal ¼ cup. Return fat to skillet and heat over medium heat until shimmering. Add flour and cook, whisking constantly, until flour is well coated with fat and browned, about 1 minute. Add wine, whisking to scrape up any browned bits, and cook until wine has evaporated, 1 to 2 minutes. Slowly whisk in reserved broth. Increase heat to medium-high and cook, whisking occasionally, until sauce is thickened and reduced to 2 cups, about 20 minutes. Season with salt and pepper to taste. Carve turkey and serve, passing gravy separately.

removing the backbone from a turkey breast

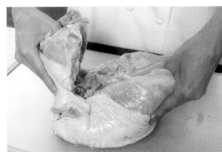  

1 Using kitchen shears, cut through ribs following vertical line of fat where breast meets back, from tapered end of breast to wing joint.

2 Using your hands, bend back away from breast to pop shoulder joint out of socket. Cut through joint to remove back.

3 Pull back skin to evenly season breast meat.

SPICE-RUBBED ROAST TURKEY BREAST WITH GREEN BEANS

serves 6 to 8

1 (5- to 7-pound) bone-in turkey breast

Kosher salt and pepper

2 teaspoons five-spice powder

1½ teaspoons ground cumin

1 teaspoon garlic powder

¼ teaspoon cayenne pepper

¼ teaspoon ground cardamom

2 tablespoons unsalted butter, melted

1 large shallot, sliced thin

2 pounds green beans, trimmed

Why This Recipe Works To turn our perfectly roasted whole turkey breast into a one-pan non-holiday meal, we kicked up the meat's mild flavor with an interesting spice rub and introduced an easy, fresh side. We added five-spice powder, cumin, cayenne, and cardamom to the salt rub and applied it directly to the meat before refrigerating the breast for 24 hours. This added immense flavor and the salt helped the meat stay moist during roasting. Brushing the skin with melted butter and cranking the oven to 500 degrees at the end of roasting guaranteed a crisp exterior. Because we roasted the breast in a 12-inch skillet, we were able to contain the drippings for use in sautéing our vegetable: a helping of crisp, verdant green beans. You will need a 12-inch ovensafe skillet for this recipe. Note that this recipe requires refrigerating the seasoned breast for 24 hours. If using a self-basting turkey (such as a frozen Butterball) or a kosher turkey, do not add salt to rub in step 2.

1 Using kitchen shears, cut through ribs following vertical line of fat where breast meets back, from tapered end of breast to wing joint. Using your hands, bend back away from breast to pop shoulder joint out of socket. With paring knife, cut through joint between bones to separate back from breast; discard back. Trim excess fat from breast.

2 Place turkey, breast side up, on counter. Combine 2 teaspoons salt, five-spice powder, cumin, garlic powder, cayenne, and cardamom in bowl. Using your fingers or handle of spoon, gently loosen and separate turkey skin from each side of breast. Peel skin back, leaving it attached at top and center of breast. Rub 2 teaspoons spice mixture onto each side of breast, then lay skin back in place. Rub remaining spice mixture into underside of bird's cavity. Refrigerate turkey, uncovered, for 24 hours.

3 Adjust oven rack to middle position and heat oven to 325 degrees. Pat turkey dry with paper towels. Arrange turkey breast, skin side up, in 12-inch ovensafe skillet, tucking ribs under breast and arranging so narrow end of breast is not touching skillet. Brush melted butter evenly over turkey and sprinkle with 1 teaspoon salt. Roast until thickest part of breast registers 130 degrees, 1 to 1¼ hours.

4 Remove turkey from oven (skillet handle will be hot) and increase temperature to 500 degrees. When oven reaches 500 degrees, return turkey to oven and roast until skin is deeply browned and thickest part of breast registers 160 degrees, 15 to 30 minutes. Using spatula, loosen turkey from skillet and transfer to carving board. Let rest for 30 minutes.

5 Meanwhile, being careful of hot skillet handle, pour off all but 1 tablespoon fat from skillet. Add shallot and cook over medium heat until softened, about 1 minute. Add green beans, ¼ cup water, and 1 teaspoon salt and toss to combine. Reduce heat to medium-low, cover, and cook until green beans are just tender, 12 to 15 minutes.

6 Uncover, increase heat to medium, and cook until water evaporates and beans are tender, 3 to 5 minutes. Season with salt and pepper to taste. Carve turkey and serve with green beans.

STUFFED ROAST TURKEY BREAST

serves 6 to 8

1 (3- to 4-pound) boneless, skinless turkey breast, trimmed

1 recipe stuffing (recipes follow)

2 tablespoons vegetable oil

1 tablespoon sugar

2 teaspoons pepper

1 teaspoon salt

Why This Recipe Works A stuffed turkey breast makes a nice change from the usual plain roast turkey. Stuffed, rolled, and roasted, our turkey breast looks as good as it tastes. Without skin and bones this cut can turn out bland and dry, but a simple rub and rich stuffing provided plenty of flavor. After butterflying and pounding the breast to an even thickness, we spread the turkey with an assertive vegetable and cheese stuffing and rolled it into a tight cylinder. Applying a sugar rub to the breast and roasting it in a moderate oven added both color and flavor and kept the turkey moist. Some stores sell only boneless turkey breasts with the skin still attached; the skin can be removed with a paring knife. This recipe calls for one turkey breast half; an entire breast with two lobes of meat is too large for this recipe. Before stuffing the turkey, make sure that the stuffing is completely chilled.

1 With turkey smooth side down, slice into thickest part, keeping knife ½ inch above cutting board and stopping ½ inch from edge of breast. Lay butterflied meat flat on cutting board, cover with plastic wrap, and pound lightly with meat mallet until about ½ inch thick. Spread stuffing in even layer over turkey. Starting with short side nearest you, roll up turkey and tie with kitchen twine at 1½-inch intervals.

2 Adjust oven rack to middle position and heat oven to 325 degrees. Rub roast with oil and sprinkle evenly with sugar, pepper, and salt. Place on wire rack set in rimmed baking sheet and roast, turning every 30 minutes, until turkey registers 160 degrees, about 2 hours. Transfer roast to carving board, tent with aluminum foil, and let rest for 20 minutes. Remove twine and slice into ½-inch-thick slices. Serve.

MUSHROOM-MARSALA STUFFING
makes about 2 cups
To avoid flare-ups, remove the pan from the heat before adding the Marsala.

2 tablespoons unsalted butter

1 onion, chopped fine

1 pound white mushrooms, trimmed and chopped fine

2 garlic cloves, minced

2 teaspoons minced fresh thyme

¼ cup sweet Marsala

2 ounces Parmesan cheese, grated (1 cup)

2 tablespoons minced fresh parsley

Salt and pepper

Melt butter in 12-inch skillet over medium-high heat. Add onion and cook until softened, about 5 minutes. Reduce heat to medium, add mushrooms, and cook until liquid has evaporated, 10 to 15 minutes. Add garlic and thyme and cook until fragrant, 30 seconds. Off heat, stir in Marsala. Return to heat and cook until mushrooms are dry and golden brown, about 5 minutes. Remove from heat and let cool for 10 minutes. Stir in Parmesan, parsley, and salt and pepper to taste. Stuffing can be refrigerated for up to 3 days.

LEMON, SPINACH, AND FONTINA STUFFING
makes about 2 cups
Soggy spinach can make for a watery filling, so wring out excess moisture in cheesecloth or a dish towel.

2 tablespoons extra-virgin olive oil

1 onion, chopped fine

8 ounces frozen spinach, thawed, squeezed dry, and chopped

3 garlic cloves, minced

¼ teaspoon grated lemon zest

8 ounces fontina cheese, shredded (2 cups)

Salt and pepper

Heat oil in 12-inch skillet over medium-high heat until shimmering. Add onion and cook until softened, about 5 minutes. Stir in spinach, garlic, and lemon zest and cook until fragrant, 30 seconds. Remove from heat and let cool for 10 minutes. Stir in fontina and season with salt and pepper to taste. Stuffing can be refrigerated for up to 3 days.

PERFECT ROAST TURKEY AND GRAVY

serves 10 to 12

Kosher salt and pepper

4 teaspoons sugar

1 (12- to 14-pound) turkey, neck and giblets removed and reserved for gravy

2½ tablespoons vegetable oil

1 teaspoon baking powder

1 small onion, chopped fine

1 carrot, sliced thin

5 sprigs fresh parsley

2 bay leaves

5 tablespoons all-purpose flour

3¼ cups water

¼ cup dry white wine

Why This Recipe Works To produce a fuss-free classic roast turkey and a fast, richly flavored gravy, we borrowed a tool from pizza making. To prep the turkey, we first rubbed it with a salt and sugar blend and refrigerated it for 24 hours. Over time, the salt mixed with the moisture from the meat to form a concentrated brine; this both seasoned the turkey and helped to keep it juicy and also dried out the skin. To roast the turkey, we preheated a roasting pan on a baking stone to create an extra-hot oven. Roasting the bird directly in the preheated pan (with no V-rack) helped the dark meat finish cooking at the same time as the white meat. Adding an aluminum foil shield over the breast protected it during the initial roasting; removing the foil and finishing the turkey in a cooler oven ensured a browned exterior and moist meat. The juices reduced in the pan, laying the foundation for a rich gravy. Note that this recipe requires refrigerating the salted turkey for at least 24 hours or up to 2 days before cooking (a longer chilling time is preferable). If using a self-basting turkey (such as a frozen Butterball) or a kosher turkey, omit salt from rub in step 1.

1 Combine ¼ cup salt and sugar in bowl. Place turkey, breast side up, on counter. Using your fingers or handle of spoon, gently loosen skin covering breast, thighs, and drumsticks. Rub 4 teaspoons salt mixture under skin of each side of breast, 2 teaspoons under skin of each leg, and remaining salt mixture inside cavity. Tie legs together with kitchen twine and tuck wings behind back. Place turkey on wire rack set in rimmed baking sheet and refrigerate, uncovered, for at least 24 hours or up to 2 days.

2 At least 30 minutes before roasting turkey, adjust oven rack to lowest position, set baking stone on rack, set roasting pan on baking stone, and heat oven to 500 degrees. Combine 1½ teaspoons oil and baking powder in small bowl. Pat turkey dry with paper towels. Rub oil mixture evenly over turkey. Cover turkey breast with double layer of aluminum foil.

3 Remove pan from oven and drizzle remaining 2 tablespoons oil into pan. Place turkey, breast side up, in pan and return pan to oven. Reduce oven temperature to 425 degrees and roast for 45 minutes.

4 Remove foil, reduce oven temperature to 325 degrees, and continue to roast until breast registers 160 degrees and drumsticks/thighs register 175 degrees, 1 to 1½ hours longer.

5 Using spatula, loosen turkey from pan; transfer to carving board and let rest for 45 minutes. While turkey rests, scrape up any browned bits from bottom of pan. Strain mixture through fine-mesh strainer set over bowl. Transfer drippings to fat separator and let rest for 10 minutes. Reserve 3 tablespoons fat and defatted liquid (you should have 1 cup of liquid; add water as needed to equal 1 cup). Discard remaining fat.

6 Heat reserved fat in large saucepan over medium-high heat until shimmering. Add reserved neck and giblets and cook until well browned, 10 to 12 minutes. Transfer neck and giblets to large plate. Reduce heat to medium; add onion, carrot, parsley sprigs, and bay leaves; and cook, stirring frequently, until vegetables are softened, 5 to 7 minutes. Add flour and cook, stirring constantly, until flour is well coated with fat, about 1 minute. Slowly whisk in reserved defatted liquid and cook until thickened, about 1 minute. Whisk in water and wine, return neck and giblets to saucepan, and bring to simmer. Simmer for 10 minutes, then season with salt and pepper to taste. Discard neck. Strain gravy through fine-mesh strainer, discarding solids, and transfer to serving bowl. Carve turkey and serve, passing gravy separately.

HERBED ROAST TURKEY

Turkey and Brine

1 cup salt

1 (12- to 14-pound) turkey, neck and giblets discarded

Herb Paste

1¼ cups chopped fresh parsley

1 shallot, minced

4 teaspoons minced fresh thyme

2 garlic cloves, minced

2 teaspoons chopped fresh sage

1½ teaspoons minced fresh rosemary

1 teaspoon pepper

¾ teaspoon grated lemon zest

¾ teaspoon salt

¼ cup extra-virgin olive oil

1 teaspoon Dijon mustard

Why This Recipe Works Incorporating a bounty of fresh herbs into a roast turkey provides a flavorful alternative to a plain roasted bird. Adding the herbs seemed straightforward, but it was not easy to get their flavor to go more than skin deep; we wanted serious herb flavor through and through. We first brined the turkey to infuse the meat with salt and moisture; then, to ensure crisp skin, we dried and refrigerated the turkey, uncovered, for 30 minutes. To add intense herb flavor, we spread a potent herb paste on and beneath the skin of the turkey and inside its cavity, but the deepest flavor infusion came from cutting two pockets into the breast and rubbing them with more of the paste. This created an attractive swirl of herbs in every slice. We ensured that our turkey would roast evenly by starting it breast side down in a V-rack and flipping it partway through, giving the slow-cooking dark meat extra exposure to the pan's heat in the last hour or so in the oven. A 45-minute rest redistributed the juices. Note that this recipe requires refrigerating the brined turkey for at least 6 hours or up to 12 hours before cooking (a longer brining time is preferable). If using a self-basting turkey (such as a frozen Butterball) or a kosher turkey, do not brine in step 1. For a turkey with extra-crisp skin, refrigerate, uncovered, for 8 to 24 hours in step 2.

1 For the turkey and brine Dissolve salt in 2 gallons cold water in large container. Submerge turkey in brine, cover, and refrigerate for at least 6 hours or up to 12 hours.

2 Remove turkey from brine and pat dry, inside and out, with paper towels. Transfer turkey, breast side up, to wire rack set in rimmed baking sheet and refrigerate, uncovered, for 30 minutes.

3 For the herb paste Pulse parsley, shallot, thyme, garlic, sage, rosemary, pepper, lemon zest, and salt in food processor until coarse paste is formed, about 10 pulses. Add oil and mustard and continue to pulse until mixture forms smooth paste, 10 to 12 pulses, scraping down sides of bowl with rubber spatula after 5 pulses. Transfer herb paste to bowl.

4 Adjust oven rack to lowest position and heat oven to 400 degrees. Line V-rack with heavy-duty aluminum foil and poke several holes in foil. Set V-rack in roasting pan and spray foil with vegetable oil spray.

5 Transfer turkey to large cutting board. Using your fingers or handle of spoon, gently loosen skin covering breast, thighs, and drumsticks. Place 1½ tablespoons herb paste under skin of each side of breast. Gently press on skin to distribute paste over breast, thigh, and drumstick meat.

6 Using sharp paring knife, cut 1½-inch vertical slit into thickest part of each side of breast. Starting from top of incision, swing knife tip down to create 4- to 5-inch pocket within flesh. Place 1 tablespoon herb paste in each pocket; using your fingers, rub paste in thin, even layer.

7 Rub 1 tablespoon herb paste inside turkey cavity. Flip turkey breast side down; apply half of remaining herb paste to turkey skin; flip turkey breast side up and apply remaining herb paste to skin, pressing and patting to make paste adhere; reapply herb paste that falls onto cutting board. Tie legs together with kitchen twine and tuck wings behind back.

8 Place turkey, breast side down, on prepared V-rack. Roast turkey for 45 minutes. Remove pan from oven. Using 2 large wads of paper towels, rotate turkey breast side up. Continue to roast until breast registers 160 degrees and thighs register 175 degrees, 50 minutes to 1 hour longer. Transfer turkey to carving board and let rest for 45 minutes. Carve turkey and serve.

applying an herb paste

1 After rubbing herb paste under skin directly onto flesh, make 1½-inch slit in each side of breast. Swing knife tip through breast, creating large pocket.

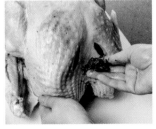

2 Apply layer of paste inside each pocket. Rub remaining paste inside turkey cavity and on skin.

OLD-FASHIONED STUFFED ROAST TURKEY

serves 10 to 12

Turkey

1 (12- to 14-pound) turkey, neck and giblets discarded

Kosher salt

2 teaspoons baking powder

1 (36-inch) square cheesecloth, folded into quarters

12 ounces salt pork, sliced ¼ inch thick and rinsed

Classic Herb Stuffing

1½ pounds hearty white sandwich bread, cut into ½-inch cubes (12 cups)

4 tablespoons unsalted butter

1 onion, chopped fine

2 celery ribs, chopped fine

2 teaspoons salt

1 teaspoon pepper

2 tablespoons minced fresh thyme

1 tablespoon minced fresh marjoram

1 tablespoon minced fresh sage

1½ cups chicken broth

2 large eggs

Why This Recipe Works For some people, an unstuffed roast turkey is heresy. Food safety concerns aside, stuffing a turkey generally complicates the matter of properly roasting it. Our method makes it possible to have it all—moist meat, crisp skin, and plenty of classic bread stuffing. We salted the turkey for at least 24 hours to season the meat and keep it moist. Next we poked holes in the fatty deposits of the skin to speed up the rendering process; just before roasting we rubbed the skin with baking powder and salt to encourage browning. To make removing the stuffing easier, we lined the turkey cavity with cheesecloth first and then packed it with as much stuffing as would fit (reserving the rest). Laying the bird breast side down in a V-rack and draping strips of salt pork on the back infused the turkey with deep flavor as it roasted. Once the breast was nearly cooked through, we removed the salt pork, mixed the cooked stuffing with the uncooked stuffing, and flipped the turkey breast side up to finish roasting in a hotter oven. We finished baking our turkey-infused stuffing, enriching it with broth and eggs, while the finished bird rested. Look for salt pork that is roughly equal parts fat and lean meat. The bread can be toasted up to 24 hours in advance. Note that this recipe requires refrigerating the salted turkey for at least 24 hours or up to 2 days before cooking (a longer salting time is preferable). Do not use table salt for dry-brining the turkey; it's too fine. If using a self-basting turkey (such as a frozen Butterball) or a kosher turkey, do not salt in step 1, but do include the salt in step 5.

1 For the turkey Using your fingers or handle of spoon, gently loosen skin covering breast, thighs, drumsticks, and back. Rub 1 tablespoon kosher salt evenly inside cavity of turkey, 1½ teaspoons kosher salt under skin of each side of breast, and 1½ teaspoons kosher salt under skin of each leg. Wrap turkey tightly in plastic wrap and refrigerate for at least 24 hours or up to 2 days.

2 For the classic herb stuffing Adjust oven rack to lowest position and heat oven to 250 degrees. Spread bread in single layer on rimmed baking sheet; bake until edges have dried but centers are slightly moist (cubes should yield to pressure), about 45 minutes, stirring several times during baking. Transfer to large bowl. Increase oven temperature to 325 degrees.

3 Meanwhile, melt butter in 12-inch skillet over medium-high heat. Add onion, celery, salt, and pepper; cook, stirring occasionally, until vegetables are softened and lightly browned, 5 to 7 minutes. Stir in thyme, marjoram, and sage and cook until fragrant, about 1 minute. Add vegetable mixture to bowl with bread; add 1 cup broth and toss until bread is thoroughly moistened.

4 Remove turkey from refrigerator and pat dry, inside and out, with paper towels. Using metal skewer, poke 15 to 20 holes in fat deposits on top of breast halves and thighs, 4 to 5 holes in each deposit. Tuck wings behind back.

5 Combine 2 teaspoons kosher salt and baking powder in small bowl. Sprinkle surface of turkey with salt mixture and rub in mixture with your hands, coating entire surface evenly. Line turkey cavity with cheesecloth, pack with 4 to 5 cups stuffing, and tie ends of cheesecloth together. Cover remaining stuffing with plastic and refrigerate. Using kitchen twine, loosely tie turkey legs together. Place turkey breast side down in V-rack set in roasting pan and drape salt pork slices over back.

6 Roast turkey until thickest part of breast registers 130 degrees, 2 to 2½ hours. Remove roasting pan from oven and increase oven temperature to 450 degrees. Transfer turkey in V-rack to rimmed baking sheet. Remove and discard salt pork. Using 2 large wads of paper towels, rotate turkey breast side up. Cut twine binding legs and remove stuffing bag; empty into reserved stuffing in bowl.

7 Once oven has come to temperature, return turkey in V-rack to roasting pan and roast until skin is golden brown and crisp, breast registers 160 degrees, and thighs register 175 degrees, about 45 minutes, rotating pan halfway through cooking. Transfer turkey to carving board and let rest for 45 minutes.

8 While turkey rests, reduce oven temperature to 400 degrees. Whisk eggs and remaining ½ cup broth together in small bowl. Pour egg mixture over stuffing and toss to combine, breaking up any large chunks; spread in buttered 13 by 9-inch baking dish. Bake until stuffing registers 165 degrees and top is golden brown, about 15 minutes. Carve turkey and serve with stuffing.

ROAST TURKEY FOR A CROWD

3 onions, chopped coarse

3 carrots, peeled and chopped coarse

3 celery ribs, chopped coarse

1 lemon, quartered

6 sprigs fresh thyme

5 tablespoons unsalted butter, melted

1 (18- to 22-pound) frozen Butterball or kosher turkey, neck and giblets removed and reserved for gravy

1 cup water, plus extra as needed

Salt and pepper

Why This Recipe Works When you've got a crowd coming to dinner, only a very large turkey will do so we aimed for the Norman Rockwell picture of perfection. Since brining a big bird can be tricky, we chose a Butterball turkey, which has already been brined (a kosher turkey, which has been salted, works well, too). After brushing the turkey with butter to add richness, we used a combination of high and low heat to produce a tender turkey with beautiful brown skin. Roasting it first at 425 degrees, breast side down, crisped the exterior, while a more moderate 325 degrees with breast side up kept the white meat moist and the dark meat rich and tender. Filling the cavity with an aromatic mix of vegetables and scattering more in the roasting pan added subtle flavor to the meat and contributed to the accompanying gravy. Serve with Giblet Pan Gravy for a Crowd (recipe follows). Rotating the bird helps produce evenly cooked meat, but for the sake of ease, you may opt not to rotate it. In that case, skip the step of lining the V-rack with foil and roast the turkey breast side up for the entire cooking time. Because we do not brine this bird, we had the best results with a frozen Butterball turkey or a kosher turkey.

1 Adjust oven rack to lowest position. Heat oven to 425 degrees. Line V-rack with heavy-duty aluminum foil and poke several holes in foil. Set V-rack in roasting pan and spray foil with vegetable oil spray.

2 Toss half of vegetables, half of lemon, and thyme sprigs with 1 tablespoon melted butter in bowl and place inside turkey. Tie legs together with kitchen twine and tuck wings behind back. Scatter remaining vegetables into pan.

3 Pour water over vegetable mixture in pan. Brush turkey breast with 2 tablespoons melted butter, then sprinkle with ½ teaspoon salt and ½ teaspoon pepper. Place turkey, breast side down, on prepared V-rack. Brush with remaining 2 tablespoons melted butter and sprinkle with ½ teaspoon salt and ½ teaspoon pepper.

4 Roast turkey for 1 hour. Baste turkey with juices from pan. Using 2 large wads of paper towels, turn turkey breast side up. If liquid in pan has evaporated, add ½ cup water. Lower oven temperature to 325 degrees. Continue to roast until breast registers 160 degrees and thighs register 175 degrees, about 2 hours longer.

5 Remove turkey from oven. Gently tip turkey up so that any accumulated juices in cavity run into pan. Transfer turkey to carving board. Let rest for 35 to 40 minutes. Carve turkey and serve.

GIBLET PAN GRAVY FOR A CROWD
makes about 8 cups

Complete step 1 up to a day ahead, if desired. Begin step 3 once the bird has been removed from the oven and is resting on a carving board.

1 tablespoon vegetable oil

Reserved turkey neck and giblets

1 onion, unpeeled and chopped

6 cups chicken broth

3 cups water

2 sprigs fresh thyme

8 sprigs fresh parsley

5 tablespoons unsalted butter

6 tablespoons all-purpose flour

1½ cups dry white wine

Salt and pepper

1 Heat oil in Dutch oven over medium heat until shimmering. Add neck and giblets and cook until golden and fragrant, about 5 minutes. Stir in onion and cook until softened, about 5 minutes. Reduce heat to low, cover, and cook until turkey parts and onion release their juices, about 15 minutes. Stir in broth, water, and herbs; bring to boil then reduce heat to low. Simmer, uncovered, skimming any impurities that may rise to surface, until broth is rich and flavorful, about 30 minutes longer. Strain broth into large container and reserve giblets. When cool enough to handle, chop giblets. Refrigerate giblets and broth until ready to use. (Broth can refrigerated for up to 24 hours.)

2 While turkey is roasting, return reserved turkey broth to simmer in medium saucepan. Melt butter in large saucepan over medium-low heat. Add flour and cook, whisking constantly (the mixture will froth and then thin out again),

until nutty brown and fragrant, 10 to 15 minutes. Vigorously whisk all but 2 cups of hot broth into flour mixture. Bring to boil, then continue to simmer, stirring occasionally, until gravy is slightly thickened and very flavorful, about 35 minutes longer. Set aside until turkey is done.

3 When turkey has been transferred to carving board to rest, spoon out and discard as much fat as possible from roasting pan, leaving caramelized herbs and vegetables. Place pan over 2 burners set on medium-high heat. Return gravy to simmer. Add wine to pan of caramelized vegetables, scraping up any browned bits. Bring to boil and cook until reduced by half, about 7 minutes. Add remaining 2 cups turkey broth, bring to simmer, and cook for 15 minutes; strain pan juices into gravy, pressing as much juice as possible out of vegetables. Stir reserved giblets into gravy and return to boil. Season with salt and pepper to taste, and serve.

ROAST BUTTERFLIED TURKEY WITH CRANBERRY-MOLASSES GLAZE

serves 10 to 12

Turkey

1 (12- to 14-pound) turkey, neck and giblets discarded

Kosher salt and pepper

2 teaspoons baking powder

2 large onions, peeled and halved

Glaze

3 cups apple cider

1 cup frozen or fresh cranberries

½ cup light or mild molasses

½ cup apple cider vinegar

1 tablespoon Dijon mustard

1 tablespoon grated fresh ginger

2 tablespoons unsalted butter

Why This Recipe Works Glazing a roast turkey is great way to bring a holiday centerpiece to the next level, if the glaze enhances an already stellar bird. Butterflying the turkey, though an untraditional step, flattened it; this created a more level surface so the glaze wouldn't slide off and also promoted even cooking. A dry rub of salt and baking powder dehydrated the skin and encouraged browning while an hour rest at room temperature air-dried the turkey, further wicking away moisture from the skin. We made a makeshift roasting rack for the turkey, propping it up on halved onions in a large roasting pan so it would brown properly. Starting the turkey roasting low and slow created moist, tender meat and allowed maximum fat to render from the skin. Waiting to apply the coats of glaze until the turkey was fully cooked allowed the skin to crisp up first. Cranking the oven to 450 degrees thickened and concentrated the glaze. As an added bonus, the remaining glaze, reduced along with some of the drippings and finished with butter, produced a silky serving sauce. If using a self-basting turkey (such as a frozen Butterball) or kosher turkey, omit the salt in step 1.

1 For the turkey With turkey breast side down, use kitchen shears to cut through bones on either side of backbone; discard backbone. Flip turkey over and press on breastbone to flatten. Using your fingers or handle of spoon, gently loosen skin covering breast and thighs. Using metal skewer, poke 15 to 20 holes in fat deposits on breast halves and thighs. Rub underside (bone side) of turkey evenly with 2 teaspoons salt and 1 teaspoon pepper. Flip turkey skin side up and rub 1 tablespoon salt evenly under skin. Tuck wings behind turkey. Push legs up to rest on lower portion of breast and tie legs together with kitchen twine. Combine baking powder, 1 tablespoon salt, and 1 teaspoon pepper in small bowl. Pat skin side of turkey dry with paper towels. Sprinkle surface of turkey with baking powder mixture and rub in mixture with your hands, coating skin evenly. Transfer turkey to large roasting pan, skin side up. Place 1 onion half under each side of breast and each thigh to elevate turkey off bottom of pan. Let stand at room temperature for 1 hour.

2 Adjust oven rack to lower-middle position and heat oven to 275 degrees. Roast turkey until breast registers 160 degrees and thighs register 175 degrees, 2½ to 3 hours. Remove pan from oven and let turkey rest in pan for at least 30 minutes or up to 1½ hours. Thirty minutes before returning turkey to oven, increase oven temperature to 450 degrees.

3 For the glaze While turkey rests, bring cider, cranberries, molasses, vinegar, mustard, and ginger to boil in medium saucepan over medium-high heat. Cook, stirring occasionally, until reduced to 1½ cups, about 30 minutes. Strain mixture through fine-mesh strainer into 2-cup liquid measuring cup, pressing on solids to extract as much liquid as possible. Discard solids (you should have about 1¼ cups glaze). Transfer ½ cup glaze to small saucepan and set aside.

4 Brush turkey with one-third of glaze from measuring cup, transfer to oven, and roast for 7 minutes. Brush turkey with half of remaining glaze from measuring cup and roast 7 minutes longer. Brush turkey with remaining glaze from measuring cup and roast until skin is evenly browned and crispy, 7 to 10 minutes. Transfer turkey to carving board and let rest for 45 minutes.

5 While turkey rests, remove onions from roasting pan and discard. Strain liquid from pan through fine-mesh strainer into fat separator (you should have about 2 cups liquid) and let settle for 5 minutes; pour liquid into saucepan with reserved glaze, discarding any remaining fat. Bring mixture to boil over medium-high heat and cook until slightly syrupy, about 10 minutes. Remove pan from heat and whisk in butter. Carve turkey and serve, passing sauce separately.

butterflying a turkey

1 Using kitchen shears, cut through bones on either side of backbone, staying as close as possible to backbone, then remove and discard it.

2 Flip turkey over and press down firmly with heels of your hands to flatten breastbone.

3 After poking skin and seasoning it, tuck wings behind turkey and push legs up to rest on breast, tying together with kitchen twine.

CRISP ROAST DUCK WITH PORT WINE GLAZE

1¼ cups port wine

2 garlic cloves, sliced thin

4 sprigs fresh thyme

1 (4½- to 5-pound) whole duck, neck and giblets discarded

Salt and pepper

Why This Recipe Works Wild ducks are quite lean but the ducks available in the supermarket are another story; they are superfatty. What is the secret to knockout roast duck with crisp skin and moist meat? Steam it first and then cut it into parts and roast it. Removing the large clumps of fat by hand only took us so far; steaming the duck proved the best (and easiest) way to eliminate more of the fat. We found that the steam couldn't penetrate the fat in the meaty legs though, so before roasting the duck, we cut it into parts. No longer protected from the heat, the fat in the legs just melted away. By periodically collecting the rendered fat in the pan and removing the parts as soon as they'd taken on enough color, we wound up with perfectly cooked, perfectly browned duck. Adding a glaze and letting it caramelize for a few minutes before serving produced a glossy, appealing finish. We like the contrasting flavor of a glaze with duck, but the meat is so flavorful it can also be seasoned with just salt and pepper. Pekin ducks, also called Long Island ducks, are the only choice in most supermarkets. Almost always sold frozen, the duck must defrost in the refrigerator for at least one day before cooking. Port comes in many styles, but we prefer to use an inexpensive tawny port here. Steaming the duck for 40 minutes produces very moist, tender meat and slightly crisp skin once roasted; for somewhat denser meat and very crisp skin after roasting, steam for an additional 10 minutes in step 2.

1 Bring port, garlic, and thyme sprigs to simmer in small saucepan and cook until thickened and measures ¼ cup, 25 to 30 minutes. Discard garlic and thyme sprigs; set glaze aside until ready to use.

2 Meanwhile, spray V-rack with vegetable oil spray and set in roasting pan; place duck, breast side up, on rack. Add water to just below bottom of duck, place pan over 2 burners, and bring to boil. Reduce heat to medium, cover pan tightly with aluminum foil, and steam until skin has pulled away from at least 1 leg, about 40 minutes (add more hot water to maintain water level if necessary). Transfer duck to carving board, let cool slightly, then carve into 6 pieces (2 boneless breasts, 2 legs, 2 wings). Remove rack and discard steaming liquid. Wipe out pan with paper towels.

3 Adjust oven rack to lowest position and heat oven to 425 degrees. Lightly spray now-empty pan with oil spray. Season duck pieces with salt and pepper and place skin side down in prepared pan. Roast duck, carefully removing fat if more than 2 tablespoons accumulate in pan, until skin on breast pieces is rich golden brown and crisp, about 25 minutes. Transfer breast pieces to plate.

4 Again, carefully remove excess fat from pan, turn leg and wing pieces skin side up, and continue roasting until skin is deep golden brown and crisp, 15 to 20 minutes. Again, carefully remove excess fat from pan. Return breast pieces to pan and brush both sides of each piece with glaze; position pieces skin side up once glazed. Roast until glaze is hot and richly colored on duck pieces, 3 to 4 minutes. Serve immediately.

Crisp Roast Duck with Orange Glaze
The lime juice keeps this thick, syrupy glaze from being too sweet.

Substitute 1 cup orange juice (2 oranges), 2 tablespoons lime juice, and 2 tablespoons honey for port, and omit garlic and thyme.

ROAST POMEGRANATE-GLAZED QUAIL

serves 4

Salt and pepper

8 (5- to 7-ounce) whole quail, giblets discarded

2 tablespoons extra-virgin olive oil

6 tablespoons pomegranate molasses

1 tablespoon minced fresh thyme

1 teaspoon ground cinnamon

Why This Recipe Works Quail are prized for their delicate flavor, which is milder and sweeter than that of many other game birds. Since they are so small, roasting these tiny birds is a delicate balancing act between achieving golden brown skin and preventing the meat from overcooking. A 20-minute brine offered some insurance against dry meat. The direct heat from a just-smoking skillet allowed all the surface moisture to be shed and jump-started the browning process. Finishing the birds in a 500-degree oven allowed the quail to bronze further without drying out. Sweet, sour, and fruity pomegranate molasses made a great glaze for our quail because it clung nicely and its sugars helped the skin to brown. Quail is often sold with the neck still attached; you can remove it with kitchen shears, if desired.

1 Adjust oven rack to upper-middle position and heat oven to 500 degrees. Set wire rack in aluminum foil–lined rimmed baking sheet and spray with vegetable oil spray. Dissolve ½ cup salt in 2 quarts water in large container. Submerge quail in brine and refrigerate for 20 minutes.

2 Remove quail from brine, pat dry with paper towels, and season with pepper. Working with 1 quail at a time, make incision through meat of 1 drumstick using tip of paring knife, about ½ inch from tip of drumstick bone. Carefully insert other drumstick through incision so legs are securely crossed. Tuck wingtips behind back.

3 Heat 1 tablespoon oil in 12-inch skillet over medium-high heat until just smoking. Brown 4 quail on all sides, about 4 minutes; transfer to prepared rack. Repeat with remaining 1 tablespoon oil and remaining 4 quail.

4 Combine pomegranate molasses, thyme, cinnamon, and ⅛ teaspoon salt in bowl. Brush quail evenly with half of pomegranate molasses mixture and roast for 5 minutes. Brush quail with remaining pomegranate molasses mixture and continue to roast until well browned and breasts register 160 degrees and thighs register 175 degrees, 7 to 13 minutes. Transfer quail to serving dish and let rest for 5 minutes. Serve.

preparing quail for roasting

1 Using tip of paring knife, make incision through meat of 1 drumstick, about ½ inch from tip of drumstick bone.

2 Carefully insert other drumstick through incision so legs are securely crossed.

3 Tuck wingtips behind back.

ROASTED CORNISH HENS

serves 4

4 (1¼- to 1½-pound) whole Cornish game hens, giblets discarded

Kosher salt and pepper

¼ teaspoon vegetable oil

1 teaspoon baking powder

Vegetable oil spray

Why This Recipe Works Cornish game hens deliver more flavor than regular chickens. The hens, weighing less than 2 pounds, cook fast, but given their small dimensions the meat finishes cooking long before the skin crisps. To successfully roast these little birds, we split them in half. Poking holes in the skin allowed the fat to drain during cooking and aided crisping. Rubbing the birds with salt and baking powder and then chilling them evaporated moisture. Searing the birds skin side down on a preheated baking sheet efficiently crisped their skin and we finished them skin side up under the broiler. Note that this recipe requires refrigerating the salted hens for at least 4 hours or up to 24 hours before cooking (a longer salting time is preferable). If your hens weigh 1½ to 2 pounds, cook three instead of four and extend the cooking time in step 5 to 15 minutes. If your hens are frozen, be sure to thaw them in the refrigerator for 24 to 36 hours before salting.

1 Working with 1 hen at a time, use kitchen shears to cut along both sides of backbone to remove it. Flatten hens and lay breast side up on counter. Using sharp chef's knife, cut through center of breast to make 2 halves.

2 Using your fingers, gently separate skin from breast and thighs. Using metal skewer or tip of paring knife, poke 10 to 15 holes in fat deposits on top of breast halves and thighs. Tuck wingtips behind back. Pat hens dry with paper towels.

3 Sprinkle 1 tablespoon salt on underside (bone side) of hens. Combine 1 tablespoon salt and oil in small bowl and stir until salt is evenly coated with oil. Add baking powder and stir until well combined. Turn hens skin side up and rub salt mixture evenly over surface. Transfer hens, skin side up, to wire rack set in rimmed baking sheet, and refrigerate, uncovered, for at least 4 hours or up to 24 hours.

4 Adjust oven racks to upper-middle and lower positions, place rimmed baking sheet on lower rack, and heat oven to 500 degrees.

5 Once oven is fully heated, spray skin side of hens with oil spray and season with pepper to taste. Carefully transfer hens, skin side down, to baking sheet and cook for 10 minutes.

6 Remove hens from oven and heat broiler. Flip hens skin side up. Transfer baking sheet with hens to upper rack and broil until well browned and breasts register 160 degrees and thighs register 175 degrees, about 5 minutes, rotating as necessary to promote even browning. Transfer to serving dish or individual plates and serve.

Herb-Roasted Cornish Hens
In step 3, combine 2 tablespoons kosher salt with 1 teaspoon dried thyme, 1 teaspoon dried marjoram, and 1 teaspoon dried crushed rosemary. Sprinkle half of salt mixture on underside of hens; stir oil into remaining salt-herb mixture until mixture is evenly coated with oil. Add baking powder to oil-salt mixture and proceed with recipe.

Oregano-Anise Roasted Cornish Hens
In step 3, combine 2 tablespoons kosher salt with 1 teaspoon dried oregano, ½ teaspoon anise seeds, and ½ teaspoon hot smoked paprika. Sprinkle half of salt mixture on underside of hens; stir oil into remaining salt mixture until mixture is evenly coated with oil. Add baking powder to oil-salt mixture and proceed with recipe.

Cumin-Coriander Roasted Cornish Hens
In step 3, combine 2 tablespoons kosher salt with 2 teaspoons ground cumin, 2 teaspoons ground coriander, 1 teaspoon paprika, and ¼ teaspoon cayenne pepper. Sprinkle half of salt mixture on underside of hens; add oil to remaining salt mixture until mixture is evenly coated with oil. Add baking powder to oil-salt mixture and proceed with recipe.

STUFFED ROAST CORNISH HENS

serves 6

Hens

Salt and pepper

6 (1¼- to 1½-pound) whole Cornish game hens, giblets discarded

6 tablespoons balsamic vinegar

3 tablespoons extra-virgin olive oil

1 cup chicken broth

¼ cup dry vermouth or dry white wine

Stuffing

2 cups chicken broth

1 cup wild rice blend

2 tablespoons unsalted butter

1 onion, chopped fine

½ celery rib, minced

¼ cup pecans, toasted and chopped coarse

¼ cup dried cranberries

2 tablespoons minced fresh parsley

2 teaspoons minced fresh thyme

Salt and pepper

Why This Recipe Works Whole roast Cornish game hens make an elegant individual-size entrée. Our mission was to introduce a stuffing into these petite birds, making sure to keep the skin crisp and the meat tender in the process. Brining the Cornish hens was the first step; the salt water seasoned and deepened their flavor. Carefully pricking the skin on the breasts and legs prevented it from ballooning when the juices built up. Heating the stuffing before packing it into the birds' cavities reduced the oven time, and tying the legs together secured the stuffing in place. Roasting the birds on a wire rack–lined baking sheet and placing them as far apart as possible helped them to brown, and brushing them with a balsamic glaze ensured good color as the sugar in the glaze caramelized in the high oven heat. One application partway through roasting and another before the 450-degree blast added sheen and flavor to the skin. We made good use of the pan drippings by pouring in broth before the final stage of roasting. This concentrated mixture, later reduced with vermouth while the hens rested, provided a rich accompanying sauce. If your Cornish hens are frozen, be sure to thaw them in the refrigerator for 24 to 36 hours before brining.

1 For the hens Dissolve ½ cup salt in 4 quarts cold water in large container. Submerge hens, breast side down, in brine; cover; and refrigerate for at least 30 minutes or up to 1 hour. Prick skin all over breast and legs with tip of paring knife.

2 For the stuffing Bring broth to boil in medium saucepan. Add rice and return to boil. Reduce heat to low, cover, and simmer until rice is fully cooked, 40 to 50 minutes. Transfer rice to bowl and fluff with fork.

3 Meanwhile, melt butter in 10-inch skillet over medium heat. Add onion and celery and cook, stirring occasionally, until softened, about 5 minutes. Stir onion mixture into rice, along with pecans, cranberries, parsley, and thyme. Season with salt and pepper to taste. (Stuffing can be refrigerated for up to 24 hours.)

4 Adjust oven rack to middle position and heat oven to 400 degrees. Set wire rack in aluminum foil–lined rimmed baking sheet. Remove hens from brine and pat dry with paper towels. Season hens with pepper and tuck wingtips behind back.

5 Whisk vinegar and oil together in small bowl and set aside. Place stuffing in bowl and microwave, covered, until very hot, about 2 minutes. Spoon ½ cup hot stuffing into cavity of each hen, then tie each hen's legs together with kitchen twine. Arrange hens, breast side down and with wings facing out, on prepared rack.

6 Roast hens until backs are golden brown, about 25 minutes. Remove sheet from oven and brush back side of each hen with vinegar glaze. Rotate hens breast side up and with wings facing out and brush with more glaze. Add ½ cup broth to sheet and continue to roast until stuffed cavity registers 150 degrees, 15 to 20 minutes.

7 Remove sheet from oven and increase oven temperature to 450 degrees. Brush each hen with glaze, add remaining ½ cup broth to sheet, and continue to roast until hens are spotty brown and cavity registers 160 degrees, 5 to 10 minutes. Remove hens from oven, transfer to carving board, and let rest for 10 minutes. Remove twine.

8 Meanwhile, pour juices from sheet into small saucepan and let settle for 5 minutes. Remove fat from surface using large spoon. Add vermouth, bring to simmer, and cook until sauce thickens slightly and flavors meld, 3 to 5 minutes. Season with salt and pepper to taste. Serve hens, passing sauce separately.

pricking poultry skin

To prevent skin from "ballooning" when juices build up, carefully prick skin (but not meat) on breasts and legs with tip of paring knife before roasting.

ROAST BEEF SIRLOIN WITH CARAMELIZED CARROTS AND POTATOES

serves 8

2 pounds carrots, peeled and cut into 2-inch pieces

2 pounds red potatoes, unpeeled, cut into 1½-inch pieces

¼ cup vegetable oil

1 tablespoon minced fresh thyme or 1 teaspoon dried

Salt and pepper

1 (4-pound) center-cut boneless top sirloin roast, fat trimmed to ¼ inch and tied at 1½-inch intervals

Why This Recipe Works When most people think of a beef roast, prime rib or tenderloin comes to mind. But those premium cuts are expensive. We wanted a comparatively affordable roast paired with root vegetables for an impressive roast beef dinner that was also easy and economical. Boneless top sirloin roast fit the bill because it offered beefy flavor and enough marbling to keep the meat tender, but not so much that it would require an extended cooking time to break down its fat. Carrots and potatoes were a natural pairing with roast beef, and precooking them in the microwave ensured that they would be done at roughly the same time as the roast. Searing one side of the meat on the stovetop gave us some browning, and doing it in the roasting pan meant there were no extra dishes to clean. We then started the pan of meat and vegetables in a low, 250-degree oven for 45 minutes so everything cooked through gently before cranking the heat up to 500 degrees for the last 10 minutes in the oven for great browning. At that point, we took the meat out to rest and gave the veggies a little more time in the oven for extra flavor. Top sirloin is our favorite cut for this recipe, but any boneless roast from the sirloin will work well. If your carrots are very thick, slice them in half lengthwise first to ensure even cooking. For how to tie a roast, see page 12. We prefer this roast cooked to medium-rare, but if you prefer it more or less done, see our guidelines on page 24.

1 Adjust oven rack to lower-middle position and heat oven to 250 degrees. Microwave carrots, potatoes, and 3 tablespoons water in covered bowl, stirring occasionally, until vegetables are nearly tender, 15 to 20 minutes. Drain well, then toss with 3 tablespoons oil and thyme and season with salt and pepper.

2 Pat roast dry with paper towels and season with salt and pepper. Heat remaining 1 tablespoon oil in large roasting pan over medium heat (over 2 burners, if possible) until just smoking. Brown roast well on fat side, about 3 minutes.

3 Off heat, flip roast browned side up and spread vegetables around roast. Roast beef and vegetables until beef registers 110 degrees, 45 minutes to 1 hour.

4 Remove pan from oven and increase oven temperature to 500 degrees. Continue to roast beef and vegetables until beef registers 120 to 125 degrees (for medium-rare), 10 to 15 minutes.

5 Transfer roast to carving board and let rest for 20 minutes. Meanwhile, continue to roast vegetables until nicely browned, 10 to 20 minutes. Remove twine and slice into ¼-inch-thick slices. Serve with vegetables.

Roast Beef Sirloin with Caramelized Parsnips and Brussels Sprouts

If your parsnips are very thick, slice them in half lengthwise first to ensure even cooking.

Substitute 2 pounds parsnips, peeled and cut into 2-inch lengths, and 2 pounds Brussels sprouts, trimmed and halved, for carrots and potatoes. Microwave vegetables with water as directed until just tender, 10 to 15 minutes.

HERBED ROAST BEEF

serves 8

⅓ cup minced fresh parsley

1 shallot, minced

2 tablespoons minced fresh thyme

2 tablespoons extra-virgin olive oil

1 tablespoon Dijon mustard

4 tablespoons unsalted butter, softened

1 (4-pound) center-cut boneless
top sirloin roast, fat trimmed to ¼ inch

2 tablespoons kosher salt

1 tablespoon pepper

Why This Recipe Works To transform a top sirloin roast, we used two flavor-packed additions: an herb-mustard mixture spread inside the roast before cooking and an herb butter slathered on the outside after cooking. The preparation was simple: We butterflied the roast, spread the herb mustard over the meat, and then folded and tied it back together. We seared the beef before roasting it in a low oven to get the perfect mix of crisp crust and juicy meat. The herb butter, spread over the resting roast, melted and mingled with the meat juices and created an instant sauce. If you don't have a V-rack, cook the roast on a wire rack set in a rimmed baking sheet. This recipe requires refrigerating the salted beef for at least 1 hour or up to 24 hours before cooking (a longer time is preferable). We prefer this roast cooked to medium-rare, but if you prefer it more or less done, see our guidelines on page 24.

1 Combine parsley, shallot, and thyme in bowl. Transfer 2 tablespoons herb mixture to second bowl and stir in 1 tablespoon oil and mustard until combined. Add butter to remaining herb mixture and mash with fork until combined.

2 Position roast fat side up. Insert knife one-third of way up from bottom of roast along 1 long side and cut horizontally, stopping ½ inch before edge. Open up flap. Keeping knife parallel to cutting board, cut through thicker portion of roast about ½ inch from bottom of roast, keeping knife level with first cut and stopping about ½ inch before edge. Open up this flap. If uneven, cover with plastic wrap and use meat pounder to even out. Rub inside and out with salt and pepper. Spread herb-mustard mixture over interior of beef, fold back together, and tie securely with kitchen twine at 1½-inch intervals. Refrigerate, uncovered, for at least 1 hour or up to 24 hours.

3 Adjust oven rack to middle position and heat oven to 275 degrees. Set V-rack in large roasting pan and spray with vegetable oil spray. Pat roast dry with paper towels. Heat remaining 1 tablespoon oil in 12-inch skillet over medium-high heat until just smoking. Brown roast well on all sides, 8 to 12 minutes, then arrange, fat side up, on prepared V-rack. Roast until beef registers 120 to 125 degrees (for medium-rare), 1½ to 2 hours.

4 Transfer roast to carving board, spread top with herb-butter mixture and let rest for 20 minutes. Remove twine and slice into ¼-inch-thick slices. Serve.

butterflying and filling a top sirloin roast

1 Slice roast horizontally through middle of meat, leaving about ½ inch of meat intact.

2 After seasoning meat, spread herb mixture over interior surface of meat.

3 Fold meat back together, then tie securely at 1½-inch intervals with kitchen twine.

SUNDAY-BEST GARLIC ROAST BEEF

serves 8

Beef

8 large garlic cloves, unpeeled, plus 3 large garlic cloves, minced

1 (4-pound) center-cut boneless top sirloin roast, fat trimmed to ¼ inch and tied at 1½-inch intervals

1 teaspoon dried thyme

1 teaspoon kosher salt

Garlic Paste

½ cup extra-virgin olive oil

12 large garlic cloves, peeled and cut in half lengthwise

2 sprigs fresh thyme

2 bay leaves

1 teaspoon kosher salt

Pepper

Jus

1½ cups beef broth

1½ cups chicken broth

Why This Recipe Works For a version of affordable, beefy top sirloin roast where every bite is thoroughly infused with complex sweet-savory garlic flavor, we took a multipronged approach. We studded the beef with nutty toasted garlic, rubbed it with garlic salt, and let it sit before roasting. We also rubbed it with garlic oil before it went into the oven and finally coated it with a garlic paste partway through cooking. Cooking the garlic for the paste in oil over low heat took the bite out of it and also created our deeply flavored garlic oil. To simplify cooking, we skipped a stovetop sear, but we still wanted a well-browned roast. Starting it at a high temperature in a preheated roasting pan and then reducing the heat for the majority of the cooking time accomplished this goal and also resulted in a perfectly pink interior. Look for a top sirloin roast that has a thick, substantial fat cap still attached. The rendered fat will help to keep the roast moist. When making the jus, taste the reduced broth before adding any of the accumulated meat juices from the roast. The meat juices are well seasoned and may make the jus too salty. This recipe requires refrigerating the salted beef for at least 1 hour or up to 24 hours before cooking (a longer time is preferable). For how to tie a roast, see page 12. We prefer this roast cooked to medium-rare, but if you prefer it more or less done, see our guidelines on page 24.

1 For the beef Toast unpeeled garlic in 8-inch skillet over medium-high heat, tossing frequently, until spotty brown, about 8 minutes. Set aside. When cool enough to handle, peel and cut into ¼-inch slivers. Using paring knife, make 1-inch-deep slits all over roast and insert toasted garlic into slits.

2 Combine minced garlic, thyme, and salt in small bowl and rub all over roast. Refrigerate, uncovered, for at least 1 hour or up to 24 hours.

3 For the garlic paste Heat oil, garlic, thyme sprigs, bay leaves, and salt in small saucepan over medium-high heat until bubbles start to rise to surface. Reduce heat to low and cook until garlic is soft, about 30 minutes. Let cool completely, then strain, reserving oil. Discard herbs and transfer garlic to small bowl. Mash garlic with 1 tablespoon garlic oil until paste forms. Cover and refrigerate paste until ready to use. Cover and reserve remaining garlic oil.

4 Adjust oven rack to middle position, place large roasting pan on rack, and heat oven to 450 degrees. Using paper towels, wipe garlic-salt rub off roast. Rub with 2 tablespoons reserved garlic oil and season with pepper. Transfer roast, fat side down, to preheated pan and roast, turning as needed until browned on all sides, 10 to 15 minutes.

5 Reduce oven temperature to 300 degrees. Remove pan from oven, turn roast fat side up, and coat top with garlic paste. Roast until beef registers 120 to 125 degrees (for medium-rare), 50 to 70 minutes. Transfer to carving board and let rest for 20 minutes.

6 For the jus Pour off fat from pan and place pan over high heat. Add broths and bring to boil, scraping up any browned bits. Simmer, stirring occasionally, until reduced to 2 cups, about 5 minutes. Add accumulated meat juices and cook for 1 minute. Pour through fine-mesh strainer into bowl. Remove twine. Slice into ¼-inch-thick slices. Serve with jus.

CHICAGO-STYLE ITALIAN ROAST BEEF

4 teaspoons kosher salt

1 (4-pound) center-cut boneless top sirloin roast, fat trimmed to ¼ inch and tied at 1½-inch intervals

4 teaspoons garlic powder

4 teaspoons dried basil

4 teaspoons dried oregano

1 tablespoon pepper

2 tablespoons vegetable oil

1 onion, chopped fine

3 garlic cloves, minced

1 tablespoon all-purpose flour

2 cups beef broth

2 cups chicken broth

1½ cups water

1 teaspoon red pepper flakes

Why This Recipe Works Bold Italian-style roast beef relies on the presence of strong herb flavors, usually achieved with a marinade. In Chicago, meat prepared this way is served with a spicy jus. To build flavor in our version of this roast without inhibiting browning, we turned to a spicy rub rather than a marinade. Before cooking, we salted the meat and let it sit, which helped season it through and through and keep it moist. We seared the salted roast in a skillet to jump-start browning and build a flavorful crust; we then made a rich base for the jus by cooking onion, garlic, flour, and some of our spice rub in the roast's rendered fat. With our roast elevated in a V-rack, we poured the jus into the roasting pan below. Next, we rubbed the meat with a flavorful blend of garlic powder, dried basil and oregano, black pepper, pepper flakes, and oil. As the meat roasted in the oven, its drippings landed right in the jus, reinforcing its meaty flavor, and the jus was done at exactly the same time that the roast was, with no need for last-minute fuss. This recipe requires refrigerating the salted beef for at least 1 hour or up to 24 hours before cooking (a longer time is preferable). For how to tie a roast, see page 12. We prefer this roast cooked to medium-rare, but if you prefer it more or less done, see our guidelines on page 24.

1 Rub salt on roast and refrigerate, uncovered, for at least 1 hour or up to 24 hours.

2 Adjust oven rack to lower-middle position and heat oven to 300 degrees. Set V-rack in large roasting pan and spray with vegetable oil spray. Combine garlic powder, basil, oregano, and pepper in small bowl; set aside.

3 Pat roast dry with paper towels. Heat 1 tablespoon oil in 12-inch skillet over medium-high heat until just smoking. Brown roast on all sides, 8 to 12 minutes; transfer to prepared V-rack.

4 Add onion to fat in skillet and cook over medium heat until softened, about 5 minutes. Stir in garlic, flour, and 1 teaspoon reserved spice mixture and cook until fragrant,

about 1 minute. Whisk in beef broth, chicken broth, and water, scraping up any browned bits and smoothing out any lumps. Bring mixture to boil, then pour into roasting pan.

5 Stir pepper flakes and remaining 1 tablespoon oil into remaining spice mixture. Rub mixture all over roast, transfer to oven fat side up, and cook until beef registers 120 to 125 degrees (for medium-rare), 1¼ to 1½ hours. Transfer roast to carving board and let rest for 20 minutes.

6 Pour jus from roasting pan through fine-mesh strainer into bowl and keep warm. Remove twine and slice into ¼-inch-thick slices. Serve with jus.

COFFEE-CHIPOTLE-RUBBED ROAST BEEF

1 (5- to 6-pound) center-cut boneless top sirloin roast, fat trimmed to ¼-inch

2 tablespoons kosher salt

4 teaspoons plus ¼ cup extra-virgin olive oil

4 garlic cloves, minced

6 anchovy fillets, rinsed and patted dry

1 tablespoon ground coffee

1 tablespoon minced canned chipotle chile in adobo sauce

2 teaspoons ground coriander

2 teaspoons paprika

1 teaspoon unsweetened cocoa powder

1 teaspoon dry mustard

1 teaspoon pepper

Why This Recipe Works This extraordinarily flavorful top sirloin roast is special enough to get star billing at a holiday meal. To keep this centerpiece dish manageable, we cut the large, oddly shaped roast in half and then tied it along its length to create two round, attractive cylinders that cooked through in just 2 hours (half of the time a prime rib would require). This method also offered the convenience of cooking each roast to a different degree of doneness to accommodate guest preferences. Salting the roasts overnight seasoned them well and helped keep them moist during cooking, while roasting them in a low 225-degree oven avoided overcooking the exterior before the interior cooked through. We took a three-step approach to creating a flavorful, attractive exterior. First, we seared the roasts on all sides and then we coated them with an aromatic paste of garlic, anchovy, coffee, chipotle, and spices. Finishing with a brief stint in a 500-degree oven deepened the paste's color and flavor and helped crisp up the crust. Do not omit the anchovies; they provide great depth of flavor with no overt fishiness. This recipe requires refrigerating the salted beef for at least 24 hours or up to four days before cooking (a longer time is preferable). For how to tie a roast, see page 12. We prefer this roast cooked to medium-rare, but if you prefer it more or less done, see our guidelines on page 24.

1 Cut roast lengthwise along grain into 2 equal pieces. Rub 1 tablespoon salt over each piece and tie securely with kitchen twine at 1½-inch intervals. Refrigerate, uncovered, for at least 24 hours or up to 4 days.

2 Adjust oven rack to middle position and heat oven to 225 degrees. Heat 2 teaspoons oil in 12-inch skillet over high heat until just smoking. Brown 1 roast on all sides, 6 to 8 minutes; transfer to large plate. Repeat with 2 teaspoons oil and remaining roast; transfer to large plate. Let roasts cool for 10 minutes.

3 Meanwhile, process garlic, anchovies, coffee, chipotle, coriander, paprika, cocoa, mustard, pepper, and remaining ¼ cup oil in food processor until smooth paste forms, about 30 seconds, scraping down sides of bowl as needed. Transfer roasts, fat side up, to wire rack set in rimmed baking sheet and rub evenly with paste.

4 Roast until beef registers 120 to 125 degrees (for medium-rare), 2 to 2¼ hours. Remove roasts from oven and let rest on rack for 30 minutes.

5 Heat oven to 500 degrees. Remove twine. Return roasts to oven and cook until exteriors are well browned, 6 to 8 minutes. Transfer roasts to carving board and slice into ¼-inch-thick slices. Serve.

Fennel-Coriander-Rubbed Roast Beef
Substitute 2 teaspoons ground fennel and 2 teaspoons dried oregano for coffee, chipotle chile, cocoa powder, and mustard.

BOTTOM ROUND ROAST BEEF WITH ZIP-STYLE SAUCE

Beef

1 (4-pound) boneless beef bottom round roast, trimmed and tied at 1½-inch intervals

Kosher salt and pepper

1 tablespoon minced fresh rosemary

1 tablespoon minced fresh thyme

2 tablespoons vegetable oil

Zip-Style Sauce

8 tablespoons unsalted butter

½ cup Worcestershire sauce

2 garlic cloves, minced

2 teaspoons minced fresh rosemary

1 teaspoon minced fresh thyme

½ teaspoon kosher salt

½ teaspoon pepper

Why This Recipe Works Top sirloin roast isn't the only inexpensive beef cut that can make a first-rate roast if you treat it correctly. Bottom round roast is typically a fairly bland, chewy cut, but by using a combination of a salting-and-resting step plus a slow-roasting technique, we transformed it into a tender, juicy showstopper. Salting the meat and letting it rest before roasting ensured that it was thoroughly seasoned. Sprinkling a woodsy mixture of thyme, rosemary, salt, and pepper over the roast created an herbed crust and contributed enough flavor to make browning the roast unnecessary. Instead of searing, we headed straight for the oven. Roasting the beef slowly in a 250-degree oven turned the meat supremely tender by slowly breaking down its tough connective tissue. After about 2 hours, we turned off the oven and let the roast gradually reach medium doneness as the oven cooled. We served the roast with our take on Zip Sauce, a winning combination of butter, Worcestershire sauce, garlic, rosemary, and thyme that was invented in Detroit as a steak sauce with a kick. We recommend cooking this roast to medium, which makes it easier to slice the meat paper-thin. Because the sauce contains butter, it will solidify as it cools, so it's best kept warm for serving. This recipe requires refrigerating the rubbed beef for at least 1 hour or up to 24 hours before cooking (a longer time is preferable). For how to tie a roast, see page 12.

1 For the beef Pat roast dry with paper towels and rub with 2 teaspoons salt. Refrigerate, uncovered, for at least 1 hour or up to 24 hours.

2 Adjust oven rack to middle position and heat oven to 250 degrees. Set wire rack in rimmed baking sheet. Combine rosemary, thyme, 2 teaspoons pepper, and 1 teaspoon salt in bowl.

3 Pat roast dry with paper towels. Rub roast all over with oil and sprinkle with herb mixture; place fat side up on prepared rack. Transfer to oven and cook until beef registers 120 degrees, 1¾ hours to 2¼ hours. Turn off oven and leave beef in oven, without opening door, until beef registers 130 to 135 degrees (for medium), 20 to 30 minutes. Transfer roast to carving board and let rest for 30 minutes.

4 For the zip-style sauce Meanwhile, bring butter, Worcestershire, garlic, rosemary, thyme, salt, and pepper to bare simmer in small saucepan over medium heat, whisking constantly. Remove from heat, cover, and keep warm. Slice roast thin against grain. Serve with sauce.

ROAST BEEF TENDERLOIN

serves 4

Beef

1 (2-pound) center-cut beef tenderloin roast, trimmed, tail end tucked, and tied at 1½-inch intervals

2 teaspoons kosher salt

1 teaspoon pepper

2 tablespoons unsalted butter, softened

1 tablespoon vegetable oil

Shallot and Parsley Butter

4 tablespoons unsalted butter, softened

½ shallot, minced

1 tablespoon minced fresh parsley

1 garlic clove, minced

¼ teaspoon salt

¼ teaspoon pepper

Why This Recipe Works The center-cut tenderloin comes from the middle of the whole tenderloin, which sits beneath the spine of the cow and gets no exercise at all, making it the most tender piece of beef you can buy. We knew that a simple preparation would let the exceptional texture shine. Tying the roast at intervals with kitchen twine made it more compact and helped give it an even shape, which promoted even cooking. To up the tenderloin's mild flavor and help it hold on to its juices, we salted the roast before cooking. A smear of softened butter added before cooking also helped counteract the leanness and mildness of this cut with a minimum of fuss. We then used a reverse-sear method, roasting the meat first and then finishing it by searing it in a skillet. Starting the roast in a fairly cool 300-degree oven minimized the temperature differential between the exterior and interior, allowing for gentle, even cooking. This approach also dried out the surface of the meat so it then seared very quickly in the skillet—leaving no chance for it to overcook. We finished by slathering the roast with a flavored butter as it rested. As the savory butter melted it became an instant sauce. Center-cut beef tenderloin roasts are sometimes sold as Châteaubriand. Ask your butcher to prepare a trimmed center-cut Châteaubriand, as this cut is not usually available without special ordering. For how to tie a roast, see page 12. We prefer this roast cooked to medium-rare, but if you prefer it more or less done, see our guidelines on page 24.

1 **For the beef** Sprinkle roast evenly with salt, cover loosely with plastic wrap, and let stand at room temperature for 1 hour. Adjust oven rack to middle position and heat oven to 300 degrees.

2 **For the shallot and parsley butter** Meanwhile, combine all ingredients in bowl and let rest to blend flavors, about 10 minutes. Wrap in plastic wrap, roll into log, and refrigerate until serving.

3 Pat roast dry with paper towels. Sprinkle roast evenly with pepper and spread softened butter evenly over surface. Transfer roast to wire rack set in rimmed baking sheet. Roast until beef registers 120 to 125 degrees (for medium-rare), 40 to 55 minutes, flipping roast halfway through roasting.

4 Heat oil in 12-inch skillet over medium-high heat until just smoking. Brown roast well on all sides, about 8 minutes. Transfer roast to carving board and spread 2 tablespoons flavored butter evenly over top of roast; let rest for 30 minutes. Remove twine and slice into ½-inch-thick slices. Serve, passing remaining flavored butter separately.

HERB-CRUSTED ROAST BEEF TENDERLOIN

1 (6-pound) whole beef tenderloin, trimmed, tail end tucked, and tied at 1½-inch intervals

Kosher salt and cracked peppercorns

2 teaspoons sugar

2 slices hearty white sandwich bread, torn into pieces

2½ ounces Parmesan cheese, grated (1¼ cups)

½ cup chopped fresh parsley

6 tablespoons extra-virgin olive oil

2 teaspoons plus 2 tablespoons chopped fresh thyme

4 garlic cloves, minced

Why This Recipe Works Though beef tenderloin offers incomparable tenderness, it is not known for its beefy flavor. To give this mild cut a boost here, we turned to a thick herbed crust. But applying herbs to a raw roast before it goes into the oven is tricky, and if they're exposed to heat for too long, herbs can burn, lose their flavor in a hot oven, or just fall off the meat. Cooking the roast in the oven at a high temperature for part of the time gave it a perfectly caramelized exterior that made applying an herb paste for the second half of the cooking time easy. Adding grated Parmesan cheese to the paste gave it nutty flavor and helped the paste adhere to the meat. Fresh parsley and thyme provided a flavorful coating and for a crisp texture, we relied on bread crumbs. Make sure to begin this recipe at least 1 hour before you plan to put the roast in the oven. The tenderloin can be trimmed, tied, rubbed with the salt mixture, and refrigerated up to 24 hours in advance; bring the roast back to room temperature before putting it into the oven. For how to tie a roast, see page 12. We prefer this roast cooked to medium-rare, but if you prefer it more or less done, see our guidelines on page 24. Serve with Horseradish Sauce (page 27), if desired.

1 Set wire rack in rimmed baking sheet. Pat roast dry with paper towels. Combine 1 tablespoon salt, 1 tablespoon peppercorns, and sugar in small bowl and rub all over roast. Transfer to prepared sheet and let sit at room temperature for at least 1 hour or up to 2 hours.

2 Meanwhile, pulse bread in food processor to fine crumbs, about 15 pulses. Transfer bread crumbs to medium bowl and toss with ½ cup Parmesan, 2 tablespoons parsley, 2 tablespoons oil, and 2 teaspoons thyme until evenly combined. Wipe out food processor with paper towels and process remaining ¾ cup Parmesan, 6 tablespoons parsley, ¼ cup oil, 2 tablespoons thyme, and garlic until smooth paste forms. Transfer herb paste to small bowl.

3 Adjust oven rack to upper-middle position and heat oven to 400 degrees. Roast beef for 20 minutes, then remove from oven. Remove twine. Coat beef with herb paste, then bread-crumb topping. Roast until beef registers 120 to 125 degrees (for medium-rare) and topping is golden brown, 20 to 25 minutes. (If topping browns before beef reaches preferred internal temperature, lightly cover with aluminum foil for remainder of roasting time and remove while beef rests.) Transfer to carving board and let rest for 30 minutes. Slice roast into ½-inch-thick slices. Serve.

ROAST BEEF TENDERLOIN WITH SMOKY POTATOES AND PERSILLADE RELISH

serves 6

Beef and Potatoes

1 (3-pound) center-cut beef tenderloin roast, trimmed

Kosher salt and pepper

1 teaspoon baking soda

3 tablespoons extra-virgin olive oil

3 pounds extra-small red potatoes, unpeeled

5 scallions, minced

4 garlic cloves, minced

1 tablespoon smoked paprika

½ cup water

Persillade Relish

¾ cup minced fresh parsley

½ cup extra-virgin olive oil

6 tablespoons minced cornichons plus 1 teaspoon brine

¼ cup capers, rinsed and chopped coarse

3 garlic cloves, minced

1 scallion, minced

1 teaspoon sugar

¼ teaspoon salt

¼ teaspoon pepper

Why This Recipe Works One of the beauties of oven roasting as a technique is the opportunity to roast vegetables alongside a large cut of meat, taking advantage of the heat of the oven and the flavorful drippings from the meat. Small whole red potatoes paired perfectly with a simple roast beef tenderloin, gaining deep flavor from sharing the pan with the meat. The addition of smoked paprika gave the potatoes a pleasant smokiness that complemented the roasted meat. Tying the roast helped to ensure even cooking and a hot oven delivered rich, roasted flavor and perfectly rosy meat without overcooking the lean cut. The tender meat needed a zesty sauce to boost its mild flavor, so we made a simple yet bold persillade relish featuring parsley, capers, and cornichons. The brightness of the sauce against the buttery meat and smoky potatoes was the perfect finishing touch to a one-pan meal worthy of a special occasion. We prefer to use extra-small red potatoes measuring less than 1 inch in diameter. Larger potatoes can be used, but it may be necessary to return the potatoes to the oven to finish cooking while the roast is resting in step 5. Center-cut beef tenderloin roasts are sometimes sold as Châteaubriand. Ask your butcher to prepare a trimmed center-cut Châteaubriand, as this cut is not usually available without special ordering. We prefer this roast cooked to medium-rare, but if you prefer it more or less done, see our guidelines on page 24.

1 For the beef and potatoes Pat roast dry with paper towels. Combine 2¼ teaspoons salt, 1 teaspoon pepper, and baking soda in small bowl. Rub salt mixture evenly over roast and let stand for 1 hour. Tuck tail end and tie roast with kitchen twine at 1½-inch intervals. Adjust oven rack to middle position and heat oven to 425 degrees.

2 Heat 2 tablespoons oil in large roasting pan over medium-high heat (over 2 burners, if possible) until shimmering. Add potatoes, scallions, garlic, paprika, 1 teaspoon salt, and ¼ teaspoon pepper and cook until scallions are softened, about 1 minute. Off heat, stir in water, scraping up any browned bits. Transfer roasting pan to oven and roast potatoes for 15 minutes.

3 Brush remaining 1 tablespoon oil over surface of roast. Remove roasting pan from oven, stir potato mixture, and lay beef on top. Reduce oven temperature to 300 degrees. Return pan to oven and roast until beef registers 120 to 125 degrees (for medium-rare), 45 to 55 minutes, rotating roasting pan halfway through cooking.

4 For the persillade relish While beef roasts, combine all ingredients in bowl.

5 Remove pan from oven. Transfer roast to carving board, tent with aluminum foil, and let rest for 15 minutes. Cover potatoes in pan with foil to keep warm. Remove twine, slice into ½-inch-thick slices, and serve with potatoes and relish.

ROAST BEEF TENDERLOIN WITH MUSHROOM AND CARAMELIZED ONION STUFFING

serves 4 to 6

Stuffing

8 ounces cremini mushrooms, trimmed and broken into rough pieces

1 tablespoon unsalted butter

2 teaspoons extra-virgin olive oil

1 onion, halved and sliced ¼ inch thick

½ teaspoon kosher salt

⅛ teaspoon pepper

1 garlic clove, minced

½ cup Madeira or sweet Marsala wine

Roast

1 (2- to 3-pound) center-cut beef tenderloin roast, trimmed

Kosher salt and pepper

½ cup baby spinach

3 tablespoons extra-virgin olive oil

Herb Butter

4 tablespoons unsalted butter, softened

1 tablespoon whole-grain mustard

1 tablespoon chopped fresh parsley

1 garlic clove, minced

¾ teaspoon chopped fresh thyme

¼ teaspoon kosher salt

⅛ teaspoon pepper

Why This Recipe Works Incorporating a rich stuffing is an ideal way to add flavor to mild, buttery beef tenderloin and help dress it up for special occasions. For a stuffed beef tenderloin with a deeply charred crust, a tender, rosy-pink interior, and an intensely flavored stuffing that stayed neatly rolled in the meat, we started by butterflying a center-cut tenderloin. This cut's cylindrical shape made it easy to stuff and encouraged even cooking. After we stuffed, rolled, and tied it, we rubbed the roast with salt, pepper, and oil, which helped develop a good crust when we seared the meat. We could fit just a cupful of stuffing in the meat, so we knew the flavors had to be intense—no room for filler like bread crumbs. We landed on woodsy cremini mushrooms and caramelized onions seasoned with Madeira and garlic; this combination made a savory-sweet jam-like filling that spread easily on the meat and held together well. Baby spinach added color and freshness. Center-cut beef tenderloin roasts are sometimes sold as Châteaubriand. The roast can be stuffed, rolled, tied, and refrigerated up to 24 hours in advance; make sure to bring it back to room temperature before putting it into the oven. This recipe can be doubled to make two roasts. Sear the roasts one after the other, cleaning the pan and adding new oil after searing the first roast. Both pieces of meat can be roasted on the same rack. We prefer this roast cooked to medium-rare, but if you prefer it more or less done, see our guidelines on page 24.

1 For the stuffing Pulse mushrooms in food processor until coarsely chopped, about 6 pulses. Heat butter and oil in 12-inch nonstick skillet over medium-high heat until butter is melted. Add onion, salt, and pepper; cook, stirring occasionally, until onion is softened, about 5 minutes. Add mushrooms and cook, stirring occasionally, until all moisture has evaporated, 5 to 7 minutes. Reduce heat to medium and continue to cook, stirring frequently, until vegetables are deeply browned and sticky, about 10 minutes. Stir in garlic and cook until fragrant, 30 seconds. Stir in Madeira,

scraping bottom of skillet to loosen any browned bits, and cook until liquid has evaporated, 2 to 3 minutes. Transfer mushroom mixture to plate and let cool completely.

2 For the roast Position roast fat side up. Insert knife one-third of way up from bottom of roast along 1 long side and cut horizontally, stopping ½ inch before edge. Open up flap. Keeping knife parallel to cutting board, cut through thicker portion of roast about ½ inch from bottom of roast, keeping knife level with first cut and stopping about ½ inch before edge. Open up this flap. If uneven, cover with plastic wrap and use meat pounder to even out. Season cut side of roast with salt and pepper. Spread cooled mushroom mixture over interior of roast, leaving ½-inch border on all sides; lay spinach on top of stuffing. Roll roast lengthwise and tie at 1½-inch intervals with kitchen twine.

3 Stir 1 tablespoon oil, 1½ teaspoons salt, and 1½ teaspoons pepper together in small bowl. Rub roast with oil mixture and let stand at room temperature for at least 1 hour or up to 2 hours.

4 Adjust oven rack to middle position and heat oven to 450 degrees. Heat remaining 2 tablespoons oil in 12-inch skillet over medium-high heat until just smoking. Brown roast well on all sides, 8 to 10 minutes. Transfer to wire rack set in rimmed baking sheet and place in oven. Roast until beef registers 120 to 125 degrees (for medium-rare), 20 to 22 minutes.

5 For the herb butter Meanwhile, combine all ingredients in bowl. Transfer roast to carving board; spread half of butter evenly over top of roast and let rest for 20 minutes. Remove twine and slice into ½-inch-thick slices. Serve with remaining butter.

butterflying a beef tenderloin

1 Insert chef's knife about 1 inch from bottom of roast and cut horizontally, stopping just before edge. Open meat like book.

2 Make another cut diagonally into thicker portion of roast. Open up this flap, smoothing out rectangle of meat.

BEST ROAST PRIME RIB

serves 8 to 10

1 (7-pound) first-cut beef standing rib roast (3 bones), with ½-inch fat cap

Kosher salt and pepper

2 teaspoons vegetable oil

Why This Recipe Works Prime rib is a hefty, expensive cut of beef with an extraordinary amount of flavor. It is best prepared with a simple roasting technique following a few key steps along the way. We started by salting the roast and then refrigerating it uncovered for at least 24 hours. This not only seasoned the meat but also dried out the exterior so it developed great browning and a nice thick crust when we seared it in a superhot skillet. We removed the meat from the bones first to make searing easier, and then tied the seared roast back to the bones for more even cooking. To further enhance tenderness, we cooked the roast at a very low temperature, which allowed the meat's enzymes to act as natural tenderizers. A quick trip under the broiler right before serving restored the crispness the crust lost while the meat was resting. Look for a roast with an untrimmed fat cap, ideally ½ inch thick. We prefer the flavor and texture of prime-grade beef, but choice grade will work as well. This recipe requires refrigerating the salted beef for at least 24 hours or up to four days before cooking (a longer time is preferable). If the roast has not reached the correct temperature in the time range specified in step 4, reheat the oven to 200 degrees for 5 minutes, shut it off, and continue to cook the roast until it reaches the desired temperature. We prefer this roast cooked to medium-rare, but if you prefer it more or less done, see our guidelines on page 24. Serve with Horseradish Sauce (page 27), Garlic-Herb Compound Butter (page 28), or one of the other accompaniments on pages 27–29.

1 Using sharp knife, cut beef from bones. Cut slits 1 inch apart in crosshatch pattern in fat cap of roast, being careful not to cut into beef. Rub 2 tablespoons salt thoroughly over roast and into slits. Place beef back on bones (to save space in refrigerator), and refrigerate, uncovered, for at least 24 hours or up to 4 days.

2 Adjust oven rack to middle position and heat oven to 200 degrees. Heat oil in 12-inch skillet over high heat until just smoking. Remove beef from bones. Sear top and sides of roast until browned, 6 to 8 minutes; do not sear side of roast that was cut from bones.

3 Fit roast back onto bones, let cool for 10 minutes, then tie together with kitchen twine between ribs. Transfer roast, fat side up, to wire rack set in rimmed baking sheet and season with pepper. Roast until beef registers 110 degrees, 3 to 4 hours.

4 Turn oven off and leave roast in oven, without opening door, until beef registers 120 to 125 degrees (for medium-rare), 30 minutes to 1¼ hours.

5 Remove roast from oven (leave roast on sheet) and let rest for at least 30 minutes or up to 1¼ hours.

6 Adjust oven rack 8 inches from broiler element and heat broiler. Place 3-inch aluminum foil ball under ribs to elevate fat cap. Broil until top of roast is well browned and crisp, 2 to 8 minutes. Transfer roast to carving board, remove twine, and remove beef from ribs. Slice roast into ¾-inch-thick slices. Serve.

preparing prime rib for roasting

1 Using sharp knife, cut meat from bones in single piece.

2 Cut a crosshatch pattern in fat cap of roast. Rub with kosher salt, place meat back on bones, and refrigerate for 1 to 4 days.

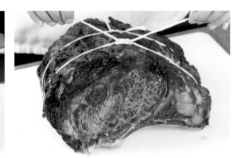

3 After searing roast, fit browned meat back onto bones, let cool for 10 minutes, then tie meat and bones together with twine.

BONELESS RIB ROAST WITH YORKSHIRE PUDDING AND JUS

serves 10 to 12

Roast and Pudding

1 (5- to 5½-pound) first-cut boneless beef rib roast, with ½-inch fat cap

Kosher salt and pepper

2½ cups all-purpose flour

4 cups milk

4 large eggs

1 tablespoon vegetable oil, plus extra as needed

Jus

1 onion, chopped fine

1 teaspoon cornstarch

2½ cups beef broth

1 sprig fresh thyme

Why This Recipe Works For our take on a traditional British Sunday roast dinner, we started with a richly marbled, easy-to-carve boneless rib roast and used rendered fat from the roast and trimmings to make a Yorkshire pudding infused with meaty flavor. For an ultrajuicy, well-seasoned boneless rib roast, we salted the beef a day in advance and cooked it in a low, 250-degree oven. Letting the Yorkshire pudding batter sit while the roast was in the oven allowed time for the gluten in the batter to relax, so the pudding could rise more quickly in the oven when we poured it into a searing-hot roasting pan. A quick, deeply savory jus was the perfect complement to the buttery roast and golden York-shire pudding. If you're using a dark roasting pan, reduce the pudding's cooking time by 5 minutes. Look for a roast with an untrimmed fat cap, ideally ½ inch thick. This recipe requires refrigerating the salted beef for at least 24 hours or up to four days before cooking (a longer time is preferable). We prefer this roast cooked to medium-rare, but if you prefer it more or less done, see our guidelines on page 24. Serve with Horseradish Sauce (page 27), if desired.

1 For the roast and pudding Using sharp knife, trim roast's fat cap to ¼-inch thickness; refrigerate trimmings. Cut 1-inch crosshatch pattern in fat cap, being careful not to cut into beef. Rub 2 tablespoons salt thoroughly over roast and into slits. Refrigerate, uncovered, for at least 24 hours or up to 4 days.

2 Adjust oven rack to lower-middle position and heat oven to 250 degrees. Spray large roasting pan with vegetable oil spray. Cut reserved trimmings into ½-inch pieces. Place 3 ounces (about ¾ cup) trimmings in bottom of pan. Set V-rack over trimmings in pan and spray with oil spray.

3 Season roast with pepper and place fat side up on V-rack. Roast until beef registers 120 to 125 degrees (for medium-rare), 2½ to 3 hours.

4 Meanwhile, combine flour and 1 tablespoon salt in large bowl. Whisk milk and eggs in second bowl until fully combined. Slowly whisk milk mixture into flour mixture until smooth. Cover with plastic wrap and let rest at room temperature for 1 hour.

5 Transfer V-rack with roast to carving board and let rest for 1 hour. Remove solids in pan, leaving liquid fat behind (there should be about 6 tablespoons; if not, supplement with vegetable oil). Increase oven temperature to 425 degrees.

6 When oven reaches 425 degrees, return pan to oven and heat until fat is just smoking, 3 to 5 minutes. Rewhisk batter and pour into center of pan. Bake until pudding is dark golden brown and edges are crisp, 40 to 45 minutes.

7 Meanwhile, pat roast dry with paper towels. Heat oil in 12-inch skillet over medium-high heat until just smoking. Brown roast well on all sides, 8 to 12 minutes. Transfer roast to carving board.

8 For the jus Return now-empty skillet to medium-high heat, add onion, and cook until softened, about 5 minutes, scraping up any browned bits. Whisk cornstarch into broth. Add broth mixture and thyme sprig to skillet and bring to boil. Reduce heat to medium-low and simmer until reduced by half, about 7 minutes. Strain jus through fine-mesh strainer set over small saucepan; discard solids. Cover and keep warm.

9 Slice roast into ¾-inch-thick slices. Cut pudding into squares in pan. Serve roast with pudding and jus.

ROASTED PRIME RIB AND POTATOES

serves 8 to 10

1 (7-pound) first-cut beef standing rib roast (3 bones), with ½-inch fat cap

Kosher salt and pepper

4 pounds Yukon Gold potatoes

1 tablespoon minced fresh rosemary

1 tablespoon vegetable oil, plus extra as needed

Why This Recipe Works Juicy rib roast cooked on a bed of crispy potatoes infused with deep flavor from the drippings. . . there's a reason meat and potatoes are such a classic pairing. However, we like to cook bone-in rib roasts slowly at a low temperature while potatoes are best when roasted at a high temperature, so in order to cook everything to just the right doneness, we had to think outside the roasting pan. We placed the trimmed fat from the meat under the roast as it cooked, creating intensely flavored drippings. Once the meat had finished roasting, we precooked the potatoes in the microwave, tossed them with the rendered fat, cranked the oven up to 450 degrees, and roasted them (while the meat rested) until they were crisp and full of beefy flavor. Searing the cooked roast in a hot skillet added some last-minute browning to the roast's exterior without overcooking it. Look for a roast with an untrimmed fat cap, ideally ½ inch thick. Wait until the roast is done cooking before peeling and cutting the potatoes so they don't discolor. It is crucial to use a sturdy rimmed baking sheet for this recipe. This recipe requires refrigerating the salted beef for at least 24 hours or up to four days before cooking (a longer time is preferable). We prefer this roast cooked to medium-rare, but if you prefer it more or less done, see our guidelines on page 24. Serve with Red Wine–Orange Sauce (page 28), if desired.

1 Using sharp knife, trim roast's fat cap to ¼-inch thickness; refrigerate trimmings. Cut 1-inch crosshatch pattern in fat cap, being careful not to cut into beef. Rub 2 tablespoons salt thoroughly over roast and into slits. Refrigerate, uncovered, for at least 24 hours or up to 4 days.

2 Adjust oven rack to lower-middle position and heat oven to 250 degrees. Cut reserved trimmings into ½-inch pieces. Place 4 ounces (about 1 cup) of trimmings in rimmed baking sheet, then set wire rack in sheet. Season roast with pepper and place, fat side up, on prepared rack.

3 Roast until beef registers 120 to 125 degrees (for medium-rare), 3 to 3½ hours. Transfer roast to carving board and let rest for 1 hour. Carefully remove wire rack. Using fork, remove solids in pan, leaving liquid fat behind (there should be about ½ cup; if not, supplement with vegetable oil).

4 Increase oven temperature to 450 degrees. Peel potatoes and cut into 1½-inch pieces. Microwave potatoes, covered, in large bowl until they begin to release moisture and surfaces look wet, about 7 minutes. Pat potatoes dry with paper towels. Toss potatoes with rosemary, 2 teaspoons salt, and ½ teaspoon pepper. Transfer potatoes to sheet and carefully toss with reserved fat (fat may be hot). Roast until tender and browned, 35 to 40 minutes, redistributing halfway through cooking. Season potatoes with salt and pepper to taste.

5 Pat roast dry with paper towels. Heat oil in 12-inch skillet over medium-high heat until just smoking. Brown roast well on all sides, 8 to 12 minutes. Transfer roast to carving board. Carve beef from bones and cut into ¾-inch-thick slices. Serve with potatoes.

ONE-PAN ROASTED PRIME RIB AND VEGETABLES

serves 8 to 10

1 (7-pound) first-cut beef standing rib roast (3 bones), with ½-inch fat cap

Kosher salt and pepper

Vegetable oil

2 pounds carrots, peeled, cut into 2-inch lengths, halved or quartered lengthwise to create ½-inch-diameter pieces

1 pound parsnips, peeled and sliced ½ inch thick on bias

1 pound Brussels sprouts, trimmed and halved

1 red onion, halved and sliced through root end into ½-inch wedges

2 teaspoons minced fresh thyme

Why This Recipe Works Cooking vegetables alongside a big roast is a classic way to take your dinner to the next level. By using our preferred low-and-slow method for prime rib and then roasting a mix of root vegetables and Brussels sprouts in the flavorful beef drippings as the meat rested, we put together a simple, foolproof path to an impressive dinner. We began by scoring and salting a standing rib roast and refrigerating it for at least 24 hours to ensure tender beef. Roasting the beef in a low oven for 3 hours yielded evenly pink and juicy meat. Adding the meat back to the pan with the browned, tender vegetables for a final stint under the broiler turned the outside of the roast crispy and golden and brought the whole dish together. We ended up with a feast fit for a holiday—with only one pan to wash. Look for a roast with an untrimmed fat cap, ideally ½ inch thick. This recipe requires refrigerating the salted beef for at least 24 hours or up four days before cooking (a longer time is preferable). We prefer this roast cooked to medium-rare, but if you prefer it more or less done, see our guidelines on page 24.

1 Using sharp knife, cut 1-inch crosshatch pattern in roast's fat cap, being careful not to cut into beef. Rub 2 tablespoons salt over entire roast and into slits. Refrigerate, uncovered, for at least 24 hours or up to 4 days.

2 Adjust oven rack to lower-middle position and heat oven to 250 degrees. Set V-rack in large roasting pan and spray with vegetable oil spray. Season roast with pepper and arrange, fat side up, on prepared V-rack. Roast until beef registers 120 to 125 degrees (for medium-rare), 3 to 3½ hours. Transfer V-rack with roast to carving board and let rest for 1 hour.

3 Meanwhile, increase oven temperature to 425 degrees. Using fork, remove solids in pan, leaving liquid fat behind (there should be about 2 tablespoons; if not, supplement with vegetable oil). Toss carrots, parsnips, Brussels sprouts, onion, thyme, 1 teaspoon salt, and ½ teaspoon pepper with fat in pan. Roast vegetables until tender and browned, 45 to 50 minutes, redistributing halfway through cooking.

4 Remove pan from oven and heat broiler. Carefully nestle V-rack with roast among vegetables in pan. Broil roast until fat cap is evenly browned, rotating pan as necessary, about 5 minutes. Transfer roast to carving board, carve beef from bones, and cut into ¾-inch-thick slices. Season vegetables with salt and pepper to taste. Serve beef with vegetables.

OVEN-BARBECUED BEEF BRISKET

serves 8 to 10

Brisket

4 teaspoons packed light brown sugar

4 teaspoons paprika

2 teaspoons dry mustard

2 teaspoons pepper

2 teaspoons salt

1 teaspoon onion powder

1 teaspoon garlic powder

1 teaspoon ground cumin

¼ teaspoon cayenne pepper

1 (4- to 5-pound) beef brisket, flat cut, fat trimmed to ¼ inch

1 pound bacon

Smoky Bacon Barbecue Sauce

1 onion, chopped fine

½ cup cider vinegar

⅓ cup packed light brown sugar

1–2 cups chicken broth

½ cup ketchup

4 teaspoons minced canned chipotle chile in adobo sauce

Why This Recipe Works Brisket is a notoriously tough cut, but the right cooking technique can turn it tender and juicy. One common treatment for brisket is barbecuing; Texas pit masters will tell you that the secret to blue-ribbon barbecued brisket is hours and hours of low, smoky heat penetrating the beef. This is because as the internal temperature of the brisket climbs, collagen—a tough connective tissue inside the meat—begins to melt, turning into soft gelatin. For an oven-roasting approach that could mimic the low-and-slow heat and complex flavors of authentic barbecue, we started by rubbing a spicy-sweet blend of brown sugar and seasonings onto a brisket roast. Poking its surface with a fork readied the meat to absorb flavor. Covering the brisket in smoky-sweet bacon mimicked the flavors imparted by wood chips on the grill. Covered with aluminum foil, the brisket cooked to a fully tender texture in 4 hours. Rather than letting the brisket's flavorful renderings and the bacon go to waste, we incorporated them into a quick barbecue sauce, brushed it over the brisket, and put the meat under the broiler. The sauce glazed the top, turning the brisket a rich mahogany color. With its authentic appearance and robust smoky, seasoned flavor, we had a brisket with all the appeal of real barbecue without having to step outside. You can substitute 3½ cups of bottled barbecue sauce, if desired. You will need a broiler-safe baking dish here; glass (such as Pyrex) may crack under the high heat.

1 For the brisket Adjust oven rack to upper-middle position and heat oven to 275 degrees. Combine sugar, paprika, mustard, pepper, salt, onion powder, garlic powder, cumin, and cayenne in small bowl, breaking up any lumps of sugar. Massage rub into roast and prick all over with fork. Arrange half of bacon strips, overlapping slightly, crosswise on bottom of 13 by 9-inch broiler-safe baking dish. Place roast, fat side down, in prepared dish, and place remaining bacon strips on top, tucking ends of strips underneath roast. Cover with aluminum foil and roast until fork slips easily in and out of beef, about 4 hours.

2 Remove dish from oven and carefully flip roast fat side up. Replace foil and return roast to oven. Turn off oven and let roast rest in warm oven for 1 hour.

3 For the smoky bacon barbecue sauce Pour any accumulated juices from baking dish into 4-cup liquid measuring cup and set aside. Remove bacon from roast and chop into small pieces. Cook bacon in medium saucepan over medium heat until fat has rendered, about 5 minutes. Add onion and cook until softened, about 5 minutes. Off heat, add vinegar and sugar and stir to combine. Return to medium heat and reduce to syrupy consistency, about 5 minutes.

4 Meanwhile, skim fat from reserved juices and discard. Add broth to juices as needed to equal 3 cups, then add to saucepan and reduce until mixture measures 3 cups, about 8 minutes. Off heat, stir in ketchup and chipotle. Strain sauce through fine-mesh strainer into bowl; discard solids.

5 Heat broiler. Brush roast with 1 cup sauce and broil until top is lightly charred and fat is crisped, 5 to 7 minutes. Transfer to carving board and slice against grain into ¼-inch-thick slices. Serve, passing remaining sauce separately.

adding smoky flavor to oven-barbecued brisket

Arrange half of bacon strips, overlapping slightly, crosswise on bottom of 13 by 9-inch broiler-safe baking dish. Place brisket, fat side down, in bacon-lined pan, and place remaining strips of bacon on top.

DEVILED BEEF SHORT RIBS

serves 4 to 6

⅔ cup yellow mustard

⅓ cup orange juice

⅓ cup packed light brown sugar

1–2 jalapeño chiles, stemmed, seeds reserved, and roughly chopped

4 teaspoons dry mustard

1 teaspoon grated lemon zest plus 1 tablespoon juice

Salt and pepper

½ teaspoon cayenne pepper

5 pounds bone-in English-style short ribs, bones 4 to 5 inches long, 1 to 1½ inches of meat on top of bone, trimmed

2 tablespoons unsalted butter

1½ cups panko bread crumbs

1 tablespoon chopped fresh parsley

Why This Recipe Works Braising and barbecuing are usually the cooking methods of choice for beef short ribs since they allow the connective tissue in the ribs to break down, making them fall-off-the-bone tender. For a different take on this cut, we turned to oven roasting. A modified multistep roasting technique allowed us to build up great flavor while still ensuring completely tender ribs. We first roasted the seasoned ribs meat side down in a covered baking dish, allowing the meat to cook in its own rendered fat and juices. After cranking the heat and pouring off the juices, we brushed the ribs with a spicy sauce of dry and prepared mustards, citrus, brown sugar, and jalapeños. These hot and spicy flavors are typical of "deviled" food and they made a perfect counterpoint to the rich meat. A few rounds of brushing and roasting created a browned crust, and for a crunchy finish we coated the ribs with buttery toasted panko bread crumbs. English-style short ribs contain a single rib bone. For a milder sauce, use only one jalapeño and discard the seeds.

1 Adjust oven rack to middle position and heat oven to 325 degrees. Process yellow mustard, orange juice, sugar, jalapeños and reserved seeds, dry mustard, lemon juice, and 2 teaspoons pepper in food processor until smooth, scraping down sides of bowl, about 30 seconds; set aside. (Mustard mixture can be refrigerated for up to 1 week.)

2 Combine 1 tablespoon salt, 1 tablespoon pepper, and cayenne in bowl. Sprinkle ribs all over with spice mixture. Arrange ribs, meat side down, in 13 by 9-inch baking dish. Cover dish tightly with aluminum foil and roast until beef is nearly tender, about 3 hours.

3 Meanwhile, melt butter in 12-inch skillet over medium-high heat. Add panko and cook, stirring often, until golden brown, about 3 minutes. Off heat, stir in parsley and lemon zest and transfer to shallow dish.

4 Remove baking dish from oven and increase oven temperature to 425 degrees; transfer ribs to plate. Discard rendered fat and juices from dish. Brush beef (not bones) all over with one-fourth of mustard sauce and return ribs to dish, meat side up. Roast, uncovered, until beginning to brown, about 10 minutes. Brush beef again with one-third of remaining mustard sauce and continue to roast until well browned and completely tender, 10 to 15 minutes. Transfer ribs to serving dish and let rest for 15 minutes.

5 Brush beef once more with half of remaining mustard sauce and roll in panko mixture, taking care to entirely coat beef. Serve, passing remaining mustard sauce separately.

ROASTED THICK-CUT RIB-EYE STEAKS

2 (1¾- to 2-pound) bone-in rib-eye steaks, 2 inches thick, trimmed

Kosher salt and pepper

3 tablespoons vegetable oil

4 tablespoons unsalted butter

1 large shallot, peeled and quartered through root end

2 garlic cloves, lightly crushed and peeled

5 sprigs fresh thyme

Why This Recipe Works When roasting mammoth cuts of steak like extra-thick rib eye, it can be especially hard to achieve an even mahogany crust while maintaining a rosy interior. To serve up thick-cut steaks with a burnished crust and a juicy, tender center, we began by roasting them gently in a low oven until they were almost cooked through. To impart a distinct crust, we then moved to the stovetop. Searing the steaks in abundant oil over high heat and flipping them frequently imparted the deeply browned exterior we wanted. To give these premium steaks some extra finesse, we added butter and aromatics to the pan toward the end of cooking and used the hot fat to baste the steaks, further boosting flavor and adding incomparable richness. Not wanting to waste a drop of the flavored butter, we strained out the aromatics and served it with the steak as a sauce. This recipe moves quickly once you start searing, so have everything prepared and within arm's reach before you start. We prefer these steaks cooked to medium-rare, but if you prefer them more or less done, see our guidelines on page 24.

1 Adjust oven rack to middle position and heat oven to 250 degrees. Set wire rack in rimmed baking sheet. Pat steaks dry with paper towels and season liberally with salt and pepper. Place steaks on prepared rack and roast until thermometer inserted into side of steak registers 90 to 95 degrees, 30 to 50 minutes, flipping steaks halfway through roasting.

2 Heat oil in 12-inch skillet over high heat until just smoking. Pat steaks dry with paper towels. Cook steaks, without moving, for 30 seconds. Flip steaks and continue to cook, flipping every 30 seconds, until lightly browned, about 3 minutes.

3 Slide steaks to back of skillet, opposite handle, and add butter to front of skillet. Once butter has melted, add shallot, garlic, and thyme sprigs. Holding skillet handle, tilt skillet so butter pools near base of handle. Using metal spoon, baste steaks with butter and aromatics, concentrating on areas where crust is less browned. Continuously baste steaks, flipping every 30 seconds, until steaks register 120 to 125 degrees (for medium-rare), 1 to 3 minutes.

4 Transfer steaks to carving board and let rest for 10 minutes. Strain seasoned butter into small bowl; discard solids. Carve steaks off bones, then slice into ¼-inch-thick slices. Serve with seasoned butter.

Roasted Thick-Cut Rib-Eye Steaks with Coffee-Chile Butter

Substitute 2 tablespoons whole coffee beans, cracked, for garlic cloves and ½ teaspoon red pepper flakes for thyme.

Roasted Thick-Cut Rib-Eye Steaks with Rosemary-Orange Butter

Substitute 8 (2-inch) strips orange zest for garlic and 1 sprig fresh rosemary for thyme.

Roasted Thick-Cut Rib-Eye Steaks with Green Peppercorn–Star Anise Butter

Substitute 2 teaspoons whole green peppercorns, cracked, for garlic and 5 star anise pods, cracked, for thyme.

PORK AND LAMB

ROASTED THICK-CUT PORK CHOPS

serves 4

4 (12-ounce) bone-in pork rib chops,
1½ inches thick, trimmed

Kosher salt and pepper

1–2 tablespoons vegetable oil

Why This Recipe Works Most recipes offer one of two approaches for cooking thick, bone-in pork chops: searing them in a smoking skillet or roasting them in a blazing-hot oven. Unfortunately, neither approach yields the perfect combination of rich, brown crust alongside plump, juicy meat that's full of flavor down to the last gnaw of the bone. To achieve that goal, we used a reverse-sear hybrid approach. We started by cooking the chops in a gentle oven before searing them in a smoking-hot pan. We chose thick-cut bone-in rib chops for their meaty texture and relatively high fat content. The bone acted as an insulator and helped the chops cook gently. The low oven helped break down the collagen in the chops, tenderizing the meat. It also dried out the exterior of the meat so that we got a gratifyingly crisp crust when we seared the chops. Salting the chops before roasting them also improved flavor and juiciness. We strongly prefer natural pork in this recipe. If the pork is enhanced (injected with a salt solution), do not salt in step 1. Serve with Salsa Verde (page 27), if desired.

1 Adjust oven rack to middle position and heat oven to 275 degrees. Pat chops dry with paper towels. Cut 2 slits, about 2 inches apart, through outer layer of fat and silverskin on each chop. Sprinkle each chop with 1 teaspoon salt. Place chops on wire rack set in rimmed baking sheet and let sit at room temperature for 45 minutes.

2 Season chops with pepper; transfer sheet to oven. Roast until pork registers 120 to 125 degrees, 30 to 45 minutes.

3 Heat 1 tablespoon oil in 12-inch skillet over high heat until just smoking. Place 2 chops in skillet and sear until well browned and crusty, 2 to 3 minutes, lifting once halfway through to redistribute fat underneath each chop. Turn chops and cook until well browned on second side, 2 to 3 minutes. Transfer chops to plate and repeat with remaining 2 chops, adding 1 tablespoon oil if pan is dry.

4 Reduce heat to medium. Use tongs to stand 2 pork chops on their sides. Holding chops together with tongs, return to skillet and sear sides of chops (with exception of bone side) until browned and pork registers 145 degrees, about 2 minutes. Repeat with remaining 2 chops. Transfer chops to serving dish and let rest for 10 minutes. Serve.

ROASTED THICK-CUT PORK CHOPS WITH RED ONION JAM STUFFING

serves 4

4 (12-ounce) bone-in pork rib chops, 1½ inches thick, trimmed

Salt and pepper

¼ cup packed light brown sugar

¾ cup ruby port

⅓ cup chopped dates

⅓ cup dried tart cherries

2 tablespoons vegetable oil

1 red onion, halved and sliced thin

1 orange, cut into 4 wedges

3 tablespoons white wine vinegar

2 teaspoons minced fresh thyme

⅓ cup pecans, toasted and chopped

3 ounces blue cheese, crumbled (¾ cup)

Why This Recipe Works Stuffing isn't just for whole birds and giant Sunday roasts—it's also a great way to add flavor and moisture to bland pork chops. We started with thick-cut rib chops, which have an unbroken eye of meat big enough for us to cut a wide pocket into with a sharp paring knife. For a stuffing that would add much needed moisture and assertive flavor to our chops, we combined dates, dried cherries, port, brown sugar, red onion, orange juice, vinegar, and pecans, making a rich, sticky, jam-like stuffing that was easy to pack into the chops. The best cooking results came from searing the brined, stuffed chops in a hot skillet and then transferring them to a preheated baking sheet to finish cooking in the oven. We strongly prefer natural pork in this recipe. If the pork is enhanced (injected with a salt solution), omit salt from brine in step 1. The stuffing can be made a day in advance, but it must be microwaved to room temperature before being packed into the chops.

1 Using sharp paring knife, cut 1-inch opening into side of each chop, then cut pocket for stuffing by swinging blade through middle of chop. Dissolve 3 tablespoons salt and 3 tablespoons sugar in 1½ quarts cold water in large container. Submerge chops in brine, cover, and refrigerate for 1 hour.

2 Meanwhile, microwave port, dates, and cherries in covered bowl until simmering, about 1 minute. Heat 1 tablespoon oil in medium saucepan over medium heat until shimmering. Add onion and remaining 1 tablespoon sugar and cook, stirring occasionally, until beginning to brown, 20 to 25 minutes. Squeeze juice from orange wedges into small bowl, then trim spent peels to 2-inch lengths; set aside trimmed peels.

3 When onion is soft, add dried fruit mixture, ¼ cup orange juice, 2 tablespoons vinegar, thyme, ¼ teaspoon salt, and ¼ teaspoon pepper; continue to cook, stirring occasionally, until mixture is jam-like, 10 to 12 minutes. Stir in remaining 1 tablespoon vinegar and pecans; transfer to bowl and let cool until just warm, about 15 minutes.

4 Adjust oven rack to lower-middle position, place rimmed baking sheet on rack, and heat oven to 450 degrees. Remove chops from brine and thoroughly pat dry with paper towels. Place one-quarter of stuffing in pocket of each chop (enlarge pocket opening to 1-inch, if necessary). Insert one reserved orange wedge into each pocket to contain stuffing. Season chops with pepper.

5 Heat remaining 1 tablespoon oil in 12-inch skillet over medium-high heat until just smoking. Brown chops well on both sides, about 6 minutes.

6 Transfer chops to preheated sheet in oven; roast until stuffing registers 145 degrees, 15 to 20 minutes, flipping chops halfway through roasting. Transfer chops to serving dish and let rest for 10 minutes. Sprinkle chops with blue cheese and serve.

ONE-PAN ROAST PORK TENDERLOIN WITH GREEN BEANS AND POTATOES

serves 4

4 tablespoons unsalted butter, softened

2 tablespoons minced fresh chives

1 garlic clove, minced to paste

Salt and pepper

1 pound green beans, trimmed

3 tablespoons extra-virgin olive oil

1½ pounds fingerling potatoes, unpeeled, halved lengthwise

2 (12- to 16-ounce) pork tenderloins, trimmed

¼ cup hoisin sauce

Why This Recipe Works Tender, inexpensive pork tenderloin takes well to an array of flavors because of its relatively mild flavor. Because it cooks so quickly, it is also easy to pair with vegetables for a simple, satisfying one-pan meal perfect for weeknights. We started with a base of green beans and halved fingerling potatoes on a rimmed baking sheet and then perched two tenderloins on top of the vegetables. Keeping them up off the metal pan helped protect the lean meat from drying out while the vegetables developed great browning. Brushing a layer of hoisin sauce over the meat before roasting gave it a flavor boost and an appealing caramelized layer. The thick, salty-sweet-spicy paste of soybeans, sugar, vinegar, garlic, and chiles added complexity to this simple dish. After just 20 minutes of roasting, we took the tenderloins out to rest and gave the vegetables a little extra time in the oven to pick up some color. An easy garlic-chive butter, melted over the resting pork and tossed with the vegetables, made for a rich, flavorful finish. To ensure that the tenderloins don't curl during cooking, remove the silverskin from the meat (see page 15). We strongly prefer natural pork in this recipe. If the pork is enhanced (injected with a salt solution), do not salt in step 3. A rasp-style grater makes quick work of turning the garlic into a paste.

1 Adjust oven rack to lower-middle position and heat oven to 450 degrees. Combine butter, chives, garlic, ¼ teaspoon salt, and ¼ teaspoon pepper in bowl; set aside for serving.

2 Toss green beans with 1 tablespoon oil, ¼ teaspoon salt, and ¼ teaspoon pepper in separate bowl. Arrange beans crosswise down center of rimmed baking sheet, leaving room on both sides for potatoes. Toss potatoes with remaining 2 tablespoons oil, ¼ teaspoon salt, and ¼ teaspoon pepper in now-empty bowl. Place potatoes, cut side down, on either side of green beans.

3 Pat tenderloins dry with paper towels, season with salt and pepper, and brush thoroughly with hoisin sauce. Lay tenderloins lengthwise, without touching, on top of green beans. Roast until pork registers 145 degrees, 20 to 25 minutes.

4 Remove sheet from oven and transfer tenderloins to carving board. Dot each tenderloin with 1 tablespoon chive butter and let rest while vegetables finish cooking. Gently stir vegetables on sheet to combine and continue to roast until tender and golden, 5 to 10 minutes.

5 Remove sheet from oven, add remaining 2 tablespoons butter to vegetables, and toss to coat. Slice pork into ½-inch-thick slices. Serve with vegetables.

PEPPER-CRUSTED ROAST PORK TENDERLOIN WITH ASPARAGUS AND BALSAMIC PAN SAUCE

serves 4

1 tablespoon minced fresh rosemary

Salt and pepper

2 (12- to 16-ounce) pork tenderloins, trimmed

2 tablespoons vegetable oil

2 pounds asparagus, trimmed and cut on bias into 2-inch lengths

¼ cup chicken broth

2 ounces goat cheese, crumbled (½ cup)

¼ cup balsamic vinegar

2 tablespoons unsalted butter

Why This Recipe Works This elegant take on pork tenderloin uses a skillet-to-oven roasting method similar to our Pan-Seared Oven-Roasted Pork Tenderloin (page 48). We added a coating of salt, pepper, and fresh rosemary before searing the pork to give it potent flavor. Then, we took advantage of the flavorful fond left behind in the pan to build a quick side dish of sautéed asparagus after the pork was transferred to the oven. Once the asparagus was tender, we topped it with a sprinkle of creamy goat cheese to complement its fresh green flavors. We finished this easy dinner by making a quick balsamic vinegar–butter sauce in the same triple-duty skillet. The sauce added just enough richness and tang to the roasted meat. To ensure that the tenderloins don't curl during cooking, remove the silverskin from the meat (see page 15). We strongly prefer natural pork in this recipe. If the pork is enhanced (injected with a salt solution), omit salt in step 1.

1 Adjust oven rack to middle position and heat oven to 450 degrees. Set wire rack in rimmed baking sheet. Combine rosemary, 1 tablespoon pepper, and 1 teaspoon salt in bowl. Pat tenderloins dry with paper towels and sprinkle with rosemary mixture.

2 Heat 1 tablespoon oil in 12-inch skillet over medium-high heat until just smoking. Brown tenderloins well on all sides, about 10 minutes. Transfer tenderloins to prepared rack and roast until pork registers 145 degrees, about 15 minutes. Transfer tenderloins to carving board and let rest for 10 minutes.

3 Meanwhile, heat remaining 1 tablespoon oil in now-empty skillet over medium-high heat until shimmering. Add asparagus, broth, ¼ teaspoon salt, and ¼ teaspoon pepper and cook, covered, until tender, about 5 minutes; transfer asparagus to serving dish and top with goat cheese. Reduce heat to medium-low, add vinegar to now-empty skillet, and simmer until thickened, scraping up any browned bits, about 1 minute. Off heat, whisk in butter. Slice pork into ½-inch-thick slices, arrange on serving dish with asparagus, and drizzle with sauce. Serve.

CRUMB-CRUSTED ROAST PORK TENDERLOIN

serves 4 to 6

5 tablespoons unsalted butter, melted

¼ cup whole-grain mustard

1½ tablespoons white wine vinegar

2 garlic cloves, minced

2 teaspoons minced fresh rosemary

Salt and pepper

Pinch cayenne pepper

1½ cups panko bread crumbs

¼ cup all-purpose flour

3 large egg whites

⅓ cup grated Parmesan cheese

2 (1- to 1¼-pound) pork tenderloins, trimmed

Why This Recipe Works Pork tenderloin has a lot to recommend it, but this lean cut can often end up dry, overcooked, and just plain boring. To introduce flavor and textural interest to inexpensive, quick-cooking tenderloin without a ton of extra fuss, we coated the meat with a crunchy bread-crumb mixture including savory powerhouse ingredients like mustard, garlic, and rosemary. Egg whites and flour helped it adhere. Baking the tenderloins on a wire rack set in a rimmed baking sheet enhanced the crunchy texture of the coating and also guaranteed that the meat cooked evenly. To ensure that the tenderloins don't curl during cooking, remove the silverskin from the meat (see page 15). We strongly prefer natural pork in this recipe. If the pork is enhanced (injected with a salt solution), do not salt in step 3.

1 Adjust oven rack to middle position and heat oven to 350 degrees. Whisk melted butter, mustard, vinegar, garlic, rosemary, ½ teaspoon salt, ½ teaspoon pepper, and cayenne in bowl until combined. Stir in panko until fully combined.

2 Spread panko mixture in even layer on rimmed baking sheet, breaking up any clumps. Bake, stirring every 5 minutes, until golden brown, 15 to 18 minutes. Transfer crumbs to 13 by 9-inch baking dish and let cool completely, about 10 minutes. Break up any large clumps with your fingers. Increase oven temperature to 400 degrees.

3 Set wire rack in now-empty sheet. Place flour in shallow dish. Whisk egg whites together in second shallow dish. Stir Parmesan into cooled crumb mixture. Pat tenderloins dry with paper towels and season with salt and pepper.

4 Working with 1 tenderloin at a time, dredge in flour, shaking off excess; dip in egg whites to thoroughly coat, letting excess drip back into dish; then coat with crumbs, pressing gently to adhere. Transfer tenderloins to prepared rack. Roast until pork registers 145 degrees, 25 to 30 minutes. Transfer tenderloins to carving board and let rest for 10 minutes. Slice pork into ½-inch-thick slices. Serve.

CIDER-GLAZED ROAST PORK LOIN

serves 6

1 (2½- to 3-pound) boneless center-cut pork loin roast, trimmed and tied at 1½-inch intervals, brined if desired

Salt and pepper

2 tablespoons vegetable oil

6 small shallots, peeled

2 cups apple cider

½ cup apple butter

1 bay leaf

1 sprig fresh thyme

1 teaspoon cider vinegar

Why This Recipe Works Pork is very lean, and less fat means less flavor and moisture, putting even large roasts at risk of turning out dry and bland. One of our favorite ways to ensure a flavorful exterior and moist, juicy interior for a pork loin roast is to use a sweet glaze. The glaze keeps the outside of the roast from becoming tough and dry in the oven, and when the roast is carved, the glaze coats each slice, making every bit tastier and juicier. After tying the roast to give it an even shape, we browned it in a skillet to create a flavorful crust. We then transferred the roast to a moderate oven to finish cooking through, and turned our attention to the glaze. Pork pairs beautifully with the sweet-tart flavors of apple, so we used apple cider and apple butter as our key ingredients, along with browned shallots. We added these to the flavorful juices that the pork left behind in the skillet to make a thick and glossy sweet-savory glaze. We applied the glaze to the pork in the oven to caramelize in the last 20 minutes of roasting, the excess glaze pooling in the baking dish and mingling with the drippings. With a little boost of cider vinegar, the leftover glaze from the bottom of the pan made a perfect finishing sauce for the sliced pork. We strongly prefer natural pork in this recipe. If the pork is enhanced (injected with a salt solution), omit the salt in step 1. For brining instructions, see page 22. For how to tie a pork loin, see page 15.

1 Adjust oven rack to middle position and heat oven to 375 degrees. Pat roast dry with paper towels and season with salt and pepper.

2 Heat 1 tablespoon oil in 12-inch skillet over medium-high heat until just smoking. Brown roast well on all sides, 8 to 10 minutes. Transfer roast fat side down to 13 by 9-inch baking dish and roast until pork registers 85 degrees, about 25 minutes.

3 Meanwhile, add remaining 1 tablespoon oil and shallots to now-empty skillet and cook over medium heat until golden brown, 3 to 5 minutes. Increase heat to high, add cider, apple butter, bay leaf, and thyme sprig and bring to boil. Cook until thickened, about 8 minutes.

4 After pork has roasted for 25 minutes, pour glaze over pork and, using tongs, roll pork to coat with glaze. Cook until pork registers 140 degrees, 20 to 30 minutes, turning once halfway through roasting to recoat with glaze. Transfer roast to carving board and let rest for 20 minutes. Transfer glaze to small saucepan and whisk in vinegar.

5 Before slicing roast, pour accumulated juices into glaze and warm glaze over low heat. Discard bay leaf and thyme sprig. If desired, remove shallots from sauce and transfer to serving dish. Remove twine and slice roast into ¼-inch-thick slices. Transfer to serving dish and spoon ½ cup glaze over top. Serve, passing remaining glaze at table.

MARMALADE-GLAZED ROAST PORK LOIN WITH PARSNIPS AND ONIONS

serves 6

1 (2½- to 3-pound) boneless center-cut pork loin roast, trimmed, tied at 1½-inch intervals, brined if desired

Salt and pepper

⅓ cup orange marmalade

1 tablespoon chopped fresh rosemary

½ cup orange juice

1 tablespoon vegetable oil

1 pound parsnips, peeled and cut into 3-inch pieces

2 red onions, peeled and cut into 1-inch wedges

Why This Recipe Works For another quick, flavor-packed take on glazed roast pork loin, we turned to orange marmalade. The bittersweet marmalade made an incredibly simple glaze—all we had to do was stir in some chopped rosemary and brush the mixture on the pork. Additional marmalade, combined with orange juice and oil, was the perfect complement for parsnips and red onions, which we roasted around the pork. The glaze gave them a glossy look and tart sweetness. We finished cooking the vegetables while the meat rested for a final dish that featured the perfect combination of juicy pork with a deep golden crust and vegetables with complex, caramelized flavor. We strongly prefer natural pork in this recipe. If the pork is enhanced (injected with a salt solution), omit the salt in step 1. If your parsnips are very thick, slice them in half lengthwise first to ensure even cooking. For brining instructions, see page 22. For how to tie a pork loin, see page 15.

1 Adjust oven rack to middle position and heat oven to 375 degrees. Pat roast dry with paper towels and season with salt and pepper. Place roast in center of large roasting pan.

2 Combine marmalade and rosemary in bowl. Spread half of marmalade mixture on roast. Add orange juice and oil to remaining marmalade mixture. Toss parsnips and onions with 2 tablespoons juice mixture and season with salt and pepper. Arrange vegetables around roast. Roast until pork registers 120 degrees, 30 to 45 minutes. Pour remaining juice mixture over roast, increase oven temperature to 450 degrees, and roast until pork registers 140 degrees, 15 to 20 minutes. Transfer roast to carving board and let rest for 20 minutes.

3 Meanwhile, toss vegetables and pan juices and redistribute evenly over pan bottom. Roast until juices thicken and vegetables caramelize, about 10 minutes. Remove twine from roast and slice pork into ½-inch-thick slices. Serve with vegetables, pouring pan juices over meat.

BACON-WRAPPED PORK LOIN WITH PEACH SAUCE

serves 6 to 8

Pork

Kosher salt and pepper

1 tablespoon sugar

1 (3½- to 4-pound) boneless center-cut pork loin roast, trimmed

2 teaspoons herbes de Provence

10 slices bacon

Peach Sauce

20 ounces frozen peaches, cut into ½-inch pieces (3 cups)

1 cup dry white wine

½ cup sugar

⅓ cup cider vinegar

4 sprigs fresh thyme

½ teaspoon kosher salt

2 tablespoons whole-grain mustard

Why This Recipe Works One way to counteract the inherent leanness of pork loin is to make it imitate a fattier cut of pork by wrapping it in bacon. Not only does this add big, smoky flavor to the mild meat, but it also creates a layer of protective fat that bastes the meat as it renders, just as the fat cap would on a different cut. To add even more flavor and juiciness, we started by rubbing the pork loin with a mixture of salt and sugar and letting it chill in the refrigerator. Achieving a rosy, moist roast with a browned bacon crust required a two-pronged cooking approach: We roasted the pork in a low 250-degree oven until it reached 90 degrees and then cranked the oven to 475 degrees to brown the bacon and finish cooking the pork. Brushing the whole thing with a quick-cooking peach sauce before the final stage in the oven gave it a rich, lacquered appearance and rounded out the dish. We strongly prefer natural pork in this recipe. If the pork is enhanced (injected with a salt solution), omit the salt in step 1. This recipe requires refrigerating the salted pork for at least 1 hour or up to 24 hours before cooking (a longer time is preferable). Oscar Mayer Naturally Hardwood Smoked Bacon is our winning thin-sliced bacon. Do not use thick-cut bacon here. You don't need to thaw the peaches before making the sauce.

1 **For the pork** Combine 4 teaspoons salt and sugar in bowl. Rub roast with salt-sugar mixture, wrap in plastic wrap, and refrigerate for at least 1 hour or up to 24 hours.

2 **For the peach sauce** Bring peaches, wine, sugar, vinegar, thyme sprigs, and salt to simmer in medium saucepan over medium-high heat. Reduce heat to medium and cook at strong simmer, stirring occasionally, until reduced to about 2 cups and spatula leaves trail when dragged through sauce, about 30 minutes. Off heat, discard thyme sprigs. Reserve 2 table-spoons of liquid portion of sauce (without peach segments) in small bowl for glazing. Cover and set aside remaining sauce.

3 Meanwhile, adjust oven rack to upper-middle position and heat oven to 250 degrees. Line rimmed baking sheet with aluminum foil and spray with vegetable oil spray. Pat roast dry with paper towels and sprinkle with herbes de Provence and 1 teaspoon pepper.

4 Arrange bacon slices on cutting board parallel to counter's edge, overlapping them slightly to match length of roast. Place roast in center of bacon, perpendicular to slices. Bring ends of bacon up and around sides of roast, overlapping ends of slices as needed.

5 Place bacon-wrapped roast, seam side down, in center of prepared sheet. Roast until pork registers 90 degrees, 30 to 40 minutes. Remove roast from oven and increase oven temper-ature to 475 degrees.

6 Brush top and sides of roast with reserved 2 tablespoons sauce. Once oven reaches temperature, return pork to oven and roast until bacon is well browned and pork registers 135 degrees, 15 to 20 minutes. Transfer roast to wire rack and let rest for 20 minutes.

7 Stir mustard into sauce and rewarm over low heat. Transfer roast to carving board and slice into ½-inch-thick slices. Serve with peach sauce.

HERB-CRUSTED PORK LOIN ROAST

serves 6

1 (2½- to 3-pound) boneless center-cut pork loin roast, brined if desired

1 slice hearty white sandwich bread, torn into quarters

1 ounce Parmesan or Pecorino Romano cheese, grated (½ cup)

1 shallot, minced

¼ cup plus 2 teaspoons extra-virgin olive oil

Salt and pepper

⅓ cup fresh parsley or basil leaves

2 tablespoons minced fresh thyme

1 teaspoon minced fresh rosemary or ½ teaspoon dried

1 garlic clove, minced

Why This Recipe Works A fresh herb crust is another classic way to enliven a boneless pork roast and infuse the meat with bold herb presence in every bite. In order to add flavor from the inside out, we started by cutting a deep, wide pocket in the roast and filling it with a paste packed full of fresh herbs, garlic, and nutty Parmesan. We also scored the fat cap on top of the roast before searing it briefly in a very hot skillet. The seared, crosshatched layer provided the perfect canvas for our bread-crumb and herb paste crust. It gave the paste something to grip on to and helped unify the crust and meat. After applying the crust to our seared roast, we transferred the whole dish to a relatively low oven, which allowed the roast to cook evenly and the crust to get beautifully crisp and golden brown. Center-cut pork loin roast is also called center-cut roast. Look for a roast with a thin fat cap (about ¼ inch thick) and don't trim this thin layer of fat. We strongly prefer natural pork in this recipe. If the pork is enhanced (injected with a salt solution), omit the salt in step 4. For brining instructions, see page 22. For how to tie a pork loin, see page 15.

1 Using sharp knife, cut slits 1 inch apart in crosshatch pattern in fat cap of roast, being careful not to cut into meat. Create pocket in roast by inserting knife ½ inch from end of roast and cutting along side of pork, stopping ½ inch short of other end. Pull open roast and use gentle strokes to cut deeper pocket.

2 Adjust oven rack to lower-middle position and heat oven to 325 degrees. Set wire rack in rimmed baking sheet lined with aluminum foil. Pulse bread in food processor until coarsely ground, about 16 pulses (you should have 1 cup crumbs). Transfer crumbs to bowl and add 2 tablespoons Parmesan, shallot, 1 tablespoon oil, ⅛ teaspoon salt, and ⅛ teaspoon pepper. Using fork, toss mixture until crumbs are evenly coated with oil.

3 Pulse parsley, thyme, rosemary, garlic, remaining 6 table-spoons Parmesan, 3 tablespoons oil, ⅛ teaspoon salt, and ⅛ teaspoon pepper in now-empty processor until smooth, about 12 pulses. Transfer herb paste to bowl.

4 Spread ¼ cup herb paste inside roast and tie roast at 1½-inch intervals with kitchen twine. Season roast with salt and pepper.

5 Heat remaining 2 teaspoons oil in 12-inch skillet over medium-high heat until just smoking. Brown roast well on all sides, about 10 minutes. Transfer roast, fat side up, to prepared sheet.

6 Remove twine from roast. Spread remaining herb paste over roast and top with bread-crumb mixture. Transfer sheet with roast to oven and cook until pork registers 140 degrees, 50 to 75 minutes. Remove roast from oven and let rest on sheet for 20 minutes. Transfer roast to carving board, taking care not to squeeze juices out of pocket in roast. Slice roast into ½-inch-thick slices. Serve.

Herb-Crusted Pork Loin Roast with Mustard and Caraway

Substitute 1 tablespoon minced garlic for shallot in bread-crumb mixture, substitute 4 teaspoons whole-grain mustard and 1 tablespoon toasted caraway seeds for rosemary, and reduce oil in step 3 to 2 tablespoons.

stuffing a pork loin roast

1 Starting ½ inch from end of roast, cut along side of pork, stopping ½ inch short of other end. Pull open roast and use gentle strokes to cut deeper pocket.

2 To stuff roast, spread ¼ cup herb paste evenly into pocket, using spatula and your fingers to make sure paste reaches corners of pocket.

3 Fold roast over to original shape and tie it at 1½-inch intervals along its length with kitchen twine.

TUSCAN-STYLE ROAST PORK WITH GARLIC AND ROSEMARY (ARISTA)

serves 6

1 lemon

⅓ cup extra-virgin olive oil

8 garlic cloves, minced

¼ teaspoon red pepper flakes

1 tablespoon chopped fresh rosemary

2 ounces pancetta, cut into ½-inch pieces

1 (2½- to 3-pound) boneless center-cut pork loin roast, trimmed, brined if desired

Kosher salt

Why This Recipe Works Our version of the Tuscan roast pork dish known as *arista* uses a few key tricks to turn lean, mild boneless pork loin into a juicy roast flavored with plenty of garlic and rosemary and featuring a deeply browned crust. To boost both flavor and juiciness, we salted the meat for 1 hour before cooking, using a double-butterfly technique to expose plenty of surface area and then salting both sides and rolling it back up. The double-butterflied roast and rolling technique also allowed us to maximize the distribution of our garlic and rosemary mixture. Briefly simmering the herbs and garlic before processing them into a smooth paste and spreading it over the pork tempered any raw flavors, and using plenty of oil (which we then strained off) and a non-stick skillet kept the garlic from browning, for a fresher flavor. To boost richness and enhance the overall porky flavor of the dish, we added pancetta (plus red pepper flakes and lemon zest for brightness) to the paste. Using a low oven ensured that the meat was evenly cooked from edge to center. Instead of roasting, browning, and then resting the roast, we let it rest after it came out of the oven and then browned it and served it immediately; this helped the crust stay crisp. For a finishing touch, we made a simple sauce by combining the strained garlic-rosemary oil with the juice from a halved lemon that we quickly caramelized in the skillet for more complex flavor. We strongly prefer natural pork in this recipe, but if enhanced pork (injected with a salt solution) is used, reduce the salt to 2 teaspoons (1 teaspoon per side) in step 3. For brining instructions, see page 22. For how to tie a pork loin, see page 15.

1 Finely grate 1 teaspoon zest from lemon. Cut lemon in half and reserve. Combine lemon zest, oil, garlic, and pepper flakes in 10-inch nonstick skillet. Cook over medium-low heat, stirring frequently, until garlic is sizzling, about 3 minutes. Add rosemary and cook until fragrant, about 30 seconds. Strain mixture through fine-mesh strainer set over bowl, pushing on garlic-rosemary mixture to extract oil. Set oil aside and let garlic-rosemary mixture cool. Wipe skillet clean with paper towels.

2 Process pancetta in food processor until smooth paste forms, 20 to 30 seconds, scraping down sides of bowl as needed. Add garlic-rosemary mixture and continue to process until mixture is homogeneous, 20 to 30 seconds longer, scraping down sides of bowl as needed.

3 Position roast fat side up. Insert knife one-third of way up from bottom of roast along 1 long side and cut horizontally, stopping ½ inch before edge. Open up flap. Keeping knife parallel to cutting board, cut through thicker portion of roast about ½ inch from bottom of roast, keeping knife level with first cut and stopping about ½ inch before edge. Open up this flap. If uneven, cover with plastic wrap and use meat pounder to even out. Sprinkle 1 tablespoon salt over both sides of roast (½ tablespoon per side) and rub into pork to adhere. Spread inside of roast evenly with pancetta-garlic paste, leaving about ¼-inch border on all sides. Starting from short side, roll roast (keeping fat on outside) and tie with kitchen twine at 1½-inch intervals. Set wire rack in rimmed baking sheet and spray with vegetable oil spray. Set roast fat side up on prepared rack and refrigerate for 1 hour.

4 Adjust oven rack to middle position and heat oven to 275 degrees. Transfer roast to oven and cook until pork registers 135 degrees, 1½ to 2 hours. Remove roast from oven and let rest for 20 minutes.

5 Heat 1 teaspoon reserved oil in now-empty skillet over high heat until just smoking. Add reserved lemon halves, cut side down, and cook until softened and cut surfaces are browned, 3 to 4 minutes. Transfer lemon halves to small plate.

6 Pat roast dry with paper towels. Heat 2 tablespoons reserved oil in now-empty skillet over high heat until just smoking. Brown roast on fat side and sides (do not brown bottom of roast), 4 to 6 minutes. Transfer roast to carving board and let rest while finishing vinaigrette.

7 Once lemon halves are cool enough to handle, squeeze into fine-mesh strainer set over bowl. Press on solids to extract juice; discard solids. Whisk 2 tablespoons strained lemon juice into bowl with remaining reserved oil. Remove twine from roast and slice roast into ½-inch-thick slices. Serve, passing vinaigrette separately.

double butterflying a pork loin

With roast fat side up, cut horizonally through meat, one-third above bottom, stopping ½ inch from edge. Open roast and press flat; 1 side will be twice as thick. Repeat, cutting thicker side of roast in half horizontally, stopping ½ inch from edge.

ROAST PORK LOIN WITH SWEET POTATOES AND CILANTRO SAUCE

serves 6

Pork and Potatoes

1 (2½- to 3-pound) boneless center-cut pork loin roast, trimmed, tied at 1½-inch intervals, brined if desired

Salt and pepper

1 teaspoon ground coriander

1 teaspoon ground cumin

3 pounds sweet potatoes, peeled, quartered, and cut into 2-inch pieces

3 tablespoons extra-virgin olive oil

⅛ teaspoon cayenne pepper

Cilantro Sauce

2½ cups fresh cilantro leaves and stems, trimmed (2 bunches)

½ cup extra-virgin olive oil

4 teaspoons lime juice

2 garlic cloves, minced

½ teaspoon sugar

Salt and pepper

Why This Recipe Works This modern take on a roast pork dinner features meat and potatoes paired with fresh flavors: a tender spice-rubbed pork loin, caramelized sweet potatoes, and a lively green herb sauce. And, as an added bonus, it's a one-pan dinner—no piles of dishes to wash on a Sunday night. Roasting the meat in a moderate 375-degree oven and turning it halfway through roasting ensured juicy, perfectly cooked pork. A mixture of ground coriander, cumin, and salt gave the pork's exterior color and flavor and complemented a lively cilantro sauce. To complete the meal, we tossed sweet potato chunks with some olive oil and a pinch of cayenne pepper and roasted them along with the pork. By the time the pork was done, the potatoes were tender but a little pale, so we set the pork aside to rest, turned up the heat, and returned the roasting pan to the oven to give them some extra time to caramelize. A ¼-inch-thick layer of fat on top of the roast is ideal; if your roast has a thicker fat cap, trim it back accordingly. If the pork is enhanced (injected with a salt solution), do not brine but do season with salt in step 1. This sauce uses two entire bunches of cilantro, including the stems. For brining instructions, see page 22. For how to tie a pork loin, see page 15.

1 For the pork and potatoes Adjust oven rack to lower-middle position and heat oven to 375 degrees. Pat roast dry with paper towels. Season with salt and sprinkle with coriander and cumin.

2 Toss sweet potatoes in bowl with oil and cayenne, season with salt and pepper, and spread evenly into large roasting pan. Lay roast, fat side up, on top of potatoes. Roast until pork registers 140 degrees, 50 to 70 minutes, turning roast over halfway through roasting.

3 For the cilantro sauce Meanwhile, pulse all ingredients in food processor until cilantro is finely chopped, 10 to 15 pulses, scraping down sides of bowl as needed. Season with salt and pepper to taste.

4 Remove pan from oven. Transfer roast to carving board and let rest for 20 minutes. While roast rests, increase oven temperature to 450 degrees and continue to roast potatoes until nicely browned, about 10 minutes. Remove twine from roast and slice into ½-inch-thick slices. Serve with potatoes and cilantro sauce.

CROWN ROAST OF PORK

serves 10 to 12

Kosher salt and pepper

3 tablespoons minced fresh thyme

2 tablespoons minced fresh rosemary

5 garlic cloves, minced

1 (8- to 10-pound) pork crown roast, trimmed

2 pounds small red potatoes, scrubbed

10 ounces shallots, peeled and halved

2 Golden Delicious apples, peeled, cored, and halved

8 tablespoons unsalted butter, melted

½ cup apple cider

1 cup chicken broth

Why This Recipe Works The ultimate showstopping centerpiece, a crown roast of pork consists of two bone-in pork loin roasts that have been tied together. Its unique shape requires a few unusual steps in order to get rosy, perfectly seasoned meat. First, it was too unwieldy to brine, so we started by salting the roast for at least 6 hours. The addition of thyme, rosemary, and garlic to the salt helped season the meat and also made for delicious pan drippings during cooking. For even cooking, we turned the roast upside down for the first hour of cooking, which allowed more air to circulate through the hard-to-cook center of the crown and better exposed the thickest part of the roast to the oven's heat. We then flipped the meat right side up and turned the oven down to finish cooking the roast gently. Instead of a fussy stuffing that would slow down cooking, we opted to integrate a side dish into our recipe by adding potatoes, shallots, and apples that roasted in the pan alongside the meat. Pureeing the cooked apples into our pan sauce gave it fruity flavor and a perfectly thick consistency. A crown roast is two bone-in pork loin roasts, with the rib bones frenched and chine bones removed, that have been tied into a crown shape. This can be difficult to do, so ask your butcher to make this roast for you. We wrap extra kitchen twine around the widest part of the roast to provide more support when flipping. Use potatoes that measure 1 to 2 inches in diameter. This recipe requires refrigerating the salted pork for at least 6 hours or up to 24 hours before cooking (a longer time is preferable). We strongly prefer natural pork in this recipe. If the pork is enhanced (injected with a salt solution), omit salt in step 1.

1 Combine 3 tablespoons salt, 1 tablespoon pepper, thyme, rosemary, and garlic in bowl; reserve 2 teaspoons for vegetables. Pat roast dry with paper towels and rub with remaining herb salt. Wrap kitchen twine twice around widest part of roast and tie tightly. Refrigerate roast, covered, for at least 6 hours or up to 24 hours.

2 Adjust oven rack to lower-middle position and heat oven to 475 degrees. Place V-rack inside large roasting pan and spray with vegetable oil spray. Toss potatoes, shallots, apples, 4 tablespoons melted butter, and reserved herb salt in large bowl and transfer to pan. Arrange roast bone side down in V-rack and brush with remaining 4 tablespoons melted butter. Roast until pork is well browned and registers 110 degrees, about 1 hour.

3 Remove roast from oven and reduce oven temperature to 300 degrees. Using 2 wads of paper towels, flip roast bone side up. Add apple cider to pan and return to oven, rotating direction of pan. Roast until pork registers 140 degrees, 30 to 50 minutes. Transfer roast to carving board and let rest for 20 minutes.

4 Transfer apple halves to blender and potatoes and shallots to bowl. Pour pan juices into fat separator, let liquid settle for 5 minutes, and pour into blender, discarding fat. Add broth to blender with apples and pan juices and process until smooth, about 1 minute. Transfer sauce to medium saucepan and bring to simmer over medium heat. Season with salt and pepper to taste. Cover and keep warm. Remove twine from roast and slice between bones. Serve with vegetables and sauce.

SLOW-ROASTED PORK SHOULDER WITH PEACH SAUCE

serves 8 to 12

Pork Roast

1 (6- to 8-pound) bone-in pork butt roast

⅓ cup kosher salt

⅓ cup packed light brown sugar

Pepper

Peach Sauce

10 ounces frozen peaches, cut into 1-inch pieces, or 2 fresh peaches, peeled, pitted, and cut into ½-inch wedges

2 cups dry white wine

½ cup granulated sugar

¼ cup plus 1 tablespoon unseasoned rice vinegar

2 sprigs fresh thyme

1 tablespoon whole-grain mustard

Why This Recipe Works Slow roasting can take a simple cut of pork and turn it into something magical. We began by rubbing a bone-in pork butt roast with a mixture of salt and sugar and letting it rest overnight. As a result of this extended rest, the salt was able to penetrate deep into the meat, enhancing juiciness and seasoning it throughout, while the sugar caramelized to create a crackling-crisp crust. We then roasted the pork for the better part of a day. Cooking the pork for 5 to 6 hours pushed the meat well beyond its "done" mark, but because there is so much collagen and fat in a pork butt roast, the results were ultratender and moist. The shoulder roast may take longer to cook than other cuts of pork, but it's also inexpensive and loaded with flavorful intramuscular fat; plus, it boasts a thick fat cap that renders to a bronze, bacon-like crust. Elevating the pork shoulder on a V-rack and pouring water into the roasting pan kept the pork's drippings from burning as the meat roasted. Finally, a fruity sauce with sweet and tart elements cut the pork's richness. Pork butt roast is often labeled Boston butt in the supermarket. Add more water to the roasting pan as necessary to prevent the fond from burning. Serve the pork with the accompanying peach or cherry sauce or Fennel-Apple Chutney (page 28).

1 For the pork roast Using sharp knife, cut slits 1 inch apart in crosshatch pattern in fat cap of roast, being careful not to cut into meat. Combine salt and sugar in bowl. Rub salt mixture over entire roast and into slits. Wrap roast tightly in double layer of plastic wrap and refrigerate for at least 12 hours or up to 24 hours.

2 Adjust oven rack to lowest position and heat oven to 325 degrees. Line large roasting pan with aluminum foil. Unwrap roast and brush any excess salt mixture from surface. Season roast with pepper. Set V-rack in roasting pan, spray with vegetable oil spray, and place roast on rack. Add 1 quart water to roasting pan.

3 Cook roast, basting twice during cooking, until roast is extremely tender and pork near (but not touching) bone registers 190 degrees, 5 to 6 hours. (If pan begins to smoke and sizzle, add additional water.) Transfer roast to carving board and let rest for 1 hour. Transfer liquid in roasting pan to fat separator and let liquid settle for 5 minutes. Pour off ¼ cup jus and set aside; discard fat and reserve remaining jus for another use.

4 For the peach sauce Bring peaches, wine, sugar, ¼ cup vinegar, ¼ cup defatted jus, and thyme sprigs to simmer in small saucepan; cook, stirring occasionally, until reduced to 2 cups, about 30 minutes. Stir in remaining 1 tablespoon vinegar and mustard. Discard thyme sprigs, cover, and keep warm.

5 Using sharp paring knife, cut around inverted T-shaped bone until it can be pulled free from pork (use clean dish towel to grasp bone). Slice pieces of pork into ¼-inch-thick slices. Serve, passing sauce separately.

Slow-Roasted Pork Shoulder with Cherry Sauce

Substitute 10 ounces fresh or frozen pitted cherries for peaches, red wine for white wine, and red wine vinegar for rice vinegar, and add ¼ cup ruby port along with defatted jus. Increase granulated sugar to ¾ cup, omit thyme sprigs and mustard, and reduce mixture to 1½ cups.

CUBAN-STYLE OVEN-ROASTED PORK SHOULDER

serves 8 to 12

Pork and Brine

1 (7- to 8-pound) bone-in, skin-on pork picnic shoulder

3 cups sugar

2 cups salt

4 cups orange juice

2 garlic heads, unpeeled cloves separated and crushed

Garlic-Citrus Paste

12 garlic cloves, chopped coarse

2 tablespoons ground cumin

2 tablespoons dried oregano

1 tablespoon salt

1½ teaspoons pepper

6 tablespoons orange juice

2 tablespoons distilled white vinegar

2 tablespoons extra-virgin olive oil

Why This Recipe Works Roast pork marinated in citrus juices, garlic, olive oil, and spices, or *lechon asado*, might just be the star of Cuban cuisine. Traditionally, it's a whole spit-roasted pig, but we wanted to re-create this bold-flavored dish—with its crackling-crisp skin, tender meat, and bracing garlic-citrus sauce—using a smaller cut and an indoor cooking method. We started by choosing picnic shoulder, an inexpensive, fatty, bone-in cut that comes with a generous amount of skin attached. We used both a brine-marinade hybrid and a wet paste to flavor our pork; the "brinerade" penetrated deep into the meat, while the paste held fast to the exterior of the pork and yielded a crisp crust. Cooking the pork in the oven instead of on the grill made it much more hands-off; we could leave it on a wire rack set in a rimmed baking sheet for 6 hours at a relatively low temperature (325 degrees) without needing to replenish any charcoal or constantly adjust the heat. The only work that needed to happen while the meat was in the oven was a single flip-over halfway through the cooking time, which gave us plenty of time to make the traditional accompaniment, a bright citrusy sauce full of garlic and seasonings. Note that this recipe requires refrigerating the brined pork for at least 18 hours or up to 24 hours before cooking (a longer time is preferable). Let the meat rest for a full hour before serving it or it will not be sufficiently tender. The pork's crisp skin should be served along with the meat. Traditional accompaniments include black beans, rice, and fried plantains. Serve with Mojo Sauce (recipe follows).

1 For the pork and brine Cut 1-inch-deep slits (about 1 inch long), spaced about 2 inches apart, all over pork. Dissolve sugar and salt in 6 quarts cold water in large container. Stir in orange juice and garlic. Submerge roast in brine, cover, and refrigerate for at least 18 hours or up to 24 hours. Remove roast from brine and pat dry with paper towels.

2 For the garlic-citrus paste Pulse garlic, cumin, oregano, salt, and pepper in food processor until coarse paste forms, about 10 pulses. With processor running, add orange juice, vinegar, and oil and process until smooth, about 20 seconds. Rub paste all over roast and into slits. Wrap roast in plastic wrap and let sit at room temperature for 1 hour.

3 Adjust oven rack to lower-middle position and heat oven to 325 degrees. Line rimmed baking sheet with aluminum foil. Place paste-rubbed roast, skin side down, on wire rack and roast for 3 hours. Flip roast skin side up and continue to roast until extremely tender and pork near (but not touching) bone registers 190 degrees, about 3 hours, lightly tenting with aluminum foil if skin begins to get too dark.

4 Transfer roast to carving board and let rest for 1 hour. Remove skin in 1 large piece. Scrape off and discard top layer of fat, then cut pork away from bone in 3 or 4 large pieces. Slice pieces of pork into ¼-inch-thick slices. Scrape excess fat from underside of skin and cut skin into strips. Serve.

MOJO SAUCE
makes 1 cup

The sauce can be made while the pork is resting.

½ cup extra-virgin olive oil
4 garlic cloves, minced
4 teaspoons salt
½ teaspoon ground cumin
¼ cup distilled white vinegar
¼ cup orange juice
¼ teaspoon dried oregano
⅛ teaspoon pepper

Heat oil in medium saucepan over medium heat until shimmering. Add garlic, salt, and cumin and cook, stirring, until fragrant, about 30 seconds. Off heat, whisk in vinegar, orange juice, oregano, and pepper. Transfer to bowl and let cool completely. Whisk sauce to recombine before serving.

removing skin from oven-roasted pork shoulder

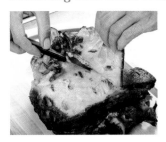

Remove skin from roast in 1 large piece. Scrape off and discard top layer of fat.

CHINESE BARBECUED ROAST PORK SHOULDER

serves 8 to 12

1 (6- to 8-pound) bone-in pork butt roast

1¾ cups sugar

1 cup soy sauce

¾ cup hoisin sauce

½ cup Chinese rice wine or dry sherry

¼ cup grated fresh ginger

2 tablespoons toasted sesame oil

4 garlic cloves, minced

2 teaspoons five-spice powder

½ teaspoon ground white pepper

2 scallions, sliced thin on bias

2 teaspoons rice vinegar, plus extra as needed

Why This Recipe Works Chinese barbecued pork, also known as *char siu*, is a classic Cantonese dish that features succulent pork slathered in a sticky, sweet-salty glaze. Ultraflavorful bone-in pork butt is the traditional cut for this dish, so we followed suit for our homemade version, soaking the meat in a bold marinade of soy sauce, hoisin, Chinese rice wine, ginger, sesame oil, five-spice powder, and white pepper. The sugars in the marinade threatened to overbrown during roasting, so we covered the pork with foil and basted it twice with the drippings collected in the pan below. An hour or so uncovered allowed the pork to take on plenty of flavor-boosting color, and before pulling the roast from the oven we brushed it with a sticky, sweet glaze we prepared by cooking down some additional marinade mixed with extra sugar. While the pork rested, we combined the remaining glaze with the meaty pan drippings and rice vinegar to create a potent sauce for serving. You can substitute dry sherry for Chinese rice wine. Let the meat rest for a full hour before serving or it will not be sufficiently tender. Pork butt roast is often labeled Boston butt in the supermarket. This recipe requires refrigerating the marinated pork for at least 12 hours or up to 24 hours before cooking (a longer time is preferable).

1 Using sharp knife, cut slits 1 inch apart in crosshatch pattern in fat cap of roast, being careful not to cut into meat. Whisk 1 cup sugar, soy sauce, hoisin, rice wine, ginger, oil, garlic, five-spice powder, and pepper together in bowl. Measure out and reserve 1½ cups marinade. Transfer pork butt to 1-gallon zipper-lock bag and pour in remaining marinade. Press out as much air as possible from bag and seal; refrigerate roast for at least 12 hours or up to 24 hours, flipping pork butt halfway through marinating.

2 Whisk reserved marinade and remaining ¾ cup sugar together in medium saucepan. Bring to simmer over medium heat and cook, stirring occasionally, until sugar has dissolved and glaze has thickened and measures about 2 cups, about 2 minutes.

3 Adjust oven rack to lowest position and heat oven to 325 degrees. Set V-rack in large roasting pan and spray with vegetable oil spray. Remove pork butt from marinade, letting excess drip off, and place fat side up on prepared V-rack. Add 4 cups water to pan.

4 Cover pan with aluminum foil and roast for 4 hours, basting pork butt halfway through roasting. Uncover, baste pork butt, and continue to roast until extremely tender and pork near (but not touching) bone registers 190 degrees, 1 to 2 hours. (If pan begins to smoke and sizzle, add additional water.)

5 Brush pork butt with ⅓ cup glaze and roast for 20 minutes, brushing pork with glaze twice more during roasting. Transfer pork butt to carving board and let rest for 1 hour.

6 Transfer liquid in roasting pan to fat separator and let settle for 5 minutes. Combine remaining glaze, ¼ cup defatted liquid, scallions, and vinegar in serving bowl; discard remaining liquid. Season sauce with extra vinegar to taste. Using sharp paring knife, cut around inverted T-shaped bone until it can be pulled free from pork (use clean dish towel to grasp bone). Slice pieces of pork into ¼-inch-thick slices. Serve, passing sauce separately.

PORCHETTA

serves 8 to 10

3 tablespoons fennel seeds

½ cup fresh rosemary leaves
(2 bunches)

¼ cup fresh thyme leaves (2 bunches)

12 garlic cloves, peeled

Kosher salt and pepper

½ cup extra-virgin olive oil

1 (5- to 6-pound) boneless pork
butt roast

¼ teaspoon baking soda

Why This Recipe Works In this recipe, we took Italy's *porchetta*—aromatic, tender, rich, slow-cooked pork that is traditionally served with pieces of crisp skin on a crusty roll—and turned it into a holiday-worthy roast. As a substitute for the whole pig that is usually slow-roasted over a wood fire, we opted for easy-to-find pork butt, which offered the right balance of meat and fatty richness. For quicker cooking we cut the roast into two pieces and tied each into a compact cylinder. To season the meat we cut slits in the exterior; coated it with salt and an intensely flavored paste of garlic, rosemary, and fennel; and let it sit overnight in the refrigerator. A two-stage cooking method gave us the perfect combination of moist, juicy meat and crispy crust. We also cut a crosshatch in the fat cap and rubbed it with a mixture of salt and baking soda to help dry it out and crisp up. Pork butt roast is often labeled Boston butt in the supermarket. Look for a roast with a substantial fat cap. If fennel seeds are unavailable, substitute ¼ cup of ground fennel. This recipe requires refrigerating the rubbed pork for at least 6 hours or up to 24 hours before cooking (a longer time is preferable). For how to tie a roast, see page 15.

1 Grind fennel seeds in spice grinder or mortar and pestle until finely ground. Transfer ground fennel to food processor and add rosemary, thyme, garlic, 1 tablespoon pepper, and 2 teaspoons salt. Pulse mixture until finely chopped, 10 to 15 pulses. Add oil and process until smooth paste forms, 20 to 30 seconds.

2 Using sharp knife, cut slits 1 inch apart in crosshatch pattern in fat cap of roast, being careful not to cut into meat. Cut roast in half with grain into 2 equal pieces.

3 Turn each roast on its side so fat cap is facing away from you, bottom of roast is facing toward you, and newly cut side is facing up. Starting 1 inch from short end of each roast, use boning or paring knife to make slit that starts 1 inch from top of roast and ends 1 inch from bottom, pushing knife completely through roast. Repeat making slits, spaced 1 to 1½ inches apart, along length of each roast, stopping 1 inch from opposite end (you should have 6 to 8 slits, depending on size of roast).

4 Turn roast so fat cap is facing down. Rub sides and bottom of each roast with 2 teaspoons salt, taking care to work salt into slits from both sides. Rub herb paste onto sides and bottom of each roast, taking care to work paste into slits from both sides. Flip roast so that fat cap is facing up. Tie each roast with kitchen twine at 1½-inch intervals into compact cylinder.

5 Combine 1 tablespoon salt, 1 teaspoon pepper, and baking soda in small bowl. Rub fat cap of each roast with salt–baking soda mixture, taking care to work mixture into crosshatches. Refrigerate roasts, uncovered, for at least 6 hours or up to 24 hours.

6 Adjust oven rack to middle position and heat oven to 325 degrees. Transfer roasts, fat side up, to large roasting pan, leaving at least 2 inches between roasts. Cover tightly with aluminum foil. Cook until extremely tender and pork registers 180 degrees, 2 to 2½ hours.

7 Remove pan from oven and increase oven temperature to 500 degrees. Carefully remove and discard foil and transfer roasts to large plate. Discard liquid in pan. Line pan with foil. Remove twine from roasts; return roasts to pan, directly on foil; and return pan to oven. Cook until well browned and pork registers 190 degrees, 20 to 30 minutes. Transfer roasts to carving board and let rest for 20 minutes. Slice roasts into ½-inch-thick slices. Serve.

CRISPY SLOW-ROASTED PORK BELLY

serves 8 to 10

Pork

1 (3-pound) skin-on center-cut fresh pork belly, about 1½ inches thick

Kosher salt

2 tablespoons packed dark brown sugar

Vegetable oil

Mustard Sauce

⅔ cup Dijon mustard

⅓ cup cider vinegar

¼ cup packed dark brown sugar

1 tablespoon hot sauce

1 teaspoon Worcestershire sauce

Why This Recipe Works Pork belly is a boneless cut featuring alternating layers of deeply flavorful, well-marbled meat and buttery fat which, when properly cooked, turn silky and sumptuous, with a crisp crown of skin. To tackle this special cut, we started by scoring the skin and rubbing it with a mixture of salt and brown sugar. We then air-dried the belly overnight in the refrigerator to dehydrate the skin. Roasting the pork belly low and slow further dried the skin and broke down the tough collagen, making the meat juicy and supple. We finished by frying the belly skin side down, which caused it to dramatically puff up and crisp. A quick, bracing mustard sauce balanced the richness of the belly. This recipe requires refrigerating the seasoned pork belly for at least 12 hours or up to 24 hours before cooking (a longer time is preferable). Be sure to ask for a flat, rectangular center-cut section of skin-on pork belly that's 1½ inches thick with roughly equal amounts of meat and fat. Serve with white rice and steamed greens or boiled potatoes and salad.

1 For the pork Using sharp chef's knife, slice pork belly lengthwise into 3 strips about 2 inches wide, then cut slits, spaced 1 inch apart in crosshatch pattern, in surface fat layer, being careful not to cut into meat. Combine 2 tablespoons salt and sugar in bowl. Rub salt mixture into bottom and sides of pork belly (do not rub into skin). Season skin of each strip evenly with ½ teaspoon salt. Place pork belly, skin side up, in 13 by 9-inch baking dish and refrigerate, uncovered, for at least 12 hours or up to 24 hours.

2 Adjust oven rack to middle position and heat oven to 250 degrees. Set wire rack in rimmed baking sheet and spray with vegetable oil spray. Transfer pork belly, skin side up, to wire rack and roast until pork registers 195 degrees and paring knife inserted in pork meets little resistance, 3 to 3½ hours, rotating sheet halfway through roasting.

3 For the mustard sauce Whisk all ingredients together in bowl; set aside.

4 Transfer pork belly, skin side up, to large plate. (Pork belly can be held at room temperature for up to 1 hour.) Pour fat from sheet into 1-cup liquid measuring cup. Add vegetable oil as needed to equal 1 cup and transfer to 12-inch skillet. Arrange pork belly, skin side down, in skillet (strips can be sliced in half crosswise if skillet won't fit strips whole) and place over medium heat until bubbles form around pork belly. Continue to fry, tilting skillet occasionally to even out hot spots, until skin puffs, crisps, and turns golden, 6 to 10 minutes. Transfer pork belly, skin side up, to carving board and let rest for 5 minutes. Flip pork belly skin side down and slice ½ inch thick (being sure to slice through original score marks). Reinvert slices and serve with sauce.

Crispy Slow-Roasted Pork Belly with Tangy Hoisin Sauce

Omit mustard sauce. Whisk ½ cup hoisin, 4 teaspoons rice vinegar, 1 teaspoon grated fresh ginger, and 2 thinly sliced scallions together in bowl and serve with pork.

ROAST COUNTRY HAM

serves 12 to 15

Ham

1 (13- to 15-pound) 3- to 6-month-old bone-in country ham

½ cup packed light brown sugar

1 tablespoon dry mustard

2 teaspoons pepper

Jezebel Sauce

⅓ cup pineapple preserves

⅓ cup apple jelly

⅓ cup yellow mustard

⅓ cup prepared horseradish

1½ teaspoons pepper

¼ teaspoon cayenne pepper

Why This Recipe Works Tradition dictates that country ham—the South's salty, aged cousin to today's spiral-cut hams—requires lengthy soaking before it gets scored and roasted in the oven. We were ready to follow suit until we discovered that soaking the ham neither drew out excess salt nor increased moisture—the long-accepted reasoning behind this time-consuming prep. Working with country hams aged between three and six months, we skipped the soaking altogether. We scrubbed off the mold (a normal result of the aging process), trimmed off the skin, and scored the surface, and then moved the ham right to the oven. We placed the ham fat side up in a roasting pan and ensured plenty of moisture-boosting steam by pouring in water and covering the pan with aluminum foil. After baking the ham for 4 to 5 hours, we mixed together a glaze of brown sugar, dry mustard, and pepper and rubbed it over the ham's surface. We returned the ham to the oven for a few more minutes to set the glaze and then let it rest on a carving board before slicing. In record time, we had moist slices of country ham with a crusty sugar coating on our plates, which paired perfectly with the traditional spicy-sweet Jezebel sauce. Use hams aged six months or less for this recipe. Mold on country ham is not a sign of spoilage; it is a natural effect of the curing and aging process. Serve the ham on biscuits. Leftover ham is delicious in scrambled eggs, cheese grits, and macaroni and cheese.

1 **For the ham** Adjust oven rack to middle position and heat oven to 325 degrees. Using clean, stiff-bristled brush, scrub ham under cold running water to remove any surface mold. Transfer ham to cutting board and trim off dry meat, skin, and all but ¼ inch of fat. Using sharp knife, cut slits ½ inch apart in crosshatch pattern in fat cap of ham, being careful not to cut into meat.

2 Transfer ham to large roasting pan fat side up, add 4 cups water, and cover pan tightly with aluminum foil. Roast until thickest part of meat registers 140 degrees, 4 to 5 hours. Remove ham from oven, discard foil, and increase oven temperature to 450 degrees.

3 Combine sugar, mustard, and pepper in bowl and rub over top of ham. Return ham to oven and cook, uncovered, until glazed and lacquered, 12 to 17 minutes. Transfer ham to carving board and let rest for 30 minutes.

4 **For the Jezebel sauce** Combine all ingredients in blender and process until smooth, 20 to 30 seconds. Carve ham into thin slices and serve with sauce.

cutting a crosshatch pattern into the fat cap

Using sharp knife, cut slits ½ inch apart and ¼ inch deep in cross-hatch pattern in fat cap of ham, being careful not to cut into meat.

SLOW-ROASTED FRESH HAM

serves 12 to 14

1 (8- to 10-pound) skin-on bone-in shank-end fresh ham

⅓ cup packed brown sugar

⅓ cup kosher salt

3 tablespoons minced fresh rosemary

1 tablespoon minced fresh thyme

1 turkey-size oven bag

2 tablespoons maple syrup

2 tablespoons molasses

1 tablespoon soy sauce

1 tablespoon Dijon mustard

1 teaspoon pepper

Why This Recipe Works Unlike the hams that most people are familiar with, fresh ham is neither cured nor smoked. This big cut is basically just an oddly shaped bone-in, skin-on pork roast, and slow roasting turned it tender and flavorful. In order to make it easier to season the meat, we removed its thick skin, cut slits into the fat underneath (including one bigger pocket in the meat end of the ham), and rubbed it all over with salt, sugar, and herbs. Roasting the ham in an oven bag helped it retain plenty of moisture. A simple tangy glaze brushed on toward the end of roasting made for a flavorful finish. Be sure to cut a slit in the oven bag so it doesn't burst. This recipe requires a turkey-size oven bag. This recipe requires refrigerating the rubbed ham for at least 12 hours or up to 24 hours before cooking (a longer time is preferable).

1 Place ham flat side down on cutting board. Using sharp knife, remove skin, leaving ½- to ¼-inch layer of fat intact. Cut slits 1 inch apart in crosshatch pattern in surface fat layer, being careful not to cut into meat. Place ham on its side. Cut one 4-inch horizontal pocket about 2 inches deep in center of flat side of ham, being careful not to poke through opposite side.

2 Combine sugar, salt, rosemary, and thyme in bowl. Rub half of sugar mixture in ham pocket. Tie 1 piece of kitchen twine tightly around base of ham. Rub exterior of ham with remaining sugar mixture. Wrap ham tightly in plastic wrap and refrigerate for at least 12 hours or up to 24 hours.

3 Adjust oven rack to lowest position and heat oven to 325 degrees. Set V-rack in large roasting pan and spray with vegetable oil spray. Unwrap ham and place in oven bag flat side down. Tie top of oven bag closed with kitchen twine. Place ham, flat side down, on V-rack and cut ½-inch slit in top of oven bag. Roast until extremely tender and pork near (but not touching) bone registers 160 degrees, 3½ to 5 hours. Remove ham from oven and let rest in oven bag on V-rack for 1 hour. Heat oven to 450 degrees.

4 Whisk maple syrup, molasses, soy sauce, mustard, and pepper together in bowl. Cut off top of oven bag and push down with tongs, allowing accumulated juices to spill into roasting pan; discard oven bag. Leave ham sitting flat side down on V-rack.

5 Brush ham with half of glaze and roast for 10 minutes. Brush ham with remaining glaze, rotate pan, and roast until deep amber color, about 10 minutes. Move ham to carving board, flat side down, and let rest for 30 minutes. Pour pan juices into fat separator and let liquid settle 5 minutes. Carve ham into ¼-inch-thick slices, arrange on serving dish, and moisten lightly with defatted pan juices. Serve, passing remaining pan juices separately.

seasoning a fresh ham

1 Place ham on its side. With sharp knife, carefully cut a horizontal pocket about 2 inches deep in center of flat side of ham.

2 For deep seasoning, rub half of sugar mixture into ham pocket.

GLAZED SPIRAL-SLICED ROAST HAM

serves 12 to 14

Ham

1 (7- to 10-pound) spiral-sliced bone-in ham

1 turkey-size oven bag

Cherry-Port Glaze

½ cup ruby port

1 cup packed dark brown sugar

½ cup cherry preserves

1 teaspoon pepper

Why This Recipe Works Cooking a spiral-sliced ham is appealingly simple; you just throw it in the oven, brush on a sweet glaze, and wait. To guarantee moist, tender meat and a glaze that complemented (but didn't overwhelm) the ham, we knew we had to start with the right ham. Bone-in hams labeled "with natural juices" have the best flavor. Using an oven bag reduced the cooking time and also helped the ham retain moisture. We determined that it was best to apply our simple, syrupy glaze toward the end of cooking and then again once the ham came out of the oven for the best savory-sweet lacquer. Be sure to cut slits in the oven bag so it doesn't burst. This recipe requires a turkey-size oven bag. You can bypass the 1½-hour sitting time, but the roasting time will increase to 18 to 20 minutes per pound for a cold ham. Our favorite spiral-sliced ham is Johnston County Spiral-Sliced Smoked Ham.

1 **For the ham** Place ham in oven bag. Gather top of bag tightly so bag fits snugly around ham, tie bag with kitchen twine, and trim excess plastic. Set ham, cut side down, in large roasting pan and cut 4 slits in top of bag with paring knife. Let ham sit at room temperature for 1½ hours.

2 Adjust oven rack to lowest position and heat oven to 250 degrees. Roast ham until center registers 100 degrees, 1 to 1½ hours (about 10 minutes per pound).

3 **For the cherry-port glaze** Simmer port in small saucepan over medium heat until reduced to 2 tablespoons, about 5 minutes. Add sugar, preserves, and pepper and cook, stirring occasionally, until sugar dissolves and mixture is thick, syrupy, and reduced to 1 cup, 5 to 10 minutes; set aside.

4 Remove ham from oven and increase oven temperature to 350 degrees. Cut open oven bag and roll back sides to expose ham. Brush ham with one-third of glaze and return to oven until glaze becomes sticky, about 10 minutes (if glaze is too thick to brush, return to heat to loosen).

5 Remove ham from oven, transfer to carving board, brush entire ham with one-third of glaze, and let rest for 30 minutes. While ham rests, add 4 to 6 tablespoons ham juices to remaining one-third of glaze and cook over medium heat until thick but fluid sauce forms. Carve ham and serve, passing sauce separately.

Maple-Orange Glaze

Omit cherry-port glaze. Combine ¾ cup maple syrup, ½ cup orange marmalade, 2 tablespoons unsalted butter, 1 tablespoon Dijon mustard, 1 teaspoon pepper, and ¼ teaspoon cinnamon in small saucepan and simmer over medium heat until mixture is thick, syrupy, and reduced to 1 cup, 5 to 10 minutes.

Apple-Ginger Glaze

Omit cherry-port glaze. Combine 1 cup packed dark brown sugar, ¾ cup apple jelly, 3 tablespoons apple butter, 1 tablespoon grated fresh ginger, and a pinch ground cloves in small saucepan and simmer over medium heat until sugar dissolves and mixture is thick, syrupy, and reduced to 1½ cups, 5 to 10 minutes.

CRUMB-COATED ROAST HAM

serves 12 to 14

1 (7- to 10-pound) spiral-sliced, bone-in ham
1 turkey-size oven bag
1 cup packed brown sugar
½ cup spicy brown mustard
½ cup balsamic vinegar
2 tablespoons dry mustard
2 teaspoons ground ginger
¼ teaspoon ground cloves
1½ cups panko bread crumbs
½ cup minced fresh parsley
3 tablespoons vegetable oil
¼ teaspoon salt
¼ teaspoon pepper

Why This Recipe Works For a fresh take on spiral-sliced ham, we added a crispy, well-seasoned crumb coating to the exterior. In order to keep the meat moist and avoid any sogginess in the bread crumbs, we started the ham on its own in a low oven. We baked the ham under—not in—an oven bag so we could easily pull it off and apply our crumb coating once the meat was thoroughly warmed through. We then painted on a superconcentrated spicy-sweet glaze and pressed on a mixture of crunchy panko bread crumbs, salt, pepper, and fresh parsley. Once the ham was in the oven, we stirred together a slightly spicy no-cook mustard sauce that was the perfect complement to the flavors of the glazed and coated ham. Our favorite spiral-sliced ham is Johnston County Spiral-Sliced Smoked Ham. This recipe requires a turkey-size oven bag. You can bypass the 1½-hour sitting time, but the roasting time will increase to 18 to 20 minutes per pound for a cold ham. Serve the ham with Hot Mustard Sauce (recipe follows).

1 Set wire rack in aluminum foil–lined rimmed baking sheet. Place 12-inch square of foil in center of wire rack. Set ham on foil, flat side down, and cover with oven bag, tucking bag under ham to secure it. Let ham sit at room temperature for 1½ hours.

2 Adjust oven rack to lowest position and heat oven to 325 degrees. Roast ham until center registers 100 degrees, about 2 hours. (Lift bag to take temperature; do not puncture.)

3 Meanwhile, combine sugar, brown mustard, vinegar, dry mustard, ginger, and cloves in medium saucepan and bring to boil over medium-high heat. Reduce heat to medium-low and simmer until reduced to ¾ cup, 15 to 20 minutes. Let cool while ham cooks.

4 Combine panko, parsley, oil, salt, and pepper in bowl. Remove ham from oven, remove and discard oven bag, and let ham cool for 5 minutes. Increase oven temperature to 400 degrees.

5 Brush ham all over with brown sugar–mustard glaze. Press panko mixture against sides of ham to coat evenly. Roast until crumbs are deep golden brown, 20 to 30 minutes. Transfer ham, flat side down, to carving board and let rest for 30 minutes. Carve and serve.

HOT MUSTARD SAUCE
makes about 1 cup
The longer this sauce sits, the milder it becomes.

3 tablespoons water
2 tablespoons dry mustard
½ teaspoon salt
½ cup Dijon mustard
2 tablespoons honey

Whisk water, dry mustard, and salt in bowl until smooth; let sit for 15 minutes. Whisk in Dijon mustard and honey. Cover and let sit at room temperature for at least 2 hours before using. (Sauce can be refrigerated for up to 2 months.)

ROASTED RACK OF LAMB

serves 4 to 6

Lamb

2 (1¾- to 2-pound) racks of lamb, fat trimmed to ⅛ to ¼ inch and rib bones frenched

Kosher salt

1 teaspoon ground cumin

1 teaspoon vegetable oil

Red Pepper Relish

½ cup jarred roasted red peppers, rinsed, patted dry, and chopped fine

½ cup minced fresh parsley

¼ cup extra-virgin olive oil

¼ teaspoon lemon juice

⅛ teaspoon garlic, minced to paste

Kosher salt and pepper

Why This Recipe Works With elegantly curved rib bones attached to a long, lean loin, rack of lamb is as grand as any beef roast or whole bird, but it cooks much faster and its small size makes it ideal for fewer guests. Its tenderness and mild flavor also make it approachable for those who may be wary of lamb. Our roasting method delivers uniformly rosy meat and is as simple as arranging the lamb on a wire rack set in a baking sheet. We first cut a shallow crosshatch into the racks' fat caps and rubbed the surface with a blend of kosher salt and ground cumin to give the lamb deep flavor. While the meat roasted, we pulled together a bold relish to serve alongside it. Then, to give the racks a flavorful brown crust, we seared them quickly in a skillet just before serving. We prefer the subtler flavor and larger size of lamb labeled "domestic" or "American," but you may substitute lamb imported from New Zealand or Australia. Since imported racks are generally smaller, in step 1 season each rack with ½ teaspoon of the salt mixture and reduce the cooking time to 50 minutes to 1 hour 10 minutes. We prefer this rack of lamb cooked to medium-rare, but if you prefer it more or less done, see our guidelines on page 24.

1 For the lamb Adjust oven rack to middle position and heat oven to 250 degrees. Using sharp knife, cut slits ½ inch apart in crosshatch pattern in fat cap of lamb, being careful not to cut into meat. Combine 2 tablespoons salt and cumin in bowl. Rub ¾ teaspoon salt mixture over entire surface of each rack and into slits. Reserve remaining salt mixture. Place racks, bone side down, on wire rack set in rimmed baking sheet. Roast until lamb registers 125 degrees (for medium-rare), 1 hour 5 minutes to 1 hour 25 minutes.

2 For the red pepper relish Meanwhile, combine red peppers, parsley, oil, lemon juice, and garlic in bowl. Season with salt and pepper to taste. Set aside at room temperature for at least 1 hour.

3 Heat oil in 12-inch skillet over high heat until just smoking. Place 1 rack, bone side up, in skillet and cook until well browned, 1 to 2 minutes. Transfer to carving board. Pour off all but 1 teaspoon fat from skillet and repeat browning with second rack. Let racks rest 20 minutes. Cut between ribs to separate chops and sprinkle cut side of chops with ½ teaspoon salt mixture. Serve, passing relish and remaining salt mixture separately.

Sweet Mint-Almond Relish

Substitute ground anise for cumin in salt mixture. Omit red pepper relish. Combine ½ cup minced fresh mint; ¼ cup sliced almonds, toasted and chopped fine; ¼ cup extra-virgin olive oil; 2 tablespoons red currant jelly; 4 teaspoons red wine vinegar; and 2 teaspoons Dijon mustard in bowl. Season with salt and pepper to taste. Let sit at room temperature for at least 1 hour before serving.

ROAST BONELESS LEG OF LAMB WITH GARLIC, HERB, AND BREAD-CRUMB CRUST

serves 6 to 8

1 slice hearty white sandwich bread

¼ cup extra-virgin olive oil

¼ cup minced fresh parsley

3 tablespoons minced fresh rosemary

2 tablespoons minced fresh thyme

3 garlic cloves, peeled

1 ounce Parmesan cheese, grated (½ cup)

1 (3½- to 4-pound) boneless half leg of lamb, trimmed, and pounded to ¾-inch thickness

Salt and pepper

1 tablespoon Dijon mustard

Why This Recipe Works A boneless leg of lamb is an easy shortcut to a great roast dinner—as long as you treat it correctly. We started by pounding it to an even thickness. Next we introduced extra flavor and textural interest to the roast. First, we made a potent herb and garlic paste. We spread a portion of the paste over the lamb before rolling up and tying the roast so it would infuse the lamb with flavor from the inside out. The rest of the herb paste was combined with fresh bread crumbs and Parmesan. A quick sear on the stovetop jump-started the cooking process and ensured our lamb would have a golden-brown crust. After searing, we moved the roast to a 375-degree oven, which was perfect for cooking the meat to a juicy, tender medium-rare. Partway through cooking, we took the roast out of the oven, removed the twine, brushed the meat with zingy Dijon mustard, and applied the bread-crumb mixture. This ensured that the crust wouldn't peel off with the twine but also gave the tied lamb enough roasting time to hold its shape when we removed the twine, resulting in perfect slices with a crunchy, savory crust. We prefer the sirloin end rather than the shank end for this recipe, though either will work well. We prefer the subtler flavor and larger size of lamb labeled "domestic" or "American," but you may substitute lamb imported from New Zealand or Australia. Leg of lamb is often sold in elastic netting that must be removed. We prefer this roast cooked to medium-rare, but if you prefer it more or less done, see our guidelines on page 24. For how to tie a roast, see page 12.

1 Adjust oven rack to lower-middle position and heat oven to 375 degrees. Pulse bread in food processor until coarsely ground, about 10 pulses (you should have about 1 cup crumbs). Transfer to bowl and set aside. Process 1 teaspoon oil, parsley, rosemary, thyme, and garlic in now-empty processor until minced, scraping down sides of bowl as needed, about 1 minute. Transfer 1½ tablespoons herb mixture to bowl and reserve. Scrape remaining mixture into bowl of bread crumbs; stir in Parmesan and 1 tablespoon oil and set aside.

2 Lay roast on cutting board with rough interior side (which was against bone) facing up, rub with 2 teaspoons oil, and season with salt and pepper. Spread reserved herb mixture evenly over lamb, leaving 1-inch border around edge. Roll roast and tie with kitchen twine at 1½-inch intervals. Season roast with salt and pepper, then rub with 1 tablespoon oil.

3 Set wire rack in rimmed baking sheet. Heat remaining 1 tablespoon oil in 12-inch skillet over medium-high heat until just smoking. Brown roast well on all sides, about 10 minutes. Transfer to prepared rack and roast until lamb registers 120 degrees, 30 to 35 minutes. Transfer roast to carving board; remove twine. Brush roast exterior with mustard, then carefully press bread-crumb mixture onto top and sides of roast with your hands, pressing firmly to form solid, even coating that adheres to roast. Return coated roast to prepared rack; roast until lamb registers 125 degrees (for medium-rare), 15 to 25 minutes. Transfer roast to carving board and let for rest 20 minutes. Slice roast into ½-inch-thick slices. Serve.

HARISSA-RUBBED ROAST BONELESS LEG OF LAMB WITH WARM CAULIFLOWER SALAD

serves 6 to 8

½ cup extra-virgin olive oil

6 garlic cloves, minced

2 tablespoons paprika

1 tablespoon ground coriander

1 tablespoon ground dried Aleppo pepper

1 teaspoon ground cumin

¾ teaspoon caraway seeds

Salt and pepper

1 (3½- to 4-pound) boneless half leg of lamb, trimmed, and pounded to ¾-inch thickness

1 head cauliflower (2 pounds), cored and cut into 1-inch florets

½ red onion, sliced ¼ inch thick

1 cup shredded carrots

½ cup raisins

¼ cup fresh cilantro leaves

2 tablespoons sliced almonds, toasted

1 tablespoon lemon juice, plus extra for seasoning

Why This Recipe Works The robust, fragrant flavor profile of North African cuisine is another perfect pairing with rich, meaty lamb. We again took advantage of the broad surface area of a boneless leg of lamb by rubbing it with Tunisian-inspired harissa paste. We bloomed paprika, coriander, Aleppo pepper, cumin, caraway, and garlic in oil in the microwave and applied our quick homemade harissa to the inside of the leg before rolling it up and tying it to make a compact roast. We seared the exterior of the meat on all sides to build up some browning before moving the lamb to the oven where it finished roasting to a juicy medium-rare. We also applied more of the harissa to the outside of the roast in between the two cooking steps. Then, to keep the flavorful fat and fond from going to waste, we prepared a quick vegetable side while the roast rested by tossing cauliflower florets with the pan drippings and roasting them until they were tender and browned. Combining the warm cauliflower with shredded carrots, sweet raisins, cilantro, and toasted almonds produced a side that paired perfectly with the fragrant, richly spiced lamb. If you can't find Aleppo pepper, you can substitute ¾ teaspoon paprika and ¾ teaspoon finely chopped red pepper flakes. Leg of lamb is often sold in elastic netting that must be removed. We prefer this roast cooked to medium-rare, but if you prefer it more or less done, see our guidelines on page 24. For how to tie a roast, see page 12.

1 Combine 6 tablespoons oil, garlic, paprika, coriander, Aleppo pepper, cumin, caraway seeds, and 1 teaspoon salt in bowl and microwave until bubbling and very fragrant, about 1 minute, stirring halfway through microwaving. Let cool to room temperature.

2 Adjust oven rack to lower-middle position and heat oven to 375 degrees. Set V-rack in large roasting pan and spray with vegetable oil spray. Lay roast on cutting board with rough interior side (which was against bone) facing up and rub with 2 tablespoons spice paste. Roll roast and tie with kitchen twine at 1½-inch intervals, then rub exterior with 1 table-spoon oil.

3 Heat remaining 1 tablespoon oil in 12-inch skillet over medium-high heat until just smoking. Brown lamb on all sides, about 8 minutes. Brush lamb all over with remaining spice paste and place fat side down in prepared V-rack.

Roast until thickest part registers 125 degrees (for medium-rare), flipping lamb halfway through roasting. Transfer lamb to carving board, tent with aluminum foil, and let rest while making salad.

4 Increase oven temperature to 475 degrees. Pour all but 3 tablespoons fat from pan; discard any charred drippings. Add cauliflower, ½ teaspoon salt, and ½ teaspoon pepper to pan and toss to coat. Cover with aluminum foil and roast until cauliflower is softened, about 5 minutes.

5 Remove foil and spread onion evenly over cauliflower. Roast until vegetables are tender and cauliflower is golden brown, 10 to 15 minutes, stirring halfway through roasting. Transfer vegetable mixture to serving bowl, add carrots, raisins, cilantro, almonds, and lemon juice and toss to combine. Season with salt, pepper, and lemon juice to taste. Slice leg of lamb into ½-inch-thick slices and serve with salad.

ROAST BUTTERFLIED LEG OF LAMB WITH CORIANDER, CUMIN, AND MUSTARD SEEDS

serves 10 to 12

Lamb

1 (6- to 8-pound) butterflied leg of lamb

Kosher salt

⅓ cup vegetable oil

3 shallots, sliced thin

4 garlic cloves, peeled and smashed

1 (1-inch) piece ginger, sliced into ½-inch-thick rounds and smashed

1 tablespoon coriander seeds

1 tablespoon cumin seeds

1 tablespoon mustard seeds

3 bay leaves

2 (2-inch) strips lemon zest

Sauce

⅓ cup chopped fresh mint

⅓ cup chopped fresh cilantro

1 shallot, minced

2 tablespoons lemon juice

Salt and pepper

Why This Recipe Works Boneless butterflied leg of lamb is pretty much the simplest cut of lamb you can cook. No bones, no tying or rolling, and carving is incredibly simple. The uniform thickness of this cut also encourages even cooking. Our favorite roasting method for boneless butterflied leg of lamb is to start it in a very low oven (just 250 degrees) and then finish with a blast under the broiler for juicy, tender roasted lamb with a burnished, crisp crust. Before cooking, we made sure to remove the sinew and pockets of fat that can hide on this cut. Scoring the fat cap, rubbing the roast with salt and letting it sit for an hour gave us well-seasoned, tender meat. We ditched the usual spice rub (which had a tendency to scorch under the broiler) in favor a slow-cooked spice-infused oil that both seasoned the lamb during cooking and provided the basis for a quick sauce. We prefer the subtler flavor and larger size of lamb labeled "domestic" or "American," but you may substitute lamb imported from New Zealand or Australia. The 2 tablespoons of salt in step 1 is for a 6-pound leg. If using a larger leg (7 to 8 pounds), add an additional teaspoon of salt for every pound. We prefer this roast cooked to medium-rare, but if you prefer it more or less done, see our guidelines on page 24.

1 For the lamb Place roast on cutting board with fat cap facing down. Using sharp knife, trim any pockets of fat and connective tissue from underside of roast. Flip roast over, trim fat cap to between ⅛ and ¼ inch thick, and pound to even 1-inch thickness. Using sharp knife, cut slits ½ inch apart in crosshatch pattern in fat cap of roast, being careful not to cut into meat. Rub 2 tablespoons salt over entire roast and into slits. Let sit, uncovered, at room temperature for 1 hour.

2 Meanwhile, adjust oven racks to upper-middle and lower-middle positions and heat oven to 250 degrees. Stir oil, shallots, garlic, ginger, coriander seeds, cumin seeds, mustard seeds, bay leaves, and lemon zest together in rimmed baking sheet and bake on lower rack until spices are softened and fragrant and shallots and garlic turn golden, about 1 hour. Remove sheet from oven and discard bay leaves.

3 Thoroughly pat roast dry with paper towels and transfer, fat side up, to sheet (directly on top of spices). Roast on lower rack until lamb registers 120 degrees, 30 to 40 minutes. Remove sheet from oven and heat broiler. Broil roast on upper rack until surface is well browned and charred in spots and lamb registers 125 degrees (for medium-rare), 3 to 8 minutes.

4 Remove sheet from oven and transfer roast to carving board (some spices will cling to roast); let rest for 20 minutes.

5 For the sauce Meanwhile, carefully pour pan juices through fine-mesh strainer into medium bowl, pressing on solids to extract as much liquid as possible; discard solids. Stir in mint, cilantro, shallot, and lemon juice. Add any accumulated lamb juices to sauce and season with salt and pepper to taste.

6 With long side facing you, slice roast with grain into 3 equal pieces. Turn each piece and slice against grain into ¼-inch-thick slices. Serve with sauce. (Briefly warm sauce in microwave if it has cooled and thickened.)

Roast Butterflied Leg of Lamb with Coriander, Fennel, and Black Pepper
Substitute 1 tablespoon fennel seeds for cumin seeds and 1 tablespoon black peppercorns for mustard seeds in step 2. Substitute parsley for mint in sauce.

trimming butterflied leg of lamb

Place butterflied lamb on cutting board with fat cap facing down. Using sharp knife, trim fat from meat and remove big pockets of intermuscular fat and connective tissue.

POMEGRANATE-GLAZED ROAST BONE-IN LEG OF LAMB

serves 8 to 10

Lamb

1 (6- to 8-pound) semi-boneless leg of lamb, trimmed

1 tablespoon vegetable oil

Kosher salt and pepper

Pomegranate Glaze

2 cups pomegranate juice

⅓ cup sugar

3 sprigs fresh thyme

Why This Recipe Works A roast bone-in leg of lamb makes an impressive centerpiece for your dinner table. When properly cooked, this hefty cut sports a browned, crusty exterior and juicy, ultrarich meat. Because of its large, awkward shape, stovetop searing isn't an option for this cut, but we found that we got great results using a combination of a low-and-slow roasting technique plus an "oven sear," where we started the lamb in a 250-degree oven before cranking up the heat to 450 degrees for the last 20 minutes so we got exceptionally tender meat as well as a beautifully browned, crisp crust. Adding water to the roasting pan during the high-heat finish helped prevent the pan drippings from burning and smoking out the kitchen. To flavor the lamb, we used a simple Middle Eastern–inspired pomegranate glaze, which we brushed on the meat twice during cooking and a final time before serving for a perfectly lacquered roast. This recipe actually uses a semi-boneless leg of lamb, which is what you most commonly find at the market; if, by chance, the leg has the full bone, have the butcher remove the hipbone and aitchbone for you. We prefer the subtler flavor and larger size of lamb labeled "domestic" or "American," but you may substitute lamb imported from New Zealand or Australia. We prefer this roast cooked to medium-rare, but if you prefer it more or less done, see our guidelines on page 24.

1 **For the lamb** Pat roast dry with paper towels, rub with oil, and season with salt and pepper. Cover roast with plastic wrap and let sit at room temperature for at least 1 hour or up to 2 hours.

2 **For the pomegranate glaze** Meanwhile, simmer pomegranate juice, sugar, and thyme sprigs together in small saucepan over medium heat until thickened and mixture measures about ½ cup, about 20 minutes. Discard thyme sprigs. Measure out and reserve half of glaze for serving.

3 Adjust oven rack to lowest position and heat oven to 250 degrees. Set wire rack inside aluminum foil–lined rimmed baking sheet. Transfer roast to prepared rack, fat side up, and brush with about half of remaining glaze. Roast until meat registers 100 degrees, about 1¾ hours.

4 Brush roast with remaining glaze and pour ¼ cup water into sheet. Increase oven temperature to 450 degrees and roast until lamb registers 125 degrees (for medium-rare), about 20 minutes.

5 Transfer roast to carving board and brush with half of glaze reserved for serving. Let rest for 30 minutes. Brush with remaining glaze reserved for serving and carve roast. Serve.

SEAFOOD

PAN-ROASTED FISH FILLETS

serves 4

4 (6- to 8-ounce) skinless white fish fillets, 1 to 1½ inches thick

Salt and pepper

½ teaspoon sugar

1 tablespoon vegetable oil

Why This Recipe Works Mild-mannered white fish turns flavorful and tender when roasted, and our simple pan-roasting method guarantees moist fillets with an appealing chestnut-brown crust every time. To impart a deep sear without overcooking the fish, we began by browning just one side of thick fillets in a hot nonstick skillet before roasting them in the oven. Sprinkling on some sugar before searing encouraged rapid caramelization on the fillets, trimming the stovetop cooking time down to around a minute. We flipped the fillets browned side up and moved the skillet to a hot 425-degree oven to briefly roast the fish. Within minutes, the fillets were perfectly cooked, emerging nicely browned but still plenty succulent. Thick white fish fillets with a meaty texture, like halibut, cod, sea bass, or red snapper, work best in this recipe. Because most fish fillets differ in thickness, some pieces may finish cooking before others— be sure to immediately remove any fillet that reaches 140 degrees. You will need a 12-inch ovensafe nonstick skillet for this recipe. Serve with lemon wedges, Chermoula Sauce (page 27), Salsa Verde (page 27), Garlic-Herb Compound Butter (page 28), or one of the other accompaniments on pages 27–29, if desired.

1 Adjust oven rack to middle position and heat oven to 425 degrees. Pat fish dry with paper towels, season with salt and pepper, and sprinkle sugar lightly over 1 side of each fillet.

2 Heat oil in 12-inch ovensafe nonstick skillet over high heat until just smoking. Lay fillets sugared side down in skillet and press lightly to ensure even contact with skillet. Cook until browned on first side, 1 to 1½ minutes.

3 Turn fish over using 2 spatulas and transfer skillet to oven. Roast until fish flakes apart when gently prodded with paring knife and registers 140 degrees, 7 to 10 minutes. Serve.

searing and flipping fish fillets

1 Heat oil until just smoking. Place fillets sugared side down and press lightly to ensure even contact with pan.

2 Cook until fillets are just browned, 1 to 1½ minutes. Use 2 spatulas to flip fillets carefully.

LEMON-HERB ROAST COD WITH CRISPY GARLIC POTATOES

serves 4

3 tablespoons extra-virgin olive oil

1½ pounds russet potatoes, unpeeled, sliced into ¼-inch-thick rounds

3 garlic cloves, minced

Salt and pepper

4 (6- to 8-ounce) skinless cod fillets, 1 to 1½ inches thick

3 tablespoons unsalted butter, cut into ¼-inch pieces

4 sprigs fresh thyme

1 lemon, sliced thin

Why This Recipe Works When you want to make something fancier than simple roast cod, look no further than this ingenious recipe, which delivers perfectly roasted fillets and potatoes—all in one sheet pan. We roasted the cod fillets atop beds of shingled sliced spuds to give the quick-cooking fish some insulation. Slicing and microwaving starchy russets with garlic and oil before roasting jump-started their cooking so the potatoes and fish finished at the same time. To infuse the mild cod with flavor, we topped each fillet with butter, thyme sprigs, and slices of lemon, allowing the three components to gently baste and season the cod as it roasted. In the end, we were met with four elegant portions of rich, tender cod and fragrant, crisp potatoes. You can substitute haddock or halibut for the cod.

1 Adjust oven rack to lower-middle position and heat oven to 425 degrees. Brush rimmed baking sheet with 1 tablespoon oil. Combine potatoes, garlic, and remaining 2 tablespoons oil in bowl and season with salt and pepper. Microwave, uncovered, until potatoes are just tender, 12 to 14 minutes.

2 Shingle potatoes into 4 rectangular piles that measure roughly 4 by 6 inches on prepared sheet. Pat cod dry with paper towels, season with salt and pepper, and lay on top of potatoes skinned side down. Place butter, thyme sprigs, and lemon slices on top of cod.

3 Roast until cod flakes apart when gently prodded with paring knife and registers 140 degrees, 15 to 18 minutes. Slide spatula underneath potatoes and cod, gently transfer to plates, and serve.

ROAST COD WITH ARTICHOKES, OLIVES, AND SUN-DRIED TOMATOES

serves 4

3 cups jarred whole baby artichokes packed in water, halved, rinsed, and patted dry

¾ cup oil-packed sun-dried tomatoes, drained, ¼ cup oil reserved

Salt and pepper

½ cup pitted kalamata olives, chopped coarse

1 teaspoon grated lemon zest plus 1 tablespoon juice

4 (6- to 8-ounce) skinless cod fillets, 1 to 1½ inches thick

2 tablespoons chopped fresh basil

Why This Recipe Works For a bold take on roast cod, we created a one-dish meal inspired by the flavors of the Mediterranean. Using the pantry-friendly combination of tender jarred baby artichokes, sweet sun-dried tomatoes, and briny kalamata olives as our base kept prep work light and promised to infuse the mild fish with multiple layers of flavor. We roasted the artichokes first, tossing them with the tomatoes' packing oil to deepen their subtle flavor. We stirred in the sun-dried tomatoes and chopped olives as well as some grated lemon zest before finally nestling in the cod fillets, brushing them with more of the potent tomato oil. The vegetables' flavors melded and flavored the cod as it gently roasted, cooking to perfect tenderness. By the end of its brief roasting time, this fuss-free cod dinner boasted incredible complexity. While we prefer the flavor and texture of jarred whole baby artichokes, you can substitute 18 ounces frozen artichoke hearts, thawed and patted dry, for the jarred. You can substitute haddock or halibut for the cod.

1 Adjust oven rack to middle position and heat oven to 450 degrees. Toss artichokes with 2 tablespoons tomato oil in bowl, season with salt and pepper, and spread into 13 by 9-inch baking dish. Roast artichokes until lightly browned, about 15 minutes.

2 Remove baking dish from oven and stir in olives, lemon zest, tomatoes, and 1 tablespoon tomato oil. Pat cod dry with paper towels and nestle into vegetables. Brush cod with remaining 1 tablespoon tomato oil and season with salt and pepper.

3 Roast until cod flakes apart when gently prodded with paring knife and registers 140 degrees, 15 to 18 minutes. Drizzle with lemon juice, sprinkle with basil, and serve.

ROAST HALIBUT WITH RED POTATOES, CORN, AND ANDOUILLE

serves 4

4 tablespoons unsalted butter, softened

2 teaspoons Old Bay seasoning

1 teaspoon lemon juice

4 (6- to 8-ounce) skinless halibut fillets, 1 to 1½ inches thick

Salt and pepper

¼ cup vegetable oil

1½ pounds small red potatoes, unpeeled, halved

4 ears corn, husks and silk removed, cut into thirds

12 ounces andouille sausage, sliced 1 inch thick

1 tablespoon minced fresh parsley

Why This Recipe Works Much like roasting cod, the best thing about roasting halibut is that it concentrates the mild fish's sweetness in mere minutes, and this dish keeps things efficient even while incorporating multiple sides. Inspired by the spicy, rich flavors of Lowcountry shrimp boils, we paired our roast halibut with smoky andouille sausage, sweet corn, and tender red potatoes. We managed to keep the meal mostly hands-off without letting anything overcook by first roasting the halved potatoes, corn, and andouille in a 500-degree oven. Once the corn's kernels were nicely plumped, we removed the cobs, lowered the temperature to 425 degrees, and made room on the sheet pan for the halibut fillets; the hot pan helped brown the fish as it cooked through. We gave the corn and halibut a rich, authentic finish by slathering them with a citrusy Old Bay compound butter. Use small red potatoes 1 to 2 inches in diameter. You can substitute haddock or cod for the halibut.

1 Adjust oven rack to lowest position and heat oven to 500 degrees. Mash butter, Old Bay, and lemon juice together in bowl; set aside. Pat halibut dry with paper towels and season with salt and pepper; refrigerate until needed.

2 Brush rimmed baking sheet with 1 tablespoon oil. Toss potatoes with 2 tablespoons oil, ¼ teaspoon salt, and ¼ teaspoon pepper in bowl. Arrange potatoes, cut side down, on half of sheet. Toss corn in now-empty bowl with remaining 1 tablespoon oil, ¼ teaspoon salt, and ⅛ teaspoon pepper, then place on empty side of sheet. Nestle andouille onto sheet around corn. Roast until potatoes and andouille are lightly browned and corn kernels are plump, 20 to 25 minutes, rotating sheet halfway through roasting.

3 Remove sheet from oven and reduce oven temperature to 425 degrees. Transfer corn to clean bowl, leaving andouille and potatoes on sheet. Add 2 tablespoons Old Bay butter to corn, toss to coat, and cover bowl tightly with aluminum foil; set aside.

4 Slide andouille to side of sheet with potatoes, then place halibut on now-empty side of sheet. Roast potatoes, andouille, and halibut until fish flakes apart when gently prodded with paring knife and registers 140 degrees, 8 to 10 minutes, rotating sheet halfway through roasting.

5 Remove sheet from oven. Transfer potatoes, andouille, and halibut browned side up to serving dish. Dot remaining Old Bay butter over halibut. Add corn to serving dish, sprinkle with parsley, and serve.

ROASTED CRAB-STUFFED FLOUNDER

serves 6

6 tablespoons unsalted butter

½ onion, chopped fine

½ red bell pepper, chopped fine

1 teaspoon Old Bay seasoning

Salt and pepper

⅛ teaspoon cayenne pepper

1 garlic clove, minced

½ cup heavy cream

1 pound lump crabmeat, picked over for shells and pressed dry between paper towels

¼ cup minced fresh parsley

1 tablespoon lemon juice, plus lemon wedges for serving

12 (2- to 3-ounce) skinless flounder fillets, ¼ to ½ inch thick

1 cup panko bread crumbs

Why This Recipe Works Flounder is a thin, delicate fish, but a measured approach and the right stuffing make it a perfect candidate for roasting. Our version of this New England classic pairs gently roasted fish with a fresh, nuanced crab filling. We kept the filling simple by sautéing some aromatics, cayenne, and Old Bay on the stovetop, adding cream for richness, and folding in the crabmeat before chilling the mixture to meld its flavors. We placed a small mound of the crab stuffing on each flounder fillet, rolled them up, sprinkled them with buttered panko bread crumbs, and roasted the stuffed fillets in a hot oven. In 15 minutes or so we had tender, flaky fillets filled with a creamy stuffing and a touch of crunch from the buttery panko. Do not substitute canned or imitation crab here. Do not use fillets thinner than ¼ inch, as they will overcook quickly. You can substitute sole for the flounder.

1 Melt 3 tablespoons butter in 12-inch nonstick skillet over medium heat. Add onion, bell pepper, Old Bay, ½ teaspoon salt, and cayenne. Cook until vegetables are softened, about 5 minutes. Stir in garlic and cook until fragrant, about 30 seconds. Stir in cream. Bring mixture to boil and cook until very thick, about 3 minutes.

2 Transfer vegetable mixture to bowl and gently fold in crabmeat, 2 tablespoons parsley, and lemon juice. Season with salt and pepper to taste. Refrigerate filling until chilled, about 30 minutes.

3 Adjust oven rack to middle position and heat oven to 400 degrees. Pat flounder dry with paper towels and season with salt and pepper. Place skinned side up on cutting board and mound ¼ cup of filling in middle of each fillet. Fold tapered end of flounder tightly over filling and then fold thicker end of fish over top to make tidy bundle.

4 Spray 13 by 9-inch baking dish with vegetable oil spray and lay fish bundles seam side down in baking dish. Melt remaining 3 tablespoons butter and toss together with panko and remaining 2 tablespoons parsley; sprinkle over bundles.

Roast until panko is golden brown and flounder flakes apart when gently prodded with a paring knife, 15 to 20 minutes. Serve with lemon wedges.

stuffing flounder fillets

1 Place fillets, skinned side up, on cutting board and mound ¼ cup of filling in middle of each fillet.

2 Fold tapered end of flounder tightly over filling and then fold thicker end of fish over top to make tidy bundle.

HONEY-LIME GLAZED ROAST SALMON

serves 4

Honey-Lime Glaze

¼ cup honey

1 teaspoon grated lime zest plus 2 tablespoons juice

1 teaspoon chili powder

½ teaspoon cornstarch

⅛ teaspoon cayenne pepper

Salmon

1 teaspoon packed light brown sugar

¼ teaspoon salt

¼ teaspoon cornstarch

⅛ teaspoon pepper

1 (1¾- to 2-pound) center-cut skin-on salmon fillet, 1½ inches thick

1 teaspoon vegetable oil

Why This Recipe Works While an oven-only approach served our classic roasted salmon fillets (page 54) well, pairing perfectly roasted salmon with a spiced-up honey-lime glaze required a cooking technique all its own. Slashing the skin encouraged it to render and crisp quickly, but we also needed to give the flesh a strong, flavorful crust that would stand up to (as well as hold on to) a thick coating of glaze. Applying a rub of cornstarch and brown sugar to the flesh and searing it in a hot skillet provided that browned crust and firm texture on the double. Once flipped, the skin side needed just a minute to crisp. We spooned the thickened glaze over the fillets and transferred the skillet to a moderate oven where our salmon hit its target temperature in less than 10 minutes. Glossy and appealingly sweet-tart, these fillets were an easy, satisfying upgrade. To ensure uniform pieces of fish, buy a whole center-cut fillet and cut it into four pieces. If your knife is not sharp enough to cut through the skin easily, try a serrated knife. You will need a 12-inch ovensafe nonstick skillet for this recipe.

1 **For the honey-lime glaze** Whisk all ingredients together in small saucepan and simmer over medium-high heat until thickened, about 1 minute; remove from heat and cover to keep warm.

2 **For the salmon** Adjust oven rack to middle position and heat oven to 300 degrees. Combine sugar, salt, cornstarch, and pepper in bowl. Cut salmon crosswise into 4 fillets. Make 3 or 4 shallow slashes diagonally, about 1 inch apart, on skin side of each fillet, being careful not to cut into flesh. Pat salmon dry with paper towels, and rub sugar mixture evenly over flesh side of salmon.

3 Heat oil in 12-inch ovensafe nonstick skillet over medium-high heat until just smoking. Lay salmon flesh side down in skillet and cook until well browned, about 1 minute. Carefully flip salmon and cook on skin side for 1 minute.

4 Off heat, spoon glaze over salmon fillets. Transfer skillet to oven and roast until center is still translucent when checked with tip of paring knife and registers 125 degrees (for medium-rare), 7 to 10 minutes. Serve.

Soy-Mustard Glazed Roast Salmon
Substitute following ingredients for glaze and cook as directed: 3 tablespoons packed light brown sugar, 2 tablespoons soy sauce, 2 tablespoons mirin, 1 tablespoon sherry vinegar, 1 tablespoon whole-grain mustard, 1 tablespoon water, 1 teaspoon cornstarch, and ⅛ teaspoon red pepper flakes.

Pomegranate-Balsamic Glazed Roast Salmon
Substitute following ingredients for glaze and cook as directed: 3 tablespoons packed light brown sugar, 3 tablespoons pomegranate juice, 2 tablespoons balsamic vinegar, 1 tablespoon whole-grain mustard, 1 teaspoon cornstarch, and pinch cayenne pepper.

ROAST SALMON AND BROCCOLI RABE

serves 4

¼ cup shelled pistachios, toasted and chopped fine

2 tablespoons minced fresh parsley

2 garlic cloves, minced

1 teaspoon grated lemon zest

1 pound broccoli rabe, trimmed and cut into 1½-inch pieces

2 tablespoons plus 2 teaspoons extra-virgin olive oil

Salt and pepper

Pinch red pepper flakes

4 (6- to 8-ounce) center-cut skinless salmon fillets, 1 to 1½ inches thick

Why This Recipe Works Salmon cooks quickly and doesn't flood the pan with rendered juices, so roasting it right alongside an equally quick-cooking vegetable is a great way to streamline dinner. We decided to pair the rich salmon with pleasantly bitter broccoli rabe, using skinless fillets for fish that readily cooked through as the sheet pan heated up. We reinforced the broccoli rabe's bite with some red pepper flakes and minced garlic but kept the seasoning of the salmon simple, rubbing the flesh with oil and sprinkling on salt and pepper before placing the fish on one half of the sheet pan and the broccoli rabe on the other. Roasted in a hot oven, the fillets cooked through to a silky medium-rare right as the broccoli rabe turned tender. A fresh, nutty pistachio gremolata spooned over the finished dish added some crunch and even more flavor. Broccoli rabe is sometimes called rapini.

1 Adjust oven rack to middle position and heat oven to 450 degrees. Combine pistachios, parsley, half of garlic, and lemon zest in small bowl; set gremolata aside.

2 Toss broccoli rabe, 2 tablespoons oil, ¼ teaspoon salt, ¼ teaspoon pepper, pepper flakes, and remaining garlic together in bowl. Arrange on half of rimmed baking sheet. Pat salmon dry with paper towels, rub all over with remaining 2 teaspoons oil, and season with salt and pepper. Arrange salmon skinned side down on empty half of sheet.

3 Roast until center of fillets is still translucent when checked with tip of paring knife and registers 125 degrees (for medium-rare) and broccoli rabe is tender, about 10 minutes. Sprinkle with gremolata and serve.

ROAST SIDE OF SALMON WITH ORANGE BEURRE BLANC

serves 4 to 6

Salmon

15 juniper berries, toasted

¾ teaspoon fennel seeds, toasted

1 teaspoon grated orange zest

½ teaspoon sugar

½ teaspoon salt

½ teaspoon pepper

1 (1¾- to 2-pound) center-cut skin-on side of salmon, pinbones removed

1 tablespoon vegetable oil

Orange Beurre Blanc

3 tablespoons dry white wine

2 tablespoons white wine vinegar

1 small shallot, minced

Salt

1 tablespoon heavy cream

8 tablespoons unsalted butter, cut into 8 pieces and chilled

⅛ teaspoon sugar

⅛ teaspoon grated orange zest

Why This Recipe Works Roasting a side of salmon makes serving rich, silky fish a foolproof, almost hands-off affair, and this recipe's fragrant rub and elegant sauce make it dinner party–perfect. Rather than searing the salmon on the stovetop, we kept everything in the oven, using the rub in conjunction with a hot cooking environment to impart crisp skin, firm flesh, and appealing browning. While the oven and baking pan heated to 500 degrees, we prepared an aromatic rub, grinding floral yet bitter toasted juniper berries and fennel seeds. A touch of sugar balanced out any bitterness and promoted browning while orange zest added brightness. We slashed the skin to encourage the fat to render, applied the rub, dropped the oven temperature to 275 degrees, and transferred the salmon to the hot pan in a protective foil sling. The salmon roasted in the gradually cooling oven, the heat further toasting the rub. An orange beurre blanc sauce offered a sophisticated complement to the fish; we prepared it while the salmon roasted by reducing white wine and vinegar on the stovetop, enriching it with cream and butter, and finishing with orange zest. Toast the juniper and fennel seeds in a dry skillet over medium heat until fragrant, about 1 minute, and then remove the skillet from the heat so the spices won't scorch. If your knife is not sharp enough to cut through the skin easily, try a serrated knife. Heavy-duty aluminum foil measuring 18 inches wide is essential for creating a sling that aids in transferring the cooked fish to a cutting board or serving dish.

1 For the salmon Adjust oven rack to lowest position, place rimmed baking sheet on rack, and heat oven to 500 degrees. Grind juniper and fennel in spice grinder or in mortar and pestle until coarsely ground. Transfer spices to small bowl and stir in orange zest, sugar, salt, and pepper.

2 Cut piece of heavy-duty aluminum foil to be 1 foot longer than side of salmon and fold lengthwise into thirds. Make 8 shallow slashes, about 3 inches long and 1 inch apart, on skin side of salmon, being careful not to cut into flesh. Pat salmon dry with paper towels and lay skin side down on foil. Rub flesh side of salmon with oil, then rub with spice mixture.

3 Reduce oven temperature to 275 degrees. Using foil sling, lay salmon on preheated sheet and roast until center is still translucent when checked with tip of paring knife and registers 125 degrees (for medium-rare), 14 to 18 minutes.

4 For the orange beurre blanc Meanwhile, bring wine, vinegar, shallot, and pinch salt to simmer in small saucepan over medium heat and cook until about 2 scant tablespoons of liquid remain, 3 to 5 minutes. Reduce heat to medium-low and whisk in cream. Add butter, 1 piece at a time, whisking vigorously after each addition until butter is incorporated and forms thick, pale yellow sauce, 30 to 60 seconds. Off heat, whisk in sugar. Strain sauce through fine mesh strainer into bowl. Stir in orange zest and season with salt to taste.

5 Using foil sling, transfer salmon to cutting board (or serving dish). Run thin metal spatula between salmon skin and salmon to loosen. Using spatula to hold salmon in place on cutting board or serving dish, gently pull foil out from underneath salmon. Serve with beurre blanc.

prepping and serving roast side of salmon

1 Cut piece of heavy-duty aluminum foil 1 foot longer than side of salmon and fold lengthwise into thirds.

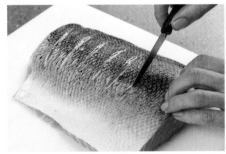

2 Make 8 shallow slashes, 3 inches long and about 1 inch apart, on skin side of salmon, being careful not to cut into flesh.

3 Run thin metal spatula between salmon skin and salmon to loosen. Use spatula to hold salmon in place on cutting board or serving dish and gently pull foil out from underneath salmon.

WHOLE ROAST SNAPPER WITH CITRUS VINAIGRETTE

serves 4

6 tablespoons extra-virgin olive oil

¼ cup minced fresh cilantro

2 teaspoons grated lime zest plus 2 tablespoons juice

2 teaspoons grated orange zest plus 2 tablespoons juice

1 small shallot, minced

⅛ teaspoon red pepper flakes

Salt and pepper

2 (1½- to 2-pound) whole red snapper, scaled, gutted, and fins snipped off with scissors

Why This Recipe Works It would seem that nothing could possibly be easier than roasting fish fillets, but roasting a fish whole is absolutely foolproof: The skin and bones allow for deeply flavorful, perfectly moist fish with minimal effort. To serve up an impressive dish of roasted red snapper, we started by making shallow slashes in the skin to ensure even cooking and seasoning; this step also allowed us to gauge the doneness of the fish easily. Applying an intense citrusy salt to both the fish's cavities and outside skin infused their mild flesh with flavor. A quick citrus vinaigrette made for a punchy accompaniment. We roasted the fish on a rimmed baking sheet for even air circulation, and after a brief stint in a hot oven, they emerged firm, flaky, and still plenty moist. You can substitute whole sea bass for the snapper. Fish weighing more than 2 pounds will be hard to maneuver on the baking sheet and should be avoided.

1 Adjust oven rack to middle position and heat oven to 500 degrees. Line rimmed baking sheet with parchment paper and spray parchment with vegetable oil spray. Whisk ¼ cup oil, cilantro, lime juice, orange juice, shallot, and pepper flakes together in bowl. Season with salt and pepper to taste; set aside.

2 In separate bowl, combine lime zest, orange zest, 1½ teaspoons salt, and ½ teaspoon pepper. Rinse each snapper under cold running water and pat dry with paper towels inside and out. Using sharp knife, make 3 or 4 shallow slashes, about 2 inches apart, on both sides of snapper. Open cavity of each snapper and sprinkle 1 teaspoon salt mixture on flesh. Brush 1 tablespoon oil on outside of each snapper and season with remaining salt mixture; transfer to prepared sheet and let sit for 10 minutes.

3 Roast until snapper flakes apart when gently prodded with paring knife and registers 140 degrees, 15 to 20 minutes.

4 Carefully transfer snapper to cutting board and let rest for 5 minutes. Fillet each snapper by making vertical cut just behind head from top of fish to belly. Make another cut along top of snapper from head to tail. Use spatula to lift meat from bones, starting at head end and running spatula over bones to lift out fillet. Repeat on other side of snapper. Discard head and skeleton. Whisk vinaigrette to recombine and serve with fillets.

filleting a whole snapper

1 Make vertical cut just behind head from top to belly, then cut along back of fish from head to tail.

2 Starting at head and working toward tail, use metal spatula to lift meat away from bones. Repeat on second side.

WHOLE ROAST TROUT WITH WHITE BEAN SALAD

serves 4

4 (7- to 10-ounce) boneless, butterflied whole trout

Salt and pepper

½ cup extra-virgin olive oil, plus extra for drizzling

2 (15-ounce) cans cannellini beans, rinsed

2 shallots, minced

¼ cup chopped fresh parsley

¼ cup lemon juice (2 lemons)

2 tablespoons capers, rinsed and chopped

4 teaspoons minced fresh rosemary

2 garlic cloves, minced

Why This Recipe Works If you buy them already butterflied, roasting whole trout proves fast and totally foolproof. With the deboning and butterflying taken care of by the fishmonger, our main concern became cooking the delicate fish evenly and pairing its rich flavor with a complementary side. To crisp the skin, we preheated a baking sheet in a hot oven, coated it with oil, and then gave the oil a few minutes to heat up before placing the fish on the pan. The skin immediately began to crisp on contact and the oven's dry, all-encompassing heat cooked the thin flesh to flaky perfection within minutes. Given the trout's brief roasting time, we partnered it with an equally quick accompaniment: creamy cannellini beans tossed with the bright, fresh flavors of shallots, parsley, lemon juice, capers, rosemary, and garlic. Served with a drizzle of olive oil, this roasted trout proved to be as elegant as it was fast. We like cannellini beans for this salad, but any canned small white beans will work.

1 Adjust oven rack to middle position, place rimmed baking sheet on rack, and heat oven to 450 degrees. Pat trout dry with paper towels and season with salt and pepper. Add ¼ cup oil to preheated sheet, tilting to coat evenly, and return to oven for 4 minutes. Carefully place trout skin side down on hot sheet and cook until trout flakes apart when gently prodded with paring knife, 7 to 9 minutes.

2 Meanwhile, combine beans, shallots, parsley, lemon juice, capers, rosemary, garlic, and remaining ¼ cup oil in bowl. Season with salt and pepper to taste. Drizzle trout with extra oil and serve with bean salad.

WHOLE ROAST MACKEREL WITH RED PEPPER AND PRESERVED LEMON STUFFING

serves 4

3 tablespoons extra-virgin olive oil

1 red bell pepper, stemmed, seeded, and chopped fine

1 red onion, chopped fine

½ preserved lemon, pulp and white pith removed, rind rinsed and minced (2 tablespoons)

⅓ cup pitted brine-cured green olives, chopped

1 tablespoon minced fresh parsley

Salt and pepper

4 (8- to 10-ounce) whole mackerel, scaled, gutted, and fins snipped off with scissors

Lemon wedges

Why This Recipe Works Like snapper, mackerel maintains its tender, moist texture best when roasted whole, and because each slender fish is enough to serve one person, we decided to double down on flavor by pairing this already pungent, rich fish with an impactful stuffing. Inspired by the aromatic ingredients in Moroccan cuisine, we tucked a combination of sweet red bell pepper, fragrant preserved lemon, and briny green olives into each fish. With our stuffed fish lined up on a rimmed baking sheet for optimum air circulation, we roasted them in a hot oven. After 10 minutes or so, we had four perfectly cooked, superflavorful fish. If you can't find preserved lemons, you can substitute 2 tablespoons of finely grated lemon zest. You can substitute whole trout for the mackerel. The mackerel heads can be removed before serving, if desired.

1 Adjust oven rack to middle position and heat oven to 500 degrees. Heat 2 tablespoons oil in 12-inch skillet over medium-high heat until shimmering. Add bell pepper and onion and cook until vegetables are softened and well browned, 8 to 10 minutes. Stir in preserved lemon and cook until fragrant, about 30 seconds. Off heat, stir in olives and parsley and season with salt and pepper to taste.

2 Grease rimmed baking sheet with remaining 1 tablespoon oil. Rinse each mackerel under cold running water and pat dry with paper towels inside and out. Open cavity of each mackerel, season flesh with salt and pepper, and spoon one-quarter of filling into opening. Place mackerel on prepared sheet, spaced at least 2 inches apart. Roast until thickest part of mackerel registers 130 to 135 degrees, 10 to 12 minutes. Carefully transfer mackerel to serving dish and let rest for 5 minutes. Serve with lemon wedges.

ROASTED STUFFED LOBSTER TAILS

serves 4

6 tablespoons unsalted butter

½ cup panko bread crumbs

2 celery ribs, chopped fine

1 shallot, minced

¼ teaspoon salt

3 tablespoons dry sherry

8 ounces medium-large shrimp (31 to 40 per pound), peeled, deveined, tails removed, and chopped

¼ cup chopped fresh parsley

1½ teaspoons grated lemon zest

4 (5- to 6-ounce) lobster tails

Lemon wedges

Why This Recipe Works Classic as it may be, steaming fresh lobster washes out its natural sweetness. Roasting, on the other hand, heightens and concentrates that delicate flavor. By stuffing and roasting readily available lobster tails (often sold frozen), we capitalized on this technique's strengths and took the dish's flavor over the top. Lobster tails turn chewy when overcooked, so after splitting the shell's underside and loosening the meat to make room for the stuffing, we kept the rest of the protective shell intact. In preparing the filling, we combined chopped shrimp and buttery panko to mirror the rich, sweet lobster taste; chopped parsley, grated lemon zest, and dry sherry offered a fresh, well-rounded profile. We mounded the stuffing into the tails and roasted them in a baking dish; the panko became more gorgeously browned as the meat gently cooked through. These tails were full-flavored and totally indulgent; plus, this approach made it possible to tuck into a lobster feast any day of the year. To thaw frozen lobster tails, let them sit either in the refrigerator for 24 hours or submerged in cold water for 30 minutes to 1 hour.

1 Adjust oven rack to middle position and heat oven to 350 degrees. Melt 4 tablespoons butter in 10-inch skillet over medium heat. Add panko and cook, stirring often, until crumbs are dark golden brown, about 2 minutes. Transfer panko to large bowl and let cool slightly. Wipe skillet clean with paper towels.

2 Melt remaining 2 tablespoons butter in now-empty skillet over medium heat. Add celery, shallot, and salt and cook until softened, 3 to 5 minutes. Stir in sherry and cook until reduced slightly, about 30 seconds. Transfer vegetable mixture to bowl with panko. Stir in shrimp, parsley, and lemon zest until well combined.

3 Using kitchen shears, cut lengthwise through soft shell on underside of lobster tail. Cut meat in half using paring knife, taking care not to cut through outer shell. With lobster tail cut side up, grasp each side with your hands and crack outer shell, opening cut side to expose meat. Lift meat from shell to loosen, then tuck back into shell.

4 Arrange lobster tails cut side up in 13 by 9-inch baking dish, alternating tails front to back. Spoon stuffing evenly into tails, mounding stuffing slightly. Roast until stuffing is golden brown and lobster registers 140 degrees, 20 to 25 minutes. Serve with lemon wedges.

Roasted Stuffed Lobster Tails with Fennel and Pernod

Substitute 1 finely chopped fennel bulb (about 1 cup) for celery. Substitute minced fennel fronds, if available, for parsley and 3 tablespoons Pernod for sherry.

butterflying a lobster tail

1 Using kitchen shears, cut lengthwise through soft shell on underside of lobster tail. Cut meat in half using paring knife; do not cut through outer shell.

2 With lobster tail cut side up, grasp each side with your hands and crack outer shell, opening cut side to expose meat.

GARLICKY ROASTED SHRIMP WITH PARSLEY AND ANISE

serves 4 to 6

¼ cup salt

2 pounds shell-on jumbo shrimp
(16 to 20 per pound)

4 tablespoons unsalted butter, melted

¼ cup extra-virgin olive oil

6 garlic cloves, minced

1 teaspoon anise seeds

½ teaspoon red pepper flakes

¼ teaspoon pepper

2 tablespoons minced fresh parsley

Lemon wedges

Why This Recipe Works Lobster is not the only crustacean that benefits from roasting. Shrimp, too, see their sweet flavor concentrating and deepening, but those benefits are only worth it if the quick-cooking flesh stays tender and moist. Aiming for that ideal balance of profound flavor and perfect doneness, we took every precaution against overcooking, starting by brining hefty jumbo shrimp for extra moisture and thorough seasoning. Butterflying the shrimp offered an easy route to flavor-infused flesh, and although we sliced through the shells, we didn't remove them, as they proved key to boosting flavor while also adding an extra layer of protection. After tossing the shrimp in melted butter and olive oil boosted with garlic, spices, and herbs, we elevated them on a wire rack set in a rimmed baking sheet and slid them under the broiler. Within minutes, our shrimp emerged tender and deeply fragrant beneath flavorful, browned shells. Don't use smaller shrimp with this cooking technique; they will be overseasoned and prone to overcooking.

1 Dissolve salt in 1 quart cold water in large container. Using kitchen shears or sharp paring knife, cut through shell of shrimp and devein but do not remove shell. Using paring knife, continue to cut shrimp ½ inch deep, taking care not to cut in half completely. Submerge shrimp in brine, cover, and refrigerate for 15 minutes.

2 Adjust oven rack 4 inches from broiler element and heat broiler. Combine melted butter, oil, garlic, anise seeds, pepper flakes, and pepper in large bowl. Remove shrimp from brine and pat dry with paper towels. Add shrimp and parsley to butter mixture; toss well, making sure butter mixture gets into interior of shrimp. Arrange shrimp in single layer on wire rack set in rimmed baking sheet.

3 Broil shrimp until opaque and shells are beginning to brown, 2 to 4 minutes, rotating sheet halfway through broiling. Flip shrimp and continue to broil until second side is opaque and shells are beginning to brown, 2 to 4 minutes longer, rotating sheet halfway through broiling. Transfer shrimp to serving dish and serve with lemon wedges.

Garlicky Roasted Shrimp with Cilantro and Lime

Annatto powder, also called achiote, can be found with the Latin American foods at your supermarket. An equal amount of paprika can be substituted.

Omit butter and increase oil to ½ cup. Omit anise seeds and pepper. Add 2 teaspoons lightly crushed coriander seeds, 2 teaspoons grated lime zest, and 1 teaspoon annatto powder to oil mixture in step 2. Substitute ¼ cup minced fresh cilantro for parsley and lime wedges for lemon wedges.

Garlicky Roasted Shrimp with Cumin, Ginger, and Sesame

Omit butter and increase oil to ½ cup. Decrease garlic to 2 cloves and omit anise seeds and pepper. Add 2 teaspoons toasted sesame oil, 1½ teaspoons grated fresh ginger, and 1 teaspoon cumin seeds to oil mixture in step 2. Substitute 2 thinly sliced scallion greens for parsley and omit lemon wedges.

ROASTED MUSSELS

1 tablespoon extra-virgin olive oil

3 garlic cloves, minced

Pinch red pepper flakes

1 cup dry white wine

3 sprigs fresh thyme

2 bay leaves

4 pounds mussels, scrubbed and debearded

¼ teaspoon salt

2 tablespoons unsalted butter, cut into 4 pieces

2 tablespoons minced fresh parsley

Why This Recipe Works Ask almost anyone how to prepare mussels and they will no doubt recite the standard stovetop steaming steps. But here in the test kitchen, we learned that roasting them is far better. Mussels come in a range of sizes, making it a real challenge to cook them evenly, so rather than piling them into a Dutch oven (where the mussels closest to the stove's burner will inevitably overcook), we roasted them en masse in the generous space afforded by a roomy roasting pan. After infusing white wine with garlic, thyme, and bay leaves on the stovetop, we stirred in the mussels and sealed them under a sheet of aluminum foil. The all-encompassing heat of a 500-degree oven gently heated the shellfish through so the majority of the mussels, both big and small, yawned open in about 15 minutes, their liquid mingling with the reduced wine for an irresistibly briny-sweet broth. A hit of butter melted into the concentrated cooking liquid before serving offered a rich complement to these simple but spectacular mussels. Discard any mussel with an unpleasant odor or with a cracked shell or a shell that won't close. Serve with crusty bread.

1 Adjust oven rack to lowest position and heat oven to 500 degrees. Heat oil, garlic, and pepper flakes in large roasting pan over medium heat (over 2 burners, if possible) and cook, stirring constantly, until fragrant, about 30 seconds. Stir in wine, thyme sprigs, and bay leaves and boil until wine is slightly reduced, about 1 minute.

2 Stir in mussels and salt. Cover pan tightly with aluminum foil and transfer to oven. Roast until most mussels have opened (a few may remain closed), 15 to 18 minutes.

3 Remove pan from oven. Push mussels to sides of pan. Being careful of hot pan handles, add butter to center and whisk until melted. Discard thyme sprigs and bay leaves. Stir in parsley and serve.

Roasted Mussels with Leeks and Pernod

Omit pepper flakes and increase oil to 3 tablespoons. Heat oil; 1 pound leeks, white and light green parts only, halved lengthwise, sliced thin, and washed thoroughly; and garlic in roasting pan until leeks are wilted, about 3 minutes. Proceed with recipe as directed, omitting thyme sprigs and substituting ½ cup Pernod and ¼ cup water for wine, ¼ cup crème fraîche for butter, and chives for parsley.

Roasted Mussels with Tomato and Chorizo

Omit pepper flakes and increase oil to 3 tablespoons. Heat oil, 12 ounces chopped Spanish-style chorizo, and garlic in roasting pan until chorizo starts to brown, about 5 minutes. Proceed with recipe as directed, omitting thyme sprigs and substituting 1 (28-ounce) can crushed tomatoes for wine.

Roasted Mussels with Hard Cider and Bacon

Omit garlic and red pepper flakes. Heat oil and 4 slices thick-cut bacon, cut into ½-inch pieces, in roasting pan until bacon has rendered and is starting to crisp, about 5 minutes. Proceed with recipe as directed, substituting dry hard cider for wine and ¼ cup heavy cream for butter.

GRILL ROASTING

GRILL-ROASTED SPICE-RUBBED CHICKEN DRUMSTICKS

serves 6

½ cup salt

5 pounds chicken drumsticks

1 recipe spice rub (recipes follow)

Why This Recipe Works With their built-in handles and small size, economical chicken drumsticks are tailor-made for a cookout. So we decided to devise a foolproof way to roast them on the grill to ultra-tender perfection with nicely browned skin and wonderfully juicy meat. We usually don't brine fattier dark meat, but since we were roasting the drumsticks for a fairly long time in the grill's dry heat we brined them first in salt water to help them retain their juices as well as to season them. A light coating of spice rub also upped their flavor. We set up a half-grill fire with two zones: On the cooler side we roasted the drumsticks beyond their usual doneness temperature of 175 degrees to 190 degrees, at which point most of their connective tissue had turned into rich gelatin and their skin had rendered gently. Indirect grilling is largely hands off, but halfway through roasting we rearranged the drumsticks, moving those closer to the heat to the outside and those on the outside closer to the heat to ensure all of the drumsticks were done at the same time. We moved them to the hotter side until the skin was nicely charred and crisp, which took only 5 minutes. Before applying the spice rub, smooth the skin over the drumsticks so it is covering as much surface area as possible. This will help the skin render evenly and prevent the meat from drying out.

1 Dissolve salt in 2 quarts cold water in large container. Submerge drumsticks in brine, cover, and refrigerate for 30 minutes to 1 hour.

2 Place spice rub on plate. Remove drumsticks from brine and pat dry with paper towels. Holding 1 drumstick by bone end, press lightly into rub on all sides. Pat gently to remove excess rub. Repeat with remaining drumsticks.

3A For a charcoal grill Open bottom vent halfway. Light large chimney starter filled with charcoal briquettes (6 quarts). When top coals are partially covered with ash, pour evenly over half of grill. Set cooking grate in place, cover, and open lid vent halfway. Heat grill until hot, about 5 minutes.

3B For a gas grill Turn all burners to high, cover, and heat grill until hot, about 15 minutes. Leave primary burner on high and turn off other burner(s). (Adjust primary burner as needed to maintain grill temperature between 325 and 350 degrees.)

4 Clean and oil cooking grate. Place drumsticks, skin side down, on cooler side of grill. Cover and cook for 25 minutes. Rearrange pieces so that drumsticks that were closest to edge are now closer to heat source and vice versa. Cover and cook until drumsticks register 185 to 190 degrees, 20 to 30 minutes.

5 Move all drumsticks to hotter side of grill and cook, turning occasionally, until skin is nicely charred, about 5 minutes. Transfer to serving dish and let rest for 10 minutes. Serve.

BARBECUE SPICE RUB

makes about ⅓ cup

You can substitute granulated garlic for the garlic powder, if desired.

3 tablespoons packed brown sugar

1 tablespoon paprika

1 tablespoon chili powder

2 teaspoons garlic powder

¾ teaspoon salt

¾ teaspoon pepper

¼ teaspoon cayenne pepper

Combine all ingredients in small bowl.

JERK-STYLE SPICE RUB

makes about ¼ cup

If you can't find whole allspice berries, substitute 2 teaspoons of ground allspice.

1 tablespoon allspice berries

1 tablespoon black peppercorns

1½ teaspoons dried thyme

2 tablespoons packed brown sugar

2 teaspoons garlic powder

1½ teaspoons dry mustard

¾ teaspoon salt

¾ teaspoon cayenne pepper

Grind allspice, peppercorns, and thyme in spice grinder or mortar and pestle until coarsely ground. Transfer to bowl and stir in sugar, garlic powder, mustard, salt, and cayenne.

GRILL-ROASTED CORNELL CHICKEN

serves 8

Chicken

¼ cup salt

3½ cups cider vinegar

2 (3½- to 4-pound) whole chickens, giblets discarded

Seasoning and Sauce

1 tablespoon ground poultry seasoning

Salt and pepper

½ cup cider vinegar

3 tablespoons Dijon mustard

1 tablespoon chopped fresh sage

1 tablespoon chopped fresh rosemary

½ cup extra-virgin olive oil

Why This Recipe Works A longtime New York State Fair favorite, Cornell chicken gets its signature tangy, herby flavor from plenty of vinegar, sage, and rosemary. Half chickens are basted with a tangy sauce while they grill-roast over low heat to crisp-skinned perfection. To serve up an authentic version at home, we butterflied and halved two chickens and soaked them in a cider vinegar–salt brine. Half chickens cook more quickly and are easier to maneuver on the grill. We seasoned the chicken with a spice rub containing poultry seasoning, an essential flavoring for Cornell chicken. A single-level fire proved the ideal setup for direct but gentle heat. We started the chickens skin side up so the fat could render slowly, later flipping them over to brown the skin. While the meat was roasting, we basted the birds' exterior three times with a bright, bold sauce made with more vinegar, fresh sage, fresh rosemary, and Dijon mustard to help the sauce stay put. Served with extra sauce, these crisp chickens boasted tangy flavor in every bite. Do not brine the chicken longer than 2 hours or the vinegar will turn the meat mushy. Poultry seasoning is a mix of herbs and spices that can be found in the supermarket spice aisle.

1 **For the chicken** Dissolve salt in vinegar and 2 quarts cold water in large container. With 1 chicken breast side down, use kitchen shears to cut along both sides of backbone. Discard backbone and trim any excess fat or skin at neck. Flip chicken over and, using chef's knife, cut through breastbone to separate chicken into halves. Tuck wingtips behind back. Repeat with second chicken. Submerge chickens in brine, cover, and refrigerate for 1 to 2 hours.

2 **For the seasoning and sauce** Combine poultry seasoning, 2 teaspoons salt, and 2 teaspoons pepper in small bowl; set aside. Process vinegar, mustard, sage, rosemary, ½ teaspoon salt, and ½ teaspoon pepper in blender until smooth, about 1 minute. With blender running, slowly add oil until incorporated. Measure out ¾ cup vinegar sauce and set aside for cooking; reserve remaining sauce for serving.

3A **For a charcoal grill** Open bottom vent completely. Light large chimney starter three-quarters filled with charcoal briquettes (4½ quarts). When top coals are partially covered with ash, pour evenly over grill. Set cooking grate in place, cover, and open lid vent completely. Heat grill until hot, about 5 minutes.

3B **For a gas grill** Turn all burners to high, cover, and heat grill until hot, about 15 minutes. Turn all burners to medium-low. (Adjust burners as needed to maintain grill temperature around 350 degrees.)

4 Clean and oil cooking grate. Remove chicken from brine and pat dry with paper towels. Rub chicken evenly with poultry seasoning mixture. Place chickens skin side up on grill and brush with 6 tablespoons vinegar sauce for cooking. Cover and cook chickens until well browned on bottom and thighs register 120 degrees, 25 to 30 minutes, brushing with more sauce for cooking halfway through cooking.

5 Flip chickens skin side down and brush with remaining sauce for cooking. Cover and continue to cook chickens until skin is golden brown and crisp, breasts register 160 degrees, and thighs register 175 degrees, 20 to 25 minutes. Transfer chickens to carving board and let rest for 20 minutes. Carve chickens and serve with reserved sauce.

GRILL-SMOKED BOURBON CHICKEN

serves 8

1¼ cups bourbon

1¼ cups soy sauce

½ cup packed brown sugar

1 shallot, minced

4 garlic cloves, minced

2 teaspoons pepper

2 (3½- to 4-pound) whole chickens, giblets discarded

1 cup wood chips

4 (12-inch) wooden skewers

Why This Recipe Works Grill smoking is grill roasting with the addition of wood chips to infuse the food with smoky flavor. To get both rich smoke and bourbon flavor into chicken, we needed a few tricks. To add deep flavor, we slashed the skin and meat of two halved chickens so a marinade could soak in. We made a marinade of equal parts bourbon and salty soy sauce and heated it to enhance the bourbon flavor. Skewering the chicken halves through the breast and thigh kept them together on the grill. We concentrated the grill's heat to one side and arranged the birds skin side up on the cooler side with their meaty legs facing the coals. Using reserved marinade as a basting sauce, we basted the chicken every 15 minutes since moist skin attracts more smoke. The basting also built up an attractive lacquered surface on the outside of the chicken. Use all of the basting liquid in step 5. This recipe requires refrigerating the marinated chickens for at least 1 hour or up to 24 hours before cooking (a longer time is preferable).

1 Bring bourbon, soy sauce, sugar, shallot, garlic, and pepper to boil in medium saucepan over medium-high heat and cook for 1 minute. Remove from heat and let cool completely. Measure out ¾ cup bourbon mixture and set aside for cooking. (Bourbon mixture can be refrigerated for up to 3 days.)

2 With 1 chicken breast side down, use kitchen shears to cut along both sides of backbone. Discard backbone and trim any excess fat or skin at neck. Flip chicken over and, using chef's knife, cut through breastbone to separate chicken into halves. Cut ½-inch-deep slits across breast, thigh, and leg of each half, about ½ inch apart. Tuck wingtips behind back. Repeat with second chicken. Divide remaining bourbon mixture between two 1-gallon zipper-lock bags. Add chickens to bags and toss to coat. Press out as much air as possible, seal bags, and refrigerate for at least 1 hour or up to 24 hours, flipping occasionally.

3 Just before grilling, soak wood chips in water for 15 minutes, then drain. Using large piece of heavy-duty aluminum foil, wrap soaked chips in 8 by 4½-inch foil packet. (Make sure chips do not poke holes in sides or bottom of packet.) Cut 2 evenly spaced 2-inch slits in top of packet. Remove chicken halves from marinade and pat dry with paper towels; discard marinade. Insert 1 skewer lengthwise through thickest part of breast down through thigh of each chicken half.

4A For a charcoal grill Open bottom vent halfway. Light large chimney starter filled with charcoal briquettes (6 quarts). When top coals are partially covered with ash, pour into steeply banked pile against side of grill. Place wood chip packet on coals. Set cooking grate in place, cover, and open lid vent halfway. Heat grill until hot and wood chips are smoking, about 5 minutes.

4B For a gas grill Remove cooking grate and place wood chip packet directly on primary burner. Set cooking grate in place, turn all burners to high, cover, and heat grill until hot and wood chips are smoking, about 15 minutes. Leave primary burner on high and turn off other burner(s). (Adjust primary burner as needed to maintain grill temperature between 350 and 375 degrees.)

5 Clean and oil cooking grate. Place chicken halves skin side up on cooler side of grill with legs pointing toward heat source. Cover and cook for 45 minutes, basting every 15 minutes with reserved bourbon mixture for cooking.

6 Switch placement of chickens, with legs still pointed toward heat source, and continue to cook, covered, until breasts register 160 degrees and thighs register 175 degrees, 30 to 45 minutes. Transfer chickens to carving board and let rest for 20 minutes. Remove skewers, carve chickens, and serve.

GRILL-SMOKED HULI HULI CHICKEN

serves 8

Chicken

2 cups soy sauce

1 tablespoon vegetable oil

6 garlic cloves, minced

1 tablespoon grated fresh ginger

2 (3½- to 4-pound) whole chickens, giblets discarded

Glaze

3 (6-ounce) cans pineapple juice

¼ cup packed light brown sugar

¼ cup soy sauce

¼ cup ketchup

¼ cup rice vinegar

2 tablespoons grated fresh ginger

4 garlic cloves, minced

2 teaspoons Asian chili-garlic sauce

2 cups wood chips

Why This Recipe Works Sweet and tangy *huli huli* chicken is a Hawaiian specialty. There, the birds are continually basted with a sticky-sweet glaze as they turn (or "huli") on a specialized rotisserie over local kiawe wood. To develop a recipe for the home grill we had to change both the sauce and the technique. For the teriyaki-like glaze, we reduced brown sugar, soy sauce, ketchup, rice vinegar, chili-garlic sauce, and lots of pineapple juice on the stovetop until it was thick and glossy, and used it to brush on the cooked chicken and as an accompanying sauce. Prior to grilling, we infused the chicken with flavor and moisture by soaking it in a soy sauce brine boosted with fresh ginger and garlic. To mimic a Hawaiian rotisserie, we spread the coals in a single layer and deployed a packet of wood chips (mesquite came closest to kiawe wood in flavor). The direct heat rendered the fat and crisped the skin, but the chicken was far enough from the coals to avoid burning. Starting the halved chickens skin side up helped the fat to render and the meat to absorb the smoke; finishing skin side down allowed the skin to brown and crisp. Rather than burn our glaze on the grill, we brushed it on the still-hot chickens while they rested. This recipe requires refrigerating the brined chickens for at least 1 hour or up to 8 hours before cooking (a longer time is preferable). We prefer mesquite wood chips in this recipe.

1 For the chicken Combine soy sauce and 2 quarts cold water in large container. Heat oil in large saucepan over medium-high heat until shimmering. Add garlic and ginger and cook until fragrant, about 30 seconds. Stir into soy sauce mixture. With 1 chicken breast side down, use kitchen shears to cut along both sides of backbone. Discard backbone and trim any excess fat or skin at neck. Flip chicken over and, using chef's knife, cut through breastbone to separate chicken into halves. Tuck wingtips behind back. Repeat with second chicken. Submerge chickens in brine, cover, and refrigerate for at least 1 hour or up to 8 hours.

2 For the glaze Combine pineapple juice, sugar, soy sauce, ketchup, vinegar, ginger, garlic, and chili-garlic sauce in empty saucepan and bring to boil. Reduce heat to medium and simmer until thick and syrupy (you should have about 1 cup), 20 to 25 minutes. (Glaze can be refrigerated for up to 3 days.) Just before grilling, soak wood chips in water for 15 minutes, then drain. Using large piece of heavy-duty aluminum foil, wrap soaked chips in 8 by 4½-inch foil packet. (Make sure chips do not poke holes in sides or bottom of packet.) Cut 2 evenly spaced 2-inch slits in top of packet.

3A For a charcoal grill Open bottom vent halfway. Light large chimney starter three-quarters filled with charcoal briquettes (4½ quarts). When top coals are partially covered with ash, pour evenly over grill. Place wood chip packet on coals. Set cooking grate in place, cover, and open lid vent open halfway. Heat grill until hot and wood chips are smoking, about 5 minutes.

3B For a gas grill Remove cooking grate and place wood chip packet directly on primary burner. Set cooking grate in place, turn all burners to high, cover, and heat grill until hot and wood chips are smoking, about 15 minutes. Turn all burners to medium-low. (Adjust burners as needed to maintain grill temperature around 350 degrees.)

4 Clean and oil cooking grate. Remove chickens from brine and pat dry with paper towels. Place chickens skin side up on grill (do not place chicken directly above wood chip packet). Cover and cook chicken until well browned on bottom and thighs register 120 degrees, 25 to 30 minutes. Flip chickens skin side down. Cover and continue to cook until skin is well browned and crisp, breasts register 160 degrees, and thighs register 175 degrees, 20 to 25 minutes. Transfer chickens to serving dish, brush with half of glaze, and let rest for 20 minutes. Carve chickens and serve, passing remaining glaze separately.

GRILL-SMOKED SINALOA-STYLE CHICKEN

serves 8

2 (3½- to 4-pound) whole chickens, giblets discarded

2 onions, chopped

1 (12-ounce) can frozen orange juice concentrate, thawed

¼ cup extra-virgin olive oil

2 garlic heads, cloves separated and peeled (20 cloves)

Salt and pepper

1 tablespoon chopped fresh oregano

1 tablespoon minced fresh thyme

2 teaspoons minced canned chipotle chile in adobo sauce

1½ cups wood chips

Lime wedges

Why This Recipe Works Along Mexico's Sinaloa coast, chickens are split in half, marinated in a bitter orange, garlic, and herb mixture, and grilled over smoky embers. To bring all the earthy flavor of this dish home, we prepared a potent marinade using frozen orange juice concentrate and 20 garlic cloves. Slashing the skin and meat allowed the marinade to fully penetrate the chicken; we reserved some of the marinade to baste the chicken and help keep the meat moist. The sugars in the marinade and basting liquid caramelized to produce really crisp skin. Skewering the chicken halves helped them keep their shape on the grill and made them easier to maneuver. We roasted the chickens on the cooler side of a banked fire with the legs toward the heat and brushed on more marinade for deep flavor. You will need four 12-inch metal skewers for this recipe. This recipe requires refrigerating the marinated chickens for at least 2 hours or up to 24 hours before cooking (a longer time is preferable).

1 With 1 chicken breast side down, use kitchen shears to cut along both sides of backbone. Discard backbone and trim any excess fat or skin at neck. Flip chicken over and, using chef's knife, cut through breastbone to separate chicken into halves. Cut ½-inch deep slits across breast, thigh, and leg of each half, about ½ inch apart. Tuck wingtips behind back. Repeat with second chicken.

2 Process onions, orange juice concentrate, oil, garlic, and 2 tablespoons salt in blender until smooth, about 1 minute. Transfer ¾ cup marinade to bowl and stir in oregano, thyme, and chipotle; set aside for cooking. Divide remaining marinade between two 1-gallon zipper-lock bags. Add chickens to bags and toss to coat. Press out as much air as possible, seal bags, and refrigerate for at least 2 hours or up to 24 hours, flipping occasionally.

3 Just before grilling, soak wood chips in water for 15 minutes, then drain. Using large piece of heavy-duty aluminum foil, wrap soaked chips in 8 by 4½-inch foil packet. (Make sure chips do not poke holes in packet.) Cut 2 evenly spaced 2-inch slits in top of packet. Remove chickens from marinade and pat dry with paper towels; discard marinade. Insert one 12-inch metal skewer lengthwise through thickest part of breast down through thigh of each chicken half.

4A For a charcoal grill Open bottom vent halfway. Light large chimney starter filled with charcoal briquettes (6 quarts). When top coals are partially covered with ash, pour into steeply banked pile against side of grill. Place wood chip packet on coals. Set cooking grate in place, cover, and open lid vent halfway. Heat grill until hot and wood chips are smoking, about 5 minutes.

4B For a gas grill Remove cooking grate and place wood chip packet directly on primary burner. Set cooking grate in place, turn all burners to high, cover, and heat grill until hot and wood chips are smoking, about 15 minutes. Leave primary burner on high and turn off other burner(s). (Adjust primary burner as needed to maintain grill temperature between 350 to 375 degrees.)

5 Clean and oil cooking grate. Place chicken halves skin side up on cooler side of grill with legs pointing toward heat source. Cover and cook for 45 minutes, basting every 15 minutes with reserved marinade for cooking.

6 Switch placement of chickens, with legs still pointed toward heat source, and continue to cook, covered, until breasts register 160 degrees and thighs register 175 degrees, 30 to 45 minutes. Transfer chickens to carving board and let rest for 20 minutes. Remove skewers, carve chickens, and serve with lime wedges.

GRILL-SMOKED CHICKEN

serves 4

½ cup salt

1 (3½- to 4-pound) whole chicken, giblets discarded

3 tablespoons spice rub (recipes follow)

2 cups wood chips

1 (16 by 12-inch) disposable aluminum roasting pan (if using charcoal)

Why This Recipe Works For a whole chicken with serious smoke flavor, we turned to the grill to make the ideal chicken with moist meat and crisp skin. Often the bird's exterior chars before the interior gets a chance to cook through, but our approach overcame that challenge in a few easy steps. First, we brined the chicken for well-seasoned meat and additional moisture to keep it from drying out on the grill. An aromatic spice rub applied directly onto the meat added another layer of flavor while encouraging the skin to crisp more and look better, too. Arranging the coals on either side of the grill with a disposable roasting pan in the center provided plenty of indirect heat to cook the chicken through, without burning, in about an hour and gave it time to pick up plenty of smoke. We left the legs untied, letting them splay to readily cook through. The chicken needed only one turn halfway through cooking to get perfect, evenly roasted meat. If using a kosher chicken, do not brine.

1 Dissolve salt in 2 quarts cold water in large container. Submerge chicken in brine, cover, and refrigerate for 1 hour. Remove chicken from brine and pat dry with paper towels. Using your fingers or handle of spoon, gently loosen skin covering breast and thighs. Rub spice rub all over chicken and underneath skin of breast directly onto meat. Tuck wingtips behind back.

2 Just before grilling, soak wood chips in water for 15 minutes, then drain. Using large piece of heavy-duty aluminum foil, wrap 1 cup soaked chips in 8 by 4½-inch foil packet. (Make sure chips do not poke holes in sides or bottom of packet.) Repeat with remaining 1 cup chips. Cut 2 evenly spaced 2-inch slits in top of each packet.

3A For a charcoal grill Open bottom vent halfway and place disposable pan in center of grill. Light large chimney starter filled with charcoal briquettes (6 quarts). When top coals are partially covered with ash, pour into 2 even piles on either side of disposable pan. Place 1 wood chip packet on each pile of coals. Set cooking grate in place, cover, and open lid vent halfway. Heat grill until hot and wood chips are smoking, about 5 minutes.

3B For a gas grill Remove cooking grate and place wood chip packets directly on primary burner. Set cooking grate in place, turn all burners to high, cover, and heat grill until hot and wood chips are smoking, about 15 minutes. Turn all burners to medium. (Adjust burners as needed to maintain grill temperature around 325 degrees.)

4 Clean and oil cooking grate. Place chicken on center of grill (over disposable pan if using charcoal), breast side down, cover (position lid vent over chicken if using charcoal), and cook for 30 minutes.

5 Working quickly, remove lid and, using 2 large wads of paper towels, turn chicken breast side up. Cover and continue to cook until breast registers 160 degrees and thighs register 175 degrees, 25 to 35 minutes. Transfer chicken to carving board and let rest for 20 minutes. Carve chicken and serve.

FRAGRANT DRY SPICE RUB
makes about ½ cup
Store leftover spice rub for up to 3 months.

2 tablespoons ground cumin
2 tablespoons curry powder
2 tablespoons chili powder
1 tablespoon ground allspice
1 tablespoon pepper
1 teaspoon ground cinnamon

Combine all ingredients in bowl.

CITRUS-CILANTRO WET SPICE RUB
makes about 3 tablespoons
For more heat, add up to ½ teaspoon cayenne pepper.

1 tablespoon minced fresh cilantro
1 tablespoon orange juice
1½ teaspoons lime juice
1½ teaspoons extra-virgin olive oil
1 small garlic clove, minced
½ teaspoon ground cumin
½ teaspoon chili powder
½ teaspoon paprika
½ teaspoon ground coriander

Combine all ingredients in bowl. Use immediately.

GRILL-ROASTED GLAZED CHICKEN

serves 8

2 (3½- to 4-pound) whole chickens, giblets discarded

1 tablespoon sugar

1 tablespoon salt

1 teaspoon pepper

1 recipe glaze (recipes follow)

Why This Recipe Works A bronzed grill-roasted chicken finished with a sweet, sticky glaze is universally appealing. To get some low direct heat on the chickens (we cooked two since it was no more work than cooking one) while keeping them a safe distance from the fire, we poured our coals into a single layer and elevated the birds head to tail on a V-rack on the cooking grate. Pricking the skin gave the fat an escape route and adding some sugar to a simple rub helped the rendered skin to crisp and brown. Flipping the chickens halfway through roasting ensured the white and dark meat cooked evenly. So as not to slow the cooking process by opening and closing the lid, and to keep the glaze from burning, we waited until the last 15 minutes of roasting to brush on the thick glaze, turning the chickens at least three times for a substantial coating. If using kosher chickens, omit the salt in the rub.

1 Spray V-rack with vegetable oil spray. Pat chickens dry with paper towels and prick skin all over with tip of paring knife. Combine sugar, salt, and pepper in small bowl, then rub seasoning mixture all over chickens. Tie legs together with kitchen twine and tuck wingtips behind back. Arrange chickens breast side up head to tail on prepared V-rack.

2A **For a charcoal grill** Open bottom vent completely. Light large chimney starter filled with charcoal briquettes (6 quarts). When top coals are partially covered with ash, pour evenly over grill. Set cooking grate in place, cover, and open lid vent completely. Heat grill until hot, about 5 minutes.

2B **For a gas grill** Turn all burners to high, cover, and heat grill until hot, about 15 minutes. Turn all burners to low. (Adjust burners as needed to maintain grill temperature around 325 degrees.)

3 Arrange V-rack on cooking grate, cover, and cook until back of each chicken is well browned, about 30 minutes, carefully rotating V-rack 180 degrees after 15 minutes. Flip chickens and repeat until breasts are well browned and thighs register 155 degrees, 30 to 40 minutes. Brush chickens with glaze, cover, and continue to cook, flipping and glazing chickens every 5 minutes, until lightly charred in spots and breasts register 160 degrees and thighs register 175 degrees, 15 to 25 minutes.

4 Transfer chickens to carving board and let rest for 20 minutes; remove twine. Carve chickens, drizzle with any remaining glaze, and serve.

HONEY-MUSTARD GLAZE
makes about ½ cup
Simmer ⅓ cup honey, ¼ cup Dijon mustard, and ¼ teaspoon salt in small saucepan over medium heat until thickened, 3 to 5 minutes. (Glaze can be refrigerated for up to 3 days. Gently warm glaze in small saucepan or microwave before using.)

BROWN SUGAR–BALSAMIC GLAZE
makes about ½ cup
Simmer ⅓ cup packed dark brown sugar, ¼ cup balsamic vinegar, and ¼ teaspoon salt in small saucepan over medium heat until thickened, 3 to 5 minutes. (Glaze can be refrigerated for up to 3 days. Gently warm glaze in small saucepan or microwave before using.)

---

arranging chickens on a V-rack

Place chickens breast side up and head to tail on V-rack. Make sure they are well balanced on rack.

GRILL-ROASTED BUTTERFLIED LEMON CHICKEN

serves 8

2 (3½- to 4-pound) whole chickens, giblets discarded

5 lemons

Salt and pepper

1 (13 by 9-inch) disposable aluminum pan (if using charcoal)

1 garlic clove, minced

2 tablespoons minced fresh parsley

2 teaspoons Dijon mustard

1 teaspoon sugar

⅔ cup extra-virgin olive oil

Why This Recipe Works Butterflied chicken is made for roasting on the grill. Opening up the chicken like a book creates a flat surface that makes for even grilling. We also can easily rub seasonings directly under the skin to flavor the meat and the skin becomes especially crisp since it's all on one side. For a pair of grill-roasted birds with bright lemon flavor, we started by pounding the breasts a bit to flatten them and applied a simple rub of salt, pepper, and grated lemon zest under the skin, giving it at least an hour to penetrate. To add more lemon flavor, we decided on a lemon vinaigrette to serve with the chicken. Grilling halved lemons intensified their citrus flavor while muting the acidity of their juice. We kept the roasting brief but effective by cooking the chickens skin side down over the cooler side of a half-grill fire (a disposable pan kept the coals all on one side) with the legs facing the coals and the delicate white meat positioned further away. This setup kept the breasts moist while the dark meat cooked through. A final sear directly over the dying coals crisped and browned the skin nicely—without the risk of flare-ups. This recipe requires refrigerating the salted chicken for at least 1 hour or up to 24 hours before cooking (a longer time is preferable). If using kosher chickens, omit the salt in step 2. For butterflying instructions, see page 5.

1 Set wire rack in rimmed baking sheet. With 1 chicken breast side down, use kitchen shears to cut through bones on either side of backbone; discard backbone. Flip chicken over and press on breastbone to flatten. Cover chicken with plastic wrap and pound breast with meat pounder to even thickness. Repeat with second chicken.

2 Grate 2 teaspoons zest from 1 lemon (halve and reserve lemon) and mix with 2 teaspoons salt and 1 teaspoon pepper in bowl. Pat chickens dry with paper towels and, using your fingers or handle of wooden spoon, gently loosen skin covering breasts and thighs. Rub zest mixture underneath skin of breasts, directly onto meat, then season exterior of chicken with salt and pepper. Tuck wingtips behind back and transfer chickens to prepared rack. Refrigerate uncovered for at least 1 hour or up to 24 hours.

3A For a charcoal grill Open bottom vent completely and place disposable pan on 1 side of grill. Light large chimney starter filled with charcoal briquettes (6 quarts). When top coals are partially covered with ash, pour evenly over other side of grill. Scatter 20 unlit coals on top of lit coals. Set cooking grate in place, cover, and open lid vent completely. Heat grill until hot, about 5 minutes.

3B For a gas grill Turn all burners to high, cover, and heat grill until hot, about 15 minutes. Leave primary burner on high and turn other burner(s) to low. (Adjust primary burner as needed to maintain grill temperature between 350 and 375 degrees.)

4 Clean and oil cooking grate. Halve remaining 4 lemons and place cut side down on hotter side of grill along with reserved lemon halves. Place chickens skin side down on cooler side of grill, with legs pointing toward heat source; cover, placing lid vent over chickens on charcoal grill.

5 Cook lemons until deep brown and caramelized, 5 to 8 minutes; transfer to bowl. Cover and continue to cook until breasts register 160 degrees and thighs register 175 degrees, 40 to 50 minutes. Slide chickens to hotter side of grill and cook uncovered until skin is well browned, 2 to 4 minutes. Transfer chickens to carving board skin side up and let rest for 20 minutes.

6 Meanwhile, squeeze ⅓ cup juice from grilled lemons into bowl. (Cut any unsqueezed lemons into wedges for serving.) Using flat side of knife, mash garlic and ½ teaspoon salt into paste and add to bowl with lemon juice. Whisk in parsley, mustard, sugar, and ½ teaspoon pepper. Slowly whisk in oil until emulsified.

7 Carve chickens, transfer to serving dish, and pour ⅓ cup vinaigrette over chicken. Serve, passing remaining vinaigrette and grilled lemon wedges separately.

pounding and flavoring lemon chicken

1 Use meat pounder to gently pound breasts to even thickness.

2 Rub zest mixture under skin and season chicken all over with salt and pepper.

GRILL-SMOKED BONELESS TURKEY BREAST

serves 6 to 8

1 (5- to 7-pound) bone-in whole turkey breast, trimmed

Salt and pepper

½ cup wood chips

1 teaspoon vegetable oil

Why This Recipe Works The smoky fire of a grill can turn mild-mannered turkey into a richly flavored, juicy roast. We were determined to deliver a grill-smoked breast with crisp, well-rendered skin and moist white meat. We started with a bone-in whole turkey breast, removed the skin and bones, and then salted the meat to add flavor and moisture. (This boneless roast also gave us the option of adding a filling.) Next we stacked the breast halves on top of one another thick end over tapered end to create an even thickness. We draped the halves with the turkey skin, and tied the "roast" together. The skin helped protect the meat from the fire and the stacked breasts ensured the meat roasted more slowly. When it came time to grill, we set up a half-grill fire and started the oiled and peppered turkey breast over the cooler side of the grill. A quick sear on the hotter side of the grill at the end of roasting took care of crisping the skin. A packet with just a half cup of wood chips created enough savory smoke to infuse the skin and meat with its flavor and offer a deeply burnished finish. If using a self-basting turkey (such as a frozen Butterball) or a kosher turkey, omit the salt in step 1.

1 Remove skin from breast meat and then cut along rib cage to remove breast halves; discard bones. Pat turkey breast halves dry with paper towels and season with 2 teaspoons salt. Stack breast halves on top of one another with cut sides facing each other, and alternating thick and tapered ends. Stretch skin over exposed meat and tuck in ends. Tie kitchen twine lengthwise around roast, then tie 5 to 7 pieces of twine at 1-inch intervals crosswise around roast. Transfer roast to wire rack set in rimmed baking sheet and refrigerate uncovered for 1 hour.

2 Just before grilling, soak wood chips in water for 15 minutes, then drain. Using large piece of heavy-duty aluminum foil, wrap soaked chips in 8 by 4½-inch foil packet. (Make sure chips do not poke holes in sides or bottom of packet.) Cut 2 evenly spaced 2-inch slits in top of packet.

3A For a charcoal grill Open bottom vent halfway. Light large chimney starter filled with charcoal briquettes (6 quarts). When top coals are partially covered with ash, pour evenly over half of grill. Place wood chip packet on coals. Set cooking grate in place, cover, and open lid vent halfway. Heat grill until hot and wood chips are smoking, about 5 minutes.

3B For a gas grill Remove cooking grate and place wood chip packet directly on primary burner. Set cooking grate in place, turn all burners to high, cover, and heat grill until hot and wood chips are smoking, about 15 minutes. Turn all burners to medium-low. (Adjust burners as needed to maintain grill temperature around 300 degrees.)

4 Clean and oil cooking grate. Rub surface of roast with oil and season with pepper. Place roast on grill (on cooler side if using charcoal). Cover (position lid vent over meat if using charcoal) and cook until roast registers 150 degrees, 40 minutes to 1 hour, turning roast 180 degrees halfway through cooking.

5 Slide roast to hotter side of grill (if using charcoal) or turn all burners to medium-high (if using gas). Cook until roast is browned and skin is crisp on all sides, 8 to 10 minutes, rotating every 2 minutes.

6 Transfer roast to carving board and let rest for 20 minutes. Remove twine and slice into ½-inch-thick slices. Serve.

Grill-Smoked Boneless Turkey Breast with Olives and Sun-Dried Tomatoes

Combine ¼ cup finely chopped kalamata olives, 3 tablespoons finely chopped sun-dried tomatoes, 1 minced garlic clove, 1 teaspoon minced fresh thyme, ½ teaspoon anchovy paste, and ½ teaspoon red pepper flakes in bowl. Spread olive mixture evenly over cut side of each turkey breast half before assembling roast.

turning a bone-in breast into a boneless roast

1 Remove skin from breast. Using tip of knife, cut along rib cage to remove each breast half completely.

2 Arrange 1 breast cut side up; top with second breast, cut side down, thick end over tapered end. Drape skin over breasts and tuck ends under.

GRILL-SMOKED TURKEY BREAST

serves 6 to 8

3 tablespoons packed brown sugar

1 tablespoon salt

1 (5- to 7-pound) bone-in whole turkey breast, trimmed

½ cup wood chips

2 teaspoons pepper

1 (13 by 9-inch) disposable aluminum roasting pan (if using charcoal)

Why This Recipe Works A bone-in, skin-on whole turkey breast cooks relatively quickly on the grill. We wanted plump, juicy white meat with just the right balance of sweet and smoky flavors. For deeply seasoned, crisp-skinned meat, we rubbed salt and brown sugar under and over the skin and gave it at least 8 hours wrapped in plastic in the refrigerator to penetrate and dehydrate the skin. Before grilling, we applied a second rub, replacing the salt with pepper for a spicy kick while the brown sugar helped to add some color to the skin. Piercing the skin before grilling allowed some of the fat to drain away, which helped crisp the skin. A half cup of wood chips added just enough smokiness without overwhelming the mild flavor of the breast meat, and a double-banked fire around a disposable aluminum pan offered the right amount of gentle, even heat to gradually cook the meat through while producing a rich golden skin. This recipe requires refrigerating the rubbed turkey for at least 8 hours or up to 24 hours (a longer time is preferable). If using a self-basting turkey (such as a frozen Butterball) or a kosher turkey, do not salt it in step 1, but do apply sugar.

1 Combine 2 tablespoons sugar and salt in bowl. Pat turkey dry with paper towels. Using your fingers or handle of spoon, gently loosen skin covering each side of breast and rub sugar mixture evenly over and under skin. Tightly wrap turkey with plastic wrap and refrigerate for at least 8 hours or up to 24 hours.

2 Just before grilling, soak wood chips in water for 15 minutes, then drain. Using large piece of heavy-duty aluminum foil, wrap soaked chips in 8 by 4½-inch foil packet. (Make sure chips do not poke holes in sides or bottom of packet.) Cut 2 evenly spaced 2-inch slits in top of packet. Combine remaining 1 tablespoon sugar and pepper in bowl. Unwrap turkey, pat dry with paper towels, and rub sugar-pepper mixture under and over skin. Prick skin all over with paring knife.

3A For a charcoal grill Open bottom vent halfway and place disposable pan in center of grill. Light large chimney starter filled with charcoal briquettes (6 quarts). When top coals are partially covered with ash, pour into 2 even piles on either side of disposable pan. Place wood chip packet on 1 pile of coals. Set cooking grate in place, cover, and open lid vent halfway. Heat grill until hot and wood chips are smoking, about 5 minutes.

3B For a gas grill Remove cooking grate and place wood chip packet directly on primary burner. Set cooking grate in place, turn all burners to high, cover, and heat grill until hot and wood chips are smoking, about 15 minutes. Turn all burners to medium-low. (Adjust burners as needed to maintain grill temperature around 350 degrees.)

4 Clean and oil cooking grate. Place turkey breast skin side up in center of grill (over disposable pan if using charcoal). Cover (position lid vent over turkey if using charcoal) and cook until skin is well browned and breast registers 160 degrees, about 1½ hours.

5 Transfer turkey to carving board and let rest for 30 minutes. Carve turkey and serve.

CLASSIC GRILL-SMOKED TURKEY

serves 10 to 12

1 cup salt

1 (12- to 14-pound) turkey, neck and giblets discarded

2 tablespoons unsalted butter, melted

6 cups wood chips

Why This Recipe Works For a holiday change of pace, grill smoking can produce the best-tasting, best-looking turkey, complete with crisp skin and moist meat perfumed with smoke. We chose a small turkey (no more than 14 pounds) because the skin on larger birds burns before the meat is cooked. To season the meat and add moisture, we brined our turkey. Arranging the turkey in a V-rack improved air circulation and placing it on the cooler side of the grill protected the skin and extended the cooking time. An hour in, we replenished the charcoal and wood chips and flipped the turkey. After another 45 minutes, we turned the rack to promote even browning. This recipe requires refrigerating the brined turkey for at least 6 hours or up to 12 hours before cooking (a longer time is preferable). If using a self-basting turkey (such as a frozen Butterball) or a kosher turkey, do not brine in step 1, but do season with salt after brushing with butter in step 2.

1 Dissolve salt in 2 gallons cold water in large container. Submerge turkey in brine, cover, and refrigerate for at least 6 hours or up to 12 hours.

2 Lightly spray V-rack with vegetable oil spray. Remove turkey from brine and pat dry, inside and out, with paper towels. Tuck wingtips behind back, brush entire surface of turkey with melted butter, and place breast side down in prepared V-rack.

3 Just before grilling, soak wood chips in water for 15 minutes, then drain. Using large piece of heavy-duty aluminum foil, wrap 2 cups soaked chips in 8 by 4½-inch foil packet. (Make sure chips do not poke holes in sides or bottom of packet.) Repeat twice with remaining 4 cups chips for total of 3 packets. Cut 2 evenly spaced 2-inch slits in top of each packet.

4A For a charcoal grill Open bottom vent halfway. Light large chimney mounded with charcoal briquettes (7 quarts). When top coals are partially covered with ash, pour into steeply banked pile against side of grill. Place 2 wood chip packets on pile of coals. Set cooking grate in place, cover, and open lid vent halfway. Heat grill until hot and wood chips are smoking, about 5 minutes.

4B For a gas grill Remove cooking grate and place 1 wood chip packet directly on primary burner. Set cooking grate in place, turn all burners to high, cover, and heat grill until hot and wood chips are smoking, about 15 minutes. Turn primary burner to medium-high and turn off other burner(s). (Adjust primary burner as needed to maintain grill temperature around 325 degrees.)

5 Clean and oil cooking grate. Place V-rack with turkey on cooler side of grill with leg and wing facing heat source, cover (position lid vent over turkey if using charcoal), and cook for 1 hour.

6 Using potholders, transfer V-rack with turkey to rimmed baking sheet or roasting pan. If using charcoal, remove cooking grate and add 12 new briquettes and third wood chip packet to pile of coals; set cooking grate in place. If using gas, place remaining wood chip packets directly on primary burner. With wad of paper towels in each hand, flip turkey breast side up in rack and return V-rack with turkey to cooler side of grill, with other leg and wing facing heat source. Cover (position lid vent over turkey if using charcoal) and cook for 45 minutes.

7 Using potholders, carefully rotate V-rack with turkey (breast remains up) 180 degrees. Cover and continue to cook until breast registers 160 degrees and thighs register 175 degrees, 15 to 45 minutes. Transfer turkey to carving board and let rest for 45 minutes. Carve turkey and serve.

GRILL-SMOKED DUCK

serves 4

1 (4½- to 5-pound) whole duck, neck and giblets discarded

2 cups wood chips

1 (13 by 9-inch) disposable aluminum roasting pan (if using charcoal) or
1 (9-inch) disposable aluminum pie plate (if using gas)

1 cup orange juice (2 oranges)

2 tablespoons lime juice

2 tablespoons honey

Why This Recipe Works This grill-smoked whole duck boasts rich, tender meat beneath crisp, paper-thin skin. Our method makes roasting this fatty bird on the grill totally foolproof (and flare-up-proof). We took our cue from our recipe for oven-roasted duck (see page 107) and first steamed the duck on the stovetop to render its fat. Before steaming, we pricked the duck skin all over so any fat left after steaming would render on the grill, thereby guaranteeing wonderfully crisp skin. We set up a double-banked fire, added a packet of wood chips for plenty of smoke, and placed the duck above an aluminum pan in the middle where it cooked evenly in the moderate heat without any need for turning or flipping. In about an hour, the duck reached brown and tender perfection. To elevate the flavor of the duck, we decided to add a final flourish: a citrusy glaze. Brushed on with minutes to go so it wouldn't burn, this coating created a sweet, burnished finish. Pekin ducks, also called Long Island ducks, are the only choice in most supermarkets. Almost always sold frozen, the duck must defrost in the refrigerator for at least one day before cooking.

1 Using tip of paring knife, prick skin over entire body of duck. Spray V-rack with vegetable oil spray and set in roasting pan; place duck breast side up on rack. Add water to just below bottom of duck, place pan over 2 burners, and bring to boil. Reduce heat to medium, cover pan tightly with aluminum foil, and steam until fat beads on pores of duck and skin has pulled away from at least 1 leg, about 30 minutes (add more hot water to maintain water level if necessary). Lift duck from rack and, being careful not to break skin, pat gently with paper towels to remove excess fat and moisture.

2 Just before grilling, soak wood chips in water for 15 minutes, then drain. Using large piece of heavy-duty aluminum foil, wrap soaked chips in 8 by 4½-inch foil packet. (Make sure chips do not poke holes in sides or bottom of packet.) Cut 2 evenly spaced 2-inch slits in top of packet.

3A For a charcoal grill Open bottom vent halfway and place disposable pan in center of grill. Light large chimney starter filled with charcoal briquettes (6 quarts). When top coals are partially covered with ash, pour into 2 even piles on either side of disposable pan. Place wood chip packet on 1 pile of coals. Set cooking grate in place, cover, and open lid vent halfway. Heat grill until hot and wood chips are smoking, about 5 minutes.

3B For a gas grill Remove cooking grate and place wood chip packet directly on primary burner. Place disposable pie plate over other burner(s). Set cooking grate in place, turn all burners to high, cover, and heat grill until hot and wood chips are smoking, about 15 minutes. Leave primary burner on high and turn off other burner(s). (Adjust primary burner as needed to maintain grill temperature between 325 and 350 degrees.)

4A For a charcoal grill Clean and oil cooking grate. Place duck breast side up on grill directly over disposable pan. Cover, position lid vent over duck, and cook until skin is crispy, thin, and richly brown, about 1 hour.

4B For a gas grill Clean and oil cooking grate. Place duck breast side up on grill, directly over disposable pie plate. Cover and cook until skin just begins to brown, about 30 minutes. Turn secondary burner(s) to low. (Adjust burners as needed to maintain grill temperature between 425 and 450 degrees.) Cook duck until skin is crisp, thin, and richly brown, 40 to 50 minutes.

5 Meanwhile, bring orange juice, lime juice, and honey to boil in small saucepan. Reduce heat to medium-low and simmer until slightly thickened and reduced to ¼ cup, 25 to 30 minutes.

6 Brush duck generously with glaze. Cover and continue to cook until glaze heats through, 3 to 5 minutes. (Be careful not to let glaze burn.) Transfer duck to carving board and let rest for 10 minutes. Carve duck and serve.

Chinese-Style Grill-Smoked Duck
Before proceeding with step 3, mix 1½ tablespoons soy sauce, 2 teaspoons five-spice powder, and 1 teaspoon toasted sesame oil in small bowl. Brush mixture all over duck, being careful not to tear skin. Place 3 large scallions, ends trimmed and cut into thirds, and one 1½-inch piece of ginger, peeled and sliced into thin coins, in cavity of duck. Replace orange glaze with uncooked mixture of 2 tablespoons honey, 2 tablespoons rice vinegar, and 1 tablespoon soy sauce.

GRILL-SMOKED CORNISH HENS

serves 4

4 (1¼- to 1½-pound) whole Cornish game hens, giblets discarded

Salt

2 tablespoons packed brown sugar

1 tablespoon paprika

2 teaspoons garlic powder

2 teaspoons chili powder

1 teaspoon pepper

1 teaspoon ground coriander

⅛ teaspoon cayenne pepper

4 cups wood chips

1 (16 by 12-inch) disposable aluminum roasting pan (if using charcoal)

1 recipe glaze (recipes follow)

Why This Recipe Works Cornish hens are an elegant alternative to chicken, and grill-smoking them concentrates their delicate flavor and produces really crisp skin and serious smoky flavor. To start, we butter-flied the small hens to make them an even thickness and to put all of the skin on one side for more efficient grilling. We then treated them to a short brine for maximum moisture retention. Skewering each hen from the drumstick to the wing helped to hold the skin in place and improved the bird's appearance. An aluminum pan placed in the center of the grill with the coals banked on either side created a cooler heat zone. We started the hens skin side down there, allowing them to gently cook through before moving them to the hotter sides to give them a last blast of heat to crisp the skin. A quick barbecue glaze provided the final touch. You will need four 12-inch metal skewers for this recipe.

1 With 1 hen breast side down, use kitchen shears to cut along both sides of backbone; discard backbone. With skin side down, make ¼-inch cut into bone separating breast halves. Lightly press on ribs to flatten hen. Tuck wingtips behind back. Repeat with remaining 3 hens.

2 Dissolve ½ cup salt in 4 quarts cold water in large container. Submerge hens in brine, cover, and refrigerate for at least 30 minutes or up to 1 hour.

3 Combine sugar, paprika, garlic powder, chili powder, pepper, coriander, and cayenne in bowl. Remove hens from brine and pat dry with paper towels.

4 Insert one 12-inch metal skewer ½ inch from end of drumstick through skin and meat and out other side. Turn leg so that end of drumstick faces wing, then insert tip of skewer into meaty section of thigh under bone. Press skewer completely thorough breast and second thigh. Fold end of drumstick toward wing and insert skewer ½ inch from end. Press skewer so that blunt end rests against bird and stretches skin tight over legs, thighs, and breast halves. Repeat with remaining 3 hens. Rub hens evenly with spice mixture and refrigerate while preparing grill.

5 Just before grilling, soak wood chips in water for 15 minutes, then drain. Using large piece of heavy-duty aluminum foil, wrap 2 cups soaked chips in 8 by 4½-inch foil packet. (Make sure chips do not poke holes in sides or bottom of packet.) Repeat with remaining 2 cups chips. Cut 2 evenly spaced 2-inch slits in top of each packet.

6A **For a charcoal grill** Open bottom vent completely and place disposable pan in center of grill. Light large chimney starter filled with charcoal briquettes (6 quarts). When top coals are partially covered with ash, pour into 2 even piles on either side of disposable pan. Place 1 wood chip packet on each pile of coals. Set cooking grate in place, cover, and open lid vent completely. Heat grill until hot and wood chips are smoking, about 5 minutes.

6B **For a gas grill** Remove cooking grate and place wood chip packets directly on primary burner. Set cooking grate in place, turn all burners to high, cover, and heat grill until hot and wood chips are smoking, about 15 minutes. Turn all burners to medium. (Adjust burners as needed during cooking to maintain grill temperature around 325 degrees.)

7 Clean and oil cooking grate. Place hens in center of grill (over disposable pan if using charcoal), skin side down. Cover (position lid vent over birds if using charcoal) and cook until thighs register 160 degrees, 20 to 30 minutes.

8 Using tongs, move hens to hotter sides of grill (2 hens per side if using charcoal), keeping them skin side down, or turn all burners to high (if using gas). Cover and continue to cook until browned, about 5 minutes. Brush hens with half of glaze, flip, and cook for 2 minutes. Brush remaining glaze over hens, flip, and continue to cook until breasts register 160 degrees and thighs register 175 degrees, 1 to 3 minutes.

9 Transfer hens to carving board and let rest for 10 minutes. Remove skewers, cut hens in half through breastbone, and serve.

BARBECUE GLAZE
makes about ½ cup

½ cup ketchup
2 tablespoons packed brown sugar
1 tablespoon soy sauce
1 tablespoon distilled white vinegar
1 tablespoon yellow mustard
1 garlic clove, minced

Combine all ingredients in small saucepan, bring to simmer over medium heat, and cook, stirring occasionally, until thickened, about 5 minutes.

ASIAN BARBECUE GLAZE
makes about ½ cup

¼ cup ketchup
¼ cup hoisin sauce
2 tablespoons rice vinegar
1 tablespoon soy sauce
1 tablespoon toasted sesame oil
1 tablespoon grated fresh ginger

Combine all ingredients in small saucepan, bring to simmer over medium heat, and cook, stirring occasionally, until thickened, about 5 minutes.

skewering a cornish hen

1 After inserting skewer through drumstick, turn leg so that end of drumstick faces wing, then insert tip of skewer into meaty section of thigh under bone.

2 Press skewer completely through breast and second thigh. Fold end of drumstick toward wing and insert skewer ½ inch from end.

All About Grill Roasting

The oven isn't your only option for roasting meat. For cuts that cook over moderate heat, the grill works just as well. Building a moderate, indirect fire and covering the grill turns it into an outdoor oven for cuts like prime rib, whole chicken, and pork loin.

use briquettes

We like natural hardwood charcoal for grilling, but it's not the best choice for grill roasting. Though both hardwood charcoal and briquettes burn fast and hot for the first 30 minutes, we've found that hardwood then abruptly turns to ash while the briquettes keep going, taking hours to fall below 250 degrees.

smoking is permitted

While charcoal will infuse a little smokiness into grill-roasted meat (gas adds none), adding wood chips or chunks to the fire is the only way to infuse the meat with smoke flavor. They are made from hardwoods because they burn more slowly than softer woods; hickory and mesquite are the most common. Soaking wood chips or chunks in water prevents them from igniting and burning too quickly on the hot coals, allowing them to smolder slowly. And a good soak means more smoke. Soak wood chips for 15 minutes in cold water and wood chunks for 1 hour.

wood chips or chunks?

Wood chips work on charcoal and gas grills, but use wood chunks only on a charcoal grill. They must sit on a pile of lit coals to smoke. (**Note:** 1 cup wood chips = 1 medium wood chunk) Sealing chips in a foil packet with slits prevents them from igniting while allowing smoke to escape. On a gas grill, place the packet directly on top of the primary burner; on a kettle, put it directly on the lit charcoal.

use a thermometer

Since the type of grill and even the weather can affect cooking times, the only way to ensure proper doneness is to take the meat's temperature. For more information about using a thermometer, see page 25.

making a foil packet for wood chips

1 Soak wood chips in water for 15 minutes; spread drained chips in center of 15 by 12-inch piece of heavy-duty aluminum foil. Fold to seal edges, then cut 2 evenly spaced 2-inch slits in top of packet to allow smoke to escape.

2 Place aluminum foil packet of chips on lit coals of charcoal grill or over primary burner on gas grill.

OUR FAVORITE GRILLS—AND WHY WE LIKE THEM

Well-positioned vents draw hot air over food

Solidly constructed 22-inch kettle maintains heat well

Lid holder means you don't have to set lid on ground

Roomy, easy-to-roll cart

Gas ignition system lights coals with push of button—no chimney starter needed

Charcoal storage bin holds 20 pounds of coals and keeps them dry

TOP CHARCOAL GRILL
Weber Performer Deluxe Charcoal Grill ($399.00)

Heavy-duty cookbox and narrow vent keep heat steady and distribute smoke evenly

Large, secure grease tray makes cleanup easy

Lid design keeps smoke away from your face when open

Sturdy, compact cart rolls without struggle

TOP GAS GRILL UNDER $500
Weber Spirit E-310 Gas Grill ($499.00)

setting up a charcoal grill

A charcoal grill offers some advantages over gas, including more options for creating custom fires and a better ability to impart smoke flavor. Here's how to get going.

1 Get the Coals Hot Remove cooking grate from grill and open bottom grill vent halfway or completely, according to recipe. Fill bottom section of chimney starter with crumpled newspaper, set starter on charcoal rack, and fill top of starter with charcoal briquettes according to recipe. Ignite newspaper and allow charcoal to burn until briquettes on top are partly covered with thin layer of gray ash.

2 Get the Cooking Grate Hot and Scrub It Clean Empty briquettes onto grill and distribute them as indicated in recipe. Set cooking grate in place, cover, and heat grate for about 5 minutes, but no longer, or fire will start to die. (A blast of heat makes it easier to clean cooking grate.) Use grill brush to scrape grate clean of any residual debris; a clean grate also helps to prevent flare-ups.

3 Oil the Cooking Grate Using tongs, dip wad of paper towels in vegetable oil and wipe cleaned cooking grate several times. The oil offers another layer of protection against sticking.

building the right fire

To avoid creating too much fire, add only the amount of charcoal called for in the recipe. Depending on the type of food being grill-roasted, we use one of the grill setups outlined here. You might have to adapt these setups based on the shape, depth, and/or circumference of your grill.

SINGLE-LEVEL FIRE
Charcoal Distribute lit coals in even layer across bottom of grill.
Gas After preheating grill, turn all burners to heat setting as directed in recipe.

TWO-LEVEL FIRE
Charcoal Evenly distribute two-thirds of lit coals over half of grill, then distribute remainder of coals in even layer over other half of grill.
Gas After preheating grill, leave primary burner on high and turn other burner(s) to medium.

HALF-GRILL (MODIFIED TWO-LEVEL) FIRE
Charcoal Distribute lit coals over half of grill, piling them in even layer. Leave other half of grill free of coals.
Gas After preheating grill, adjust primary burner as directed in recipe, and turn off other burner(s).

BANKED FIRE
Charcoal Bank all lit coals steeply against one side of grill, leaving rest of grill free of coals.
Gas After preheating grill, adjust primary burner as directed in recipe, and turn off other burner(s).

DOUBLE-BANKED FIRE
Charcoal Divide lit coals into two steeply banked piles on opposite sides of grill, leaving center free of coals.
Gas After preheating grill, leave primary burner and burner at opposite end of grill on medium-high, medium, or as directed in recipe, and turn off center burner(s).

GRILL-ROASTED BEEF SHORT RIBS

serves 4 to 6

Spice Rub

2 tablespoons kosher salt

1 tablespoon packed brown sugar

2 teaspoons pepper

2 teaspoons ground cumin

2 teaspoons garlic powder

1¼ teaspoons paprika

¾ teaspoon ground fennel

⅛ teaspoon cayenne pepper

Short Ribs

5 pounds bone-in English-style short ribs, bones 4 to 6 inches long, 1 to 1½ inches of meat on top of bone, trimmed

2 tablespoons red wine vinegar

1 recipe glaze (recipes follow)

Why This Recipe Works There's no need to reserve roasting beef short ribs for the winter months. We've found that their flavorful, well-marbled meat is perfect for grill roasting. To achieve both tender meat and a substantial crust, we needed to develop a hybrid roasting method. Working with bone-in ribs offered some insurance against overcooking since the bones help to insulate the meat. In order to guarantee perfectly cooked ribs, we roasted them in the even heat of the oven after prepping them with a spice rub and a sprinkle of red wine vinegar to cut their richness. Once they reached 165 degrees, the conversion of the ribs' collagen to gelatin was well under way. We then moved the ribs outside to finish them on the grill to give them a dark crusty char in roughly 2 hours. Basting the ribs with a tangy glaze on every turn developed a rich, lacquered finish. English-style short ribs contain a single bone and are preferred in this recipe to thinner-cut flanken style ribs.

1 For the spice rub Combine all ingredients in bowl. Measure out 1 teaspoon rub and set aside for glaze.

2 For the short ribs Adjust oven rack to middle position and heat oven to 300 degrees. Sprinkle ribs with spice rub, pressing into all sides of ribs. Arrange ribs bone side down in 13 by 9-inch baking dish, placing thicker ribs around perimeter of baking dish and thinner ribs in center. Sprinkle vinegar evenly over ribs. Cover baking dish tightly with aluminum foil and roast until thickest ribs register 165 to 170 degrees, 1½ to 2 hours.

3A For a charcoal grill Open bottom vent halfway. Arrange 2 quarts unlit charcoal briquettes into steeply banked pile against 1 side of grill. Light large chimney starter half filled with charcoal briquettes (3 quarts). When top coals are partially covered with ash, pour on top of unlit charcoal to cover one-third of grill with coals steeply banked against side of grill. Set cooking grate in place, cover, and open lid vent halfway. Heat grill until hot, about 5 minutes.

3B For a gas grill Turn all burners to high, cover, and heat grill until hot, about 15 minutes. Turn primary burner to medium and turn off other burner(s). (Adjust primary burner as needed to maintain grill temperature between 275 and 300 degrees.)

4 Clean and oil cooking grate. Place short ribs bone side down on cooler side of grill about 2 inches from heat source. Brush with ¼ cup glaze. Cover and cook until ribs register 195 degrees, 1¾ to 2¼ hours, rotating and brushing ribs with ¼ cup glaze every 30 minutes. Transfer ribs to large serving dish and let rest for 15 minutes. Serve.

MUSTARD GLAZE
makes about 1 cup

½ cup Dijon mustard

½ cup red wine vinegar

¼ cup packed brown sugar

1 teaspoon reserved spice rub

⅛ teaspoon cayenne pepper

Whisk all ingredients together in bowl.

BLACKBERRY GLAZE

makes about 1 cup

You can use fresh or frozen blackberries for this recipe.

10 ounces (2 cups) fresh or frozen blackberries
½ cup ketchup
¼ cup bourbon
2 tablespoons packed brown sugar
1½ tablespoons soy sauce
1 teaspoon reserved spice rub
⅛ teaspoon cayenne pepper

Bring all ingredients to simmer in small saucepan over medium-high heat. Simmer, stirring frequently to break up blackberries, until reduced to 1¼ cups, about 10 minutes. Strain through fine-mesh strainer, pressing on solids to extract as much liquid as possible. Discard solids.

HOISIN-TAMARIND GLAZE

makes about 1 cup

1 cup water
⅓ cup hoisin sauce
¼ cup tamarind paste
1 (2-inch) piece ginger, peeled and sliced
into ½-inch-thick rounds
1 teaspoon reserved spice rub
⅛ teaspoon cayenne pepper

Bring all ingredients to simmer in small saucepan over medium-high heat. Simmer, stirring frequently, until reduced to 1¼ cups, about 10 minutes. Strain through fine-mesh strainer, pressing on solids to extract as much liquid as possible. Discard solids.

GRILL-SMOKED CALIFORNIA BARBECUED TRI-TIP

serves 4 to 6

2 tablespoons vegetable oil

6 garlic cloves, minced

1½ teaspoons kosher salt

1 (2-pound) beef tri-tip roast, trimmed

1 teaspoon pepper

¾ teaspoon garlic salt

2 cups wood chips

Why This Recipe Works California tri-tip recipes typically call for cooking the triangular beef roast over high heat and seasoning it with only salt, pepper, garlic, and the sweet smoke of the grill. This produces a charred exterior and very rare center, but we wanted the outside cooked less and the inside cooked more. To achieve this we pushed all of the coals in our grill to one side. The hotter side allowed us to develop a flavorful crust on all sides of the meat before finishing roasting it gently on the cooler side. To infuse the meat with subtle smoke, we added a wood chip packet to the fire before moving the meat to the cooler side. To infuse the beef with deep flavor in just an hour, we poked holes in the meat's surface and spread on a simple garlicky marinade. We reinforced the garlic flavor by sprinkling the roast with garlic salt and pepper before firing up the grill. This recipe requires letting the rubbed beef sit for at least 1 hour or refrigerating for up to 24 hours before cooking (a longer time is preferable). We prefer this roast cooked to medium-rare, but if you prefer it more or less done, see our guidelines on page 24. Sliced thin, this garlicky, smoky beef needs no adornment but is traditionally accompanied by fresh tomato salsa; we like to serve it with Santa Maria Salsa (recipe follows).

1 Combine oil, garlic, and salt in bowl. Pat beef dry with paper towels, poke each side about 20 times with fork, then rub evenly with oil-garlic mixture. Wrap beef in plastic wrap and let sit at room temperature for 1 hour or refrigerate for up to 24 hours.

2 Unwrap beef, wipe off garlic paste using paper towels, and season with pepper and garlic salt. Just before grilling, soak wood chips in water for 15 minutes, then drain. Using large piece of heavy-duty aluminum foil, wrap soaked chips in 8 by 4½-inch foil packet. (Make sure chips do not poke holes in sides or bottom of packet.) Cut 2 evenly spaced 2-inch slits in top of packet.

3A For a charcoal grill Open bottom vent halfway. Light large chimney starter filled with charcoal briquettes (6 quarts). When top coals are partially covered with ash, pour evenly over half of grill. Set cooking grate in place, cover, and open lid vent halfway. Heat grill until hot, about 5 minutes.

3B For a gas grill Turn all burners to high, cover, and heat grill until hot, about 15 minutes. Leave all burners on high.

4 Clean and oil cooking grate. Place roast on hotter side of grill. Cook (covered if using gas), turning as needed, until well browned on all sides, 8 to 10 minutes. Transfer roast to plate.

5 Remove cooking grate and place wood chip packet directly on coals or primary burner. Set cooking grate in place, cover, and let chips begin to smoke, about 5 minutes. If using gas, leave primary burner on high and turn off other burner(s).

6 Place roast on cooler side of grill. Cover (position lid vent over meat if using charcoal) and cook until beef registers 120 to 125 degrees (for medium-rare), about 20 minutes. Transfer roast to carving board and let rest for 20 minutes. Slice meat thin and serve.

SANTA MARIA SALSA

makes about 4 cups

The distinct texture of each ingredient is part of this salsa's appeal, so we don't recommend using a food processor.

2 pounds tomatoes, cored and chopped

2 teaspoons salt

2 jalapeño chiles, stemmed, seeded, and chopped fine

1 small red onion, chopped fine

1 celery rib, chopped fine

¼ cup lime juice (2 limes)

¼ cup chopped fresh cilantro

1 garlic clove, minced

⅛ teaspoon dried oregano

⅛ teaspoon Worcestershire sauce

1 Place tomatoes in strainer set over bowl and sprinkle with salt; drain for 30 minutes. Discard liquid. Meanwhile, combine jalapeños, onion, celery, lime juice, cilantro, garlic, oregano, and Worcestershire in large bowl.

2 Add drained tomatoes to jalapeño mixture and toss to combine. Cover with plastic wrap and let stand at room temperature for 1 hour. (Salsa can be refrigerated for up to 2 days.)

GRILL-SMOKED TEXAS CHUCK ROAST

serves 10 to 12

1½ tablespoons kosher salt

1½ teaspoons pepper

¼ teaspoon cayenne pepper

1 (5-pound) boneless beef chuck-eye roast, trimmed

2 cups wood chips

Why This Recipe Works The regional specialty of coal-black barbecued beef shoulder clod was the inspiration for our Texas chuck roast. Shoulder clod is a large boneless cut of beef that has supremely beefy flavor but tips the scales at 13 to 21 pounds. Our first move was to swap this Texas-size roast for more manageable chuck eye, a versatile piece of meat cut from a portion of the shoulder clod. We rubbed its surface with a combination of salt, pepper, and cayenne and refrigerated it for 18 hours to deeply season and tenderize the meat. We roasted the chuck eye over the indirect heat of a half-grill fire, drawing out the cooking time until the tough meat turned tender—right around 155 degrees—and took on smoky flavor. The last key to tenderness was to slice the meat paper-thin. Our richly seasoned clod-style chuck roast was so rich and flavorful it needed no embellishing. This recipe requires refrigerating the salted beef for at least 18 hours or up to 24 hours before cooking (a longer time is preferable).

1 Combine salt, pepper, and cayenne in bowl. Pat roast dry with paper towels. Place roast on large sheet of plastic wrap and rub all over with spice mixture. Wrap tightly in plastic and refrigerate for at least 18 hours or up to 24 hours.

2 Just before grilling, soak wood chips in water for 15 minutes, then drain. Using large piece of heavy-duty aluminum foil, wrap soaked chips in 8 by 4½-inch foil packet. (Make sure chips do not poke holes in sides or bottom of packet.) Cut 2 evenly spaced 2-inch slits in top of packet.

3A For a charcoal grill Open bottom vent completely. Light large chimney starter filled with charcoal briquettes (6 quarts). When top coals are partially covered with ash, pour evenly over half of grill. Place wood chip packet on coals. Set cooking grate in place, cover, and open lid vent completely. Heat grill until hot and wood chips are smoking, about 5 minutes.

3B For a gas grill Remove cooking grate and place wood chip packet directly on primary burner. Set cooking grate in place, turn all burners to high, cover, and heat grill until hot and wood chips are smoking, about 15 minutes. Leave primary burner on high and turn off other burner(s). (Adjust primary burner as needed to maintain grill temperature around 350 degrees.)

4 Clean and oil cooking grate. Place roast on cooler side of grill. Cover (position lid vent directly over roast if using charcoal) and cook until meat registers 155 to 160 degrees, 2 to 2½ hours. Transfer roast to carving board and let rest for 20 minutes. Slice thin and serve.

GRILL-ROASTED SIRLOIN ROAST WITH GARLIC AND ROSEMARY

serves 6 to 8

6 garlic cloves, minced

2 tablespoons minced fresh rosemary

4 teaspoons kosher salt

1 tablespoon pepper

1 (3- to 4-pound) center-cut boneless top sirloin roast, trimmed

1 (13 by 9-inch) disposable aluminum roasting pan

Why This Recipe Works This recipe proves that you can get a show-stopping roast from an inexpensive cut. To serve up a standout top sirloin roast with a distinct, rich crust, we started by applying a fragrant garlic-rosemary rub, wrapping the roast in plastic wrap, and allowing the seasonings to penetrate the meat in the refrigerator for a day. We set up a moderate half-grill fire and seared the beef on the hotter side, creating a strong, caramelized crust. To shield the meat from excess heat, we moved it to a perforated aluminum roasting pan and allowed the beef to roast low and slow to a tender medium-rare on the cooler side of the grill, protected by the pan's metal walls. Rotating the roast halfway through made for evenly cooked beef and the holes in the pan allowed the juices to drain, keeping the crust crisp. Cutting the roast into wafer-thin slices against the grain helped the beef taste even more tender. A pair of kitchen shears works well for punching the holes in the aluminum pan. We prefer a top sirloin roast, but you can substitute a top round or bottom round roast. This recipe requires refrigerating the salted beef for at least 18 hours or up to 24 hours before cooking (a longer time is preferable). We prefer this roast cooked to medium-rare, but if you prefer it more or less done, see our guidelines on page 24. Serve with Horseradish Sauce (page 27), if desired.

1 Combine garlic, rosemary, salt, and pepper in bowl. Sprinkle all sides of roast evenly with garlic mixture, wrap tightly in plastic wrap, and refrigerate for at least 18 hours or up to 24 hours.

2A For a charcoal grill Open bottom vent halfway. Light large chimney starter half filled with charcoal briquettes (3 quarts). When top coals are partially covered with ash, pour evenly over one-third of grill. Set cooking grate in place, cover, and open lid vent halfway. Heat grill until hot, about 5 minutes.

2B For a gas grill Turn all burners to high, cover, and heat grill until hot, about 15 minutes. Leave all burners on high.

3 Clean and oil cooking grate. Place roast on grill (hotter side if using charcoal) and cook (covered if using gas) until well browned on all sides, 10 to 12 minutes, turning as needed. (If flare-ups occur, move roast to cooler side of grill until flames die down.)

4 Meanwhile, punch fifteen ¼-inch holes in center of disposable pan in area roughly same size as roast. Once browned, place beef in pan over holes and set pan over cooler side of grill (if using charcoal) or turn primary burner to medium and other burner(s) off (if using gas). (Adjust burners as needed to maintain grill temperature between 250 and 300 degrees.) Cover and cook until meat registers 120 to 125 degrees (for medium-rare), 40 minutes to 1 hour, rotating pan halfway through cooking.

5 Transfer roast to wire rack set in rimmed baking sheet and let rest for 20 minutes. Transfer roast to carving board, slice thin against grain, and serve.

GRILL-SMOKED EYE-ROUND ROAST

serves 6 to 8

2 tablespoons ketchup

4 teaspoons salt

2 teaspoons pepper

½ teaspoon dried thyme

½ teaspoon dried oregano

½ teaspoon dried rosemary

1 (3½- to 4½-pound) boneless eye-round roast, trimmed

1 cup wood chips

2 teaspoons vegetable oil

Why This Recipe Works To transform an inexpensive eye-round roast into a tender, smoky centerpiece, we flavored and tenderized the meat with a rub full of herbs and umami-rich ketchup. Roasted opposite a banked pile of coals under a loose foil shield, the beef developed a uniformly rosy interior. We then let it rest off the grill before deeply searing it over a refueled fire. If using charcoal, you will need to light two fires: the first to smoke the meat, and the second to sear it after a prolonged rest. If using a gas grill, simply turn it off between steps. This recipe requires refrigerating the rubbed beef for at least 6 hours or up to 24 hours before cooking (a longer time is preferable). We prefer this roast cooked to medium-rare, but if you prefer it more or less done, see our guidelines on page 24. You don't need to rest the meat again after searing it in step 6; the roast may be served immediately. Serve with Horseradish Sauce (page 27), if desired.

1 Combine ketchup, salt, pepper, thyme, oregano, and rosemary in bowl. Rub ketchup mixture all over roast, wrap roast in plastic wrap, and refrigerate for at least 6 hours or up to 24 hours.

2 Just before grilling, soak wood chips in water for 15 minutes, then drain. Using large piece of heavy-duty aluminum foil, wrap soaked chips in 8 by 4½-inch foil packet. (Make sure chips do not poke holes in sides or bottom of packet.) Cut 2 evenly spaced 2-inch slits in top of packet.

3A For a charcoal grill Open bottom vent halfway. Light large chimney starter half filled with charcoal briquettes (3 quarts). When top coals are partially covered with ash, pour into steeply banked pile against side of grill. Place wood chip packet on coals. Set cooking grate in place, cover, and open lid vent halfway. Heat grill until hot and wood chips are smoking, about 5 minutes.

3B For a gas grill Remove cooking grate and place wood chip packet directly on primary burner. Set cooking grate in place, turn all burners to high, cover, and heat grill until hot and wood chips are smoking, about 15 minutes. Turn primary burner to medium-high and turn off other burner(s). (Adjust primary burner as needed to maintain grill temperature around 325 degrees.)

4 Set wire rack in rimmed baking sheet. Unwrap roast. Arrange 18 by 12-inch sheet of foil on cooler side of grill and place roast on top of 1 end of foil. Loosely roll foil over roast, then tuck end of foil under roast to form loose cylinder around roast. Cover and cook until meat registers 120 to 125 degrees (for medium-rare), 1½ to 1¾ hours. Remove roast from grill and transfer to prepared wire rack. Let roast rest for at least 20 minutes or up to 1 hour.

5A For a charcoal grill Open bottom vent completely. Light large chimney starter filled with charcoal briquettes (6 quarts). When top coals are partially covered with ash, pour into pile over spent coals. Set cooking grate in place, cover, and open lid vent completely. Heat grill until hot, about 5 minutes.

5B For a gas grill Turn all burners to high, cover, and heat grill until hot, about 5 minutes. Leave all burners on high.

6 Clean and oil cooking grate. Brush roast all over with oil. Cook (directly over coals if using charcoal; covered if using gas), turning frequently, until charred on all sides, 8 to 12 minutes. Transfer roast to carving board, slice thin, and serve.

GRILL-ROASTED BEEF TENDERLOIN

serves 6

2¼ teaspoons kosher salt

1 teaspoon pepper

2 teaspoons vegetable oil

1 teaspoon baking soda

1 (3-pound) center-cut beef tenderloin roast, trimmed and tied at 1½-inch intervals

3 slices bacon

Why This Recipe Works Grill-roasting a beef tenderloin is great for summer entertaining, but with this cut's price tag, it's one you simply have to get right. Gentle grill roasting over a half-grill fire imparted a decent crust, but in order to add some smoky flavor to the mild meat, we had to think outside the box. First, to establish a browned crust without overcooking the buttery interior, we applied a baking soda–oil paste. This mixture increased the surface's pH, accelerating its browning, and ensured the beef wouldn't stick to the grill. Much of the signature grilled flavor in fattier cuts is created when its drippings hit the coals or heat diffusers, breaking down into flavorful compounds that condense on the food above. Lean tenderloin doesn't generate those drippings, so we added something to provide fat. We laced strips of bacon onto a skewer and allowed them to render near the beef while it roasted to generate just enough smoky grilled flavor. Before the meat had the chance to overcook, we moved it over to the cooler side, finishing it off low and slow. Center-cut beef tenderloin roasts are sometimes sold as Châteaubriand. Ask your butcher to prepare a trimmed center-cut Châteaubriand, as this cut is not usually available without special ordering. You will need one 12-inch metal skewer for this recipe. The bacon will render slowly during cooking, creating a steady stream of smoke that flavors the beef. We prefer this roast cooked to medium-rare, but if you prefer it more or less done, see our guidelines on page 24. For how to tie a roast, see page 12. Serve with Chimichurri Sauce (recipe follows) or Chermoula Sauce (page 27), if desired.

1 Combine salt, pepper, oil, and baking soda in small bowl. Rub mixture evenly over roast and let sit while preparing grill.

2 Stack bacon slices. Keeping slices stacked, thread 12-inch metal skewer through bacon 6 or 7 times to create accordion shape. Push stack together to compact into about 2-inch length.

3A **For a charcoal grill** Open bottom vent halfway. Light large chimney starter two-thirds filled with charcoal briquettes (4 quarts). When top coals are partially covered with ash, pour evenly over half of grill. Set cooking grate in place, cover, and open lid vent halfway. Heat grill until hot, about 5 minutes.

3B **For a gas grill** Turn all burners to high, cover, and heat grill until hot, about 15 minutes. Turn primary burner to medium and turn off other burner(s). (Adjust primary burner as needed to maintain grill temperature around 300 degrees.)

4 Clean and oil cooking grate. Place roast on hotter side of grill and cook until lightly browned on all sides, about 12 minutes. Slide roast to cooler side of grill, arranging so roast is about 7 inches from heat source. Place skewered bacon on hotter side of grill. (For charcoal, place near center of grill, above edge of coals. For gas, place above heat diffuser of primary burner. Bacon should be 4 to 6 inches from roast and drippings should fall on coals or heat diffuser and produce steady stream of smoke and minimal flare-ups. If flare-ups are large or frequent, slide bacon skewer 1 inch toward roast.)

5 Cover and cook until beef registers 120 to 125 degrees (for medium-rare), 50 minutes to 1¼ hours. Transfer roast to carving board and let rest for 30 minutes. Remove twine, slice roast into ½-inch-thick slices, and serve.

CHIMICHURRI SAUCE
makes about 1½ cups
To keep the sauce from becoming bitter, whisk in the olive oil by hand.

¼ cup hot water
2 teaspoons dried oregano
1 teaspoon salt
1⅓ cups fresh parsley leaves
⅔ cup fresh cilantro leaves
6 garlic cloves, minced
½ teaspoon red pepper flakes
¼ cup red wine vinegar
½ cup extra-virgin olive oil

Combine hot water, oregano, and salt in small bowl; let stand for 5 minutes to soften oregano. Pulse parsley, cilantro, garlic, and pepper flakes in food processor until coarsely chopped, about 10 pulses. Add water mixture and vinegar and pulse briefly to combine. Transfer mixture to medium bowl and slowly whisk in oil until incorporated and mixture is emulsified. Cover with plastic wrap and let stand at room temperature for at least 1 hour. (Sauce can be refrigerated for up to 2 days; bring to room temperature and rewhisk before serving.)

GRILL-SMOKED PRIME RIB

serves 8 to 10

1 (7-pound) first-cut beef standing rib roast (3 or 4 bones), with ⅛-inch fat cap

1 tablespoon vegetable oil

Kosher salt and pepper

2 cups wood chips

1 (16 by 12-inch) disposable aluminum roasting pan (if using charcoal)

Why This Recipe Works When most people think of grilling they think steaks and burgers, but grill smoking offers prime treatment for prime rib. In our hands, this deluxe cut gained a well-charred salty crust and meltingly tender meat from its time on a smoky grill. Since bones protect the meat from overbrowning, we removed the bones and then tied them back onto the meat so that we could keep the convenience of a boneless roast for easier carving. A dry rub of kosher salt not only seasoned the meat but also promoted crust development by drawing out moisture just below the surface for deeper crisping on the grill. To get the color and flavor we wanted, we quickly seared the fat-covered sides directly over the coals on the hotter side of a half-grill fire before slow roasting the meat bone side down on the cooler side. We prefer the flavor and texture of prime-grade beef, but choice grade will work as well. This recipe requires refrigerating the meat for 1 hour and then letting it rest at room temperature for 2 hours before cooking. We prefer this roast cooked to medium-rare, but if you prefer it more or less done, see our guidelines on page 24. Serve with Horseradish Sauce (page 27), if desired.

1 Using sharp knife, cut beef from bones. Pat roast dry with paper towels, rub with oil, and season with pepper. Spread ¼ cup salt on rimmed baking sheet and press roast into salt to coat evenly on all sides. Place meat back on ribs so bones fit exactly where they were cut; tie meat to bones with 2 lengths of kitchen twine. Refrigerate roast uncovered for 1 hour, then let sit at room temperature for 2 hours.

2 Just before grilling, soak wood chips in water for 15 minutes, then drain. Using large piece of heavy-duty aluminum foil, wrap soaked chips in 8 by 4½-inch foil packet. (Make sure chips do not poke holes in sides or bottom of packet.) Cut 2 evenly spaced 2-inch slits in top of packet.

3A For a charcoal grill Open bottom vent halfway and place disposable pan on 1 side of grill. Light large chimney starter two-thirds filled with charcoal briquettes (4 quarts). When top coals are partially covered with ash, pour evenly over other side of grill. Set cooking grate in place, cover, and open lid vent halfway. Heat grill until hot, about 5 minutes.

3B For a gas grill Turn all burners to high, cover, and heat grill until hot, about 15 minutes. Turn primary burner to medium and turn off other burner(s). (Adjust primary burner as needed to maintain grill temperature around 325 degrees.)

4 Clean and oil cooking grate. Place roast on hotter side of grill and cook (covered if using gas) until well browned on all sides, 10 to 15 minutes, turning as needed. (If flare-ups occur, move roast to cooler side of grill until flames die down.)

5 Transfer roast to second rimmed baking sheet. If using charcoal, remove cooking grate and place wood chip packet on pile of coals; set cooking grate in place. If using gas, remove cooking grate and place wood chip packet directly on primary burner; set cooking grate in place. Place roast on cooler side of grill, bone side down, with tips of bones pointed away from fire. Cover (position lid vent over meat if using charcoal) and cook until meat registers 120 to 125 degrees (for medium-rare), 2 to 2½ hours.

6 Transfer roast to carving board and let rest for 30 minutes. Remove twine and bones, slice roast into ½-inch-thick slices, and serve.

GRILL-SMOKED BEEF BRISKET

serves 8 to 10

1 (5- to 6-pound) beef brisket, flat cut, untrimmed

⅔ cup salt

½ cup plus 2 tablespoons sugar

2 cups wood chips

3 tablespoons kosher salt

2 tablespoons pepper

1 (13 by 9-inch) disposable aluminum roasting pan (if using charcoal) or 1 (9-inch) disposable aluminum pie plate (if using gas)

Why This Recipe Works Texas barbecue is big on flavor, especially deeply smoky beef brisket. Hours of low and slow roasting over indirect heat turns this tough cut tender. We figured out how to deliver pit master–caliber beef thanks to a hybrid grill-oven roasting method. To keep the brisket moist during extended cooking, we brined it in a sugar and salt solution. We needed to build the right fire that would essentially turn our grill into a smoker and maintain steady low heat. Layering unlit briquettes in a steeply banked pile on one side of the grill and then pouring hot coals on top kept the fire going without the need to refuel (which would lower the temperature). A pan of water placed next to the coals generated enough moisture to produce the trademark pink smoke ring below the crust's surface. A mixture of sugar, salt, and pepper rubbed into the scored fat cap, along with the smoke and keeping the lid closed, helped the brisket develop its signature thick, dark crust. To finish, we moved the brisket to a moderate oven where the steady, even heat turned it perfectly tender. Slicing the brisket thin against the grain added to that tenderness. This recipe requires refrigerating the brined brisket for 2 hours. We prefer hickory wood chips in this recipe.

1 Using sharp knife, cut slits 1 inch apart in crosshatch pattern in fat cap of brisket, being careful not to cut into meat. Dissolve salt and ½ cup sugar in 4 quarts cold water in large container. Submerge brisket in brine, cover, and refrigerate for 2 hours.

2 Just before grilling, soak wood chips in water for 15 minutes, then drain. Using large piece of heavy-duty aluminum foil, wrap soaked chips in 8 by 4½-inch foil packet. (Make sure chips do not poke holes in sides or bottom of packet.) Cut 2 evenly spaced 2-inch slits in top of packet.

3 Combine remaining 2 tablespoons sugar, kosher salt, and pepper in bowl. Remove brisket from brine and pat dry with paper towels. Transfer to rimmed baking sheet and rub salt mixture over entire brisket and into slits.

4A For a charcoal grill Open bottom vent halfway and place disposable roasting pan on 1 side of grill. Add 2 cups water to pan. Arrange 3 quarts unlit charcoal briquettes banked against other side of grill. Light large chimney starter two-thirds filled with charcoal briquettes (4 quarts). When top coals are partially covered with ash, pour on top of unlit charcoal to cover one-third of grill with coals steeply banked against side of grill. Place wood chip packet on top of coals. Set cooking grate in place, cover, and open lid vent halfway. Heat grill until hot and wood chips are smoking, about 5 minutes.

4B For a gas grill Remove cooking grate and place wood chip packet directly on primary burner. Place disposable pie plate filled with 2 cups water on other burner(s). Set cooking grate in place, turn all burners to high, cover, and heat grill until hot and wood chips are smoking, about 15 minutes. Turn primary burner to medium and turn off other burner(s). (Adjust primary burner as needed to maintain grill temperature between 250 and 300 degrees.)

5 Clean and oil cooking grate. Place brisket on cooler side of grill, fat side down, as far away from coals and flames as possible with thickest side facing heat source. Cover (position lid vent over meat if using charcoal) and cook for 3 hours. During final 30 minutes of cooking, adjust oven rack to middle position and heat oven to 325 degrees.

6 Set wire rack in foil-lined rimmed baking sheet and transfer brisket to rack. Roast in oven until tender and meat registers 195 degrees, about 2 hours.

7 Transfer brisket to carving board and let rest for 30 minutes. Slice brisket against grain into long, thin slices and serve.

GRILL-SMOKED TEXAS THICK-CUT PORK CHOPS

serves 8

Pork

Salt and pepper

3 tablespoons sugar

4 (18- to 20-ounce) bone-in pork rib chops, 2 inches thick, trimmed

2 teaspoons onion powder

2 teaspoons granulated garlic

Barbecue Sauce

2 slices bacon

¼ cup grated onion

Salt and pepper

¾ cup cider vinegar

1¼ cups chicken broth

1 cup ketchup

2 tablespoons hot sauce

½ teaspoon liquid smoke

2 cups wood chips

Why This Recipe Works Massive pork chops can deliver Texas-size pit-smoked flavor with the help of the grill and the right method. We bought extra-thick bone-in chops to help keep their lean meat from drying out on the grill, then brined them in a saltwater solution with some sugar added to promote browning and to keep them juicy. A spice mixture of salt, pepper, onion powder, and granulated garlic sprinkled on before grilling added a distinct flavor, and roasting the chops over mesquite chips infused the meat's crust with fragrant smoke. A half-grill fire allowed us to gently cook the chops through on the cooler side, retaining most of their juices along the way. For a last big shot of flavor, we called on a homemade bacon-y barbecue sauce bright with vinegar to reinforce the chops' smoky grilled taste. Each chop can easily serve two people. Grate the onion for the sauce on the large holes of a box grater. Our preferred hot sauce is Frank's RedHot Original Cayenne Pepper Sauce. We prefer mesquite wood chips in this recipe.

1 **For the pork** Dissolve 3 tablespoons salt and sugar in 1½ quarts cold water in large container. Submerge chops in brine, cover, and refrigerate for 1 hour. Combine onion powder, granulated garlic, 1½ tablespoons salt, and 2 tablespoons pepper in bowl; set aside.

2 **For the barbecue sauce** Meanwhile, cook bacon in medium saucepan over medium heat until fat begins to render and bacon begins to brown, 4 to 6 minutes. Add onion and ⅛ teaspoon salt and cook until softened, 2 to 4 minutes. Stir in vinegar, scraping up any browned bits, and cook until slightly thickened, about 2 minutes.

3 Stir in broth, ketchup, hot sauce, liquid smoke, and ¼ teaspoon pepper. Bring to simmer and cook until slightly thickened, about 15 minutes, stirring occasionally. Discard bacon and season with salt and pepper to taste. Remove from heat, cover, and keep warm.

4 Just before grilling, soak wood chips in water for 15 minutes, then drain. Using large piece of heavy-duty aluminum foil, wrap soaked chips in 8 by 4½-inch foil packet. (Make sure chips do not poke holes in sides or bottom of packet.) Cut 2 evenly spaced 2-inch slits in top of packet. Remove chops from brine and pat dry with paper towels. Season chops all over with reserved spice mixture.

5A **For a charcoal grill** Open bottom vent completely. Light large chimney starter three-quarters filled with charcoal briquettes (4½ quarts). When top coals are partially covered with ash, pour evenly over half of grill. Place wood chip packet on coals. Set cooking grate in place, cover, and, open lid vent completely. Heat grill until hot and wood chips are smoking, about 5 minutes.

5B For a gas grill Remove cooking grate and place wood chip packet directly on primary burner. Set cooking grate in place, turn all burners to high, cover, and heat grill until hot and wood chips are smoking, about 15 minutes. Turn primary burner to medium-high and turn off other burner(s). (Adjust primary burner as needed to maintain grill temperature around 325 degrees.)

6 Clean and oil cooking grate. Arrange chops on cooler side of grill with bone ends toward fire. Cover (position lid vent over chops if using charcoal) and cook until chops register 140 degrees, 45 to 50 minutes, flipping halfway through cooking.

7 Transfer chops to serving dish and let rest for 10 minutes. Brush chops generously with warm sauce and serve, passing remaining sauce separately.

GRILL-ROASTED PORK TENDERLOIN WITH GRILLED PINEAPPLE–RED ONION SALSA

serves 4

Pork

1½ teaspoons kosher salt

1½ teaspoons sugar

½ teaspoon ground cumin

½ teaspoon chipotle chile powder

2 (12- to 16-ounce) pork tenderloins, trimmed

Salsa

½ pineapple, peeled, cored, and cut lengthwise into 6 wedges

1 red onion, cut into 8 wedges through root end

4 teaspoons extra-virgin olive oil

½ cup minced fresh cilantro

1 serrano chile, stemmed, seeded, and minced

2 tablespoons lime juice, plus extra for seasoning

Salt

Why This Recipe Works To turn a midweek dinner into something special try cooking easy pork tenderloin on the grill. To produce beautifully browned pork with a rich crust and tender, juicy meat, we started with a simple dry spice rub to add flavor; sugar aided browning while cumin and chipotle chile powder added savory smokiness. The rub had some time to work its magic while we readied the grill. Searing the meat first guaranteed the best crust and a rosy interior, and turning the tenderloins every 2 minutes delivered even color. Once the meat had a good crust, we moved it to the cooler side to finish roasting. To add bright flavor and enhance the smoky char of the pork, we grilled wedges of pineapple and red onion to make a quick salsa while the meat rested. To ensure that the tenderloins don't curl during cooking, remove the silverskin from the meat (see page 15). We strongly prefer natural pork in this recipe. If the pork is enhanced (injected with a salt solution), omit the salt in step 1.

1 For the pork Combine salt, sugar, cumin, and chile powder in small bowl. Reserve ½ teaspoon spice mixture. Rub remaining spice mixture evenly over surface of both tenderloins. Refrigerate while preparing grill.

2A For a charcoal grill Open bottom vent completely. Light large chimney starter filled with charcoal briquettes (6 quarts). When top coals are partially covered with ash, pour evenly over half of grill. Set cooking grate in place, cover, and open lid vent completely. Heat grill until hot, about 5 minutes.

2B For a gas grill Turn all burners to high, cover, and heat grill until hot, about 15 minutes. Leave primary burner on high and turn off other burner(s).

3 Clean and oil cooking grate. Place tenderloins on hotter side of grill. Cover and cook, turning tenderloins every 2 minutes, until well browned on all sides, about 8 minutes.

4 For the salsa Brush pineapple and onion with 1 teaspoon oil. Move tenderloins to cooler side of grill (6 to 8 inches from heat source) and place pineapple and onion on hotter side of grill. Cover and cook until pineapple and onion are charred on both sides and softened, 8 to 10 minutes, and until pork registers 140 degrees, 12 to 17 minutes, turning tenderloins every 5 minutes. As pineapple, onion, and tenderloins reach desired level of doneness, transfer pineapple and onion to plate and transfer tenderloins to carving board and let rest for 10 minutes.

5 While tenderloins rest, coarsely chop pineapple. Pulse pineapple, onion, cilantro, serrano, lime juice, reserved spice mixture, and remaining 1 tablespoon oil in food processor until mixture is coarsely chopped, 4 to 6 pulses. Transfer to bowl and season with salt and extra lime juice to taste. Slice tenderloins into ½-inch-thick slices. Serve with salsa.

GRILL-ROASTED STUFFED PORK TENDERLOIN

serves 4 to 6

4 teaspoons packed dark brown sugar

Kosher salt and pepper

2 (1¼- to 1½-pound) pork tenderloins, trimmed

1 recipe stuffing (recipes follow)

1 cup baby spinach

2 tablespoons extra-virgin olive oil

Why This Recipe Works A savory filling gives lean pork tenderloin a helping hand on the grill by adding great flavor and keeping it moist from the inside out. To make more real estate for the stuffing, we butterflied the long, thin tenderloins and pounded them to an even thickness. Ultraflavorful filling ingredients went into a food processor to make a concentrated paste that would stay in place. We smeared the paste on one edge of the flattened tenderloin and added a handful of baby spinach for fresh color and flavor. We rolled the pork into a tidy cylinder and tied it to keep it closed on the grill. After a rubdown with oil and then brown sugar, we placed the meat on the cooler side of a half-grill fire where it cooked through gently and evenly and gained a nice smokiness. To ensure that the tenderloins don't curl during cooking, remove the silverskin from the meat (see page 15). Freezing the pork for 30 minutes will make butterflying it much easier. We strongly prefer natural pork in this recipe. If the pork is enhanced (injected with a salt solution), omit the salt in step 1. For how to tie a roast, see page 12.

1 Combine sugar, 2 teaspoons salt, and 1 teaspoon pepper in bowl. Slice each tenderloin in half horizontally, stopping ½ inch from edge so halves remain attached. Open tenderloins like book, cover with plastic wrap, and pound to ¼-inch thickness. Trim any ragged edges to make rough rectangle about 10 inches by 6 inches. Sprinkle interior of each tenderloin with ⅛ teaspoon salt and ⅛ teaspoon pepper.

2 With long side of tenderloin facing you, spread half of stuffing over bottom half of 1 tenderloin and top stuffing with ½ cup spinach. Roll tenderloin away from you into tight cylinder, taking care not to squeeze stuffing out ends. Position tenderloin seam side down and tie at 1½-inch intervals with kitchen twine. Repeat with remaining tenderloin, stuffing, and spinach.

3A For a charcoal grill Open bottom vent completely. Light large chimney starter filled with charcoal briquettes (6 quarts). When top coals are partially covered with ash, pour evenly over half of grill. Set cooking grate in place, cover, and open lid vent completely. Heat grill until hot, about 5 minutes.

3B For a gas grill Turn all burners to high, cover, and heat grill until hot, about 15 minutes. Leave primary burner on high and turn off other burner(s).

4 Clean and oil cooking grate. Coat tenderloins with oil, then rub entire surface with sugar mixture. Place tenderloins on cooler side of grill, cover, and cook until center of stuffing registers 145 degrees, 25 to 30 minutes, rotating tenderloins halfway through cooking.

5 Transfer tenderloins to carving board and let rest for 10 minutes. Remove twine, slice tenderloins into ½-inch-thick slices, and serve.

OLIVE AND SUN-DRIED TOMATO STUFFING
makes about 1 cup

½ cup pitted kalamata olives
½ cup oil-packed sun-dried tomatoes, rinsed and chopped coarse
4 anchovy fillets, rinsed
2 garlic cloves, minced
1 teaspoon minced fresh thyme
1 teaspoon grated lemon zest
Salt and pepper

Pulse all ingredients in food processor until coarsely chopped, 5 to 10 pulses; season with salt and pepper to taste.

PEPPER AND MANCHEGO STUFFING
makes about 1 cup
Roasted red peppers may be substituted for the piquillo peppers.

1 slice hearty white sandwich bread, torn into ½-inch pieces
¾ cup jarred piquillo peppers, rinsed and patted dry
2 ounces Manchego cheese, shredded (½ cup)
¼ cup pine nuts, toasted
2 garlic cloves, minced
1 teaspoon minced fresh thyme
½ teaspoon smoked paprika
Salt and pepper

Pulse all ingredients in food processor until coarsely chopped, 5 to 10 pulses; season with salt and pepper to taste.

PORCINI AND ARTICHOKE STUFFING
makes about 1 cup
You can substitute 5 ounces frozen artichoke hearts, thawed and patted dry, for the jarred.

½ ounce dried porcini mushrooms, rinsed and minced
¾ cup jarred whole baby artichokes packed in water, halved, rinsed, and patted dry
1 ounce Parmesan cheese, grated (½ cup)
¼ cup oil-packed sun-dried tomatoes, rinsed and chopped coarse
¼ cup fresh parsley leaves
2 tablespoons pine nuts, toasted
2 garlic cloves, minced
1 teaspoon grated lemon zest plus 2 teaspoons juice
Pepper

Pulse all ingredients in food processor until coarsely chopped, 5 to 10 pulses; season with pepper to taste.

GRILL-SMOKED PORK LOIN WITH DRIED FRUIT CHUTNEY

serves 6 to 8

Pork

½ cup packed light brown sugar

¼ cup kosher salt

1 (3½- to 4-pound) boneless blade-end pork loin roast, trimmed and tied at 1½-inch intervals

2 cups wood chips

1 (13 by 9-inch) disposable aluminum roasting pan (if using charcoal) or 1 (9-inch) disposable aluminum pie plate (if using gas)

Dried Fruit Chutney

¾ cup dry white wine

½ cup dried apricots, diced

½ cup dried cherries

¼ cup white wine vinegar

3 tablespoons water

3 tablespoons packed light brown sugar

1 shallot, minced

2 tablespoons grated fresh ginger

1 tablespoon unsalted butter

1 tablespoon Dijon mustard

1½ teaspoons dry mustard

Kosher salt

Why This Recipe Works Pork loin takes on new character when prepared on the grill so we developed a strategy for turning out a company-worthy pork roast. Packing an overnight rub of salt and brown sugar onto a blade-end pork loin was a triple win: It seasoned the roast, helped it retain its juices, and gave it a caramelized exterior. Low-and-slow indirect grill smoking was the way to go to allow the roast to cook through evenly and gently. We spread coals on one side of the grill and placed the roast opposite them, on the cooler side, with a disposable pan filled with water beneath it to help keep the meat moist (moist meat absorbs smoke better). The pan of water also kept the temperature in the grill stable by absorbing heat. To stretch out the life of the flame so we wouldn't have to refuel it mid-roasting, we arranged a layer of unlit coals in the grill and topped them with the lit coals. Positioning the lid vents over the meat drew the smoke up and over it. As a finishing touch, we put together a quick dried-fruit chutney to serve alongside the roast. Brightened with vinegar, ginger, and mustard, it was the perfect complement to the deeply smoky meat. A blade-end roast is our preferred cut, but a center-cut boneless loin roast can also be used. We strongly prefer natural pork in this recipe. If the pork is enhanced (injected with a salt solution), omit the salt in step 1. This recipe requires refrigerating the rubbed pork for at least 6 hours or up to 24 hours before cooking (a longer time is preferable). Any variety of wood chip except mesquite will work; we prefer hickory. For how to tie a pork loin, see page 15.

1 For the pork Combine sugar and salt in small bowl. Rub sugar mixture over entire surface of roast, making sure roast is evenly coated. Wrap roast tightly in plastic wrap, set in rimmed baking sheet, and refrigerate for at least 6 hours or up to 24 hours.

2 Just before grilling, soak wood chips in water for 15 minutes, then drain. Using large piece of heavy-duty aluminum foil, wrap soaked chips in 8 by 4½-inch foil packet. (Make sure chips do not poke holes in sides or bottom of packet.) Cut 2 evenly spaced 2-inch slits in top of packet.

3A For a charcoal grill Open bottom vent halfway. Arrange 25 unlit charcoal briquettes over half of grill and place disposable pan filled with 3 cups water on other side of grill. Light large chimney starter two-thirds filled with charcoal briquettes (4 quarts). When top coals are partially covered with ash, pour evenly over unlit briquettes. Place wood chip packet on coals. Set cooking grate in place, cover, and open lid vent halfway. Heat grill until hot and wood chips are smoking, about 5 minutes.

3B For a gas grill Remove cooking grate and place wood chip packet directly on primary burner. Place disposable pie plate filled with 1 inch water directly on other burner(s). Set grate in place, turn all burners to high, cover, and heat grill until hot and wood chips are smoking, about 15 minutes. Turn primary burner to medium and turn off other burner(s). (Adjust primary burner as needed to maintain grill temperature around 300 degrees.)

4 Clean and oil cooking grate. Unwrap roast and pat dry with paper towels. Place roast on grill directly over water pan about 7 inches from heat source. Cover (position lid vent over roast if using charcoal) and cook until meat registers 140 degrees, 1½ to 2 hours, rotating roast 180 degrees after 45 minutes.

5 For the dried fruit chutney Combine wine, apricots, cherries, vinegar, water, sugar, shallot, and ginger in medium saucepan. Bring to simmer over medium heat. Cover and cook until fruit is softened, about 10 minutes. Remove lid and reduce heat to medium-low. Add butter, Dijon, and dry mustard and continue to cook until slightly thickened, 4 to 6 minutes. Remove from heat and season with salt to taste. Transfer to bowl and let stand at room temperature.

6 Transfer roast to carving board and let rest for 20 minutes. Remove twine. Slice roast into ¼-inch-thick slices and serve with chutney.

GRILL-ROASTED ROSEMARY PORK LOIN

serves 6

⅓ cup minced fresh parsley

3 tablespoons extra-virgin olive oil

1½ tablespoons minced fresh rosemary

2 garlic cloves, minced

Salt and pepper

1 (2½- to 3-pound) boneless center-cut pork loin roast

Why This Recipe Works An elegant swirl of garlic, rosemary, and parsley turns mild-mannered boneless pork loin into a sophisticated roast. This trio provides a powerful infusion of flavor from the inside out. Garlic and rosemary taste great with pork but we needed some fresh parsley in the mix to keep the rosemary from being overpowering and tasting medicinal. To get herb flavor into every bite, we butterflied the loin and then spread the interior with our assertive filling. To coax flavor out of the pork itself, we kept a thin layer of fat on the outside and scored it to encourage it to melt and baste the meat while on the grill (also producing some smoky flavor in the process). A brush of olive oil over our tightly rolled roast encouraged browning and reduced sticking on the grill. We set up a half-grill fire, gave the roast a good sear on all sides on the hotter zone, and then finished it over the gentler heat of the cooler side. Not quite an hour later, we were rewarded with a browned, juicy pork loin with a robust yet balanced hit of garlic and herbs. Freezing the pork for 30 minutes will make butterflying it much easier. We strongly prefer natural pork in this recipe. If the pork is enhanced (injected with a salt solution), omit the salt in step 1. For how to tie a pork loin, see page 15.

1 Combine parsley, 2 tablespoons oil, rosemary, garlic, ¾ teaspoon salt, and ¾ teaspoon pepper in bowl. Using sharp knife, cut slits 1 inch apart in crosshatch pattern in fat cap of roast, being careful not to cut into meat. Position roast fat side up. Insert knife one-third of way up from bottom of roast along 1 long side and cut horizontally, stopping ½ inch before edge. Open up flap. Keeping knife parallel to cutting board, cut through thicker portion of roast about ½ inch from bottom of roast, keeping knife level with first cut and stopping about ½ inch before edge. Open up this flap. If uneven, cover with plastic wrap and use meat pounder to even out.

2 Spread inside of roast evenly with herb mixture, leaving about ¼-inch border on all sides. Starting from short side, roll roast (keeping fat on outside) and tie with kitchen twine at 1½-inch intervals. (Roast can be refrigerated for up to 24 hours.) Rub roast with remaining 1 tablespoon oil and season with salt and pepper.

3A **For a charcoal grill** Open bottom vent completely. Light large chimney starter filled with charcoal briquettes (6 quarts). When top coals are partially covered with ash, pour evenly over half of grill. Set cooking grate in place, cover, and open lid vent completely. Heat grill until hot, about 5 minutes.

3B **For a gas grill** Turn all burners to high, cover, and heat grill until hot, about 15 minutes. Leave primary burner on high and turn off other burner(s).

4 Clean and oil cooking grate. Place roast, fat side down, on hotter side of grill. Cook (covered if using gas), until well browned on all sides, about 12 minutes. Slide roast to cooler side of grill and turn fat side up. Cover and cook until meat registers 140 degrees, 35 to 45 minutes.

5 Transfer pork to carving board and let rest for 20 minutes. Remove twine, slice into ½-inch-thick slices, and serve.

GRILL-SMOKED PORK LOIN WITH APPLE-CRANBERRY FILLING

serves 6

Apple-Cranberry Filling

1½ cups (4 ounces) dried apples

1 cup apple cider

¾ cup packed light brown sugar

½ cup cider vinegar

½ cup dried cranberries

1 large shallot, halved lengthwise and sliced thin crosswise

1 tablespoon grated fresh ginger

1 tablespoon yellow mustard seeds

½ teaspoon ground allspice

⅛–¼ teaspoon cayenne pepper

Pork

1 (2½- to 3-pound) boneless center-cut pork loin roast, trimmed

Salt and pepper

2 cups wood chips

Why This Recipe Works We worked from the inside out to add a filling rich with fall flavors to plain Jane grill-smoked pork loin. Even though it's very lean, a center-cut rectangular loin roast was our preferred cut for this recipe. Since it is a solid muscle it held together when we double butterflied it to open it up to stuff. After trying a variety of stuffings, we landed on a chutney-like blend of dried fruits, spices, sugar, and vinegar. We created both the filling and a glaze by simmering dried apples, dried cranberries, and brown sugar in apple cider and cider vinegar along with shallot, fresh ginger, mustard seeds, allspice, and cayenne for some spicy contrast. We strained out the solids for a drier filling and reduced the liquid until syrupy for the glaze. We roasted our stuffed and rolled pork loin only on the cooler side of a half-grill fire, never moving it over the coals. The glaze caramelized as it heated. If mustard seeds are unavailable, stir an equal amount of whole-grain mustard into the filling after the apples have been processed. For a spicier filling, use the larger amount of cayenne. This recipe is best prepared with a loin that is 7 to 8 inches long and 4 to 5 inches wide and not enhanced (injected with a salt solution). Freezing the pork for 30 minutes will make butterflying it much easier. The pork loin can be stuffed and tied a day ahead of time, but don't season the exterior until you are ready to grill. For how to tie a pork loin, see page 15.

1 For the apple-cranberry filling Bring all ingredients to simmer in medium saucepan over medium-high heat. Cover, reduce heat to low, and cook until apples are very soft, about 20 minutes. Transfer mixture to fine-mesh strainer set over bowl and press with back of spoon to extract as much liquid as possible. Return liquid to saucepan and simmer over medium-high heat until reduced to ⅓ cup, about 5 minutes; set aside for glazing. Pulse apple mixture in food processor until coarsely chopped, about 15 pulses. Transfer filling to bowl and refrigerate until needed.

2 For the pork Position roast fat side up. Insert knife one-third of way up from bottom of roast along 1 long side and cut horizontally, stopping ½ inch before edge. Open up flap. Keeping knife parallel to cutting board, cut through thicker portion of roast about ½ inch from bottom of roast, keeping knife level with first cut and stopping about ½ inch before edge. Open up this flap. If uneven, cover with plastic wrap and use meat pounder to even out. Season interior with salt and pepper and spread filling in even layer, leaving ½-inch border on all sides. Roll tightly and tie at 1½-inch intervals with kitchen twine. Season with salt and pepper.

3 Just before grilling, soak wood chips in water for 15 minutes, then drain. Using large piece of heavy-duty aluminum foil, wrap soaked chips in 8 by 4½-inch foil packet. (Make sure chips do not poke holes in sides or bottom of packet.) Cut 2 evenly spaced 2-inch slits in top of packet.

4A For a charcoal grill Open bottom vent halfway. Light large chimney starter three-quarters filled with charcoal briquettes (4½ quarts). When top coals are partially covered with ash, pour evenly over half of grill. Place wood chip packet on coals. Set cooking grate in place, cover, and open lid vent halfway. Heat grill until hot and wood chips are smoking, about 5 minutes.

4B For a gas grill Remove cooking grate and place wood chip packet directly on primary burner. Set cooking grate in place, turn all burners to high, cover, and heat grill until hot and wood chips are smoking, about 15 minutes. Turn primary burner to medium-high and turn off other burner(s). (Adjust primary burner as needed to maintain grill temperature between 300 and 325 degrees.)

5 Clean and oil cooking grate. Place pork, fat side up, on cooler side of grill, cover (position lid vent over roast if using charcoal), and cook until meat registers 130 to 135 degrees, 55 minutes to 1 hour 10 minutes, flipping roast halfway through cooking.

6 Brush roast evenly with reserved glaze. (Reheat glaze, if necessary, to make it spreadable.) Continue to cook until glaze is glossy and meat registers 140 degrees, 5 to 10 minutes. Transfer to carving board and let rest for 20 minutes. Remove twine, slice into ½ inch-thick slices, and serve.

Grill-Smoked Pork Loin with Apple-Cherry Filling with Caraway
Substitute dried cherries for cranberries and 1 teaspoon caraway seeds for ginger, mustard seeds, and allspice. After processing filling in food processor, transfer to bowl and stir in 2 teaspoons minced fresh thyme.

GRILL-SMOKED BONE-IN PORK RIB ROAST

serves 6 to 8

1 (4- to 5-pound) center-cut bone-in pork rib roast, chine bone removed

4 teaspoons kosher salt

1 cup wood chips

1½ teaspoons pepper

Why This Recipe Works Often referred to as the pork equivalent of prime rib or rack of lamb, a lean center-cut pork rib roast turns tender, juicy, and richly flavorful when grill smoked thanks to its bones and layer of surface fat. The bones and fat also make our roasting method dead simple and largely hands-off. To prepare the pork, we scored the fat cap to help the rendered drippings baste the meat during roasting. For a deeply browned, crisp crust, we salted the roast and let it rest for 6 hours in the refrigerator before grilling. All that was left to do was to position the pork correctly, bones pointed away from the coals, on the cooler side of a banked fire and let it roast gently to perfection for a little more than an hour. A thick mahogany crust developed without the need for searing. For easier carving, ask the butcher to remove the tip of the chine bone. This recipe requires refrigerating the rubbed pork for at least 6 hours or up to 24 hours before cooking (a longer time is preferable). We strongly prefer natural pork in this recipe. If the pork is enhanced (injected with a salt solution), omit salt in step 1. Serve this roast with Orange Salsa with Cuban Flavors (recipe follows), if desired.

1 Pat roast dry with paper towels. If necessary, trim thick spots of surface fat layer to about ¼-inch thickness. Using sharp knife, cut slits spaced 1 inch apart in crosshatch pattern in surface fat layer, being careful not to cut into meat. Rub roast evenly with salt. Refrigerate for at least 6 hours or up to 24 hours.

2 Just before grilling, soak wood chips in water for 15 minutes, then drain. Using large piece of heavy-duty aluminum foil, wrap soaked chips in 8 by 4½-inch foil packet. (Make sure chips do not poke holes in sides or bottom of packet.) Cut 2 evenly spaced 2-inch slits in top of packet.

3A For a charcoal grill Open bottom vent halfway. Light large chimney starter filled with charcoal briquettes (6 quarts). When top coals are partially covered with ash, pour into steeply banked pile against side of grill. Place wood chip packet on coals. Set cooking grate in place, cover, and open lid vent halfway. Heat grill until hot and wood chips are smoking, about 5 minutes.

3B For a gas grill Remove cooking grate and place wood chip packet directly on primary burner. Set cooking grate in place, turn all burners to high, cover, and heat grill until hot and wood chips are smoking, about 15 minutes. Turn primary burner to medium-high and turn off other burner(s). (Adjust primary burner as needed to maintain grill temperature around 325 degrees.)

4 Clean and oil cooking grate. Pat roast dry with paper towels and season with pepper. Place roast on grill with meat near, but not over, heat source and bones facing away from coals and flames. Cover (position lid vent over meat if using charcoal) and cook until meat registers 140 degrees, 1¼ to 1½ hours.

5 Transfer roast to carving board and let rest for 30 minutes. Carve roast into thick slices by cutting between ribs, and serve.

ORANGE SALSA WITH CUBAN FLAVORS

makes about 2½ cups

To make this salsa spicier, add the reserved chile seeds.

½ teaspoon grated orange zest, plus 5 oranges peeled and segmented, each segment quartered crosswise

½ cup finely chopped red onion

1 jalapeño chile, stemmed, seeds reserved, and minced

2 tablespoons lime juice

2 tablespoons minced fresh parsley

1 tablespoon extra-virgin olive oil

2 teaspoons packed brown sugar

1½ teaspoons distilled white vinegar

1½ teaspoons minced fresh oregano

1 garlic clove, minced

½ teaspoon ground cumin

½ teaspoon salt

½ teaspoon pepper

Combine all ingredients in bowl.

GRILL-SMOKED LEXINGTON PULLED PORK

serves 6 to 8

Pork

2 tablespoons paprika

2 tablespoons pepper

2 tablespoons packed brown sugar

2 tablespoons kosher salt

1 (4- to 5-pound) boneless pork butt roast, trimmed

4 cups wood chips

Lexington Barbecue Sauce

1 cup water

1 cup cider vinegar

½ cup ketchup

1 tablespoon sugar

¾ teaspoon salt

½ teaspoon pepper

½ teaspoon red pepper flakes

Why This Recipe Works A large pork butt usually takes hours to smoke low and slow on the grill. Our method reduces the roasting time from all day to 4 or 5 hours by using both the grill and the oven. We treated the pork with a simple dry spice rub for flavor and used a lot of wood chips for plenty of smoke. We banked the coals against one side of the grill and placed the pork on the cooler side to cook, covered, for 2 hours. Then we moved the smoke-infused pork to the consistent heat of the oven to finish roasting. We covered the roasting pan with foil to trap heat so the meat would steam and turn fork-tender. When the pork was cool enough to handle, we used our hands to "pull" or shred it. We put together a traditional Lexington, North Carolina, vinegary sauce to mix with the shredded meat. The vinegar nicely cut through the fattiness of the pork. Pork butt roast is often labeled Boston butt in the supermarket. This recipe requires letting the rubbed pork sit for 1 hour at room temperature or refrigerating it for up to 24 hours before cooking (a longer time is preferable). For a classic presentation, serve the pulled pork on white bread with pickle chips.

1 **For the pork** Combine paprika, pepper, sugar, and salt in bowl. Pat pork dry with paper towels and rub evenly with spice mixture. Wrap roast in plastic wrap and let sit at room temperature for at least 1 hour or refrigerate for up to 24 hours.

2 Just before grilling, soak wood chips in water for 15 minutes, then drain. Using large piece of heavy-duty aluminum foil, wrap 2 cups wood chips in 8 by 4½-inch foil packet. (Make sure chips do not poke holes in sides or bottom of packet.) Repeat with remaining 2 cups chips. Cut 2 evenly spaced 2-inch slits in top of each packet.

3A **For a charcoal grill** Open bottom vent halfway. Light large chimney starter half filled with charcoal briquettes (3 quarts). When top coals are partially covered with ash, pour into steeply banked pile against side of grill. Place wood chip packets on coals. Set cooking grate in place, cover, and open lid vent halfway. Heat grill until hot and wood chips are smoking, about 5 minutes.

3B **For a gas grill** Remove cooking grate and place wood chip packets directly on primary burner. Set cooking grate in place, turn all burners to high, cover, and heat grill until hot and wood chips are smoking, about 15 minutes. Turn primary burner to medium and turn off other burner(s). (Adjust primary burner as needed to maintain grill temperature around 275 degrees.)

4 Clean and oil cooking grate. Unwrap roast and place on cooler side of grill. Cover (position lid vent over roast if using charcoal) and cook until pork has dark, rosy crust, about 2 hours. During final 30 minutes of cooking, adjust oven rack to lower-middle position and heat oven to 325 degrees.

5 **For the Lexington barbecue sauce** While pork cooks, whisk all ingredients in bowl until sugar and salt are dissolved; refrigerate until needed.

6 Transfer pork to large roasting pan, cover pan tightly with foil, and transfer to oven. Roast until fork slips easily in and out of meat, 2 to 3 hours. Remove pork from oven and let rest, still covered with foil, for 1 hour. When cool enough to handle, unwrap pork and pull meat into thin shreds, discarding excess fat and gristle, adding ½ cup barbecue sauce as you shred. Serve with remaining sauce.

streamlining pulled pork

1 Cook on cooler side of grill until pork develops dark, rosy crust.

2 Transfer pork to roasting pan and finish in 325-degree oven.

3 When cool enough to handle, shred (or "pull") pork into thin strands, adding ½ cup sauce as you go.

GRILL-SMOKED SOUTH CAROLINA PULLED PORK

serves 6 to 8

Pork

3 tablespoons dry mustard

2 tablespoons salt

1½ tablespoons packed light brown sugar

2 teaspoons pepper

2 teaspoons paprika

¼ teaspoon cayenne pepper

1 (4- to 5-pound) boneless pork butt roast, trimmed

4 cups wood chips

Mustard Barbecue Sauce

½ cup yellow mustard

½ cup packed light brown sugar

¼ cup distilled white vinegar

2 tablespoons Worcestershire sauce

1 tablespoon hot sauce

1 teaspoon salt

1 teaspoon pepper

Why This Recipe Works In South Carolina, pit masters dress pulled pork in a savory mustard-based sauce nicknamed "Carolina gold." Since we had perfected a technique for cooking pulled pork when creating our Grill-Smoked Lexington Pulled Pork (page 294), we knew it would work equally well for this Southern rendition. A combination of grill smoking and oven roasting reduced the cooking time from all day to just 4 or 5 hours. We rubbed a boneless pork butt with a spice rub which included dry mustard to highlight the mustard flavor of the sauce; the rub helped the meat develop a flavorful crust. Once the pork had taken on plenty of smoke, we covered it in foil and allowed it to gently roast to tenderness in the convenience of a low oven before shredding and saucing it. Most South Carolina barbecue sauce recipes use yellow mustard, which our tasters praised for its bright tang. Brushing the pork with the sauce before it went into the oven produced a second hit of mustard flavor while tossing the shredded pork with the remaining sauce gave the meat a final layer of flavor. Boneless pork butt (also labeled Boston butt) is often wrapped in elastic netting; be sure to remove the netting before rubbing the meat with the spices in step 1. The cooked meat can be shredded or chopped.

1 For the pork Combine dry mustard, salt, sugar, pepper, paprika, and cayenne in bowl. Pat pork dry with paper towels and rub evenly with spice mixture. Wrap roast in plastic wrap and let sit at room temperature for at least 1 hour or refrigerate for up to 24 hours.

2 Just before grilling, soak wood chips in water for 15 minutes, then drain. Using large piece of heavy-duty aluminum foil, wrap 2 cups soaked chips in 8 by 4½-inch foil packet. (Make sure chips do not poke holes in sides or bottom of packet.) Repeat with remaining 2 cups chips. Cut 2 evenly spaced 2-inch slits in top of each packet.

3A For a charcoal grill Open bottom vent halfway. Light large chimney starter half filled with charcoal briquettes (3 quarts). When top coals are partially covered with ash, pour into steeply banked pile against 1 side of grill. Place wood chip packets on coals. Set cooking grate in place, cover, and open lid vent halfway. Heat grill until hot and wood chips are smoking, about 5 minutes.

3B For a gas grill Remove cooking grate and place wood chip packets directly on primary burner. Set cooking grate in place, turn all burners to high, cover, and heat grill until hot and wood chips are smoking, about 15 minutes. Turn primary burner to medium-high and turn other burner(s) off. (Adjust primary burner as needed to maintain grill temperature around 325 degrees.)

4 Clean and oil cooking grate. Place roast on cooler side of grill. Cover (position lid vent over roast if using charcoal) and cook until pork has dark, rosy crust, about 2 hours. During final 20 minutes of grilling, adjust oven rack to lower-middle position and heat oven to 325 degrees.

5 **For the mustard barbecue sauce** Whisk mustard, sugar, vinegar, Worcestershire, hot sauce, salt, and pepper in bowl until smooth. Measure out ½ cup sauce and set aside for cooking, reserving remaining sauce for tossing with pork.

6 Transfer pork to large roasting pan and brush evenly with sauce for cooking. Cover pan tightly with foil and transfer to oven. Roast until fork slips easily in and out of meat, 2 to 3 hours. Remove pork from oven and let rest, still covered with foil, for 1 hour. When cool enough to handle, unwrap pork and pull meat into thin shreds, discarding excess fat and gristle. Toss pork with reserved sauce and serve.

flavoring south carolina pulled pork

1 Before transferring to oven, brush pork with mustard barbecue sauce.

2 Once cool enough to handle, pull meat into shreds and toss with remaining sauce.

GRILL-SMOKED SOUTH CAROLINA FRESH HAM

serves 10 to 12

Ham

1 (6- to 8-pound) bone-in, skin-on shank-end fresh ham

2 tablespoons kosher salt

2 cups wood chips

Mustard Sauce

1½ cups yellow mustard

½ cup cider vinegar

6 tablespoons packed brown sugar

2 tablespoons ketchup

2 teaspoons hot sauce

2 teaspoons Worcestershire sauce

1 teaspoon pepper

Hamburger buns

Why This Recipe Works Pulled pork may get all the attention, but lesser-known grill-smoked ham from the Carolinas is a savory revelation. Cut from the lower rear leg of the hog and sold unsmoked and unseasoned, fresh ham is just a large pork roast. We like the shank end because it has a lot of skin. We salted this lean cut overnight for good flavor and juicy meat. After much testing, we discovered that 200 degrees was the best doneness temperature, but it took up to 5 hours on the grill to reach it. So we employed the hybrid grill-to-oven method from our Grill-Smoked Lexington Pulled Pork (page 294) and built up plenty of smoky flavor on the grill before turning the ham fully tender in the controlled heat of the oven. Crunchy bits of rendered skin folded into the soft chopped ham are a trademark of this South Carolina specialty. To get crackly skin, we needed to pull the skin from the ham in one piece and roast it on its own before chopping it up and incorporating it into the chopped ham. A vinegary mustard sauce is a classic Carolina barbecue accompaniment, and our version is just the vibrant contrast the rich ham needed. This recipe requires refrigerating the salted ham for at least 18 hours or up to 24 hours before cooking (a longer time is preferable). You'll have about 2½ cups of mustard sauce.

1 For the ham Pat ham dry with paper towels. Place ham on large sheet of plastic wrap and rub all over with salt. Wrap tightly in plastic and refrigerate for at least 18 hours or up to 24 hours.

2 Just before grilling, soak wood chips in water for 15 minutes, then drain. Using large piece of heavy-duty aluminum foil, wrap soaked chips in 8 by 4½-inch foil packet. (Make sure chips do not poke holes in sides or bottom of packet.) Cut 2 evenly spaced 2-inch slits in top of packet.

3A For a charcoal grill Open bottom vent completely. Light large chimney starter three-quarters filled with charcoal briquettes (4½ quarts). When top coals are partially covered with ash, pour evenly over half of grill. Place wood chip packet on coals. Set cooking grate in place, cover, and open lid vent completely. Heat grill until hot and wood chips are smoking, about 5 minutes.

3B For a gas grill Remove cooking grate and place wood chip packet directly on primary burner. Set cooking grate in place, turn all burners to high, cover, and heat grill until hot

and wood chips are smoking, about 15 minutes. Turn primary burner to medium-high and turn off other burner(s). (Adjust primary burner as needed to maintain grill temperature around 300 degrees.)

4 Clean and oil cooking grate. Unwrap ham and place flat side down on cooler side of grill. Cover (position lid vent directly over ham if using charcoal) and cook for 2 hours. During final 30 minutes of cooking, adjust oven rack to middle position and heat oven to 300 degrees.

5 For the mustard sauce Meanwhile, whisk all ingredients together in bowl. (Sauce can be refrigerated for up to 1 week.)

6 Transfer ham flat side down to 13 by 9-inch baking pan. Cover pan tightly with foil. Transfer to oven and roast until fork slips easily in and out of pork and meat registers 200 degrees, about 2½ hours.

7 Remove ham from oven and increase oven temperature to 400 degrees. Line rimmed baking sheet with foil. Using tongs, remove ham skin in 1 large piece. Place skin fatty side

down on prepared sheet. Transfer to oven and roast until skin is dark and crispy and sounds hollow when tapped with fork, about 25 minutes, rotating sheet halfway through roasting. Tent ham with foil and let rest while skin roasts.

8 Transfer ham to carving board. Strain accumulated juices from pan through fine-mesh strainer set over bowl; discard solids. Trim and discard excess fat from ham. Remove bone and chop meat into bite-size pieces; transfer to large bowl.

9 When cool enough to handle, chop skin fine. Rewarm reserved ham juices in microwave for 1 minute. Add juices and chopped skin to ham and toss to combine. Season with salt to taste. Serve on buns, topped with mustard sauce.

crisping ham skin

Once ham is cooked through, pull off skin in 1 piece. Roast skin on foil-lined baking sheet until dark brown, then chop finely and combine with chopped ham.

GRILL-ROASTED HAM

serves 12 to 14

1 (7- to 10-pound) bone-in cured ham, preferably shank end, skin removed and fat trimmed to ¼ inch

¼ cup packed dark brown sugar

2 tablespoons paprika

1 teaspoon pepper

¼ teaspoon cayenne pepper

Why This Recipe Works Once you taste the delicious caramelized crust and juicy meat of grill-roasted ham, you'll never look at your holiday ham the same. Roasting ham on the grill reinforces its smoky flavor, and builds a crisp charred exterior. To keep the ham moist, we opted for a bone-in, uncut ham for its protective layer of fat on the outside and scant exposed meat. We treated the meat with a traditional dry barbecue rub since sugary glazes burn. The dry rub stayed put and the sugar in it caramelized nicely into a tasty, crunchy coating. We kept the ham safe from flare-ups by elevating it on a V-rack and placing it on the cooler side of a half-grill fire; when the meat reached 100 degrees we switched the ham to the hotter side. For a makeshift rotisserie, we skewered the ham to give ourselves two handles with which to safely rotate the hefty ham for a well-rounded crust. Do not use a spiral-sliced ham; it will dry out on the grill. You will need two 12-inch metal skewers for this recipe. This recipe requires letting the salted ham sit for 1½ hours before cooking.

1 Score ham at 1-inch intervals in crosshatch pattern. Combine sugar, paprika, pepper, and cayenne in small bowl. Rub spice mixture all over ham. Transfer to V-rack and let sit at room temperature for 1½ hours. Thread ham with two 12-inch metal skewers on both sides of the bone.

2A For a charcoal grill Open bottom vent halfway. Light large chimney starter filled with charcoal briquettes (6 quarts). When top coals are partially covered with ash, pour over half of grill. Set cooking grate in place, cover, and open lid vent halfway. Heat grill until hot, about 5 minutes.

2B For a gas grill Turn all burners to high, cover, and heat grill until hot, about 15 minutes. Leave primary burner on high and turn off other burner(s).

3 Clean and oil cooking grate. Place V-rack with ham on cooler side of grill. Cover and cook until meat registers 100 degrees, about 1½ hours.

4A For a charcoal grill Using potholders, transfer V-rack with ham to rimmed baking sheet or roasting pan. Light 25 coals. When coals are covered with fine gray ash, remove grill grate and scatter over top of spent coals. Replace grill grate and position V-rack directly over coals.

4B For a gas grill Turn all burners to low.

5 Cook (covered if using gas) until ham is lightly charred on all sides, about 30 minutes, turning ham every 5 minutes. Transfer to carving board and let rest for 30 minutes. Carve and serve.

---

skewering a bone-in ham

Thread 2 metal skewers through ham on either side of bone. Use skewers to securely turn ham on V-rack.

GRILL-ROASTED RACK OF LAMB

serves 4 to 6

4 teaspoons vegetable oil

4 teaspoons minced fresh rosemary

2 teaspoons minced fresh thyme

2 garlic cloves, minced

2 (1½- to 1¾-pound) racks of lamb, fat trimmed to ⅛ to ¼ inch and rib bones frenched

Salt and pepper

1 (13 by 9-inch) disposable aluminum roasting pan (if using charcoal)

Why This Recipe Works Rack of lamb and the grill have great chemistry. The intense heat of the coals produces a bold crust and melts away the meat's abundance of fat, distributing flavor throughout while imparting a smokiness that's the perfect complement to lamb's rich, gamy flavor. But the rendering fat can cause flare-ups that scorch the meat and impart sooty flavors, ruining this pricey cut. For a foolproof outcome, we trimmed the excess fat from racks of lamb and built a split fire around an aluminum pan, creating a cooler center where the fat could safely render before we moved the lamb over direct heat to brown the exterior. As a last step, we stood the racks up and leaned them together to brown their bottoms. Because lamb tastes so good on its own, it needed only a simple wet rub of robust herbs and a little oil brushed on during browning to enhance its flavor. We were rewarded with rack of lamb that was pink and juicy, with a well-browned crust that contrasted nicely with the lush, ultratender interior. We prefer the subtler flavor and larger size of lamb labeled "domestic" or "American," but you may substitute lamb imported from New Zealand or Australia. Since imported racks are generally smaller, follow the shorter cooking times given in the recipe. We prefer rack of lamb cooked to medium-rare, but if you prefer it more or less done, see our guidelines on page 24.

1 Combine 1 tablespoon oil, rosemary, thyme, and garlic in bowl; set aside. Pat lamb dry with paper towels, rub with remaining 1 teaspoon oil, and season with salt and pepper.

2A For a charcoal grill Open bottom vent completely and place disposable pan in center of grill. Light large chimney starter filled with charcoal briquettes (6 quarts). When top coals are partially covered with ash, pour into 2 even piles on either side of disposable pan. Set cooking grate in place, cover, and open lid vent completely. Heat grill until hot, about 5 minutes.

2B For a gas grill Turn all burners to high, cover, and heat grill until hot, about 15 minutes. Leave primary burner on high and turn off other burner(s).

3 Clean and oil cooking grate. Place lamb, bone side up, on cooler part of grill with meaty side of racks very close to, but not quite over, heat source. Cover and cook until meat is lightly browned, faint grill marks appear, and fat has begun to render, 8 to 10 minutes.

4 Flip racks bone side down and slide to hotter part of grill. Cook until well browned, 3 to 4 minutes. Brush racks with herb mixture, flip bone side up, and cook until well browned, 3 to 4 minutes. Stand racks up, leaning them against each other for support, and cook until bottom is well browned and meat registers 125 degrees (for medium-rare), 3 to 8 minutes.

5 Transfer lamb to carving board and let rest for 20 minutes. Cut between ribs into separate chops and serve.

Grill-Roasted Rack of Lamb with Sweet Mustard Glaze

Omit rosemary and add 3 tablespoons Dijon mustard, 2 tablespoons honey, and ½ teaspoon grated lemon zest to oil, thyme, and garlic. Reserve 2 tablespoons of glaze to brush over lamb before serving.

GRILL-SMOKED SIDE OF SALMON

5 tablespoons sugar

5 tablespoons salt

1 (2½-pound) skin-on salmon fillet

2 tablespoons vegetable oil

2 cups wood chips

1½ teaspoons paprika

1 teaspoon ground white pepper

Why This Recipe Works Grill smoking offers an easy route to perfectly moist, nicely crusted salmon full of smoked flavor—in under 2 hours. Instead of the traditional cold-smoking technique, which keeps the salmon moist but requires a commercial smoker, we developed a "hot-smoked" method and kept the salmon moist by brining it; the sugar in the brine improved the flavor of the fish. To get a firm but not overly dry texture, complemented by a strong hit of smoke, we seasoned our brined side of salmon with paprika and white pepper and then slow-roasted it on the cooler side of a half-grill fire for more than an hour. The result is salmon that has a moist but flaky texture and is just smoky enough. The cooking grate must be hot and thoroughly clean before you place the salmon on it; otherwise, the fish might stick. Serve the salmon with lemon wedges or Mustard-Dill Sauce (recipe follows), if desired.

1 Dissolve sugar and salt in 2 quarts cold water in large container. Submerge salmon in brine, cover, and refrigerate for 15 minutes. Remove salmon from brine, pat dry with paper towels, and rub thoroughly with oil. Lay salmon skin side down on baking sheet and season top and sides with paprika and pepper.

2 Just before grilling, soak wood chips in water for 15 minutes, then drain. Using large piece of heavy-duty aluminum foil, wrap soaked chips in 8 by 4½-inch foil packet. (Make sure chips do not poke holes in sides or bottom of packet.) Cut 2 evenly spaced 2-inch slits in top of packet.

3A For a charcoal grill Open bottom grill vent halfway. Light large chimney starter half filled with charcoal briquettes (3 quarts). When top coals are partially covered with ash, pour evenly over half of grill. Place wood chip packet on coals. Set cooking grate in place, cover, and open lid vent halfway. Heat grill until hot and wood chips are smoking, about 5 minutes.

3B For a gas grill Remove cooking grate and place wood chip packet directly on primary burner. Set cooking grate in place, turn all burners to high, cover, and heat grill until hot and wood chips are smoking, about 15 minutes. Turn primary burner to medium and turn off other burner(s). (Adjust primary burner as needed to maintain grill temperature around 275 degrees.)

4 Clean and oil cooking grate. Gently slide salmon from sheet onto cooler side of grill, skin-side down and perpendicular to grate bars. Cover (position lid vent over fish if using charcoal) and cook until center of salmon is translucent when checked with tip of paring knife and registers 125 degrees (for medium-rare), about 1½ hours.

5 Using 2 spatulas, gently remove salmon from grill. Let rest for 5 minutes. Serve salmon hot or at room temperature.

MUSTARD-DILL SAUCE
makes about 1 cup

Use Dijon, honey, or whole-grain mustard, as desired. Depending on your choice of mustard, this sauce can be fairly hot.

1 cup mustard

¼ cup minced fresh dill

Combine ingredients in small bowl. (Sauce can be refrigerated for up to 24 hours.)

GRILL-ROASTED CEDAR-PLANKED SALMON

serves 4 to 6

4 (6- to 8-ounce) center-cut skinless salmon fillets, 1 to 1½ inches thick

2 tablespoons packed brown sugar

1½ tablespoons kosher salt

1 tablespoon chopped fresh dill

1 teaspoon pepper

1 (16 by 7-inch) cedar plank

1 teaspoon vegetable oil

Lemon wedges

Why This Recipe Works Salmon is quite simple to roast on the grill and it cooks very quickly in just about 15 minutes. You can make plain old salmon special by roasting it on a cedar plank. Available everywhere now, cedar planks aren't just for show, they are most practical: Salmon is very delicate and tends to fall apart on the grill but stays intact set on a plank. We used minimal seasoning on the fish, including just a little fresh dill (always good with salmon) and some brown sugar, to let the salmon flavor through and let it sit while we soaked the plank to keep it from catching fire. Using skinless fillets put the salmon in direct contact with the plank and helped the subtle cedar smoke flavor the fatty salmon. You can find cedar planks near the charcoal in most grocery, big box, and hardware stores; one plank will easily hold four portions. Be sure to buy an untreated cedar plank specifically intended for cooking. This recipe requires refrigerating the rubbed salmon for at least 1 hour or up to 24 hours before cooking (a longer time is preferable). It is necessary to preheat the cedar plank on the cooking grate just until it starts smoking; a crackling noise means that the plank is hot. It should not ignite. Serve with Cucumber-Yogurt Sauce (page 29), if desired.

1 Pat salmon dry with paper towels. Combine sugar, salt, dill, and pepper in bowl. Sprinkle salmon all over with sugar mixture, and refrigerate, uncovered, for at least 1 hour or up to 24 hours. Soak cedar plank in water for 1 hour (or according to manufacturer's directions).

2A For a charcoal grill Open bottom vent completely. Light large chimney starter filled with charcoal briquettes (6 quarts). When top coals are partially covered with ash, pour evenly over grill. Set cooking grate in place. Place cedar plank in center of grill. Cover and open lid vent completely. Heat grill until plank is lightly smoking and crackling (it should not ignite), about 5 minutes.

2B For a gas grill Place cedar plank in center of grill. Turn all burners to medium-low, cover, and heat grill until plank is smoking and crackling (it should not ignite), about 15 minutes. Leave all burners on medium-low. (Adjust burners as needed to maintain grill temperature between 300 and 325 degrees.)

3 Brush skinned side of salmon fillets with oil, then place skinned side down on plank. Cover and cook until center of each fillet is translucent when checked with tip of paring knife and registers 125 degrees (for medium-rare), 12 to 15 minutes. Transfer plank with salmon to baking sheet and let rest for 5 minutes. Serve with lemon wedges.

GRILL-ROASTED WHOLE TROUT WITH ORANGE AND FENNEL

serves 4

1 teaspoon ground fennel

1 teaspoon grated orange zest

Kosher salt and pepper

4 (10- to 12-ounce) whole trout, scaled, gutted, and fins snipped off with scissors

2 tablespoons mayonnaise

½ teaspoon honey

1 (13 by 9-inch) disposable aluminum pan (if using charcoal)

Lemon wedges

Why This Recipe Works Grill-roasting whole trout is quick and easy. The grill infuses the fish with smoky flavor and the intense heat crisps the skin beautifully, perfectly complementing the mild flesh. Whole trout are fairly prep-free. They are almost always sold cleaned and scaled with their backbones and pinbones removed. And their small size means one fish can serve one person for nice portioning. As with any fish, the skin is prone to sticking to the cooking grate. To get our trout off the grill in one piece and make their skin really crisp for eating, we brushed a mixture of mayonnaise and honey, neither of which you can taste, over the fish to help it brown more quickly and release from the grill before it overcooked. To add a little flavor boost, we sprinkled ground fennel and orange zest inside each fish. We readied a concentrated fire, using an aluminum pan to corral the coals and focus their heat. We poked a few holes in the pan to increase the airflow and the trout was browned and perfectly cooked in just a few minutes per side. Do not flip the fish over in one motion. Instead, use two thin metal spatulas to gently lift the fish from the grate and then slide it from the spatula back onto the grate. The heads can be removed before serving, if desired.

1 Place fennel, orange zest, and 2 teaspoons salt on cutting board and chop until finely minced and well combined. Rinse each fish under cold running water and pat dry with paper towels inside and out. Open up each fish and sprinkle fennel mixture evenly over flesh of fish. Season each fish with pepper. Close up fish and let sit for 10 minutes. Stir mayonnaise and honey together. Brush mayonnaise mixture evenly over entire exterior of each fish.

2A For a charcoal grill Using kitchen shears, poke twelve ½ inch holes in bottom of disposable pan. Open bottom vent completely and place disposable pan in center of grill. Light large chimney starter two-thirds filled with charcoal briquettes (4 quarts). When top coals are partially covered with ash, pour into even layer in disposable pan. Set cooking grate in place with bars parallel to long side of disposable pan, cover, and open lid vent completely. Heat grill until hot, about 5 minutes.

2B For a gas grill Turn all burners to high, cover, and heat grill until hot, about 15 minutes. Leave all burners on high.

3 Clean and oil cooking grate. Lay trout on grill, perpendicular to grate bars. Cook (covered if using gas) until skin is browned and beginning to blister, 2 to 4 minutes. Using thin metal spatula, lift bottom of thick backbone edge of fish from cooking grate just enough to slide second thin metal spatula under fish. Remove first spatula, then use it to support raw side of fish as you use second spatula to flip fish over. Cook until second side is browned, beginning to blister, and thickest part of fish registers 130 to 135 degrees, 2 to 4 minutes. Transfer fish to serving dish and let rest for 5 minutes. Serve with lemon wedges.

Grill-Roasted Whole Trout with Marjoram and Lemon
Substitute 2 teaspoons minced fresh marjoram for ground fennel and lemon zest for orange zest.

Grill-Roasted Whole Trout with Lime and Coriander
Substitute 1 teaspoon ground coriander for fennel, and lime zest and wedges for orange zest and lemon wedges.

GRILL-ROASTED STUFFED TROUT

serves 4

4 slices bacon, cut into ¼-inch pieces

1 onion, halved and sliced thin

1 red bell pepper, stemmed, seeded, and chopped

Salt and pepper

8 ounces (8 cups) baby spinach

2 teaspoons cider vinegar

4 (7- to 10-ounce) whole trout, scaled, gutted, and fins snipped off with scissors

1 tablespoon vegetable oil

Lemon wedges

Why This Recipe Works Trout and bacon are a classic pairing, no doubt discovered by a camping fisherman. One of our favorite ways to prepare trout is to stuff it with a flavorful filling prior to grill-roasting it. To minimize the trout's time on the grill we precooked the stuffing, crisping chopped bacon on the stovetop and using the rendered fat to soften onion and red bell pepper. Quick-cooking baby spinach added freshness and bright color and a hit of cider vinegar rounded out the flavors. After draining the excess moisture from the filling we fired up the grill and oiled the fish and the cooking grate thoroughly to help avoid any sticking issues. With the vegetable-bacon mixture tucked into the cavity of each fish, all we had to do was brown the trout on each side. In less than 15 minutes, we had perfectly roasted trout and a smoky-sweet stuffing. The filling can be made up to a day ahead of time, but the fish should be stuffed just before grilling. Do not flip the fish over in one motion. Instead, use two thin metal spatulas to gently lift the fish from the grate and then slide it from the spatula back onto the grate.

1 Cook bacon in 12-inch skillet over medium heat until browned and crisp, about 8 minutes. Using slotted spoon, transfer bacon to paper towel–lined plate, leaving fat in skillet. Return skillet to medium-high heat, add onion, bell pepper, and ½ teaspoon salt, and cook until vegetables are softened and beginning to brown, 5 to 7 minutes.

2 Stir in spinach and vinegar and cook until spinach is wilted and all extra moisture has evaporated, about 5 minutes. Transfer mixture to colander and let drain for 10 minutes. Stir in cooked bacon and season with salt and pepper to taste.

3 Meanwhile, rinse each trout under cold running water and pat dry with paper towels inside and out, then rub exteriors with oil. Season exteriors and cavities with salt and pepper. Divide spinach mixture evenly among cavities, about generous ¼ cup per fish.

4A For a charcoal grill Open bottom vent completely. Light large chimney starter filled with charcoal briquettes (6 quarts). When top coals are partially covered with ash, pour evenly over grill. Set cooking grate in place, cover, and open lid vent completely. Heat grill until hot, about 5 minutes.

4B For a gas grill Turn all burners to high, cover, and heat grill until hot, about 15 minutes. Leave all burners on high.

5 Clean and oil cooking grate. Lay trout on grill, perpendicular to grate bars. Cook (covered if using gas) until skin is browned and beginning to blister, 5 to 7 minutes. Using thin metal spatula, lift bottom of thick backbone edge of fish from cooking grate just enough to slide second thin metal spatula under fish. Remove first spatula, then use it to support raw side of fish as you use second spatula to flip fish over. Cook until second side is browned, flesh flakes when prodded with paring knife, filling is hot, and thickest part of fish registers 130 to 135 degrees 5 to 7 minutes. Transfer trout to serving dish and let rest for 5 minutes. Serve with lemon wedges.

GRILL-ROASTED WHOLE SNAPPER

serves 4

2 (1½-pound) whole red snapper, scaled, gutted, and fins snipped off with scissors

3 tablespoons extra-virgin olive oil

Salt and pepper

Why This Recipe Works Roasting whole red snappers on the grill is just as simple as roasting them in the oven (see page 222) and easily delivers deeply flavorful, crisp-skinned fish in mere minutes. Once the fish were rinsed, we made shallow slashes in the skin to ensure even seasoning and cooking; this also allowed us to gauge the doneness of the fish easily. To prevent the skin from sticking and tearing, we greased the cooking grate and coated the fish with a film of oil and just salt and pepper to season them. We used two thin metal spatulas to flip the delicate fish once the first side was done; they also made it easier to remove the cooked fish from the grill. With a few easy cuts, we were able to lift away the meat from the bones in a single piece. You can substitute whole sea bass for the snapper. If your fish are a little larger (between 1¾ and 2 pounds), simply grill them a minute or two longer on each side. Fish weighing more than 2 pounds will be hard to maneuver on the grill and should be avoided. Serve the snapper with lemon wedges, Chermoula Sauce (page 27), or Fennel-Apple Chutney (page 28), if desired. For filleting instructions, see page 21.

1A For a charcoal grill Open bottom vent completely. Light large chimney starter filled with charcoal briquettes (6 quarts). When top coals are partially covered with ash, pour evenly over grill. Set cooking grate in place, cover, and open lid vent completely. Heat grill until hot, about 5 minutes.

1B For a gas grill Turn all burners to high, cover, and heat grill until hot, about 15 minutes. Leave all burners on high.

2 Rinse each snapper under cold running water and pat dry with paper towels inside and out. Using sharp knife, make 3 or 4 shallow slashes, about 2 inches apart, on both sides of snapper. Rub snapper with oil and season generously with salt and pepper on inside and outside.

3 Clean and oil cooking grate. Lay snapper on grill, perpendicular to grate bars. Cook (covered if using gas) until side of snapper facing heat source is browned and crisp, 6 to 7 minutes. Using thin metal spatula, lift bottom of thick backbone edge of fish from cooking grate just enough to slide second thin metal spatula under fish. Remove first spatula, then use it to support raw side of fish as you use second spatula to flip fish over. Cook (covered if using gas) until flesh is no longer translucent at center, skin on both sides of each snapper is blistered and crisp, and snapper registers 140 degrees, 6 to 8 minutes. Carefully transfer snapper to serving dish and let rest for 5 minutes.

4 Fillet each snapper by making vertical cut just behind head from top of snapper to belly. Make another cut along top of snapper from head to tail. Use spatula to lift meat from bones, starting at head end and running spatula over bones to lift out fillet. Repeat on other side of snapper. Discard head and skeleton and serve.

GRILL-ROASTED WHOLE SEA BASS WITH SALMORIGLIO SAUCE

serves 4

Salmoriglio Sauce

¼ cup extra-virgin olive oil

1½ tablespoons minced fresh oregano

1 tablespoon lemon juice

1 small garlic clove, minced

⅛ teaspoon salt

⅛ teaspoon pepper

Fish

2 (1½- to 2-pound) whole sea bass, scaled, gutted, and fins snipped off with scissors

3 tablespoons extra-virgin olive oil

Salt and pepper

Why This Recipe Works Mild-mannered sea bass comes to life on the grill, its semifirm texture turning moist and flavorful under a crisp, charred exterior. We readied the sturdy sea bass for the grill by making shallow diagonal slashes on the skin, which helped ensure even cooking and enabled us to gauge doneness more easily, and then we coated the fish (and the cooking grate) with oil to prevent any sticking and seasoned them generously with salt and pepper both inside and out. Since the fish would roast quickly over a hot single-level fire, we prepared an accompanying sauce first to turn our fish into something truly special. *Salmoriglio* is a citrusy, herbal Italian sauce bursting with bright flavor that goes well with grilled fish. After grilling the first side until browned and starting to blister, we used two thin metal spatulas to flip the fish over to cook the second side. Do not flip the fish over in one motion. Instead, use two thin metal spatulas to gently lift the fish from the grate and then slide it from the spatula back onto the grate. You can substitute whole snapper for the sea bass. Fish weighing more than 2 pounds will be hard to maneuver on the grill and should be avoided. For filleting instructions, see page 21.

1 For the salmoriglio sauce Whisk all ingredients in bowl until combined; cover and set aside for serving.

2A For a charcoal grill Open bottom vent completely. Light large chimney starter filled with charcoal briquettes (6 quarts). When top coals are partially covered with ash, pour evenly over grill. Set cooking grate in place, cover, and open lid vent completely. Heat grill until hot, about 5 minutes.

2B For a gas grill Turn all burners to high, cover, and heat grill until hot, about 15 minutes. Leave all burners on high.

3 For the fish Rinse each sea bass under cold running water and pat dry with paper towels inside and out. Using sharp knife, make 3 or 4 shallow slashes, about 2 inches apart, on both sides of sea bass. Rub sea bass with oil and season generously with salt and pepper inside and outside.

4 Clean and oil cooking grate. Lay sea bass on grill, perpendicular to grate bars. Cook (covered if using gas) until sea bass skin is browned and beginning to blister on first side, 6 to 8 minutes. Using spatula, lift bottom of thick backbone edge of sea bass from cooking grate just enough to slide second spatula under fish. Remove first spatula, then use it to support raw side of sea bass as you use second spatula to flip fish over. Cook (covered if using gas) until second side is browned, beginning to blister, and sea bass registers 140 degrees, 6 to 8 minutes. Carefully transfer sea bass to carving board and let rest for 5 minutes.

5 Fillet sea bass by making vertical cut just behind head from top of fish to belly. Make another cut on top of sea bass from head to tail. Use spatula to lift meat from bones, starting at head end and running spatula over bones to lift out fillet. Repeat on other side of sea bass. Discard head and skeleton. Serve with sauce.

GRILL-ROASTED OYSTERS WITH MIGNONETTE SAUCE

serves 4 to 6

Mignonette Sauce

¼ cup red wine vinegar

1 shallot, minced

1 tablespoon lemon juice

1 teaspoon minced fresh parsley

24 oysters

Why This Recipe Works Briny, fresh oysters are a pleasure to eat in many forms, but roasting them on the grill is a very appealing option, especially for summer entertaining. The method couldn't be easier: As soon as the shells open, they're done. The key to the best oysters on the grill is to not move the shellfish around too much and to handle them carefully once they open to preserve their natural juices (or liquor). After cleaning our oysters, we placed them directly on the cooking grate of a hot grill and covered them. From there, we left them well alone as they slowly began to open. As soon as they opened, we carefully transferred the oysters, holding them steady, to a platter to preserve their natural juices. The warm, tender oysters tasted great right off the grill, but a drizzle of mignonette sauce (or one of our punchy alternatives) mingled well with the brininess of the liquor offering the perfect complement. In general, we prefer oysters from cold northern waters because they tend to be more briny and crisp. Look for oysters with tightly closed shells. You can substitute 24 littleneck clams, scrubbed, for the oysters; grill as directed in step 3, increasing cooking time by 3 to 5 minutes. Clams may take longer to cook on a gas grill than they do on a charcoal grill.

1 For the mignonette sauce Combine all ingredients in bowl; refrigerate until ready to serve. (Mignonette can be refrigerated for up to 2 days.)

2A For a charcoal grill Open bottom vent completely. Light large chimney starter filled with charcoal briquettes (6 quarts). When top coals are partially covered with ash, pour evenly over grill. Set cooking grate in place, cover, and open lid vent completely. Heat grill until hot, about 5 minutes.

2B For a gas grill Turn all burners to high, cover, and heat grill until hot, about 15 minutes. Leave all burners on high.

3 Clean and oil cooking grate. Place oysters on grill, cover, and cook, without turning, until oysters have opened, 3 to 5 minutes. Using tongs, transfer oysters to serving dish as they open, trying to preserve juices. Discard any oysters that refuse to open. If desired, discard top shells and loosen meat in bottom shells before serving with mignonette.

Grill-Roasted Oysters with Tangy Soy-Citrus Sauce

Combine ¼ cup low-sodium soy sauce, 1½ teaspoons lemon juice, 1½ teaspoons lime juice, 1 thinly sliced scallion, and ½ teaspoon grated fresh ginger in bowl. Substitute for mignonette.

Grill-Roasted Oysters with Spicy Lemon Butter Sauce

Melt 4 tablespoons unsalted butter in small saucepan over medium-low heat. Off heat, add 1 tablespoon hot sauce, 1 teaspoon lemon juice, and ¼ teaspoon salt; cover and keep warm. Substitute for mignonette.

VEGETABLES AND FRUITS

ROASTED ARTICHOKES WITH LEMON VINAIGRETTE

serves 4

3 lemons

4 artichokes (8 to 10 ounces each)

9 tablespoons extra-virgin olive oil

Salt and pepper

½ teaspoon finely grated garlic

½ teaspoon Dijon mustard

2 tablespoons minced fresh parsley

Why This Recipe Works If you have never roasted artichokes, this recipe will be a game changer. The classic (and nearly prep-free) method of cooking artichokes with water washes out the vegetable's delicate nuttiness rather than accentuating it. But roasting concentrates that flavor and turns nearly the entire vegetable edible, so we found the prep work involved to be well worth it. Trimming the fibrous stems, snapping off tough outer leaves, halving each artichoke, and scooping out the fuzzy chokes got us on track for nicely browned and tender artichokes. To ensure that the trimmed leaves wouldn't oxidize and turn a drab gray-brown in the oven, we dropped the artichokes into a lemon water bath before roasting. We tossed them with seasoned oil, making sure to get oil between their leaves, and roasted them in a 475-degree oven sealed under foil. Gently cooking in their own steam, the artichokes' flavors deepened as the stems and hearts turned rich and velvety while the leaves—even the tough outer ones—became tender. Our rich artichokes benefited from a touch of acidity, so we roasted halved lemons alongside them and used the concentrated juicy pulp to prepare a vinaigrette. If your artichokes are larger than 10 ounces, strip away another layer or two of the toughest outer leaves. Use a rasp-style grater to finely grate the garlic. Use your teeth to scrape the flesh from the cooked tough outer leaves. The inner tender leaves, heart, and stem are entirely edible.

1 Adjust oven rack to lower-middle position and heat oven to 475 degrees. Cut 1 lemon in half, squeeze halves into 2 quarts water, and drop in spent halves.

2 Cut off most of stem of 1 artichoke, leaving about ¾ inch attached. Cut off top quarter. Pull tough outer leaves downward toward stem and break off at base; continue until first three or four rows of leaves have been removed. Using paring knife, trim outer layer of stem and rough areas around base, removing any dark green parts. Cut artichoke in half lengthwise. Using spoon, remove fuzzy choke. Pull out very inner, tiny purple-tinged leaves, leaving small cavity in center of each half. Drop prepped halves into lemon water. Repeat with remaining artichokes.

3 Brush 13 by 9-inch baking dish with 1 tablespoon oil. Remove artichokes from lemon water, shaking off some excess lemon water (some should be left clinging to leaves).

Toss artichokes with 2 tablespoons oil and ¾ teaspoon salt and season with pepper, gently working some oil and seasonings between leaves. Arrange artichoke halves cut side down in baking dish. Cut very thin slices off both ends of remaining 2 lemons and cut lemons in half crosswise. Place lemon halves, flesh side up, in baking dish with artichokes and cover tightly with aluminum foil.

4 Roast until cut sides of artichokes start to brown and both bases and leaves are tender when poked with tip of paring knife, 25 to 30 minutes. Transfer artichokes to serving dish. Once lemon halves are cool enough to handle, squeeze into fine-mesh strainer set over bowl. Press on solids to extract all pulp; discard solids. Measure 1½ tablespoons strained lemon pulp into small bowl. Whisk in garlic, mustard, and ½ teaspoon salt and season with pepper to taste. Whisking constantly, gradually drizzle remaining 6 tablespoons oil into lemon mixture. Whisk in parsley. Serve with artichokes.

ROASTED ASPARAGUS WITH MINT-ORANGE GREMOLATA

serves 4 to 6

Asparagus

2 pounds thick asparagus

2 tablespoons extra-virgin olive oil

½ teaspoon salt

¼ teaspoon pepper

Gremolata

2 tablespoons minced fresh mint

2 tablespoons minced fresh parsley

2 teaspoons grated orange zest

1 garlic clove, minced

Pinch cayenne pepper

2 teaspoons extra-virgin olive oil

Why This Recipe Works Roasted asparagus is quick and easy to make, and our technique ensures perfectly cooked spears that are crisp yet tender, verdant yet perfectly browned. We achieved this balance by selecting ½-inch-thick asparagus spears, trimming off their tough ends, and peeling away the woody skin to expose the creamy interior before spreading them on a preheated baking sheet. Tossed with oil, the prepped spears sizzled as soon as they hit the pan, and not moving them during their 10-minute cooking time allowed the spears to develop a rich sear on one side and remain vibrant green on the other. Our asparagus retained its freshness and tender snap, and a citrusy topping bright with mint, parsley, and orange zest made for a perfect finish. This recipe works best with thick asparagus spears that are between ½ and ¾ inch in diameter. To avoid harsh garlic flavor, do not mince the garlic until you are ready to mix the gremolata.

1 For the asparagus Adjust oven rack to lowest position, place rimmed baking sheet on rack, and heat oven to 500 degrees.

2 Trim bottom inch of asparagus spears and discard. Peel bottom halves of spears until white flesh is exposed. Place asparagus in large baking pan and toss with oil, salt, and pepper.

3 Transfer asparagus to preheated sheet and spread into even layer. Roast without moving asparagus until undersides of spears are browned, tops are vibrant green, and tip of paring knife inserted at base of largest spear meets little resistance, 8 to 10 minutes. Transfer asparagus to serving dish.

4 For the gremolata Combine mint, parsley, orange zest, garlic, and cayenne in bowl. Drizzle asparagus with oil, sprinkle with gremolata, and serve immediately.

Roasted Asparagus with Tarragon-Lemon Gremolata

Substitute tarragon for the mint and lemon zest for the orange zest.

Roasted Asparagus with Cilantro-Lime Gremolata

Substitute ¼ cup minced fresh cilantro for the mint and parsley. Substitute lime zest for the orange zest.

ROASTED GREEN BEANS WITH ALMONDS AND MINT

serves 4 to 6

1½ pounds green beans, trimmed

6 tablespoons extra-virgin olive oil

¾ teaspoon sugar

Kosher salt and pepper

2 garlic cloves, minced

1 teaspoon grated lime zest plus 4 teaspoons juice

1 teaspoon Dijon mustard

¼ cup fresh mint leaves, torn

¼ cup whole blanched almonds, toasted and chopped

Why This Recipe Works This technique for roasting green beans has a lot going for it: It's super simple, it frees up your stovetop, and it gives mature, tough supermarket green beans a flavor comparable to sweet, fresh-picked beans. We knew these quick-cooking beans could only handle a short stay in the oven before they overcooked, so we ensured plenty of flavor-boosting color by tossing them with some sugar along with olive oil, salt, and pepper. Spreading them over a baking sheet and sealing them under aluminum foil allowed them to steam gently to perfect doneness in the oven. We uncovered the beans for the final 10 minutes so the sugar could caramelize, turning the beans an appealing blistered, speckled brown. To add some lively bite to the flavorful beans, we tossed them with a warm lime vinaigrette and fresh mint, and topped them off with crunchy almonds. To trim green beans quickly, line up a handful so the stem ends are even and then cut off the stems with one swipe of the knife.

1 Adjust oven rack to lowest position and heat oven to 475 degrees. Combine green beans, 2 tablespoons oil, sugar, ¾ teaspoon salt, and ½ teaspoon pepper in bowl. Evenly distribute green beans on rimmed baking sheet.

2 Cover sheet tightly with aluminum foil and roast for 10 minutes. Remove foil and continue to roast until green beans are spotty brown, about 10 minutes, stirring halfway through roasting.

3 Meanwhile, combine garlic, lime zest, and remaining ¼ cup oil in large bowl and microwave until bubbling, about 1 minute; let mixture steep for 1 minute. Whisk lime juice, mustard, ¼ teaspoon salt, and ¼ teaspoon pepper into garlic mixture.

4 Transfer green beans to bowl with dressing, add mint, and toss to combine. Transfer to serving dish and sprinkle with almonds. Serve.

Roasted Green Beans with Pecorino and Pine Nuts

Substitute lemon zest and juice for lime zest and juice, 2 tablespoons chopped fresh basil for mint, and toasted pine nuts for almonds. Sprinkle green beans with ½ cup shredded Pecorino Romano before serving.

Roasted Green Beans with Goat Cheese and Hazelnuts

Substitute orange zest for lime zest; 2 teaspoons orange juice for 2 teaspoons lime juice; 2 tablespoons minced fresh chives for mint; and skinned hazelnuts for almonds. Sprinkle green beans with ½ cup crumbled goat cheese before serving.

ROASTED BEET SALAD WITH GOAT CHEESE AND PISTACHIOS

serves 4 to 6

2 pounds beets, trimmed

2 tablespoons extra-virgin olive oil

4 teaspoons sherry vinegar

Salt and pepper

2 ounces (2 cups) baby arugula

2 ounces goat cheese, crumbled (½ cup)

2 tablespoons chopped toasted pistachios

Why This Recipe Works With their sweet, earthy flavor, juicy texture, and ruby-red hue, these roasted beets are real showstoppers, and our technique to prepare them could not be simpler. Unlike boiling or steaming, roasting this tough root vegetable concentrates its sweetness and turns it perfectly tender. Wrapping each unpeeled beet in foil and roasting them in a 400-degree oven allowed the beets to cook to perfect softness off their own moisture in about 45 minutes. Peeling the beets while they were still warm was easy—the skins slid right off when rubbed with paper towels. To incorporate the beets into an elegant salad, we sliced and tossed them with a simple vinaigrette while still warm, allowing them to soak up plenty of flavor. Crumbled goat cheese, peppery arugula, and toasted pistachios rounded out our salad. When buying beets, look for bunches that have the most uniformly sized beets so that they will roast in the same amount of time. If the beets are different sizes, remove the smaller ones from the oven as they become tender. You can use either golden or red beets (or a mix of each) in this recipe.

1 Adjust oven rack to middle position and heat oven to 400 degrees. Wrap beets individually in aluminum foil and place on rimmed baking sheet. Roast beets until skewer inserted into center meets little resistance (you will need to unwrap beets to test them), 45 minutes to 1 hour.

2 Remove beets from oven and carefully open foil packets. When beets are cool enough to handle, carefully rub off skins using paper towel. Slice beets into ½-inch-thick wedges, and, if large, cut in half crosswise.

3 Whisk oil, vinegar, ¼ teaspoon salt, and ¼ teaspoon pepper together in large bowl. Add beets, toss to coat, and let cool to room temperature, about 20 minutes. Add arugula and gently toss to coat. Season with salt and pepper to taste. Transfer to serving dish, sprinkle with goat cheese and pistachios, and serve.

Roasted Beet Salad with Blood Oranges and Almonds

Navel oranges, tangelos, or Cara Caras can be substituted for the blood oranges, but since they are larger you'll need to use just one of them.

Substitute 1 cup shaved ricotta salata for goat cheese, and sliced toasted almonds for pistachios. Cut away peel and pith from 2 blood oranges; quarter oranges, then slice each quarter crosswise into ½-inch-thick pieces and add to salad with arugula.

removing the skin from roasted beets

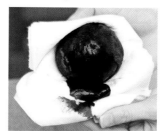

When beets are cool enough to handle, carefully rub off skins using paper towel.

ROASTED BROCCOLI WITH GARLIC

1¾ pounds broccoli

3 tablespoons extra-virgin olive oil

3 garlic cloves, minced

½ teaspoon sugar

½ teaspoon salt

Pinch pepper

Lemon wedges

Why This Recipe Works Broccoli's awkward shape, tough stems, and shrubby florets may seem to make it a poor candidate for roasting, but we found a method that delivered such great results that you may never want to steam broccoli again. Success in roasting this oddly shaped vegetable came down to how we cut it up. To maximize its direct contact with the sheet pan (thereby increasing its flavor-boosting browning), we cut the crowns into wedges and the trimmed stalks into thick planks. Preheating a baking sheet on the lowest rack of a 500-degree oven meant our broccoli pieces would begin to sizzle and sear on contact, and tossing them with some sugar along with oil, garlic, salt, and pepper sped up that caramelization even further, delivering crisp-tipped florets and blistered and browned stalks that were subtly sweet and perfectly seasoned. Make sure to trim away the outer peel from the broccoli stalks as directed; otherwise, it will turn tough when roasted.

1 Adjust oven rack to lowest position, place rimmed baking sheet on rack, and heat oven to 500 degrees. Cut broccoli horizontally at juncture of crowns and stalks. Cut crowns into 4 wedges if 3 to 4 inches in diameter or 6 wedges if 4 to 5 inches in diameter. Trim tough outer peel from stalks, then cut into ½-inch-thick planks about 2 to 3 inches long.

2 Combine oil, garlic, sugar, salt, and pepper in large bowl. Add broccoli and toss to coat. Working quickly, lay broccoli in single layer, flat sides down, on preheated sheet. Roast until stalks are well browned and tender and florets are lightly browned, 9 to 11 minutes. Transfer to serving dish and serve with lemon wedges.

Roasted Broccoli with Shallots, Fennel Seeds, and Parmesan

Omit garlic. While broccoli roasts, heat 1 tablespoon extra-virgin olive oil in 8-inch skillet over medium heat until shimmering. Add 3 thinly sliced shallots and cook, stirring often, until shallots soften and are beginning to brown, 5 to 6 minutes. Stir in 1 teaspoon coarsely chopped fennel seeds and cook until shallots are golden brown, 1 to 2 minutes; remove from heat. Toss roasted broccoli with shallot mixture and garnish with shaved Parmesan before serving.

Roasted Broccoli with Olives, Garlic, Oregano, and Lemon

While broccoli roasts, cook 2 tablespoons extra-virgin olive oil, 5 thinly sliced garlic cloves, and ½ teaspoon red pepper flakes in 8-inch skillet over medium-low heat, stirring often, until garlic softens and is beginning to brown, 5 to 7 minutes. Off heat, stir in 2 tablespoons finely chopped pitted black olives, 1 teaspoon minced fresh oregano, and 2 teaspoons lemon juice. Toss roasted broccoli with olive mixture before serving.

ROASTED BRUSSELS SPROUTS WITH BACON AND PECANS

serves 6 to 8

2¼ pounds Brussels sprouts, trimmed and halved

5 tablespoons extra-virgin olive oil

1 tablespoon water

Salt and pepper

4 slices bacon

½ cup pecans, toasted and chopped fine

Why This Recipe Works Brussels sprouts are having their moment in the spotlight and restaurant chefs are upping the ante by roasting them and adding all sorts of flavorful ingredients. Roasting turns these tough, multilayered "tiny cabbages" tender, caramelized, and nutty and eliminates any bitter, sulfurous flavors from them. Getting foolproof results at home could not be easier. To make every little leaf perfectly tender, we halved the sprouts and tossed them with a little water along with oil, salt, and pepper. After arranging the Brussels sprouts cut side down, we sealed the baking sheet with aluminum foil at the outset, which generated enough steam to soften the fibrous leaves. Removing the foil and exposing the sprouts to the dry heat of the 500-degree oven quickly crisped and caramelized them. To give our perfectly roasted sprouts some restaurant-caliber richness, we stirred in crisp bites of bacon as well as some of its smoky rendered fat and added toasted pecans for satisfying crunch. If you are buying loose Brussels sprouts, select those that are about 1½ inches long. Quarter Brussels sprouts longer than 2½ inches; do not cut sprouts shorter than 1 inch.

1 Adjust oven rack to upper-middle position and heat oven to 500 degrees. Toss Brussels sprouts, 3 tablespoons oil, water, ¾ teaspoon salt, and ¼ teaspoon pepper in bowl until sprouts are coated. Transfer sprouts to rimmed baking sheet and arrange cut sides down. Cover sheet tightly with aluminum foil and roast for 10 minutes.

2 Meanwhile, cook bacon in 10-inch skillet over medium heat until crisp, 7 to 10 minutes. Using slotted spoon, transfer bacon to paper towel-lined plate; reserve 1 tablespoon bacon fat. Finely chop bacon.

3 Remove foil and continue to roast Brussels sprouts until well browned and tender, 10 to 12 minutes. Transfer to serving dish and toss with remaining 2 tablespoons oil, reserved bacon fat, chopped bacon, and pecans. Season with salt and pepper to taste, and serve.

Roasted Brussels Sprouts with Garlic, Red Pepper Flakes, and Parmesan

Omit bacon and pecans and increase oil to 6 tablespoons. While Brussels sprouts roast, cook 3 tablespoons oil, 2 minced garlic cloves, and ½ teaspoon red pepper flakes in 8-inch skillet over medium heat until garlic is golden and fragrant, 1 to 2 minutes; remove from heat. Toss roasted Brussels sprouts with garlic oil before transferring to serving dish, then sprinkle with ¼ cup grated Parmesan cheese.

Roasted Brussels Sprouts with Walnuts and Lemon

Omit bacon and pecans and reduce oil to 3 tablespoons. Toss roasted Brussels sprouts with ⅓ cup finely chopped toasted walnuts, 3 tablespoons melted unsalted butter, and 1 tablespoon lemon juice before transferring to serving dish.

ROASTED CARROTS

serves 4 to 6

1½ pounds carrots, peeled

2 tablespoons unsalted butter, melted

Salt and pepper

Why This Recipe Works Carrots will be the star side at any meal if you use this simple roasting method. This technique is largely hands-off and also allows you to incorporate a host of interesting flavors. We found that the key was to cut the carrots into large batons, which gave us evenly cooked results and optimized their browning. Tossing the carrots with melted butter, salt, and pepper richly seasoned the spears, and sealing them under aluminum foil on a rimmed baking sheet kept their moisture in while their interiors turned tender and creamy. We then uncovered the baking sheet to finish roasting the carrots with direct exposure to the oven's heat, stirring them around periodically until their surface moisture evaporated and they took on gorgeous caramelized streaks. Seasoned with salt and pepper, these carrots are simple, sweet perfection, but we also jazzed them up with a few full-flavored variations.

1 Adjust oven rack to middle position and heat oven to 425 degrees. Cut carrots in half crosswise, then cut them lengthwise into halves or quarters as needed to create uniformly sized pieces. Toss carrots, melted butter, ½ teaspoon salt, and ¼ teaspoon pepper together in bowl.

2 Transfer carrots to parchment paper–lined rimmed baking sheet and spread into single layer. Cover baking sheet tightly with aluminum foil and roast for 15 minutes. Remove foil and roast, stirring twice, until carrots are well browned and tender, 30 to 35 minutes. Transfer to serving dish, season with salt and pepper to taste, and serve.

Roasted Carrots and Fennel with Toasted Almonds and Lemon

Reduce amount of carrots to 1 pound. Add 1 small fennel bulb, stalks discarded and bulb cored and sliced ½ inch thick, to bowl with carrots; roast as directed. Toss vegetables with ¼ cup toasted sliced almonds, 2 teaspoons minced fresh parsley, and 1 teaspoon lemon juice before serving.

Roasted Carrots and Parsnips with Rosemary

Reduce amount of carrots to 1 pound. Add 8 ounces parsnips, peeled, halved crosswise, and cut lengthwise into halves or quarters as needed to create uniformly sized pieces, and 1 teaspoon minced fresh rosemary to bowl with carrots; roast as directed. Toss vegetables with 2 teaspoons minced fresh parsley before serving.

Roasted Carrots and Shallots with Lemon and Thyme

Reduce amount of carrots to 1 pound. Add 6 shallots, peeled and halved lengthwise, and 1 teaspoon minced fresh thyme to bowl with carrots; roast as directed. Toss vegetables with 1 teaspoon lemon juice before serving.

ROASTED CARROTS WITH ORANGE GLAZE AND TOASTED ALMONDS

serves 12

3 pounds baby carrots

⅓ cup packed brown sugar

⅓ cup orange marmalade

4 tablespoons unsalted butter, cut into small pieces

Salt and pepper

Pinch cayenne pepper

½ cup sliced almonds, toasted

2 tablespoons minced fresh parsley

Why This Recipe Works When you want a carrot side dish to serve a crowd, baby carrots are the way to go since you don't have to spend time peeling and cutting. This simple and ingenious recipe transforms this ubiquitous supermarket staple by roasting them and incorporating a simple glaze. After spreading the ready-to-go carrots across a foil-lined baking sheet, creating a bright, balanced glaze was as easy as sprinkling them with brown sugar (a surefire way to boost caramelization), pieces of butter, orange marmalade for sweet-tart citrusy flavor, and a pinch of cayenne for heat. Starting the carrots under aluminum foil allowed them to cook through as the butter and marmalade melted and melded into a bubbling glaze, and finishing them uncovered gave the glaze a chance to lightly caramelize. The crunch and freshness of toasted almonds and minced parsley were all this simple side needed. Note that some of the glaze will seep underneath the foil.

1 Adjust oven rack to lowest position and heat oven to 425 degrees.

2 Line a rimmed baking sheet with aluminum foil and spray with vegetable oil spray. Spread carrots over prepared sheet and sprinkle with sugar, marmalade, butter, ½ teaspoon salt, and cayenne. Cover tightly with foil and roast, stirring occasionally, until sugar and butter have melted and sauce is bubbling, about 25 minutes.

3 Uncover carrots and continue to cook, stirring occasionally, until tender and glazed, 20 to 30 minutes. Transfer to serving bowl, stir in almonds and parsley, season with salt and pepper to taste, and serve.

ROASTED CAULIFLOWER

serves 4 to 6

1 head cauliflower (2 pounds)

¼ cup extra-virgin olive oil

Salt and pepper

Why This Recipe Works Many people think cauliflower is bland because its common preparations—steamed or served raw as crudité—do not do this sweet, nutty vegetable any justice. Roasting, on the other hand, highlights those appealing traits at every turn. To maximize the dense head's direct contact with the baking sheet, we sliced it into wedges, creating plenty of flat surfaces for browning. To keep the cauliflower from drying out in a hot oven, we started it covered and allowed it to steam in its own moisture until barely tender. Then we removed the foil and returned the pan to the oven until the wedges were caramelized and browned. Flipping each wedge halfway through roasting ensured even cooking and color. Thanks to its natural sweetness and rich flavor, our roasted cauliflower needed little enhancement—just a touch of salt and pepper did the trick. This dish stands well on its own or drizzled with extra-virgin olive oil.

1 Adjust oven rack to lowest position and heat oven to 475 degrees. Trim outer leaves off cauliflower and cut stem flush with bottom of head. Cut head into 8 equal wedges. Place wedges, with either cut side down, on aluminum foil–lined rimmed baking sheet. Drizzle with 2 tablespoons oil and season with salt and pepper. Gently rub oil and seasonings into cauliflower. Gently flip cauliflower and repeat on second cut side with remaining 2 tablespoons oil, salt, and pepper.

2 Cover baking sheet tightly with foil and roast for 10 minutes. Remove foil and continue to roast until bottoms of cauliflower wedges are golden, 8 to 12 minutes.

3 Remove sheet from oven, carefully flip wedges using spatula, and continue to roast until cauliflower is golden all over, 8 to 12 minutes. Transfer to serving dish, season with salt and pepper to taste, and serve.

Spicy Roasted Cauliflower

Stir 2 teaspoons curry powder or chili powder into oil in bowl before seasoning cauliflower in step 1.

cutting cauliflower into wedges

After trimming away any leaves, cut stem from bottom of head. Carefully slice head into 8 equal wedges, keeping core and florets intact.

ROASTED CELERY ROOT WITH YOGURT AND SESAME SEEDS

serves 6

3 celery roots (2½ pounds), peeled, halved, and sliced ½ inch thick

3 tablespoons extra-virgin olive oil

Salt and pepper

¼ cup plain yogurt

¼ teaspoon grated lemon zest plus 1 teaspoon juice

1 teaspoon sesame seeds, toasted

1 teaspoon coriander seeds, toasted and crushed

¼ teaspoon dried thyme

¼ cup fresh cilantro leaves

Why This Recipe Works Celery root may not be a looker, but this humble root vegetable boasts an herbal, earthy flavor that comes alive when roasted. To turn it into a simple but impactful vegetable side, we needed to cut the bulbous root into even-size planks. After peeling off the tough exterior, we halved the celery root and sliced it into ½-inch-thick half moons that we tossed with oil, salt, and pepper for even seasoning and ready browning. Roasting them uncovered in a single layer on a rimmed baking sheet on the bottom rack of a hot oven gradually turned their tough texture creamy; rotating the pan and flipping the slices ensured even browning as the exteriors caramelized. Tangy yogurt, with reinforced brightness from both lemon juice and zest, complemented the rich and savory celery root for a standout side dish. To finish, we sprinkled on an aromatic combination of toasted sesame seeds, coriander, and dried thyme before adding whole cilantro leaves to freshen the dish.

1 Adjust oven rack to lowest position and heat oven to 425 degrees. Toss celery root with oil, ½ teaspoon salt, and ¼ teaspoon pepper and arrange on rimmed baking sheet in single layer. Roast celery root until sides touching sheet toward back of oven are well browned, 25 to 30 minutes. Rotate sheet and continue to roast until sides touching sheet toward back of oven are well browned, 6 to 10 minutes.

2 Flip each piece and continue to roast until celery root is very tender and sides touching sheet are browned, 10 to 15 minutes.

3 Transfer celery root to serving dish. Whisk yogurt, lemon zest and juice, and pinch salt together in bowl. In separate bowl, combine sesame seeds, coriander seeds, thyme, and pinch salt. Drizzle celery root with yogurt sauce and sprinkle with seed mixture and cilantro. Serve.

peeling celery root

1 Using chef's knife, cut ½ inch from both root end and opposite end of celery root.

2 Turn celery root so 1 cut side rests on board. To peel, cut from top to bottom, rotating celery root while removing wide strips of skin.

BULGUR-STUFFED ROASTED EGGPLANT

serves 4

4 (10-ounce) Italian eggplants, halved lengthwise

2 tablespoons extra-virgin olive oil

Salt and pepper

½ cup medium-grind bulgur, rinsed

¼ cup water

1 onion, chopped fine

3 garlic cloves, minced

2 teaspoons minced fresh oregano or ½ teaspoon dried

¼ teaspoon ground cinnamon

Pinch cayenne pepper

1 pound plum tomatoes, cored, seeded, and chopped

2 ounces Pecorino Romano cheese, grated (1 cup)

2 tablespoons toasted pine nuts

2 teaspoons red wine vinegar

2 tablespoons minced fresh parsley

Why This Recipe Works A roasted, stuffed eggplant with a crown of shredded cheese is a thing of beauty and makes an appealing and satisfying entrée. Taking inspiration from Turkish cuisine, we set out to roast small eggplants and fill them with a hearty bulgur stuffing. Roasting the eggplants was the key to preventing them from turning watery: We halved them, scored their flesh, and roasted them flesh side down on a preheated baking sheet to help dry out their interiors. Letting the tender eggplants drain on paper towels eliminated excess moisture. It was then easy to push the eggplants' flesh to the sides to add our filling. Nutty bulgur made a perfect base, with chopped tomatoes, Pecorino, and pine nuts adding heft and richness that played well off the eggplant; a hit of red wine vinegar offered welcome acidity. We sprinkled on more Pecorino for good measure and melted it in the oven; minced fresh parsley finished the dish. When shopping, do not confuse bulgur with cracked wheat, which has a much longer cooking time and will not work in this recipe.

1 Adjust oven racks to upper-middle and lowest positions, place parchment paper–lined rimmed baking sheet on lower rack, and heat oven to 400 degrees.

2 Score flesh of each eggplant half in 1-inch diamond pattern, about 1 inch deep. Brush scored sides of eggplant with 1 tablespoon oil and season with salt and pepper. Lay eggplant, cut side down, on preheated sheet and roast until flesh is tender, 40 to 50 minutes. Transfer eggplant, cut side down, to paper towel–lined baking sheet and let drain.

3 Meanwhile, toss bulgur with water in bowl and let sit until grains are softened and liquid is fully absorbed, 20 to 40 minutes.

4 Heat remaining 1 tablespoon oil in 12-inch skillet over medium heat until shimmering. Add onion and cook until softened, about 5 minutes. Stir in garlic, oregano, cinnamon, cayenne, and ½ teaspoon salt and cook until fragrant, about 30 seconds. Off heat, stir in bulgur, tomatoes, ¾ cup Pecorino, pine nuts, and vinegar and let sit until heated through, about 1 minute. Season with salt and pepper to taste.

5 Return eggplant cut side up to sheet. Using 2 forks, gently push eggplant flesh to sides to make room for filling. Mound bulgur mixture into eggplant halves and pack lightly with back of spoon. Sprinkle with remaining ¼ cup Pecorino. Roast on upper rack until cheese is melted, 5 to 10 minutes. Sprinkle with parsley and serve.

ROASTED GARLIC

makes about ½ cup

4 large garlic heads
2 teaspoons extra-virgin olive oil
Salt

Why This Recipe Works Few other applications reveal roasting's power the way this garlic recipe does. Roasting turns garlic from intensely pungent to nutty, sweet, and spreadably soft with minimal work. For an easy, foolproof method, we simply trimmed off the top of each head of garlic, exposing the tops of the cloves, and drizzled them with olive oil. Sealed tightly into an aluminum foil packet, the cloves turned buttery soft in a 425-degree oven; opening up the packet for the last 20 minutes allowed the tops of the cloves to caramelize. The softened cloves are perfect for spreading onto bread; they also add rich flavor to simple condiments. This recipe can be adjusted for as many or as few garlic heads as you want. Serve the garlic with crusty bread or use in Roasted Garlic Aïoli or Creamy Roasted Garlic Dressing (recipes follow).

1 Adjust oven rack to middle position and heat oven to 425 degrees. Cut ½ inch off top of each garlic head to expose most of tops of garlic cloves. Place garlic heads, cut side up, in center of large piece of aluminum foil. Drizzle each with ½ teaspoon oil, season with salt, and gather foil tightly around garlic to form packet.

2 Place packet directly on oven rack and roast garlic for 45 minutes. Carefully open just top of foil to expose garlic and continue to roast until garlic is soft and golden brown, about 20 minutes.

3 Remove garlic from oven and let cool for 20 minutes. When cool, squeeze garlic from skins into bowl. (Roasted garlic can be refrigerated for up to 1 week.)

ROASTED GARLIC AÏOLI

makes about 1 cup

2 large egg yolks
4 teaspoons fresh lemon juice
⅛ teaspoon sugar
Salt and pepper
6 tablespoons extra-virgin olive oil
6 tablespoons vegetable oil
½ recipe Roasted Garlic (¼ cup)

Process yolks, lemon juice, sugar, ¼ teaspoon salt, and ⅛ teaspoon pepper in food processor until combined, about 10 seconds. With machine running, slowly add both oils in slow steady stream, scraping down sides of bowl as needed. Continue to process until mixture is thick and creamy, about 5 seconds. Add garlic and pulse until incorporated, about 5 pulses. Season with salt and pepper to taste.

CREAMY ROASTED GARLIC DRESSING

makes about ⅔ cup

½ recipe Roasted Garlic (¼ cup)
3 tablespoons extra-virgin olive oil
2 tablespoons water, plus extra as needed
2 tablespoons cider vinegar
1 tablespoon Dijon mustard
½ teaspoon minced fresh thyme
Salt and pepper

Process garlic, oil, water, vinegar, mustard, thyme, ½ teaspoon salt, and ⅛ teaspoon pepper in food processor until thick and smooth, about 1 minute. (If dressing is too thick, add additional water, 1 tablespoon at a time, as needed.) Season with salt and pepper to taste.

ROASTED MUSHROOMS WITH PARMESAN AND PINE NUTS

serves 4

Salt and pepper

1½ pounds cremini mushrooms, trimmed and left whole if small, halved if medium, or quartered if large

1 pound shiitake mushrooms, stemmed, caps larger than 3 inches halved

2 tablespoons extra-virgin olive oil

2 tablespoons unsalted butter, melted

1 teaspoon lemon juice

1 ounce Parmesan cheese, grated (½ cup)

2 tablespoons toasted pine nuts

2 tablespoons chopped fresh parsley

Why This Recipe Works Forget every bland, washed-out sautéed mushroom you've ever tasted; this rich, woodsy blend of cremini and shiitakes proves that roasting is a superior way to cook mushrooms. For flavorful and moist mushrooms, we discovered that brining them was the key to roasting success. This unusual step seasoned the mushrooms evenly and allowed them to absorb moisture through their gills and cut surfaces, which improved the texture of the drier shiitakes in particular. After spreading them out over a rimmed baking sheet, we roasted the brined mushrooms in a hot oven for just under an hour until they were darkly browned. To give our savory mushrooms a rich finish, we coated them in melted butter and lemon juice and tossed in Parmesan, parsley, and pine nuts. Quarter large (more than 2 inches) mushrooms, halve medium (1 to 2 inches) ones, and leave small (under 1 inch) ones whole.

1 Adjust oven rack to lowest position and heat oven to 450 degrees. Dissolve 5 teaspoons salt in 2 quarts room-temperature water in large container. Add cremini mushrooms and shiitake mushrooms to brine, cover with plate or bowl to submerge, and let sit for 10 minutes.

2 Drain mushrooms in colander and pat dry with paper towels. Spread mushrooms evenly on rimmed baking sheet, drizzle with oil, and toss to coat. Roast until liquid from mushrooms has completely evaporated, 35 to 45 minutes.

3 Carefully stir mushrooms and continue to roast until mushrooms are deeply browned, 5 to 10 minutes.

4 Combine melted butter and lemon juice in large bowl. Add mushrooms, Parmesan, pine nuts, and parsley and toss to coat. Season with salt and pepper to taste; serve immediately.

Roasted Mushrooms with Sesame and Scallions

Substitute 2 teaspoons toasted sesame oil for butter and ½ teaspoon rice vinegar for lemon juice. Omit Parmesan and substitute 2 teaspoons toasted sesame seeds for nuts and 2 thinly sliced scallions for parsley.

Roasted Mushrooms with Harissa and Mint

Substitute 1 tablespoon extra-virgin olive oil for butter and increase lemon juice to 2 teaspoons. Whisk 2 teaspoons harissa; 1 garlic clove, minced to paste; ¼ teaspoon ground cumin; and ¼ teaspoon salt into oil mixture in step 4. Omit Parmesan and pine nuts and substitute mint for parsley.

ROASTED CARAMELIZED ONIONS

makes about 2 cups

3 tablespoons unsalted butter

4 pounds onions, halved and sliced ¼ inch thick

Salt and pepper

Why This Recipe Works If there is any one ingredient that is a magic elixir, it is caramelized onions. Their uses are many—they can transform pizza, elevate a sandwich, or add interest to a cheese board. But caramelizing them on the stovetop requires patience and a watchful eye. Enter roasting. Our approach is essentially hands-off, allowing the onions to turn golden, soft, and sweet in the oven where the steady, even heat promises even cooking. After slicing up 4 pounds of onions and stirring them into melted butter in a Dutch oven, much of our work was done. The onions roasted in the covered pot, cooking down and shedding their moisture in a 400-degree oven. An hour in, we gave the pot a decisive stir, loosening any bits stuck to the sides and bottom. Leaving the lid ajar for the last hour and a half encouraged all excess moisture to evaporate, giving us deeper browning and sweet, concentrated flavor. Our finished onions boasted profound, nuanced sweetness, and scraping up and stirring the fond into the golden strands made them all the richer. Be sure to use yellow onions here; sweet onions, such as Vidalia or Walla Walla, will make this recipe overly sweet and somewhat gummy. Serve these onions alongside a wedge of cheese as an appetizer, as a side dish for steak, or as a sandwich topping.

1 Adjust oven rack to lower-middle position and heat oven to 400 degrees. Coat inside of Dutch oven with vegetable oil spray.

2 Melt butter in prepared pot over medium-low heat. Stir in onions and 1 teaspoon salt. Cover, place pot in oven, and roast for 1 hour (onions will be moist and slightly reduced in volume).

3 Working quickly, remove pot from oven and stir onions, scraping bottom and sides of pot. Partially cover, return pot to oven, and continue to roast until onions are deep golden brown, 1½ to 1¾ hours, stirring onions and scraping bottom and sides of pot every 30 minutes.

4 Remove pot from oven, stir to scrape up any browned bits, and season onions with salt and pepper. Serve warm or at room temperature. (Onions can be refrigerated for up to 1 week.)

ROASTED CARAMELIZED SHALLOTS
makes about 1 cup

Because shallots are somewhat expensive and time-consuming to prepare, we scaled this variation down.

Reduce amount of butter to 2 tablespoons; substitute 16 large shallots, peeled and quartered, for onions; and reduce amount of salt to ½ teaspoon. Reduce covered roasting time in step 2 to 45 minutes, and partially covered roasting time in step 3 to 1 hour.

ROASTED RED POTATOES

serves 4

2 pounds red potatoes, unpeeled,
cut into ¾-inch wedges

3 tablespoons extra-virgin olive oil

Salt and pepper

Why This Recipe Works These effortless roasted potatoes make it easy to prepare a standout side dish every day, delivering perfectly crisp and tender potatoes in less than an hour. To arrive at our ideal—potatoes with deep golden, crisp crusts and creamy, soft interiors—we took advantage of the naturally high moisture content of red potatoes. Rather than parboiling the potatoes (a common step that dims their subtle flavor), we arranged them cut side down on a foil-lined rimmed baking sheet and covered them with foil which turned them tender as they steamed in their own moisture. Finishing the potatoes uncovered crisped the outsides to a perfect golden brown. Contact with the baking sheet was important to browning, so we flipped the potatoes partway through for crispness on every side. This recipe was so easy, we had no trouble bringing the potatoes' flavor up a notch with a few appealing variations. If using very small potatoes, cut them in half instead of into wedges and flip them cut side up during the final 10 minutes of roasting.

1 Adjust oven rack to middle position and heat oven to 425 degrees. Line rimmed baking sheet with aluminum foil. Toss potatoes with oil in bowl and season with salt and pepper. Arrange potatoes in single layer on prepared sheet, with either cut side facing down. Cover with foil and roast for 20 minutes.

2 Remove foil and roast until sides of potatoes touching pan are crusty and golden, about 15 minutes. Flip potatoes over and roast until crusty and golden on second side, about 8 minutes. Season with salt and pepper to taste, transfer to serving dish, and serve.

Roasted Red Potatoes with Garlic and Rosemary

During final 3 minutes of roasting, sprinkle 2 tablespoons minced fresh rosemary over potatoes. Toss roasted potatoes with 1 garlic clove, minced to paste, before serving.

Roasted Red Potatoes with Shallot, Lemon, and Thyme

During final 3 minutes of roasting, sprinkle 1 teaspoon minced fresh thyme over potatoes. Toss roasted potatoes with 1 garlic clove, minced to paste; 1 minced shallot; ½ teaspoon grated lemon zest; and 1 teaspoon lemon juice before serving.

Roasted Red Potatoes with Feta, Olives, and Oregano

During final 3 minutes of roasting, sprinkle 1 tablespoon minced fresh oregano over potatoes. Combine ½ cup crumbled feta cheese; 12 pitted and chopped kalamata olives; 1 tablespoon lemon juice; and 1 garlic clove, minced to paste, in bowl. Toss roasted potatoes with feta mixture before serving.

ROASTED SMASHED POTATOES

serves 4

2 pounds small red potatoes, unpeeled

6 tablespoons extra-virgin olive oil

1 teaspoon chopped fresh thyme

Salt and pepper

Why This Recipe Works As if by magic, these roasted potatoes yield the creamy, smooth texture of mashed potatoes and the satisfying crunch of deep-fried spuds all in one foolproof recipe. Success started with choosing the right potato for the job and only small red potatoes, with their moist texture and thin skin, fit the bill. Before we could begin smashing, we needed to soften the potatoes, so we started by parcooking them on a baking sheet, adding water and covering them in aluminum foil to break down their flesh with a bit of steam. Unlike boiling, which washed out any flavor, this approach kept the potatoes tasting earthy and sweet. After a short rest (very hot potatoes crumbled apart when smashed), we drizzled them with olive oil and pressed them into patties on the baking sheet, smashing them all at once by placing a second baking sheet on top of them and pushing down evenly and firmly. In one move, we had perfect cracked potatoes. With a little chopped fresh thyme, more olive oil, and another stint in the oven, we had browned, crisped potatoes that were super creamy inside. Use small red potatoes measuring 1½ to 2 inches in diameter. Remove the potatoes from the baking sheet as soon as they are done browning—they will toughen if left for too long. A potato masher can also be used to smash the potatoes.

1 Adjust oven racks to top and lowest positions and heat oven to 500 degrees. Arrange potatoes on rimmed baking sheet, pour ¾ cup water into sheet, and wrap tightly with aluminum foil. Cook on lower rack until paring knife can be slipped into and out of center of potatoes with very little resistance (poke through foil to test), 25 to 30 minutes. Remove foil and let cool 10 minutes. If any water remains on sheet, blot dry with paper towel.

2 Drizzle 3 tablespoons oil over potatoes and roll to coat. Space potatoes evenly on sheet and place second baking sheet on top; press down firmly on second sheet, flattening potatoes until ⅓ to ½ inch thick. Sprinkle with thyme, season with salt and pepper, and drizzle evenly with remaining 3 tablespoons oil. Roast potatoes on upper rack for 15 minutes, then transfer potatoes to bottom rack and roast until well browned, 20 to 30 minutes. Serve immediately.

flattening potatoes evenly

After letting potatoes cool for 10 minutes, drizzle with oil and space evenly on rimmed baking sheet. Place second baking sheet on top and press down firmly and evenly on top sheet until potatoes are ⅓ to ½ inch thick.

CRISP ROASTED POTATOES

2½ pounds Yukon Gold potatoes, unpeeled, cut into ½-inch-thick slices

Salt and pepper

5 tablespoons extra-virgin olive oil

Why This Recipe Works Truly great roasted potatoes are every bit as good as French fries—and a lot easier to prepare. Their crunchy crust and rich creamy interior will have everyone reaching for seconds. Our unique roasting method starts on the stovetop. We tested different potatoes and Yukon Golds performed best; their balance of moisture and starch promised the perfect texture. We cut the potatoes into thick rounds to maximize contact with a hot baking sheet and minimize flipping. Keeping the skins on helped to keep their shape intact. Parcooking the potatoes first in water was the key to better crisping: Simmering brought the potatoes' starch to the surface and coated the slices with it; once the moisture evaporated in the oven the starch crisped and browned. Next, we tossed the parcooked slices with olive oil and salt to rough them up, which encouraged the release of more starch for further browning. Spread onto an oiled preheated baking sheet, the roughed-up slices began crisping on contact. We left them alone, allowing the first side to brown deeply before flipping them gently to build the same great color on the other side.

1 Adjust oven rack to lowest position, place rimmed baking sheet on rack, and heat oven to 450 degrees. Place potatoes and 1 tablespoon salt in Dutch oven, then cover with 1 inch cold water. Bring to boil over high heat, then reduce heat and gently simmer until exteriors of potatoes have softened but centers offer resistance when poked with paring knife, about 5 minutes. Drain potatoes well and transfer to large bowl.

2 Drizzle potatoes with 2 tablespoons oil and sprinkle with ½ teaspoon salt; using rubber spatula, toss to combine. Repeat with 2 tablespoons oil and ½ teaspoon salt and continue to toss until exteriors of potato slices are coated with starchy paste, 1 to 2 minutes.

3 Working quickly, remove sheet from oven and drizzle remaining 1 tablespoon oil over surface. Carefully transfer potatoes to preheated sheet and spread into even layer (place end pieces skin side up). Roast until bottoms of potatoes are golden brown and crisp, 15 to 25 minutes, rotating sheet after 10 minutes.

4 Remove sheet from oven and, using metal spatula and tongs, loosen potatoes from pan and carefully flip each slice. Continue to roast until second side is golden and crisp, 10 to 20 minutes, rotating sheet as needed to ensure potatoes brown evenly. Season with salt and pepper to taste, and serve immediately.

DUCK FAT–ROASTED POTATOES

serves 6

3½ pounds Yukon Gold potatoes, peeled and cut into 1½-inch pieces

Kosher salt and pepper

½ teaspoon baking soda

6 tablespoons duck fat

1 tablespoon chopped fresh rosemary

Why This Recipe Works For the ultimate roasted potatoes, we had to rethink the fat. When roasting most vegetables, olive oil is usually our choice, but this recipe calls for a richer option—duck fat—for potatoes that are crisp on the outside, moist on the inside, and exploding with meaty, savory flavor. Moist-yet-starchy Yukon Golds proved the best potato option; we peeled them and cut them into chunks to maximize their crispable surface area. We encouraged thorough seasoning and deeper browning by boiling the chunks with a touch of baking soda and plenty of salt and then, after draining them, vigorously stirring them to rough up their exterior before working in the duck fat. This added step was enough to coat the potatoes with a film of starchy, fatty paste for a rich, shatteringly crisp shell. All the while, we preheated a baking sheet in a hot oven for a jump start on browning. Quickly turning the potatoes partway through roasting ensured even doneness. With minutes to go, we stirred in an extra tablespoon of duck fat, this time seasoned with fresh rosemary, and roasted the potatoes until they were well browned. Aromatic, tender, and totally indulgent, these potatoes really delivered. Duck fat is available in the meat department in many supermarkets. Alternatively, substitute chicken fat, lard, or a mixture of 3 tablespoons of bacon fat and 3 tablespoons of extra-virgin olive oil.

1 Adjust oven rack to top position, place rimmed baking sheet on rack, and heat oven to 475 degrees.

2 Bring 10 cups water to boil in Dutch oven over high heat. Add potatoes, ⅓ cup salt, and baking soda. Return to boil and cook for 1 minute; drain potatoes. Return potatoes to pot and place over low heat. Cook, shaking pot occasionally, until surface moisture has evaporated, about 2 minutes. Off heat add 5 tablespoons fat and 1 teaspoon salt; mix with rubber spatula until potatoes are coated with thick paste, about 30 seconds.

3 Remove sheet from oven, transfer potatoes to sheet, and spread into even layer. Roast for 15 minutes.

4 Remove sheet from oven. Using thin metal spatula, turn potatoes. Roast until golden brown, 12 to 15 minutes. Meanwhile, combine rosemary and remaining 1 tablespoon fat in bowl.

5 Remove sheet from oven. Spoon rosemary-fat mixture over potatoes and turn again. Continue to roast until potatoes are well browned and rosemary is fragrant, 3 to 5 minutes. Season with salt and pepper to taste. Serve immediately.

ROASTED PARMESAN POTATOES

serves 4 to 6

2 pounds Yukon Gold potatoes, unpeeled, cut into ½-inch-thick slices

4 teaspoons cornstarch

Salt and pepper

1 tablespoon extra-virgin olive oil

6 ounces Parmesan cheese, cut into 1-inch pieces

2 teaspoons minced fresh rosemary

Why This Recipe Works These cheesy Parmesan potato rounds, roasted until crunchy, are irresistible. We chose creamy Yukon Gold potatoes for their balance of starch and moisture and sliced them into ½-inch rounds. Tossing them in seasoned cornstarch dried their surface, which enhanced crisping. A very hot oven achieved the best color and flavor before we introduced the cheese. Parmesan processed with rosemary, pepper, and more cornstarch created an easy savory topping that we sprinkled generously over the slices. We made sure the topping stuck by pressing it onto the potatoes and then we flipped the slices and returned them to the same place on the baking sheet to rapidly crisp the cheese during the remaining minutes of roasting. The excess Parmesan bits that crisped on the sheet pan were a salty added bonus. Once cooled, the potatoes came off the baking sheet with ease, coated in crispy cheese. Cool chive sour cream turned these cheesy spuds into a truly addictive side. Try to find potatoes that are 2½ to 3 inches long. Use a good-quality Parmesan cheese here. Serve with Chive Sour Cream (recipe follows), if desired.

1 Adjust oven rack to lower-middle position and heat oven to 500 degrees. Spray rimmed baking sheet liberally with vegetable oil spray. Place potatoes in large bowl.

2 Combine 2 teaspoons cornstarch, 1 teaspoon salt, and 1 teaspoon pepper in small bowl. Sprinkle cornstarch mixture over potatoes and toss until potatoes are thoroughly coated and cornstarch is no longer visible. Add oil and toss to coat.

3 Arrange potatoes in single layer on prepared sheet and roast until golden brown on top, about 20 minutes.

4 Meanwhile, process Parmesan, rosemary, ½ teaspoon pepper, and remaining 2 teaspoons cornstarch in food processor until cheese is finely ground, about 1 minute.

5 Remove potatoes from oven. Sprinkle Parmesan mixture evenly over and between potatoes (cheese should cover surface of baking sheet), pressing on potatoes with back of spoon to adhere. Using 2 forks, flip slices over into same spot on sheet.

6 Roast until cheese between potatoes turns light golden brown, 5 to 7 minutes. Transfer sheet to wire rack and let potatoes cool for 15 minutes. Transfer potatoes, cheese side up, and accompanying cheese to serving dish and serve.

CHIVE SOUR CREAM
makes about 1 cup

1 cup sour cream
¼ cup minced fresh chives
½ teaspoon minced fresh rosemary
½ teaspoon salt
½ teaspoon pepper
½ teaspoon garlic powder
¼ teaspoon onion powder

Combine all ingredients in bowl. Cover and refrigerate at least 30 minutes to allow flavors to blend.

BEST BAKED POTATOES

serves 4

Salt and pepper

4 (7- to 9-ounce) russet potatoes, unpeeled, each lightly pricked with fork in 6 places

1 tablespoon vegetable oil

Why This Recipe Works Baked potatoes are one of those dishes most home cooks think they don't need a recipe for, but following our precise roasting technique guarantees a perfect potato—with a fluffy interior, crispy skin, and even seasoning—every time. For starters, our tests pointed us to an ideal doneness temperature: 205 degrees. Baking russet potatoes in a hot oven propped up on a wire rack prevented a leathery ring from forming beneath the peel, and taking the potato's temperature with an instant-read thermometer ensured we hit the 205-degree sweet spot every time. Coating the potatoes in salty water before baking was all the effort required to season the skin; brushing on vegetable oil once the potatoes were cooked through and then baking the potatoes for an additional 10 minutes promised the crispest exterior possible. Potatoes this good deserve an accompaniment, so we came up with some simple but sophisticated toppings to serve with them. Open up the potatoes immediately after removal from the oven in step 3 so steam can escape. Top the potatoes as desired, or with one of our flavorful toppings (recipes follow).

1 Adjust oven rack to middle position and heat oven to 450 degrees. Dissolve 2 tablespoons salt in ½ cup water in large bowl. Place potatoes in bowl and toss so exteriors of potatoes are evenly moistened. Transfer potatoes to wire rack set in rimmed baking sheet and bake until center of largest potato registers 205 degrees, 45 minutes to 1 hour.

2 Remove potatoes from oven and brush tops and sides with oil. Return potatoes to oven and bake for 10 minutes.

3 Remove potatoes from oven and, using paring knife, make 2 slits, forming X, in each potato. Using clean dish towel, hold ends and squeeze slightly to push flesh up and out. Season with salt and pepper to taste. Serve immediately.

CREAMY EGG TOPPING
makes 1 cup
Leftover topping makes a great sandwich filling.

3 hard-cooked large eggs, chopped
4 tablespoons sour cream
1½ tablespoons minced cornichons
1 tablespoon minced fresh parsley
1 tablespoon Dijon mustard
1 tablespoon capers, rinsed and minced
1 tablespoon minced shallot
Salt and pepper

Stir all ingredients together and season with salt and pepper to taste.

HERBED GOAT CHEESE TOPPING
makes ¾ cup

Our favorite goat cheese is Laura Chenel's Chèvre Fresh Chèvre Log.

4 ounces goat cheese, softened
2 tablespoons extra-virgin olive oil
2 tablespoons minced fresh parsley
1 tablespoon minced shallot
½ teaspoon grated lemon zest
Salt and pepper

Mash goat cheese with fork. Stir in oil, parsley, shallot, and lemon zest. Season with salt and pepper to taste.

SMOKED TROUT TOPPING
makes 1 cup

We prefer trout for this recipe, but any hot-smoked fish, such as salmon or bluefish, may be substituted.

5 ounces smoked trout, chopped
⅓ cup crème fraiche
2 tablespoons minced fresh chives
4 teaspoons minced shallot
1¼ teaspoons grated lemon zest
plus ¾ teaspoon lemon juice
Salt and pepper

Stir all ingredients together and season with salt and pepper to taste.

BEST BAKED SWEET POTATOES

serves 4

4 (8-ounce) sweet potatoes, unpeeled, each lightly pricked with fork in 3 places

Salt and pepper

Why This Recipe Works The goal when baking sweet potatoes is entirely different than when baking russets: creamy not fluffy flesh with deeply complex flavor. Sweet potatoes roast differently than russets due to their lower starch level and higher sugar content. We learned that to roast a whole sweet potato to the point where its exterior was nicely tanned and its interior was silky and sweetly caramelized, the potatoes needed to reach 200 degrees and stay there for an hour, long enough for the starches to gelatinize and moisture to evaporate for concentrated flavor. To keep our recipe efficient, we microwaved the potatoes until they hit 200 degrees and then transferred them to a hot oven to linger. Putting them on a wire rack set in a rimmed baking sheet allowed air to circulate around the potatoes and also caught any sugar that oozed from the potatoes as they roasted. Any variety of orange- or red-skinned, orange-fleshed sweet potato can be used in this recipe, but we highly recommend using Garnet (also sold as Diane). Avoid varieties with tan or purple skin, which are starchier and less sweet than varieties with orange and red skins. We prefer to use sweet potatoes that are smaller, about 8 ounces. Top the potatoes as desired, or with one of our two sauces (recipes follow).

1 Adjust oven rack to middle position and heat oven to 425 degrees. Place potatoes on large plate and microwave until potatoes yield to gentle pressure and reach internal temperature of 200 degrees, 6 to 9 minutes, flipping potatoes every 3 minutes.

2 Place wire rack in aluminum foil-lined rimmed baking sheet and spray rack with vegetable oil spray. Transfer potatoes to prepared rack and bake for 1 hour (exteriors of potatoes will be lightly browned and potatoes will feel very soft when squeezed).

3 Slit each potato lengthwise; using clean dish towel, hold ends and squeeze slightly to push flesh up and out. Transfer potatoes to serving dish. Season with salt and pepper to taste. Serve.

GARLIC AND CHIVE SOUR CREAM
makes about ½ cup

This garlicky sauce adds tang to balance the potatoes' caramel-y sweetness.

½ cup sour cream
1 tablespoon minced fresh chives
1 garlic clove, minced
⅛ teaspoon salt

Combine all ingredients in bowl.

GARAM MASALA YOGURT
makes about ½ cup

The warm flavors of this Indian spice blend complement the potatoes' sweet flavor.

½ cup plain yogurt
2 teaspoons lemon juice
½ teaspoon garam masala
⅛ teaspoon salt

Combine all ingredients in bowl.

ROASTED SWEET POTATO WEDGES

serves 4 to 6

2 pounds small sweet potatoes
(8 ounces each), unpeeled, cut lengthwise into 1½-inch wedges

2 tablespoons extra-virgin olive oil

½ teaspoon salt

½ teaspoon pepper

Why This Recipe Works These roasted sweet potato wedges are as satis-fying as the sweet potato fries dished out at restaurants—without all the grease. But roasting sweet potato wedges is not as easy as it seems. Sweet potatoes release a sweet syrup-like liquid as they cook, turning the wedges mushy. The key, we learned, was to cut the sweet potatoes into wide, obtuse wedges so they would hold their shape while roasting. Cut thinner, the wedges burnt before their interiors had the chance to cook through. As for seasoning, sweet potatoes have plenty of flavor on their own, so we initially limited the seasoning to salt and pepper, tossing them with some olive oil to encourage browning. (We came up with some sweet and spicy variations later.) Arranging the wedges skin side down on a baking sheet encouraged the skins to brown while keeping the interiors pleasantly soft and tender—no turning needed. After about 30 minutes in a hot oven, the wedges were perfectly creamy and sweet, with plenty of crunch. We prefer to use small potatoes, about 8 ounces each, because it ensures that the wedges fit more uniformly on the baking sheet; they should be of similar size so they cook at the same rate. Be sure to scrub and dry the whole potatoes thoroughly before cutting them into wedges and tossing them with the oil and spices.

1 Adjust oven rack to middle position and heat oven to 450 degrees. Line rimmed baking sheet with parchment paper. Toss potatoes, oil, salt, and pepper together in bowl.

2 Arrange potatoes, skin side down, in single layer on pre-pared sheet. Roast until lightly browned and tender, about 30 minutes, rotating sheet halfway through roasting. Serve.

Cinnamon-Sugar Roasted Sweet Potato Wedges

Omit pepper. Add 2 teaspoons ground cinnamon, 2 teaspoons sugar, and pinch ground nutmeg to potato mixture in step 1.

Cumin and Chili Roasted Sweet Potato Wedges

Add 2 teaspoons ground cumin, 2 teaspoons chili powder, and 1 teaspoon garlic powder to potato mixture in step 1.

Curry Roasted Sweet Potato Wedges

Add 4 teaspoons curry powder to potato mixture in step 1.

Spicy Barbecue Roasted Sweet Potato Wedges

Add 2 teaspoons smoked paprika, 2 teaspoons packed brown sugar, 1 teaspoon garlic powder, and ⅛ teaspoon cayenne pepper to potato mixture in step 1.

ROASTED RADICCHIO, FENNEL, AND PARSNIPS WITH LEMON-BASIL SAUCE

serves 4 to 6

2 fennel bulbs, stalks discarded, bulbs halved, cored, and sliced into ½-inch-thick wedges

1 pound red potatoes, unpeeled, cut into 1-inch pieces

8 ounces parsnips, peeled and cut into 2-inch pieces

8 shallots, peeled and halved

1 head radicchio, cored and cut into 2-inch wedges

6 garlic cloves, peeled

3 tablespoons extra-virgin olive oil

2 teaspoons minced fresh thyme

1 teaspoon minced fresh rosemary

1 teaspoon sugar

Salt and pepper

2 tablespoons chopped fresh basil

2 tablespoons minced fresh chives

1 tablespoon lemon juice, plus extra for seasoning

Why This Recipe Works Roasting an array of root vegetables all together puts you on the fast track for a hearty, satisfying side. Our recipe showcases a broad range of flavors and textures and guarantees that each element shines. We combined fennel, red potatoes, parsnips, and radicchio, cutting each vegetable according to its roasting needs: We cut multilayered fennel and radicchio into wedges and sliced denser potatoes and parsnips into 1- and 2-inch pieces. Getting the different vegetables to roast at the same pace required some thoughtful arrangement: We placed the radicchio in the center of the baking sheet and hardier potatoes and other vegetables around the perimeter, which kept the more delicate radicchio from charring in the hot oven while giving the denser ones more contact with the heat. Before roasting, we tossed the vegetables with oil, thyme, rosemary, and a little sugar to promote browning. Whole garlic cloves and halved shallots softened and mellowed in the oven, lending great flavor to the finished dish. Once all of the vegetables were perfectly tender and caramelized, we tossed them with an herbal lemon vinaigrette to balance out all the deep flavors with freshness.

1 Adjust oven rack to middle position and heat oven to 450 degrees. Toss fennel, potatoes, parsnips, shallots, radicchio, garlic, 1 tablespoon oil, thyme, rosemary, sugar, ¾ teaspoon salt, and ¼ teaspoon pepper together in bowl.

2 Spread vegetables into single layer on rimmed baking sheet, arranging radicchio cut side down in center of sheet. Roast until vegetables are tender and golden brown, 30 to 35 minutes, rotating sheet halfway through roasting.

3 Whisk basil, chives, lemon juice, and remaining 2 tablespoons oil together in large bowl. Add roasted vegetables and toss to combine. Season with salt, pepper, and extra lemon juice to taste. Serve.

arranging vegetables for even roasting

Spread vegetables in single layer arranging radicchio cut side down in center of sheet and fennel, potatoes, parsnips, and shallots around perimeter.

ROASTED ROOT VEGETABLES WITH LEMON-CAPER SAUCE

serves 4 to 6

1 pound Brussels sprouts, trimmed and halved

1 pound red potatoes, unpeeled, cut into 1-inch pieces

8 shallots, peeled and halved

4 carrots, peeled and cut into 2-inch lengths, thick ends halved lengthwise

6 garlic cloves, peeled

3 tablespoons extra-virgin olive oil

2 teaspoons minced fresh thyme

1 teaspoon minced fresh rosemary

1 teaspoon sugar

Salt and pepper

2 tablespoons minced fresh parsley

1½ tablespoons capers, rinsed and minced

1 tablespoon lemon juice, plus extra for seasoning

Why This Recipe Works Pairing a hearty selection of vegetables with a vibrant caper sauce takes a humble mix of vegetables to new heights. We chose a combination of Brussels sprouts, red potatoes, and carrots to create a nice balance of deep flavors and contrasting textures. To ensure that the vegetables would roast evenly, we cut them into equal-size pieces. Arranging the vegetables with the more delicate Brussels sprouts in the center of the baking sheet protected the leaves from charring in the hot oven, while placing the denser potatoes and carrots strategically along the edges of the pan ensured that everything roasted at the same rate. To infuse the naturally flavorful vegetables with some herbaceous notes, we tossed them with olive oil, thyme, and rosemary, plus a touch of sugar to encourage browning. Softened garlic cloves and halved shallots also added flavor to the finished dish. Once all of the vegetables were perfectly tender and caramelized, we tossed them with a bright, Mediterranean-inspired dressing of parsley, capers, and lemon juice.

1 Adjust oven rack to middle position and heat oven to 450 degrees. Toss Brussels sprouts, potatoes, shallots, carrots, garlic, 1 tablespoon oil, thyme, rosemary, sugar, ¾ teaspoon salt, and ¼ teaspoon pepper together in bowl.

2 Spread vegetables into single layer on rimmed baking sheet, arranging Brussels sprouts cut side down in center of sheet. Roast until vegetables are tender and golden brown, 30 to 35 minutes, rotating sheet halfway through roasting.

3 Whisk parsley, capers, lemon juice, and remaining 2 tablespoons oil together in large bowl. Add roasted vegetables and toss to combine. Season with salt, pepper, and extra lemon juice to taste. Serve.

ROASTED BUTTERNUT SQUASH WITH TAHINI AND FETA

serves 4 to 6

Squash

1 (2½- to 3-pound) butternut squash

3 tablespoons unsalted butter, melted

½ teaspoon salt

½ teaspoon pepper

Topping

1 tablespoon tahini

1 tablespoon extra-virgin olive oil

1½ teaspoons lemon juice

1 teaspoon honey

Pinch salt

1 ounce feta cheese, finely crumbled (¼ cup)

¼ cup shelled pistachios, toasted and chopped fine

2 tablespoons chopped fresh mint

Why This Recipe Works Roasted winter squash is often a simple, if uninspired affair, but our roasting technique unlocks its true flavor potential. Peeling a large butternut squash thoroughly removed the tough outer skin as well as the rugged, fibrous layer of white flesh just beneath it, ensuring supremely tender squash. We sliced the peeled and halved squash into ½-inch-thick slices and tossed them with melted butter, which encouraged beautiful caramelization and added richness. We slid a sheet pan filled with our squash slices into a hot 425-degree oven, placing it on the lowest oven rack and roasting the squash for a generous amount of time to evaporate moisture. Rotating the pan and flipping the slices was all we needed to do to ensure the squash browned thoroughly and evenly. To finish off this simple squash side with finesse, we topped the slices with a creamy tahini sauce, some briny feta, crunchy pistachios, and fresh mint. For plain roasted squash omit the topping. This dish can be served warm or at room temperature. For the best texture it's important to remove the fibrous flesh just below the squash's skin.

1 For the squash Adjust oven rack to lowest position and heat oven to 425 degrees. Using vegetable peeler or chef's knife, remove skin and fibrous threads from squash just below skin (peel until squash is completely orange with no white flesh remaining, roughly ⅛ inch deep). Halve squash lengthwise and scrape out seeds. Place squash, cut side down, on cutting board and slice crosswise ½ inch thick.

2 Toss squash with melted butter, salt, and pepper until evenly coated. Arrange on rimmed baking sheet in single layer. Roast squash until sides touching sheet toward back of oven are well browned, 25 to 30 minutes. Rotate sheet and continue to bake until sides touching sheet toward back of oven are well browned, 6 to 10 minutes. Remove squash from oven and flip each piece. Continue to roast until squash is very tender and sides touching sheet are browned, 10 to 15 minutes.

3 For the topping While squash roasts, whisk tahini, oil, lemon juice, honey, and salt together in small bowl.

4 Transfer squash to serving dish. Drizzle tahini mixture evenly over squash. Sprinkle with feta, pistachios, and mint. Serve.

Roasted Butternut Squash with Radicchio and Parmesan

Omit topping. Whisk 1 tablespoon sherry vinegar, ½ teaspoon mayonnaise, and pinch salt together in small bowl. Gradually whisk in 2 tablespoons extra-virgin olive oil until smooth. Before serving, drizzle vinaigrette over squash and sprinkle with ½ cup coarsely shredded radicchio; ½ ounce Parmesan cheese, shaved into thin strips; and 3 tablespoons toasted pine nuts.

ROASTED TOMATOES

makes about 1½ cups

3 pounds large tomatoes, cored, bottom
⅛ inch trimmed, and sliced ¾ inch thick

2 garlic cloves, peeled and smashed

¼ teaspoon dried oregano

Kosher salt and pepper

¾ cup extra-virgin olive oil

Why This Recipe Works If you've never roasted tomatoes, you should. It's a largely hands-off technique that yields the ultimate condiment: bright, concentrated tomatoes that are soft but retain their shape. For intensely flavored tomatoes, we started by cutting them into thick slices and arranging them on a foil-lined rimmed baking sheet. Drizzling on plenty of extra-virgin olive oil infused them with fruity flavor and helped the tomatoes roast faster. Adding smashed garlic cloves lent flavor and fragrance to the tomatoes and oil. There are many ways to use savory-sweet roasted tomatoes including as a topping for crostini and pizza, in sandwiches, tossed into pasta, or added to a quiche or frittata. The flavorful tomato oil is great in salad dressings or drizzled over roasted meat, fish, or vegetables. Avoid using tomatoes smaller than 3 inches in diameter, which have a smaller ratio of flavorful jelly to skin than larger tomatoes. To double the recipe, use two baking sheets, increase the roasting time in step 2 to 40 minutes, and rotate and switch the sheets halfway through baking. In step 3, increase the roasting time to 1½ to 2½ hours.

1 Adjust oven rack to middle position and heat oven to 425 degrees. Line rimmed baking sheet with aluminum foil. Arrange tomatoes in even layer on prepared sheet, with larger slices around edge and smaller slices in center. Place garlic cloves on tomatoes. Sprinkle with oregano and ¼ teaspoon salt and season with pepper. Drizzle oil evenly over tomatoes.

2 Bake for 30 minutes, rotating sheet halfway through baking. Remove sheet from oven. Reduce oven temperature to 300 degrees and prop open door with wooden spoon to cool oven. Using thin spatula, flip tomatoes.

3 Return tomatoes to oven and continue to cook until spotty brown, skins are blistered, and tomatoes have collapsed to ¼ to ½ inch thick, 1 to 2 hours. Remove from oven and let cool completely, about 30 minutes. Discard garlic and transfer tomatoes and oil to airtight container. (Tomatoes can be refrigerated for up to 5 days or frozen for up to 2 months.)

ROASTED TOMATO RELISH
makes 1¼ cups
Use this relish to top bruschetta, chicken, or pork tenderloin or to dress up scrambled eggs or polenta.

1 cup Roasted Tomatoes, chopped coarse,
plus 1 tablespoon reserved tomato oil
1 small shallot, minced
¼ cup chopped fresh cilantro
¾ teaspoon red wine vinegar
½ teaspoon capers, rinsed and minced
Salt and pepper

Combine all ingredients in bowl and season with salt and pepper to taste.

ROASTED APPLES WITH DRIED FIGS AND WALNUTS

2½ tablespoons unsalted butter

4 Gala apples (6 to 7 ounces each), peeled, halved, and cored

1¼ cups red wine

½ cup dried Black Mission figs, stemmed and quartered

⅓ cup (2⅓ ounces) sugar

¾ teaspoon pepper

⅛ teaspoon salt

1 teaspoon lemon juice

⅓ cup walnuts, toasted and chopped

Why This Recipe Works Apples are terrific baked into a classic pie or crisp, but roasting transforms them into a more sophisticated dessert. We peeled and halved Gala apples to prevent the fruit from steaming in its own juices and started them cut side down in a skillet on the stovetop. The direct heat imparted a good bit of color and allowed the apples to absorb some of the butter's richness. From there, we moved the skillet into the oven, where the apples caramelized and roasted to perfect tenderness. When the apples were finished, we used the juices to build a lush sauce. We reduced red wine with the juices and stirred in some dried figs and sugar for extra texture and sweetness; a hit of lemon juice added another layer of flavor. A sprinkling of toasted walnuts added a little crunch. We recommend Gala apples for this recipe, but Fuji will also work. A low-tannin wine such as Pinot Noir works well. You will need a 12-inch ovensafe skillet for this recipe. The fruit can be served as is or with vanilla ice cream or plain Greek yogurt.

1 Adjust oven rack to middle position and heat oven to 450 degrees. Melt 1½ tablespoons butter in 12-inch ovensafe skillet over medium-high heat. Place apple halves, cut side down, in skillet. Cook, without moving, until apples are just beginning to brown, 3 to 5 minutes.

2 Transfer skillet to oven and roast for 15 minutes. Flip apples and continue to roast until fork easily pierces fruit, 10 to 15 minutes. Remove skillet from oven (skillet handle will be hot).

3 Transfer apples to serving dish. Being careful of hot skillet handle, return skillet to medium-high heat and add wine, figs, sugar, pepper, salt, and remaining 1 tablespoon butter. Bring to vigorous simmer, whisking to scrape up any browned bits. Cook until sauce is reduced and has consistency of maple syrup, 7 to 10 minutes. Off heat stir in lemon juice. Pour sauce over apples, sprinkle with walnuts, and serve.

CRANBERRY-PECAN-STUFFED ROASTED APPLES

serves 6

7 large Granny Smith apples (8 ounces each)

6 tablespoons unsalted butter, softened

⅓ cup dried cranberries, chopped coarse

⅓ cup pecans, toasted and chopped coarse

¼ cup packed (1¾ ounces) brown sugar

3 tablespoons old-fashioned rolled oats

1 teaspoon finely grated orange zest

½ teaspoon ground cinnamon

Pinch salt

⅓ cup maple syrup

⅓ cup plus 2 tablespoons apple cider

Why This Recipe Works Baked apples are an old-fashioned cooked fruit dessert. To freshen up this frequently frumpy dish, we looked to skillet roasting. We wanted apples that had concentrated flavor and were tender yet firm with a good amount of filling. After trying many varieties of apples, we decided that Granny Smiths, with their firm flesh and nicely tart flavor, were the best apples for the job. Removing the skin from everywhere but the top of the apple kept the flesh from steaming and turning to mush. A melon baller helped us scoop out a spacious cavity for the filling. We updated a brown sugar and chopped pecan filling by adding tangy dried cranberries, orange zest, and cinnamon and bulked up the nuttiness with chewy rolled oats and the fruitiness with diced apple pieces. Before filling the apples, we browned their flat top surface in butter on the stovetop to coax caramelized flavor from the fruit. Capping the filled apples with their unpeeled tops protected them from burning. Moving the skillet to the oven, we basted the apples with apple cider and maple syrup to infuse them with flavor and keep them moist as they finished roasting. You will need a 12-inch ovensafe nonstick skillet for this recipe. While old-fashioned rolled oats are preferable in this recipe, quick oats can be substituted; do not use instant oats. Serve with vanilla ice cream, if desired.

1 Adjust oven rack to middle position and heat oven to 375 degrees. Peel, core, and cut 1 apple into ¼-inch dice. Combine diced apple, 5 tablespoons butter, cranberries, pecans, sugar, oats, orange zest, cinnamon, and salt in bowl.

2 Shave thin slice off bottom of remaining 6 apples to allow them to sit flat. Cut top ½ inch off stem end of apples and reserve. Peel apples and use melon baller or small measuring spoon to remove 1½-inch-diameter core, being careful not to cut through bottom of apples.

3 Melt remaining 1 tablespoon butter in 12-inch ovensafe nonstick skillet over medium heat. Add apples, stem side down, and cook until cut surface is golden brown, about 3 minutes. Flip apples, reduce heat to low, and spoon filling inside, mounding excess filling over cavities. Top with reserved apple caps.

4 Add maple syrup and ⅓ cup cider to skillet. Transfer skillet to oven and roast until fork inserted into apples meets little resistance, 35 to 40 minutes, basting every 10 minutes with juices in skillet.

5 Transfer apples to serving dish. Stir up to 2 tablespoons remaining cider into sauce in skillet to adjust consistency. Pour sauce over apples and serve.

Dried Cherry–Hazelnut-Stuffed Roasted Apples
Substitute dried cherries for cranberries, skinned hazelnuts for pecans, and pepper for cinnamon.

Dried Fig–Macadamia-Stuffed Roasted Apples
Substitute dried figs for cranberries, macadamia nuts for pecans, lemon zest for orange zest, and ¼ teaspoon ground ginger for cinnamon.

Raisin-Walnut-Stuffed Roasted Apples
Substitute raisins for cranberries, walnuts for pecans, lemon zest for orange zest, and ¼ teaspoon ground nutmeg for cinnamon.

ROASTED FIGS WITH BALSAMIC GLAZE AND MASCARPONE

serves 6

½ cup balsamic vinegar

¼ cup honey

1 tablespoon unsalted butter

1½ pounds fresh figs, stemmed and halved

4 ounces (½ cup) mascarpone cheese

½ teaspoon grated lemon zest

⅓ cup shelled pistachios, toasted and chopped

Why This Recipe Works Fresh figs are a treat in their own right, but they turn wonderfully tender and rich when roasted. To take things a step further, we turned simple roasted figs into an elegant dessert by infusing them with the complex sweetness of balsamic vinegar and the floral notes of honey. Reducing the vinegar on the stovetop turned it viscous and syrupy (much like the texture of high-end drizzling balsamics), and adding honey to it banished any harshness. Roasting figs on their own can yield dry, scorched fruit, so instead we roasted the figs in the oven in the balsamic glaze. As the figs quickly roasted, they grew increasingly tender and lent their natural sweetness to the surrounding syrup. While the glazed figs were delicious on their own, we created an easy creamy topping of honeyed mascarpone cheese, flavored with lemon zest. A final sprinkle of toasted pistachios added a pleasant crunch. You will need a 12-inch ovensafe skillet for this recipe.

1 Adjust oven rack to middle position and heat oven to 450 degrees. Bring vinegar, 3 tablespoons honey, and butter to simmer in 12-inch ovensafe skillet over medium-high heat and cook until reduced to ⅓ cup, about 3 minutes. Off heat, add figs and toss to coat. Transfer skillet to oven and roast until figs are tender, 8 to 10 minutes.

2 Remove skillet from oven and let figs rest for 5 minutes. Combine mascarpone, lemon zest, and remaining 1 tablespoon honey in bowl. Divide figs among individual bowls. Dollop with mascarpone mixture, drizzle with balsamic syrup, and sprinkle with pistachios. Serve.

toasting nuts

Spread nuts in dry skillet over medium heat. Shake skillet occasionally to prevent scorching and toast until lightly browned and fragrant, 3 to 8 minutes. Watch closely since nuts can go from golden to burnt very quickly.

ROASTED ORANGES IN SPICED SYRUP

serves 6

7 oranges (6 whole, 1 juiced to yield ½ cup)

¾ cup (5¼ ounces) sugar

½ cup water

2 whole cloves

1 cinnamon stick

Why This Recipe Works Light and fragrant, glazed oranges have become a popular fruit dessert. Our method capitalizes on the caramelized flavor of roasted oranges for a simple but sophisticated way to end a meal. Slicing the oranges into thick rounds meant exposing more of the fruit to the oven's heat, which allowed the flavor to concentrate. To avoid drying out the fruit during roasting, we arranged the slices in a shallow pool of caramel syrup in a baking dish. Our syrupy sauce—a simple reduction of sugar and water—came together easily on the stovetop, and steeping a cinnamon stick and cloves in it gave the sweet sauce spicy warmth. Adding fresh orange juice to the sauce reinforced the citrus flavor. We roasted the oranges for 20 minutes, just until they were appealingly soft and tender. Serve with ice cream, pound cake, or yogurt.

1 Adjust oven rack to middle position and heat oven to 450 degrees. Cut away peel and pith from oranges, then slice crosswise into ½-inch-thick rounds. Arrange oranges evenly in 13 by 9-inch baking dish, overlapping rounds as needed.

2 Combine sugar, water, cloves, and cinnamon stick in medium saucepan. Bring to boil over medium-high heat and cook, without stirring, until mixture is amber colored, 8 to 10 minutes. Reduce heat to low and continue to cook, swirling saucepan occasionally, until dark amber, 2 to 5 minutes. (Caramel will register 350 degrees.)

3 Off heat, carefully stir in orange juice (mixture will bubble and steam). Return saucepan to medium heat and cook, stirring frequently, until caramel dissolves completely into orange juice and turns syrupy, about 2 minutes.

4 Pour syrup and spices over orange slices. Roast until syrup is bubbling and oranges are slightly wilted, 18 to 20 minutes. Transfer dish to wire rack and let cool slightly. Discard cloves and cinnamon stick. Serve warm or at room temperature.

Roasted Oranges in Vanilla-Anise Syrup
Cut vanilla bean in half lengthwise. Using tip of paring knife, scrape out seeds. Substitute vanilla bean and seeds and 2 star anise pods for cloves and cinnamon stick.

HONEY-GLAZED ROASTED PEACHES

serves 6

2 tablespoons lemon juice

1 tablespoon sugar

¼ teaspoon salt

6 firm, ripe peaches, peeled, halved, and pitted

⅓ cup water

¼ cup honey

1 tablespoon unsalted butter

¼ cup hazelnuts, toasted, skinned, and chopped coarse

Why This Recipe Works It might seem impossible to improve on a perfect peach, but we decided to try. We wanted a simple, warm dessert that amplified the peaches' flavor. To achieve tender, flavorful peaches with a lightly sweet glaze, we began by tossing peeled and halved peaches with a little sugar, salt, and lemon juice to season the fruit and extract some juice. To help the peaches heat through and still hold their shape, and to prevent the sugar from burning, we broiled the halves cut side up in a skillet, adding water to the pan to prevent sticking. Once the peaches had begun to brown, we took them out and brushed them with a mixture of honey and butter, and then slid them back under the broiler to caramelize the glaze and produce beautifully browned peaches. Lastly, we reduced the juices that had accumulated in the skillet into a thick, intensely peachy syrup to drizzle over the warm peaches and topped them with some toasted hazelnuts. Select peaches that yield slightly when pressed. You will need a 12-inch ovensafe skillet for this recipe. Use a serrated peeler to peel the peaches. These peaches are best served warm and with vanilla ice cream or plain Greek yogurt, if desired.

1 Adjust oven rack 6 inches from broiler element and heat broiler. Combine lemon juice, sugar, and salt in large bowl. Add peaches and toss to combine, making sure to coat all sides with sugar mixture.

2 Transfer peaches, cut side up, to 12-inch ovensafe skillet. Pour any remaining sugar mixture into peach cavities. Pour water around peaches in skillet. Broil until peaches are just beginning to brown, 11 to 15 minutes.

3 Combine honey and butter in bowl and microwave until melted, about 30 seconds, then stir to combine. Remove peaches from oven (skillet handle will be hot) and brush half of honey mixture over peaches. Return peaches to oven and continue to broil until spotty brown, 5 to 7 minutes.

4 Remove skillet from oven (skillet handle will be hot), brush peaches with remaining honey mixture, and transfer peaches to serving dish, leaving juices behind. Being careful of hot skillet handle, bring accumulated juices in skillet to simmer over medium heat and cook until syrupy, about 1 minute. Pour syrup over peaches. Sprinkle with hazelnuts and serve.

Currant-Glazed Roasted Peaches
Substitute red currant jelly for honey and shelled pistachios for hazelnuts.

Raspberry-Glazed Roasted Peaches
Substitute seedless raspberry jelly for honey and walnuts for hazelnuts.

ROASTED PEARS WITH DRIED APRICOTS AND PISTACHIOS

serves 4 to 6

2½ tablespoons unsalted butter

4 ripe but firm Bosc pears (6 to 7 ounces each), peeled, halved, and cored

1¼ cups dry white wine

½ cup dried apricots, quartered

⅓ cup (2⅓ ounces) sugar

¼ teaspoon ground cardamom

⅛ teaspoon salt

1 teaspoon lemon juice

⅓ cup shelled pistachios, toasted and chopped

Why This Recipe Works Pears are an excellent fruit to roast because their shape and texture hold up well. Unlike other fruit desserts, there is almost no prep work. After peeling and halving the pears, we began by cooking them in butter on the stovetop to evaporate some of their juices and concentrate their flavor; this also jump-started caramelization. We moved the pears to the oven to turn their flesh tender and brown. We then put the exuded juices to use in a quick pan sauce. We deglazed the pan with dry white wine and added the complementary flavors of dried apricots and cardamom while a little lemon added a nice burst of citrus. Select pears that yield slightly when pressed. We prefer Bosc pears in this recipe, but Comice and Bartlett pears will also work. You will need a 12-inch ovensafe skillet for this recipe. The fruit can be served as is or with vanilla ice cream or plain Greek yogurt.

1 Adjust oven rack to middle position and heat oven to 450 degrees. Melt 1½ tablespoons butter in 12-inch ovensafe skillet over medium-high heat. Place pear halves, cut side down, in skillet. Cook, without moving, until pears are just beginning to brown, 3 to 5 minutes.

2 Transfer skillet to oven and roast for 15 minutes. Flip pears and continue to roast until fork easily pierces fruit, 10 to 15 minutes.

3 Remove skillet from oven (skillet handle will be hot); transfer pears to serving dish. Being careful of hot skillet handle, return skillet to medium-high heat and add wine, apricots, sugar, cardamom, salt, and remaining 1 tablespoon butter. Bring to vigorous simmer, whisking to scrape up any browned bits. Cook until sauce is reduced and has consistency of maple syrup, 7 to 10 minutes. Off heat, stir in lemon juice. Pour sauce over pears, sprinkle with pistachios, and serve.

Roasted Pears with Golden Raisins and Hazelnuts
Omit cinnamon. Substitute golden raisins for apricots and skinned hazelnuts for pistachios. Stir 1 teaspoon grated fresh ginger into sauce with lemon juice.

RUM-GLAZED ROASTED PINEAPPLE

serves 8

2 tablespoons unsalted butter

1 pineapple, peeled, cored, and cut lengthwise into 8 wedges

1 cup plus 2 teaspoons light or dark rum

½ cup packed (3½ ounces) light brown sugar

½ teaspoon vanilla extract

⅛ teaspoon salt

⅓ cup macadamia nuts, toasted and chopped

Why This Recipe Works The tropical combination of sweet pineapple and a rum glaze is undeniably tempting. By roasting the fruit, our method takes this simple dessert to the next level. We wanted to brown and caramelize the pineapple in one fell swoop, so we cut the fruit into broad wedges that would fit into a single skillet and started them browning in butter on the stovetop for instant richness. Once the wedges were slightly browned on the first side, we moved the skillet to the oven to finish roasting the fruit, flipping the wedges when the fruit had softened so it would cook evenly and caramelize. For a boozy finish, we transferred the wedges to a serving platter and built a glaze in the empty skillet. Deglazing the pan with rum picked up all the tasty pineapple bits left behind, and we added sugar for sweetness, vanilla for complexity, and a touch of butter for even more richness before reducing it to a syrupy consistency. A little extra rum stirred in at the end reinforced the sauce's flavor. To enhance our dessert's Hawaiian profile, we sprinkled toasted macadamia nuts over the pineapple for a crunchy, buttery finish. You will need a 12-inch ovensafe skillet for this recipe.

1 Adjust oven rack to middle position and heat oven to 450 degrees. Melt 1 tablespoon butter in 12-inch ovensafe skillet over medium heat. Arrange pineapple wedges cut side down in skillet and cook, without moving, until just beginning to brown, 3 to 5 minutes.

2 Transfer skillet to oven and roast until pineapple is softened, about 12 minutes. Flip pineapple and continue to roast until golden brown on second side and fork slips easily in and out of pineapple, 15 to 20 minutes.

3 Remove skillet from oven (skillet handle will be hot); transfer pineapple to serving dish. Being careful of hot skillet handle, add 1 cup rum, sugar, vanilla, salt, and remaining 1 tablespoon butter to skillet and let warm through. Bring to simmer over medium-high heat, and cook, stirring often, until sauce is thickened and measures about ½ cup, about 4 minutes. Off heat, stir in remaining 2 teaspoons rum. Drizzle pineapple with sauce, sprinkle with macadamias, and serve.

ROASTED PLUMS WITH DRIED CHERRIES AND ALMONDS

serves 4 to 6

2½ tablespoons unsalted butter

4 ripe but firm plums (4 to 6 ounces each), halved and pitted

1¼ cups dry white wine

½ cup dried cherries

⅓ cup (2⅓ ounces) sugar

¼ teaspoon ground cinnamon

⅛ teaspoon salt

1 teaspoon lemon juice

⅓ cup sliced almonds, toasted

Why This Recipe Works Roasting plums makes for an unexpected and easy dessert. Our two-stage cooking process yields tender, beautifully caramelized fruit. The plums require almost no prep work; to help them retain their shape, we kept the skins on and simply halved and pitted them. We browned the halves cut side down in a skillet on the stovetop to build a bit of color and banish some of the plums' moisture; we then moved the skillet to the oven where the surrounding heat gently roasted the fruit and created deeper browning. After 5 minutes, we flipped the halves and allowed them to finish softening. The juices in the pan were perfect for a sauce, so we reduced them with white wine. A handful of dried cherries added the right amount of fruity sweetness and tender chew; a touch of cinnamon and a bit of lemon juice added a kick that complemented the plums. Toasted almonds supplied a contrasting crunchy garnish. This recipe works equally well with red or black plums. You will need a 12-inch ovensafe skillet for this recipe. The fruit can be served as is or with vanilla ice cream or plain Greek yogurt.

1 Adjust oven rack to middle position and heat oven to 450 degrees. Melt 1½ tablespoons butter in 12-inch ovensafe skillet over medium-high heat. Place plum halves, cut side down, in skillet. Cook, without moving, until plums are just beginning to brown, about 3 minutes.

2 Transfer skillet to oven and roast for 5 minutes. Flip plums and continue to roast until fork easily pierces fruit, about 5 minutes.

3 Remove skillet from oven (skillet handle will be hot); transfer plums to serving dish. Being careful of hot skillet handle, return skillet to medium-high heat and add wine, cherries, sugar, cinnamon, salt, and remaining 1 tablespoon butter. Bring to vigorous simmer, whisking to scrape up any browned bits. Cook until sauce is reduced and has consistency of maple syrup, 7 to 10 minutes. Off heat, stir in lemon juice. Pour sauce over plums, sprinkle with almonds, and serve.

Conversions and Equivalents

Baking is a science and an art, but geography has a hand in it, too. Flours and sugars manufactured in the United Kingdom and elsewhere will feel and taste different from those manufactured in the United States. So we cannot promise that a loaf of bread you bake in Canada or England will taste the same as a loaf baked in the States, but we can offer guidelines for converting weights and measures. We also recommend that you rely on your instincts when making our recipes. Refer to the visual cues provided. If the dough hasn't "come together in a ball" as described, you may need to add more flour—even if the recipe doesn't tell you to. You be the judge.

The recipes in this book were developed using standard U.S. measures following U.S. government guidelines. The charts below offer equivalents for U.S. and metric measures. All conversions are approximate and have been rounded up or down to the nearest whole number.

EXAMPLE

1 teaspoon = 4.9292 milliliters, rounded up to 5 milliliters
1 ounce = 28.3495 grams, rounded down to 28 grams

VOLUME CONVERSIONS

U.S.	METRIC
1 teaspoon	5 milliliters
2 teaspoons	10 milliliters
1 tablespoon	15 milliliters
2 tablespoons	30 milliliters
¼ cup	59 milliliters
⅓ cup	79 milliliters
½ cup	118 milliliters
¾ cup	177 milliliters
1 cup	237 milliliters
1¼ cups	296 milliliters
1½ cups	355 milliliters
2 cups (1 pint)	473 milliliters
2½ cups	591 milliliters
3 cups	710 milliliters
4 cups (1 quart)	0.946 liter
1.06 quarts	1 liter
4 quarts (1 gallon)	3.8 liters

WEIGHT CONVERSIONS

OUNCES	GRAMS
½	14
¾	21
1	28
1½	43
2	57
2½	71
3	85
3½	99
4	113
4½	128
5	142
6	170
7	198
8	227
9	255
10	283
12	340
16 (1 pound)	454

CONVERSIONS FOR COMMON BAKING INGREDIENTS

Because measuring by weight is far more accurate than measuring by volume, and thus more likely to produce reliable results, in our recipes we provide ounce measures in addition to cup measures for many ingredients. Refer to the chart below to convert these measures into grams.

INGREDIENT	OUNCES	GRAMS
Flour		
1 cup all-purpose flour*	5	142
1 cup cake flour	4	113
1 cup whole-wheat flour	5½	156
Sugar		
1 cup granulated (white) sugar	7	198
1 cup packed brown sugar (light or dark)	7	198
1 cup confectioners' sugar	4	113
Cocoa Powder		
1 cup cocoa powder	3	85
Butter†		
4 tablespoons (½ stick or ¼ cup)	2	57
8 tablespoons (1 stick or ½ cup)	4	113
16 tablespoons (2 sticks or 1 cup)	8	227

* U.S. all-purpose flour, the most frequently used flour in this book, does not contain leaveners, as some European flours do. These leavened flours are called self-rising or self-raising. If you are using self-rising flour, take this into consideration before adding leaveners to a recipe.

† In the United States, butter is sold both salted and unsalted. We recommend unsalted butter. If you are using salted butter, take this into consideration before adding salt to a recipe.

OVEN TEMPERATURE

FAHRENHEIT	CELSIUS	GAS MARK
225	105	¼
250	120	½
275	135	1
300	150	2
325	165	3
350	180	4
375	190	5
400	200	6
425	220	7
450	230	8
475	245	9

CONVERTING TEMPERATURES FROM AN INSTANT-READ THERMOMETER

We include doneness temperatures in many of the recipes in this book. We recommend an instant-read thermometer for the job. Refer to the table above to convert Fahrenheit degrees to Celsius. Or, for temperatures not represented in the chart, use this simple formula:

Subtract 32 degrees from the Fahrenheit reading, then divide the result by 1.8 to find the Celsius reading.

example

"Flip chicken, brush with remaining glaze, and cook until breast registers 160 degrees, 1 to 3 minutes."

To convert
160°F − 32 = 128°
128° ÷ 1.8 = 71.11°C, rounded down to 71°C

Index

Note: Page references in *italics* indicate photographs.

Grill-Smoked Huli Huli Chicken, 242–43, *243*
Grill-Smoked Lexington Pulled Pork, 294, *295*
Grill-Smoked Pork Loin
    with Apple-Cherry Filling with Caraway, 291
    with Apple-Cranberry Filling, 290–91, *291*
    with Dried Fruit Chutney, 286–87, *287*
Grill-Smoked Prime Rib, *276,* 277
Grill-Smoked Side of Salmon, 304, *305*
Grill-Smoked Sinaloa-Style Chicken, *244,* 245
Grill-Smoked South Carolina Fresh Ham, 298–99, *299*
Grill-Smoked South Carolina Pulled Pork, 296–97, *297*
Grill-Smoked Texas Chuck Roast, 268, *269*
Grill-Smoked Texas Thick-Cut Pork Chops, 280–81, *281*
Grill-Smoked Turkey, Classic, 256, *257*
Grill-Smoked Turkey Breast, *254,* 255

H

Haddock, about, 19
Halibut
    about, 19
    Roast, with Red Potatoes, Corn, and Andouille, 212, *213*
Ham
    about, 13, 14
    bone-in, skewering, 301
    Crumb-Coated Roast, *192,* 193
    fat cap, cutting crosshatch pattern into, 187
    Fresh, Grill-Smoked South Carolina, 298–99, *299*
    Fresh, Slow-Roasted, *188,* 189
    Glazed Spiral-Sliced Roast, 190, *191*
    Grill-Roasted, *300,* 301
    Roast Country, *186,* 187
    skin, crisping, 299
Harissa
    and Mint, Roasted Mushrooms with, 344
    -Rubbed Roast Boneless Leg of Lamb with Warm Cauliflower Salad, 198, *199*
Hazelnut(s)
    –Dried Cherry-Stuffed Roasted Apples, 374
    and Goat Cheese, Roasted Green Beans with, 325
    and Golden Raisins, Roasted Pears with, 382
    Honey-Glazed Roasted Peaches, 380, *381*
Herbed Goat Cheese Topping, 359
Herbed Roast Beef, *118,* 119
Herbed Roast Turkey, 98–99, *99*
Herb(s)
    Butter, 134–35, *135*
    Chicago-Style Italian Roast Beef, *122,* 123
    -Crusted Pork Loin Roast, 168, *169*
    -Crusted Pork Loin Roast with Mustard and Caraway, 168
    -Crusted Roast Beef Tenderloin, *130,* 131

Herb(s) (*cont.*)
    Garlic, and Bread-Crumb Crust, Roast Boneless Leg of Lamb with, *196,* 197
    -Garlic Compound Butter, 28
    Paste, 98
    pastes, using, 99
    -Roasted Cornish Hens, 111
    Stuffing, Classic, 100
    see also specific herbs
Hoisin (Sauce)
    Chinese Barbecued Roast Pork Shoulder, *180,* 181
    -Tamarind Glaze, 265
    Tangy, Crispy Slow-Roasted Pork Belly with, 184
Honey
    -Glazed Roasted Peaches, 380, *381*
    -Lime Glazed Roast Salmon, *216,* 217
    -Mustard Glaze, 248
    Mustard–Glazed Chicken Drumsticks, Roasted, with Sweet Potato Coins, *70,* 71
    -Orange Glaze, Roasted Chicken Breasts with, 60, *61*
    and Tahini Sauce, 36
Horseradish
    Jezebel Sauce, 187
    Sauce, *26,* 27
Hot Mustard Sauce, 193
Huli Huli Chicken, Grill-Smoked, 242–43, *243*

I

Instant-read thermometer, 31

J

Jalapeño(s)
    and Cilantro Sauce, 36
    Deviled Beef Short Ribs, *146,* 147
Jerk-Style Spice Rub, 237
Jezebel Sauce, 187

K

Kitchen shears, 33
Kitchen twine, 32
Knives, 33

Porcini and Artichoke Stuffing, 285

Pork

T

V

Vegetables
Root, and Tarragon Vinaigrette, Twin Roast
  Chickens with, 86, *87*
Root, One-Pan Roasted Chicken with, *68,* 69
Root, Roasted, with Lemon-Caper Sauce, *366, 367*
see also specific vegetables
**Vermouth-Sage Sauce, Pan-Roasted Chicken Breasts
  with, 59**
Vertical roaster, 31
V-rack, 30

W

Walnut(s)
and Dried Figs, Roasted Apples with, 372, *373*
and Lemon, Roasted Brussels Sprouts with, 330
-Raisin-Stuffed Roasted Apples, 374
Raspberry-Glazed Roasted Peaches, 380
Weeknight Roast Chicken, *40,* 41
**Whole Roast Mackerel with Red Pepper and
  Preserved Lemon Stuffing, 226, *227***
Whole Roast Snapper with Citrus Vinaigrette, 222, *223*
Whole Roast Trout with White Bean Salad, *224,* 225

Wine
Port, -Cherry Glaze, 190
Port, –Cherry Sauce, 52
Port, Glaze, Crisp Roast Duck with, *106,* 107
Red, –Orange Sauce, 28
Wire rack, 31

Y

Yogurt
-Cucumber Sauce, *26,* 29
Garam Masala, 360
Raita, 66, *67*
and Sesame Seeds, Roasted Celery Root with, 338, *339*
Tandoori Chicken with Raita, 66, *67*
**Yorkshire Pudding and Jus, Boneless Rib Roast
  with, 138, *139***

Z

**Za'atar-Rubbed Roast Chicken with Mint
  Vinaigrette, *82,* 83**
Zip-Style Sauce, 126, *127*